MARTYRS AND MIGRANTS

NORTH AMERICAN RELIGIONS

Series Editors: Tracy Fessenden (Arizona State University), Laura Levitt (Temple University), and David Harrington Watt (Haverford College)

Since its inception, the North American Religions book series has steadily disseminated gracefully written, pathbreaking explorations of religion in North America. Books in the series move among the discourses of ethnographic, textual, and historical analysis and across a range of topics, including sound, story, food, nature, healing, crime, and pilgrimage. In so doing they bring religion into view as a style and form of belonging, a set of tools for living with and in relations of power, a mode of cultural production and reproduction, and a vast repertory of the imagination. Whatever their focus, books in the series remain attentive to the shifting and contingent ways in which religious phenomena are named, organized, and contested. They bring fluency in the best of contemporary theoretical and historical scholarship to bear on the study of religion in North America. The series focuses primarily, but not exclusively, on religion in the United States in the twentieth and twenty-first centuries.

Books in the series

Ava Chamberlain, *The Notorious Elizabeth Tuttle: Marriage, Murder, and Madness in the Family of Jonathan Edwards*

Terry Rey and Alex Stepick, *Crossing the Water and Keeping the Faith: Haitian Religion in Miami*

Isaac Weiner, *Religion Out Loud: Religious Sound, Public Space, and American Pluralism*

Hillary Kaell, *Walking Where Jesus Walked: American Christians and Holy Land Pilgrimage*

Brett Hendrickson, *Border Medicine: A Transcultural History of Mexican American Curanderismo*

Jodi Eichler-Levine, *Suffer the Little Children: Uses of the Past in Jewish and African American Children's Literature*

Annie Blazer, *Playing for God: Evangelical Women and the Unintended Consequences of Sports Ministry*

Elizabeth Pérez, *Religion in the Kitchen: Cooking, Talking, and the Making of Black Atlantic Traditions*

Kerry Mitchell, *Spirituality and the State: Managing Nature and Experience in America's National Parks*

Finbarr Curtis, *The Production of American Religious Freedom*

M. Cooper Harriss, *Ralph Ellison's Invisible Theology*

Ari Y. Kelman, *Shout to the Lord: Making Worship Music in Evangelical America*

Joshua Dubler and Isaac Weiner, editors, *Religion, Law, USA*

Shari Rabin, *Jews on the Frontier: Religion and Mobility in Nineteenth-Century America*

Alyssa Maldonado-Estrada, *Lifeblood of the Parish: Men and Catholic Devotion in Williamsburg, Brooklyn*

Jenna Supp-Montgomerie, *When the Medium Was the Mission: The Atlantic Telegraph and the Religious Origins of Network Culture*

Philippa Koch, *The Course of God's Providence: Religion, Health, and the Body in Early America*

Tisa Wenger and Sylvester A. Johnson, editors, *Religion and US Empire: Critical New Histories*

Caleb Iyer Elfenbein, *Fear in Our Hearts: What Islamophobia Tells Us about America*

Rachel B. Gross, *Beyond the Synagogue: Jewish Nostalgia as Religious Practice*

Elizabeth Fenton, *Old Canaan in a New World: Native Americans and the Lost Tribes of Israel*

Deborah Dash Moore, editor, *Vernacular Religion: Collected Essays of Leonard Norman Primiano*

Katrina Daly Thompson, *Muslims on the Margins: Creating Queer Religious Community in North America*

Jennifer Scheper Hughes, *The Church of the Dead: The Epidemic of 1576 and the Birth of Christianity in the Americas*

Laura Yares, *Jewish Sunday Schools: Teaching Religion in Nineteenth-Century America*

Jonathan H. Ebel, *From Dust They Came: Government Camps and the Religion of Reform in New Deal California*

Gale L. Kenny, *Christian Imperial Feminism: White Protestant Women and the Consecration of Empire*

Leslie Beth Ribovich, *Without a Prayer: Religion and Race in New York City Public Schools*

Amanda J. Baugh, *Falling in Love with Nature: The Values of Latinx Catholic Environmentalism*

George González, *The Church of Stop Shopping and Religious Activism: Combatting Consumerism and Climate Change through Performance*

Candace Lukasik, *Martyrs and Migrants: Coptic Christians and the Persecution Politics of US Empire*

Martyrs and Migrants

Coptic Christians and the Persecution Politics of US Empire

Candace Lukasik

NEW YORK UNIVERSITY PRESS
New York

NEW YORK UNIVERSITY PRESS
New York
www.nyupress.org

© 2025 New York University
All rights reserved

Please contact the Library of Congress for Cataloging-in-Publication data.

ISBN: 9781479833191 (hardback)
ISBN: 9781479833221 (paperback)
ISBN: 9781479833252 (library ebook)
ISBN: 9781479833245 (consumer ebook)

This book is printed on acid-free paper, and its binding materials are chosen for strength and durability. We strive to use environmentally responsible suppliers and materials to the greatest extent possible in publishing our books.

Manufactured in the United States of America

10 9 8 7 6 5 4 3 2 1

Also available as an ebook

For my grandfather, Joseph Rogala
   For Saba
      Memory Eternal

CONTENTS

Introduction: Migrating Bodies/Flowing Blood ... 1

PART I: SCALES OF BLOOD

1. Persecution and Power ... 35
2. Sectarian Memory and Migration Forces ... 69
3. Religious Difference and Asylum Law ... 106

PART II: COMMUNITIES OF BLOOD

4. Affective Bodies and Security Praxis ... 151
5. Diasporic Translations and Global Culture Wars ... 178

Conclusion: Wages and Witness ... 205

Acknowledgments ... 221

Notes ... 227

Bibliography ... 255

Index ... 281

About the Author ... 294

Introduction

Migrating Bodies/Flowing Blood

This is my Body . . . broken for you.
—1 Corinthians 11:24 (New King James Version)

This is my Blood . . . poured out for many.
—Matthew 26:28 (New International Version)

In recent years, US politicians, think tanks, and NGOs have re-channeled their efforts into "saving" Middle Eastern Christians, as violence against minority communities continued to rise in the wake of the Arab Spring revolutions and the emergence of the Islamic State/Daesh. The success of these efforts to politicize Middle Eastern Christian lives has hinged on the post–Cold War remapping of the world, promoted by politicians and evangelicals, and centered on a civilizational battle between Christianity and Islam.

Coptic Orthodox are the largest community of Christians remaining in the Middle East. Their church, with roots that date back to the first century, has branched out globally since the mid-twentieth century. Though figures are contested, Copts constitute roughly 10 percent of the Egyptian population and have an ever-growing diaspora.[1] Since the 2011 Egyptian revolution and a rise in subsequent attacks on the community and their places of worship, Copts have been increasingly immigrating to the United States, which has garnered interest from American politicians and Christian religious leaders. Since the 1980s, Coptic death has been made legible to American (particularly evangelical) audiences through the global, moral imaginary of the "Persecuted Church," which argues that Christians around the globe are currently persecuted more than at any other time in history.[2] Once the objects of American missionary efforts, Coptic Orthodox Christians have been reconfigured as

Americans' Christian kin in their suffering for Christ.³ In their everyday social interactions and in their activism, Copts in the United States have woven together this geopolitical thematization of persecution with diasporic translations of homeland conditions in Egypt.

The embrace of Copts by American Christian conservatives and the US state has provided a new avenue for transnational minority activism.⁴ Yet this activism and foreign policy–level focus have produced other fraught predicaments for Christian migrants from the Middle East. Once in the United States, Copts share experiences of anti-Muslim racism with other Arab and Muslim communities in post-9/11 America. While US religio-political support for Copts hinges on their special status as victims of Islamic violence, homeland contexts of sectarian violence and minority persecution are contorted by the everyday experiences of a racially marginalized migrant community. These layered contentions of difference compel specific forms of social belonging and political organizing among American Copts that ultimately distance them racially and religiously from communities they once shared life with in Egypt—even in disaster, destruction, and discrimination, as well as hope and care.

This book focuses on the politics of scale and unpacks the transnational implications of this problem space through what I term an "economy of blood."⁵ This theopolitical economy entails the constitution of Christian communion as well as the management of kin and non-kin relations through the evaluation of blood (as martyr and as migrant).⁶ Kept inside, blood marks difference and danger; outside, blood flows toward kinship and relatedness. Blood's power separates into binarisms—life and death, kin and alien. While the body is bound, blood seeps with a fluid that is boundless, so that "death is swallowed up in victory"—that is, finds itself enclosed in a larger body.⁷ "Blood formerly *outside* the skin becomes presently blood *inside* new veins."⁸ The contentions of blood—as related to Christ's divine sacrifice for humanity's salvation—are part of a long arc of Christian theology and history, and such contentions (and contradictions) persist in the present among both Western and Eastern Christian communities.⁹

Gil Anidjar's *Blood: A Critique of Christianity* does not attend to Christian theology on blood itself; it specifically suggests that the medieval period marks the advent of an entirely new way of understanding community and kinship through blood. Anidjar maintains that all significant concepts of the modern world emerged out of the formation of a "eucharistic matrix," centering Western Christendom and excluding Eastern traditions of Christianity that formed the theological foundations of Blood theology.[10] As Daniel Steinmetz-Jenkins argued in response, "Anidjar excludes the Eastern Orthodox Church from his analysis because the concepts he is interested first emerged in the West."[11] This book both agrees with this retort and refutes it, through a response from Anidjar himself:

> Pope Francis is quoted as saying: "The blood of our Christian brothers and sisters is a testimony which cries out to be heard. . . . It makes no difference whether they be Catholics, Orthodox, Copts or Protestants. They are Christians! Their blood is one and the same. Their blood confesses Christ." Francis thus brings together (better than I have, I think) a few among the multiple dimensions of blood that bind Christians *and Christianity* and better yet, *Christianities*, for which blood also . . . testifies. The affirmation of identity ("one and the same") is a response to the differing I try to highlight, but it also abolishes and remarks that difference (the blood of Christians, all Christians). It is an *Aufhebung* that leaves the blood of others open to, say, benevolent speculations. And it finds one of its sources in the singularly pure and purifying blood of Christ, itself multifariously shared by Christians. Francis and I . . . thus appear to agree that Christianity exists, and that it has something to do with blood.[12]

This book contends that these two perspectives can be held in tension with one another—that Christianity holds theopolitical and historical variations within it as a tradition (between Protestant and Catholic traditions in Europe and Coptic Orthodox traditions in Egypt, for example), but in the contemporary moment, Christianity (as in previous ages) comes together over the blood of the persecuted, like that of the Copts.

Thus, in a (re)newed thinking about blood as martyrdom, the suffering of Coptic Christians is theologically engaged by American evangelicals and their kin as a warning call for Western Christendom (and Western civilization). Coptic martyrdom is transvalued and remapped onto an American Christian terrain, which imagines Christianity (in the United States and globally) as under threat, marginalized, and persecuted.¹³ In this reading, the American Christian experience is paralleled to the various experiences of Christian communities in the Middle East, Africa, and South Asia (mainly as minorities in Muslim-majority contexts). It is by the spilling of their blood that American Christian kinship is opened to Eastern Christian communities like the Copts. Their blood becomes shared American Christian blood, under threat of annihilation from both oppressive Islamic *and* secular, liberal anti-Christian regimes. Political discourse and communal accounts of the persecution of Copts in Egypt dually offer the grounds of claims-making practices among American Copts in their advocacy, and in their own identity formation as immigrants and citizens in a conservative American Christian landscape.¹⁴ It is the persecution of their minority-Christian kin in Egypt under Muslim rule that shapes migrant understandings of the possibilities and opportunities for flourishing in majority-Christian America.

As we think about blood as migration, American Copts, as immigrants of many different social classes, are also differentiated as "other" through processes of racialization into the figure of the Middle Eastern/Arab/Muslim, which are translated through governing practices and everyday experiences of targeting in the context of "war on terror" securitization. The reading of Coptic Christians in the United States as non-white others oscillates between the displacement of the bloody image of their martyrdom in Egypt—which gathers them into persecuted Christian kinship—and the translation of their differentiated bodies into a sensorium of suspicion.

In the context of the contemporary United States, racialization is a multi-scalar process that proliferates through these religious-racial and classed divisions within the politics of persecution. American Christians mobilize Eastern Christian suffering, yet those Christians ultimately remain "Eastern," non-white bodies in everyday interactions within American society, from the supermarket to the street. Many American Copts, including Coptic clergy and hierarchs, have reimagined Coptic collective memory of blood and persecution through the political, theological, and affective formations of the economy of blood—translating Copts' Christianity under new logics of empire and white supremacy. The power of this bloody economy shapes the contours of Coptic migration (who comes to reside in the United States and how they form lifeworlds through the binds of this economy) and the contemporary geopolitics of Christian kinship, which are the central foci of this book.

As much as Copts have been attacked and targeted as Christians in Muslim-majority Egypt, such local events are also interpreted through their interwovenness with a global politics of concern.[15] Sectarian events and their images and stories are taken up and instrumentalized in civilizational narratives of religious difference and intercommunal strife in the Middle East that impact upon internal politics and everyday life within Egypt itself. Put another way, while sectarian violence and discrimination have figured prominently in Coptic communal memory and religious life in Egypt, transnational translations of Coptic martyrdom and bloodshed have been mediated by a different kind of imperial persecution politics over the past half century.[16] In the following sections, trans-temporal scenes of the economy of blood are interwoven through the conceptual stakes of the Coptic context—in thinking about theopolitics, kinship, and empire.

Blood and Theopolitics

Blood is spilled, that's when we grow.
—Steve Haas, founder of Prayer for the Persecuted Church

If Christian sacrifice is once for all, how are the sanctifying effects forever maintained in a temporal world? If Christ is not sacrificed anew on the altar, how do Christians plug into, or keep afresh, a moment of erupting holiness that is anything but momentary?
—Caroline Walker Bynum, *Wonderful Blood*

The day before the US Capitol insurrection on January 6, 2021, conservative evangelical author Eric Metaxas tweeted an image of twenty-one Coptic martyrs, beheaded on the shores of Libya in February 2015, with the caption, "What price are you willing to pay for what you believe in?" The image was a still frame of the Coptic migrants on their knees with black-masked affiliates of ISIS behind them. At the bottom of the frame was a subtitle, "The followers of the hostile Egyptian Church" and the names of the twenty-one. The parallel was clear for Metaxas's followers, many of whom were angry over the results of the 2020 presidential

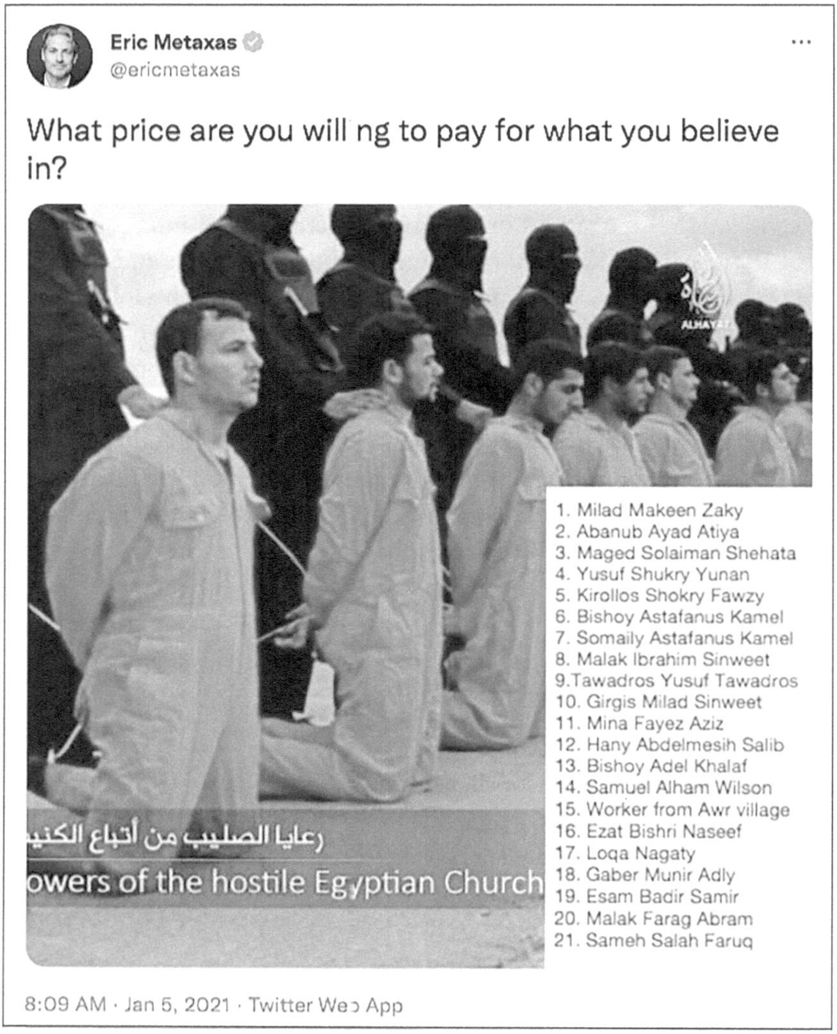

Figure 1.1. Screenshot of tweet by Eric Metaxas on January 5, 2021, with photograph of the Coptic martyrs on their knees and black-masked ISIS affiliates holding knives behind them.

election and the loss of Donald J. Trump: their struggle to save America from liberal peril was comparable to the witness of the Coptic martyrs. The juxtaposition of these images analogized the experience of Trump's supporters at the Capitol preparing for battle on January 6 and the Coptic Christian refusal to apostatize—both persecuted innocents, both victims of religious (and political) intolerance, both martyrs.

* * *

The figure of the martyr simultaneously invokes awe and anxiety, reverence and suspicion.[17] This book tracks this duality (of both the martyr and the migrant) in the contemporary geopolitical context of US empire, but also in terms of the long arc of Christian history. As much as this book threads this duality through Coptic migrants, it also gestures to broader theopolitical and transhistorical concerns as they intersect with Copts and US empire. In early Christian history, the Church (or the Body of Christians) cultivated suffering and persecution as central nodes of spiritual formation and communion in eucharistic mystery. Suffering became triumph. Judith Perkins has argued that "Christians flipped classical notions of conquest on their head by proclaiming their own deaths as triumphs, just as Christ had conquered through his crucifixion."[18] In her work on martyrdom and memory in early Christianity, Elizabeth Castelli has also argued that the politics of martyrdom (as well as persecution) can "make an ethical demand and lend legitimacy to other forms of power claims."[19] While focusing on early Christian history, both Perkins and Castelli make important, broader points on Christian power and the seemingly paradoxical theopolitics of suffering. Elayne Oliphant has explained that while an approach that takes up political theology would address "the processes through which suffering and privilege are legitimated," theopolitics, conversely, offers a means of "recognizing that some practices escape claims to sovereignty and their homogenizing effects."[20] In attending to the intersections of blood and theopolitics, then, the contemporary figuration of the martyr must be held in balance between political instrumentalization and the long arc of Christ's mystery.[21]

For Christians, Christ's death was/is in itself sufficient in salvation for all. There is nothing lacking in the saving act of Christ's passion. Yet martyrdom has long been the ultimate act of devotion and emulation of

Christ's ultimate suffering for humanity. The blood of martyrs as the seed of the Church then stands in mystery with the completion of Christ's bloody persecution, death, and resurrection. According to early Christian theologian Tertullian, the martyrs' deaths ensured the forgiveness of their sins and their place in heaven.[22] He even compared martyrdom to a second baptism in blood that could wash away any sins committed after a Christian's first baptism in water. Yet the continued ambiguity of martyrdom—in the early Church[23] as well as today—grapples with the question, Should observers react in horror, or should they desire his/her own martyrdom as well?[24] Put another way, if the blood of the martyrs is truly the seed of the Church (as Tertullian famously put it), would it be acceptable for martyrs to will their own death? If that is the case, then a collective desire for martyrdom *might* be made acceptable, and perhaps even necessary for the growth of the true Church. Are martyrdom and persecution things to be endured, or can they be desired as well? And what happens when persecution ceases and bloody martyrdom ends?[25]

In anthropology, theology has been traditionally constructed as other, given its openness to the omnipotence of the divine; recent anthropological engagements with theology have attempted to ameliorate anthropology's preoccupation with a secularized, cultural alterity.[26] Khaled Furani has noted that the concepts that theology's engagement with divine difference bring to the fore have been present in the discipline of anthropology from its beginning. However, their naming as *theos* (or omnipotent) has left them marginal within the field of anthropological knowledge.[27] In thinking about blood and theopolitics, this book moves beyond the consideration of how theological concepts permeate everyday life in tension with the Schmittian framework of secularization (where theological concepts are explained through their social use—as a system of symbols to better explain worldly phenomena).[28] Instead, martyrdom and persecution have long differentiated arcs in Christian history that weave bodies, affects, and materialities together in migration and in translation from a divine perforation.[29] By foregrounding the transhistorical role of imperial Christianity in these processes of perforation, this book brings together divine alterity with seemingly secular understandings of social difference and migration that confine theology to the domain of the supernatural and obscure "how it partakes through this history in the materiality of everyday life."[30] A conceptual deployment of theopolitics attunes the context of blood as martyrdom to an anthropology of the otherwise that considers the more-than-material properties of political and historical ruptures and transformations. In this exploration, it requires renewed thinking on the intertwinement of Christianity and empire.[31]

While this book channels the state as the site of the political—in its administrative, legal, and cultural forms—it also places it in tension with the role of the divine in the seemingly worldly processes of religious kinship and migratory translations. The enfleshing force of Christianity—in its global asymmetries—is irreducible to either difference or sameness with secular ontologies. The global idea of the Persecuted Church can be understood both as an imperial formation and as a continuing theology of suffering and persecution at the heart of the Christian tradition. The translation of that theology in-this-world has also had devastating consequences. For example, in his essays on suicide bombing, Talal Asad notes that in the Crucifixion, the violent breaking of Christ's body is not an occasion for horror, but rather the source of a transcendent truth.[32] In the worldly translation of that transcendent truth, sacrificial death constitutes the necessary foundation for the West's capacity for violence and claim to territorial sovereignty. As cited by Asad, World War I historian Richard Gamble has argued that Americans see themselves as a redemptive force through the "salvation" of others from tyranny around the globe, deploying the words of American orators themselves on divine sacrifice and the United States' war casualties. For example, "Christ gave his life upon the cross that mankind might gain the kingdom of heaven, while to-night we shall solemnly decree the sublimest sacrifice ever made by a nation for the salvation of humanity, the institution of world-wide liberty and freedom."[33] While liberal theological forms of Christianity assume in modernity that the need for bloody martyrdoms has been settled in Christian history, still other forms—most especially the red threads of the Persecuted Church—observe and admire their non-Western persistence and circulate their theopolitical power. Although Western Christian and Coptic contexts of bloody martyrdom differ considerably in terms of genealogy and connections to imperial power, they have intersected with one another in a kind of relationality, a feeling of relatedness that produces a need for accountability. This relationality is certainly asymmetrical. Through the employment of sacrificial narratives, Western Christendom gathers the Copts to mobilize their martyrdoms in an affective way that ideologically empowers contemporary global ambitions.

Historian Caroline Walker Bynum has examined the different valences of blood piety and cut in late medieval Europe. Medieval motifs of dismemberment and pouring blood in fifteenth-century devotion were often about access, not partition, and this openness was the opposite not so much of violence as of corruption.[34] While the body of Christ within these medieval image economies tended to signify community and enclosure, blood gestured to an outflow. Drop by drop, a broader Christian community was unified into an immanent, organic whole, "the community of blood."[35] This process of inclusion dually involved the exclusion of others based on bloodlines, which drew radical distinctions between bloods. Non-Christians became the carriers of impurity, hostile persecutors and defilers of Christian blood, as well as a necessary other for the purpose of revelation.

Thinking about anti-Jewish host-desecration libels, Bynum argues that these stories do not merely evidence hatred of Jews and greed for Jewish property; rather, Christians needed Jews in order to produce miraculous blood. In Bynum's reading, devotional texts constructed these narratives to culminate not in a verdict of Jewish guilt (of which Christians were convinced) but "in the wonderful blood of God made visible in matter by Jewish desecration."[36] This double movement of violation and sanctification within devotional images and text was part of an emerging moral imaginary of Western Christianity in its aesthetics and sensibilities.

The snapshot of this broader genealogy of (Western) Christian history channels how blood as theopolitics is not only a symbol of triumph over death and decay. Blood contains both access and accusation, life and separation as the paradox of Christian sacrifice. "Life lies in killing, redemption in the shedding of blood."[37]

A theopolitics of persecution collects the drops and flows of a new kind of imperial Christian kinship that has molded transnational Coptic life in the process. American Christians look to those "over there" as possessing a truer, more authentic faith. The purity of certain Christians' faith is seen only in their faithful endurance of suffering. Narratives and testimonies of pain allow American Christians as well as transnational

Copts who are otherwise separated by lines of tradition, doctrine, and geography to imagine themselves as being kin in a global community of the persecuted and of bloody martyrdom.

Blood and Kinship

> Sometimes I believe the challenge of understanding martyrdom is twofold; first to bring honor to our Lord through a willingness to die for our beloved Coptic Christianity; second it is to spread our faith through the world with the blood of the martyr.
> —Bishop Youssef, "The 21 Martyrs of Libya"

Until recently, anthropological studies of kinship have usually been considered within largely secular terms.[38] After David Schneider's critique of Western presuppositions about the biological foundations of kinship, scholars focused their research on two fields of inquiry.[39] One field focused on how kinship relations could be formed through other substances, such as shared food, land, and homes; the other considered kinship as a "process of doing," enacted in everyday practices of care, exchange, and labor.[40] While this conceptual shift allowed anthropologists to consider a much wider range of what might count as kinship, spiritual kinships as divine relation were left largely unexamined.

Taking seriously spiritual forms of kin-making requires a redirection toward important aspects of relatedness as connected to "ongoing (pious) action, affect, and context."[41] This book considers a kind of "geopolitical kinship" that threads through religious-racial and asymmetrical affects of blood. Within the earthly translation of a divine Body of Christ, there is an irresolvable tension between an inclusive sacred community and differentiated bodies. Closely linked to this tension between the universal and the particular is how relatedness entails inclusion and exclusion. An important argument of this book is that blood draws Copts into American Christian kinship through a genealogy of Christ's Body, and that US empire excludes them—as part of differentiated bodies of blood, most particularly as racialized migrants. This contemporary formulation draws on colonial divisions in Egypt, where Copts were discursively constructed as inherently different from Muslims (as civilizational heirs to the pharaohs[42]) and fundamentally the same—religiously and racially backward and ignorant. The tension between these different conceptualizations of blood encapsulates not only the polyvalence of blood as a kin-substance, but also how their asymmetrical workings are entangled with each other so that a reference in one register may carry the possibility of evoking responses in another.[43]

Martyrs are the Church's foundation in collective remembrance of Christ's death and resurrection, Christ's suffering and triumph over death by death. For the Coptic Orthodox Church, the institutional translation of this political theology of blood and sacrifice organizes relations into a temporal frame that exceeds a secular historicity.[44] New Coptic martyrs are not only incorporated into the Coptic Orthodox Church's Synaxarium as an institutional enactment, but also are divinely threaded from the sacrifice of Christ at the Crucifixion. Martyrdom is not simply a symbolic frame to give meaning to suffering and death.[45] It is a red genealogy of life that moves between life/death in this world and everlasting life in Christ in the hereafter. In this way, imagining kinship ties through spilt blood does not necessarily lend itself solely to local, interpersonal relations, or even national, communal relations. Kinship through martyrs' blood can also be forged through global imagery, social media, and religio-political policy discourse that frames spiritual kinship through geopolitics. As Todne Thomas has argued, kinship is not only a formation of similarity between members of a "family." Rather, it can also be used to narrate difference from threatening groups, traditions, and politics.[46] Geopolitical kinship through the dueling figures of the martyr and the migrant can be thought of as demarcating lines of religious belonging and racial exclusion.

As Copts migrate from Egypt to the United States, communal forms of relationality are transformed and shifted based on both their experiences as a Christian minority in Egypt and their experiences as part of the Christian majority in the United States. While theopolitically their Christianity transcends modern, national borders, the political theology of their Christianity is translated through new contexts of religious and racial difference. Central to this transformation is the idea of kinship as intersubjective being in the way people "live each other's lives and die each other's deaths."[47] Copts' communal kinship formations expand in migration as new ways of relatedness are introduced in the United States.

While much can be said on the shaping of transnational Christian kinships between homelands of the non-West and their many diasporas,[48] the more recent phenomenon of imperial (Western) Christian kinship has relied on the bloody persecution and martyrdom of Eastern Christians like the Copts. The blood of the persecuted has connected a geopolitical Body of Christ through empire building and embattlement. How Coptic death is related to and remapped in an American Christian landscape matters to how Copts between Egypt and the United States live.

With regard to communal differentiation among Copts, the blood of martyrs symbolizes both Christ's triumph over death and an eternal spiritual belonging in the Body.[49] Yet it has also represented communal otherness to ruling powers and society, as well as political belonging to the Egyptian state. The Coptic calendar dates not from the birth of Christ or the beginning of Christian Egypt, but from the "Era of the Martyrs," referring to widespread anti-Christian persecution under the rule of Roman emperor Diocletian. During early Islamic expansion in Egypt, hagiographies and narratives of persecution became especially critical to the Coptic Church's institutional coherence as the community's social constitution began to change.[50] In Coptic material culture, graphic scenes of dismemberment, blood, and martyrdom emerged as discursive nodes of communal belonging and, in turn, reinforced Coptic difference from and perseverance under Arab and Islamic rulers. Narratives and images of death not only structured the Coptic Church's institutional legitimacy, but also forged its grounds for intercommunal belonging. By the eighteenth century, Febe Armanios has argued, Coptic Orthodox clerics regularly deployed narratives of persecution and martyrdom in their sermons to prevent Muslim and interdenominational conversions increasing under Western missionary influence.[51] The Church mobilized martyrdoms and memory to authorize its power and to reinforce communal boundary making.

In contemporary Egypt, the Church avoids issues that would create antagonism among Copts toward the Muslim majority and vehemently discourages any calls for the separation of the Copts or their isolation from Egyptian society. Instead, the modern Coptic Church has depended upon these commemorative acts of witness and death for the continuous making of both religious and national contours of belonging.[52] Consequently, a Coptic moral imaginary emerges in the claims-making practices of difference that gesture to Christian endurance in Egypt.⁵³ Imperial subjugation and communal otherness have historically mapped a Coptic genealogy of blood not as enclosure but as a practice of endurance. Thus, persecution and blood define a Coptic ethos as an oscillation between similarity and difference. The spilt blood of the martyrs produced the community that would carry their distinctive religious legacy into the future. Transnational Coptic religiosity continues to be infused with memory, consecration, and desired emulation of old and new martyrs.

Under British colonial rule, structures of racialization also operationalized the oscillation between similarity and difference among Copts. Orientalist writers, Western missionaries, and colonial powers vacillated between reverence and condescension in their treatment of the Copts. Blood as a marker of belonging formed the grounds of relatedness between Western Christian and Coptic kinship (caught in the tensions between the Copts as an "ancient race"⁵⁴ and their dangerous geographic proximity to Muslims). Racial science in colonial Egypt set out to distinguish Copts from their Muslim neighbors, based on a shared Christian kinship, while at the same time denigrating the Copts for not being of an "enlightened" form of Christianity.⁵⁵ The imagined civilizational divide between a homogeneous Christian West and a Muslim East upended itself in the paradoxical logics of Coptic comprehension. In this way, blood was imagined to biogenetically tie Copts together as descendants of the ancient pharaonic race, but it also tied and continues to tie them together as martyrs to the land on which their Christian blood is spilled.⁵⁶

* * *

Sitting in a Manhattan café, Nessim, a wealthy engineer, and I drank tea and chatted about the study of Copts.⁵⁷ "The enemies of Edward Said are the heroes of the Copts,' he said. Nessim lauded the Orientalists of colonial Egypt for their accomplishments for the community. Coptologists like Gaston Maspero are noted as being partly (if not wholly) responsible for persuading elite Egyptian Copts that they are "descendants of the pharaohs" and, most importantly, that they are "racially pure."⁵⁸ In Maspero's assertion that the bloodline of the Copts has remained pure from the time of the pharaohs, the Copts secured their place in the Egyptian nation.⁵⁹ Many Coptic intellectuals, politicians, and elite laymen embraced this narrative of their timeless uniqueness and integral role in shaping Egyptian national identity, in comparison to a church-centered vision more congenial to clergy and working classes. Maspero also suggested that Egyptian Muslim populations were racially intermixed with Arabs, but largely descended from Coptic Christians who had converted to Islam. "Egyptian Muslims, then, were a substandard Copt."[60]

Nessim continued,

> If you're trying to be a part of something, and you're a Copt, you sort of stepped over back to ancient Egypt, because that was something to be proud of and the Europeans recognized it. There was always a European standard that you lived up to. So a lot of these Copts made the connection, not with Coptic culture—which they knew was inferior—but to the ancient Egyptian culture. But to do that, they needed to claim pure descent, and it fit neatly into the European attitude that Muslims were part of degenerate races, and only the pure Egyptians, these were the ones that were really a good race. All of these colonial thinkers understood the ancient Egyptians as comparable to the West. So if you [as a Copt] can claim yourself to be ethnically pure [Egyptian], you place yourself on the Western scope and you bypass all that sort of mess.

European recognition of the Copts as pure descendants of the ancient Egyptians depended on the Coptic elite distinguishing themselves from Muslims and Islam, using the criteria and rhetoric provided by the colonial thinkers and rulers.

The legacy of these colonial racial-religious hierarchies persists. Emerging out of Orientalist literature and colonial governance, "Muslim" countries were constructed as a geography that shared a common culture. In both *Mummies and Moslems* (1875) and *In the Levant* (1877), American writer Charles Dudley Warner differentiates "civilization" from "barbarism" or "savagery," always keyed to whiteness and its others. In his writings on Egypt and the Levant, he describes a meeting with a certain European traveler in Cairo. "We were civilized beings, met by chance in a barbarous place."[61] Copts are from this "barbarous" geography, but they are Christians. As Barbara Fields has pointed out, the division of peoples into Christian and heathen prior to the rise of modern racial science did not mean that all Christians were equal. In British-occupied Ireland and in the American colonies, for instance, religious and racial systems of domination overlapped and interpenetrated.[62] This logic operated in its own particular way in colonial Egypt among Coptic elites.

In *Modern Egypt* (1908), Evelyn Baring, first Earl of Cromer, describes Copts and Muslims in Egypt as the same, but different. Both Muslims and Copts have remained "stagnant." Yet Muslims are stagnant *because* they are Muslims, "because the customs which are interwoven with his religion, forbid him to change."[63] Copts are stagnant due to their improper Christianity and also because they are "Orientals," residing in a geography that prevents their progress because of its association with Islam. If they can refine their Christianity—make it modern and rational—they may be able to secure their path toward progress, yet they are still "arrested by barriers very similar to those which have applied in the case of the Moslem."[64] Baring continues, "The Copt . . . has, without knowing it, assimilated himself to the Moslem. 'The modern Copt has become from head to foot, in manners, language, and spirit, a Moslem, however unwilling he may be to recognize the fact.' . . . For all purposes of broad generalization, the only difference between the Copt and the Moslem is that the former is an Egyptian who worships in a Christian church, whilst the latter is an Egyptian who worships in a Mohammedan mosque."[65]

Yet modern Copts were also likened to mummified remains and stylized depictions of pharaohs. "Racial descent" was directly connected to Coptic status under the British.[66] The Copts were divided from other Egyptians not merely by religion, but, others argued, also by race. This was repeated by Kyriakos Mikhail, a former journalist at a Coptic newspaper who had come to London to argue for the freedom of the Egyptian press and greater Coptic representation. As part of his campaign, Mikhail edited a book about the "Coptic question" in which he enlisted the contributions of prominent individuals such as the clergyman and British Assyriologist Archibald Sayce, whose career had been focused on using archaeology to prove biblical truth and who had befriended the prominent Egyptologists Flinders Petrie and Gaston Maspero during the years he had been in Egypt. In *Copts and Muslims under British Control: A Collection of Facts and a Résumé of Authoritative Opinions on the Coptic Question*, Sayce notes,

The genuine Egyptians are the Christian Copts. They alone trace an unadulterated descent from the race to whom the civilisation and culture of the ancient world were so largely due. Thanks to their religion, they have kept their blood pure from admixture with semi-barbarous Arabs and savage Kurds, or other foreign elements whom the licentiousness of Mohammedan family life has introduced into the country. . . .

During the last thirty years I have seen a good deal of the Coptic people, more especially of the younger generation, and I have found them to compare favorably with other nations. They have inherited the aptitudes and the intellectual abilities of their forefathers; their morality and conception of the family is that of a Christian people, in other words, of Western European civilization; and I see no reason why they should not again take the same high place in the civilized world that was taken by their Pharaonic ancestors. Egypt, as Sir Gaston Maspero once said to me, is the mother of most of the ideas that have since ruled the world, and the children of that mother are still with us, under the name of Copts.[67]

Sayce's quote demonstrates an admixture of historical, racial, and religious tropes that had come to represent the European imagination of the Copts and that underlie the present politicization of Coptic suffering and migration—as an evacuation of civilization from Egypt under threat from Islam. The way race is construed and the meanings to which it is attached here demonstrate its importance in the broader Western imagination on the role of the Copts as connected to the foundations of civilization—in both its pharaonic and Christian forms.

A Western understanding of Copts as the "sons of the pharaohs" not only created difference, but also provoked anxiety over the thin lines dividing Black and white, civilized and uncivilized.[68] The disputes engendered by these debates on racial difference were ongoing. At the same time as the above statements of difference, an English-language Egyptian newspaper argued that both the Copts and the Muslims "are of the same stock, indigenous . . . and have little of any blood relationship with the foreigners who have successively exercised power on the Nile."[69] This complex structure of proximity and difference in a bloody kinship, articulated in an earlier colonial context, continues to affect Copts today in the United States as they navigate new binds of racial-religious imperial power.

Blood and Empire

American imperialist culture has seeped into Egyptian blood.
—Karas, interviewed by author

We sat on the back patio, eating watermelon in the heat of the sun on a chilly March day in 2021. Karas had moved to the United States from Egypt with his family at eight years old and settled in a suburb of Nashville, Tennessee. Having returned to Egypt in his teenage years and then again in his twenties, Karas was disheartened by what he experienced back in the "homeland":

> Drinking Starbucks and Americanos and lattes and watching *Inception* and listening to Pop Smoke, Taylor Swift, Johnny Cash, knowing about Blake Shelton and country music.... It seems like Egyptians there knew more about American culture than their own culture.

Karas focuses his life and work around community organizing and mutual aid. Part of our conversation centered on the instrumentalization of his Middle Eastern Christian identity by American conservatives, in Nashville and elsewhere. Beyond those persecution politics, though, Karas's concern concentrated on the pervasive transformation and erasure of the Egypt he once knew in the service of American capitalist expansion. Considering the explosion of American-styled beach towns, the post–Arab Spring push for the expansion of American franchises in Egypt, the interest in American clothing brands, and the overall dream of immigration to the United States by way of the Green Card Lottery, "where is America not?"[70]

Scholarship on the Middle East has approached US empire through a top-down approach, focused on America's imperial influence in the region.[71] Yet the effects of US empire in the Middle East are not solely top-down, but also operate through the multi-scalar flows of power that transcend communities, transnationally.[72] Imperial influence in the Middle East extends in and beyond it through the mobility and

Figure 1.2. An office advertises for the US Diversity Visa Program: "Submit Your Immigration Applications Here!" Cairo, Egypt, October 2017. Photo by author.

immobility of its communities.⁷³ Through a "military-political-social-economic set of practices" as well as a set of "ideologies of domination" (which the United States continues to structure in the region and globally), empire relies on *other* human beings, which it constitutes through a binary of promise and threat, utility and danger.⁷⁴

In considering US empire, we must keep in mind that imperial formations today are different from the past.⁷⁵ In *Empire*, Michael Hardt and Antonio Negri posit that the imperial expansion of empires past has ceased, since there is no singular nation-state today that plays or can play this role alone. They argue that there has been a geopolitical and neoliberal transition from the imperialism of singular empires to *empire* as a fluid apparatus of influence and power: "Whereas imperialism involved territorial expansion, empire has no territorial boundaries or fixed borders."⁷⁶ Imperial encounter, then, decenters the nation-state and flows through global connections.⁷⁷

While attending to the various considerations of the United States as an empire, this book holds in tension both the excess of the United States' power beyond territory and colonial expansion, and the influence of other tendrils of imperialism from elsewhere. In this way, there remains an analytic tendency to spatially and geographically separate US empire from the realities of life in and beyond the United States. Therefore, I argue that contemporary US imperialism requires us to reframe time and space; it is all happening together, even if in different spaces. As the assemblage that both determines global problems and articulates their solutions, America is a gatekeeper of mobility, not only of bodies, but also of ideas and sensibilities. Yet there are different ambiguities that scale and perspectives convene when brought together, generating a "tangle of potential connections."⁷⁸ Different keys of analysis yield different tractions on imperial power.

Recent scholarship has focused on US empire as a concept and lived experience for millions of subjugated populations in the United States and around the world through drone strikes, military might, structural readjustment programs, and the reformation of cultural life via new mediatized publics.⁷⁹ Empire does not only involve physical territory and the traditional understanding of colonial rule between the colony and the metropole. Rather, empire is pieced together as lived condition, opening up space to reconsider imperial thought by way of its affective dispersion; empire "emerges . . . through a differential of power, not geography."⁸⁰ Thinking about US empire as a scholarly field of inquiry and lived condition, then, allows for considering the transgressions of sovereignty, or how US imperialism seeps into the blood of other polities, cultures, and communities that are not formally part of the United States (as state, colony, or otherwise). Transgressing sovereignty is not the only form of US imperialism, as that would entail a discussion of states, policy, and diplomacy in some fashion. Rather, if we think about the intersection of empire and religion through material interests—in the extraction of natural resources and labor, as well as the extraction of cultural and economic distinctiveness and difference—imperial formations like the United States control and transform even the most ordinary movements, preferences, affective commitments, and forms of community.

* * *

One evening before a spiritual meeting, I met with Father (Abouna) James, a Coptic priest in a rural area of central New Jersey.⁸¹ A new property had been purchased by the congregation, but the church had yet to be built. We sat in what appeared to be the old office of a two-story home, used temporarily as the liturgical space. Abouna James was quite active on Facebook and had recently shared articles on then President Trump's comments that Haiti and African nations (including Egypt) were "shithole" countries. Looking through the comments on the shared article, I noticed that many Copts voiced their support for Trump's perspective. I asked him why many Copts in diaspora expressed such views on Egypt, despite their Egyptian origins and transnational kin relations. "They support those comments," he explained, "because when they support them, they are essentially saying 'shithole' refers to Islam, not to them."

While also translating "colonial trauma" as well as collective memory of discrimination and violence perpetrated by Muslims in Egypt, the work of differentiation done by some Copts, like those in these comments, gestures toward ordinary affects of US empire—as a power structure of assimilation to mold sensibilities, relationships, and practices and avoid the gaze of suspicion.⁸² Both communal and scaled trans-temporal affects can be held in tension. While such social media comments are plentiful among the diaspora, connected explicitly to Egyptian contexts, they also integrate new imperial logics of racial and civilizational difference. Sarah Gualtieri has examined how the first wave of (primarily Christian) Syrian immigrants to the United States chose to stake their claim to citizenship on the basis of membership in the "white race" because "there was something compelling, even alluring, about whiteness that went beyond the strategic and the practical."[83] Gualtieri carefully attends to the logics of the new Syrian identity in American society, constructed around striving toward white acceptance. Migrant arguments were focused on Syrian connections to Christianity to reconsider racial difference along religious lines.

Following *Dow v. United States* (1915), which defined Syrians as white, in *United States v. Cartozian* (1925), anthropologist Franz Boas testified that Armenians like defendant Tatos O. Cartozian were white because of their "European origin." The judge combined Boas's testimony with his own argumentation to rule on the division between Armenians and Turks. Ultimately emphasizing Armenian proximity to Europe and their Christian background, he ruled that they could be considered white.[84] In 1942 a judge in Detroit determined that a Muslim Yemeni immigrant could not be white. The judge noted, "Apart from the dark skin of the Arabs, it is well known that they are a part of the Mohammedan world and that a wide gulf separates their culture from that of the predominantly Christian peoples of Europe."[85] In the fall of 1943, however, Arab Muslims were deemed "white" by the Immigration and Naturalization Service, effectively casting them as partners with their Christian counterparts in the project of Western civilization. In their categorization as white, however, their religious identity was necessarily effaced. As Gualtieri writes, "Whereas the Christian identity of Syrian applicants in the racial prerequisite cases had been central to their argument for whiteness, and had indeed helped them secure it, Muslim Arabs were at their whitest when stripped of their religious affiliation."[86] Race and religion were closely tied together in the legal accession to whiteness in the United States.

The histories of other Middle Eastern Christian migrants are relevant to contemporary discussions of Coptic communal formation in the United States. In many naturalization cases that legally defined whiteness, the Christianity of such peoples was crucial to the logics of their belonging within American society. The Christianity of Middle Eastern Christians matters in different ways today, as their persecution is made visible by imagery, discourse, and policy-making efforts on their behalf. In ev-

Figure I.3. Blood of Coptic martyrs behind glass at the al-Buṭrusiyya Church, along with the written prayers of pilgrims on paper. Cairo, Egypt, February 2017. Photo by author.

eryday interactions, many Copts emphasize their distinctiveness from "Arabs"—understood as an ethno-racial but also religious identity in an America where Arab and Muslim continue to be intrinsically linked.

* * *

The economy of blood examined in this book circulates Coptic suffering to advance a theopolitics of empire that traces a red thread through Christian history and exceeds it in its reworkings by Coptic communities in the United States and Egypt. Coptic migration is layered by a collective memory of Christian persecution in the homeland. Yet Coptic collective memory is scaled beyond its specific contexts, reconfiguring Christian kinship anew through American empire building. The different scales of this book seek to address the sociopolitical transformations of Coptic migrants to the United States as they transition from being a Christian minority in Egypt to a racial minority in the United States. While the blood of Coptic martyrs relates Coptic migrants—between Egypt and the United States—as kin to American Christians, it simultaneously reconfigures community in blood and also separates them by blood.

Scale and Circuits: A Note on Method

I first traveled to Egypt in 2007 for an Arabic-language program. During that initial trip, I became well-acquainted with a Coptic Orthodox Christian family in Cairo's Masākin Sheraton neighborhood.[87] I experienced Orthodox liturgy for the first time with them, and they introduced me to a Coptic lifeworld that drew me to return to Egypt nearly every year since then. Throughout the years of travel to and from the country, I also began attending Coptic churches in the United States—from Buffalo, New York, to Hayward, California. Over those years, and most strikingly after the 2011 Egyptian revolution, church dynamics in the United States shifted, and I also noticed intergenerational tensions with new waves of Coptic migrants.[88] While I had initially begun a project on the growth and eventual decimation of Coptic political movements in post-revolutionary Egypt,[89] the renewed importance of Coptic migration to the religious and political life of this transnational community piqued my interest as an anthropologist and as a practitioner of Coptic Orthodox Christianity.[90]

In 2016 I traveled from Washington, DC, to New York to Los Angeles, and eventually Nashville, Tennessee, to choose my primary fieldsites. The Coptic Orthodox Diocese of New York and New England generously offered residence at its convent in Staten Island, New York, for the duration of my major fieldwork between 2016 and the spring of 2018. The Archdiocese of North America (in New Jersey) also gave permission and offered support for this research. During my trip to Washington, DC, in June 2016 to attend Coptic Solidarity's annual conference, I met with the founder and executive director of a Coptic-led NGO, who encouraged me to participate in their volunteer program: an opportunity to teach English for three weeks in rural Egypt.[91] On December 11, 2016, a suicide bomber killed twenty-nine and injured forty-seven at Saint Peter and Saint Paul's Coptic Orthodox Church (also known as the al-Buṭrusiyya Church), a chapel next to Saint Mark's Coptic Orthodox Cathedral in Cairo's al-ʿAbbāsiyya district. The bombing set off transnational shockwaves, and many participants in the January-February program from the diaspora withdrew their participation. Only I and three other women (Coptic and non-Egyptian evangelical) took part in the early 2017 volunteer program in Bahjūra, Upper Egypt.

During the program, almost everyone I encountered in Bahjūra noted that they had kin in the United States. One prominent interlocutor throughout this book—Amin—mentioned that his niece now lives in New Jersey, and that she was able to migrate through the US Diversity Visa Program, or Green Card Lottery. During a subsequent conversation on the matter, Amin explained over lunch one afternoon that while there are certainly issues of Muslim-Christian animosity throughout Egypt, "when Christians go to the [US] embassy, they tell them [they want to travel because of] persecution." The (dis)connection between these two comments set off my more extensive fieldwork, with guidance from Amin, on the transnational contentions and imperial encounters of minority migration between Bahjūra and Jersey City.

Centering Upper Egypt in this book is intentional. Conducting extensive fieldwork in the south of Egypt has been limited for most scholars because, outside the tourist centers of Luxor and Aswan, the region is a web of interconnected kinship relations that are difficult to navigate as an outsider. Beyond difficulty of research, though, Upper Egypt has been a region of national importance—the site of exclusion and otherness—and failed imperial ambitions. Egyptian historian Zeinab Abul-Magd details how successions of imperial conquest in the north have been substantively defeated in the southern provinces, and their control of the south has consistently been "imagined."[92] Yet the historiography and anthropology of imperialism in Egypt have long focused on Egypt's north and have been dominated by elite, Cairo-centric approaches. Martina Rieker has argued that under British colonialism, the process of building the modern state positioned the populations of Cairo and the Delta as citizens and relegated the southern population to cheap labor.[93] Upper Egypt—in its social, political, and cultural difference—has a layered story to tell about class and migration in the region's relation with imagined empires, past and present.[94]

This book centers Upper Egypt in thinking about the transnational politics of migration and the intersections of religion and empire. Using Abul-Magd's idea of "imagined empires" allows for a more nuanced understanding of the relationship between the United States and Upper Egypt in migrant circuits, through knowledge production and movement. While Upper Egypt is portrayed by Egyptian cultural media, as well as national discourse, as impenetrable and disconnected, its inhabitants are highly connected and assimilated into the globalized structure of power, reachable by the forces of multinational corporations and affiliated NGOs, but also by means of migration to the center of imperial America through the Green Card Lottery, asylum, and family reunification. For anthropologists, the remote village has long been the location of "traditional culture," a place in which to discover modernity's other and a site of redemption removed from the metropole and the global system.⁹⁵ In conversation with creative anthropological methodologies on scale and circulation, this book approaches an ostensibly remote village— Bahjūra—as the very site of empire, the heart of the economy of blood. In dialectic with this scaled conversation, though, this book tracks the refractions of empire through the communities that are in relation to it, through their desires for and imaginings about "the outside."⁹⁶

In this way, migration exceeds most scholarship that directs itself toward emigration and immigration.⁹⁷ While the method of the book traces moving bodies, kinships, and imperial formations, it centers its conceptual thrust on the spillage of migration in discourse, landscape, and memory.⁹⁸ Working in tension with the dichotomy "between the global blob and local detail," I focus on the "complex interpenetrations of different orders of magnitude" that affect my interlocutors' lives and flow through processes of migration.⁹⁹ As with recent anthropological approaches such as "transhumant ethnography," this book tracks how Coptic possibilities of belonging and community are scaled and shaped by local and global forces of violence and migration, authoritarianism and imperial intervention—from the mundane process of applying for the Green Card Lottery in rural Coptic churches in Egypt to their translations of persecution and suffering in US asylum courtrooms.¹⁰⁰

With this background, this book is based on twenty-four months (2016–2022) of ethnographic fieldwork among Coptic migrants, first-, second-, and third-generation American Copts, and Coptic Orthodox clergy members moving transnationally between Bahjūra, Najʿ Ḥammādī, Upper Egypt, and Jersey City, New Jersey, as well as conferences on Christian persecution in Washington, DC.¹⁰¹ Based on that fieldwork, this book empirically outlines how Coptic Christians, the largest Christian community in the Middle East, have increasingly immigrated to the United States since the Arab Spring and how scaled imaginations of this migration have intersected with American religious and political interest in the idea of global Christian persecution.[102] Journeying back and forth across sites of migration, everyday practices, connections, and conflict trace transnational Coptic communal formation as it interfaces with the tension between their minority status in Egypt and their racial-religious placement within an American Christian conservative landscape. Coptic migrants relate to each other through their religious tradition as well as their transnational minority condition. Their struggle to grapple with different minority positions between Egypt and the United States is what articulates their own political praxis and frames their interpellation into a broader US geopolitical frame of international religious freedom advocacy and strategies of counterterrorism, which I argue is part of a contemporary constellation of bloody theopolitics. This does not mean that Coptic migrants, positioned within these broader structures of theopolitical power, are simply conscripts of US empire or, conversely, fully outside empire's grasp.

The case of the Copts offers a window onto how empire shapes transnational minority communities in the (re)narration of their collective identity and the transformation of their political orientations, racial identification, and religious solidarities. Transnational migrants and the multi-temporal character of their diasporic lives exist within multiple realities, what anthropologist Ghassan Hage has called "diasporic lenticularity"—or a "mode of existing in multiple realities"—which allows for an accounting of how migration has impacted life beyond homeland/diaspora framings.[103] In the Coptic context, this mode of existence has foregrounded violence and bloody death as a key means through which community is remembered.[104] Coptic collective memory today is in movement, translated and entangled across different scales of recognition and geographies of empire.[105] This book threads together narratives and collective memory of diasporic communities, but takes a transnational approach to better attend to the global circuits of power that are enmeshed in multidirectional circulations and imperial remakings of knowledge, community, and kinship in both Egypt and the United States, a formulation of circuitry that Nadine Naber has described as "diasporas of empire."[106]

The ordinary affects of imperial reconfigurations of life, thought, and practice are caught both in broad transnational circuits of people and politics and in the reformations of intimate life.[107] Kathleen Stewart has elaborated that ordinary affects are "not the kind of analytic object that can be laid out on a single, static plane of analysis and they don't lend themselves to a perfect, three-tiered parallelism between analytic subject, concept, and world."[108] The idea of "ordinary affects," in this book, argues then not for clear-cut causations, but rather imperial encounters that are fractious and multiplicitous.[109] To trace such ordinary affects of empire, this book opens windows onto different analytics and lifeworlds—from Egypt to the United States, from Najʿ Ḥammādī to New Jersey. Such ordinary affects are "a problem or question emergent in disparate scenes and incommensurate forms and registers."[110] In mapping these different scales, I bring together coexisting forms of translation and event to show the interplay of minority migrant life, and the longue durée of blood theology in the Body of Christ as a theopolitical communal formation. The layered textures of the scenes scattered throughout the book—between different geographies, structures, and temporalities—speak to the elusive nature of power, where glimpses of it can be captured in its reflections and in its shadows.

Chapter Map

The book is structured by two parts, divided between the figure of the martyr and the figure of the migrant, with each chapter circulating scenes in Bahjūra and in the New York–New Jersey area to demonstrate scaled flows. Part 1, "Scales of Blood," specifically attends to the tension of the martyr in the context of diasporic political belonging, memory and migration routes, and legal translations. Chapter 1, "Persecution and Power," sets the itinerary for the study of the intersection of contemporary American persecution politics and narratives of Coptic martyrdom. It focuses on how American persecution politics of the late twentieth century fed into diasporic activism and advocacy among Copts in the United States, and shaped transnational Coptic identity in the process. The chapter briefly traces diasporic Coptic politics prior to the end of the Cold War. Starting in earnest throughout the 1970s, Coptic migrants to the United States organized to combat increasing sectarian violence impacting their brethren in Egypt. During the 1980s, new connections between diasporic activists and conservative American politicians, religious leaders, and policy makers were formed through a shared interest in Christian persecution under Islamic rule. This chapter provides historical analysis on the convergence of the Christian Right's ascendance and the emergence of the United States as the world's sole superpower and shows how that development influenced the way Eastern Christian minority migrant communities like the Copts shaped their communal narratives and political activism. Ultimately, this historical analysis provides the context for a more contemporary engagement with the transnational politics of Coptic identity and communal kinship in a new era of immigration from Egypt to the United States.

Chapter 2, "Sectarian Memory and Migration Forces," examines the contemporary conditions of Coptic emigration from Egypt to the United States, centering primarily on the Diversity Visa, or Green Card Lottery. International media, Western politicians and policy makers, and diasporic Copts themselves have argued that Christians in the region are facing extinction and are fleeing for their lives from the forces of rising religious extremism and sectarian violence. Focusing on the politics of collective memory among Copts in Egypt's rural South, this chapter examines the contentious ethnographic texture of transnational migration for a Christian minority community in the Middle East. Instead of concluding that such migration is either forced or voluntary, the chapter analyzes how the exigency to decide the validity of such a narrative of flight shapes so many lives and policies of empire.

Chapter 3, "Religious Difference and Asylum Law," focuses on processes of asylum seeking among Coptic migrants to the United States after the 2011 Egyptian revolution, and specifically addresses the paradoxes of persecution through the lens of the US asylum system. Western news media described post-revolutionary Coptic migration from Egypt as an "exodus," and focused on the suffering of Copts at the hands of Islamist groups, the Egyptian government, and everyday Muslims. Such media narratives and discursive formations—of Christian victim and Muslim perpetrator—have affected the adjudication of Coptic asylum cases in the United States. The chapter attends to the idea of "commonsense legality," which tracks how shifts in legal rationalization and bureaucracy altered how Coptic cases were made to be persuasive, and ethnographically follows Coptic asylum seekers as they apply, interview, sit in courtrooms awaiting decision, and anticipate a return to Egypt.

In part 2, "Communities of Blood," the book scales downward to focus on how Coptic Christians have navigated these broader structures that shape political belonging and communal movements—through processes of racialization, transmissions of morality around issues of gender and sexuality, and the upending of martyr narratives in the shadows of Coptic migration. Chapter 4, "Affective Bodies and Security Praxis," illustrates how Copts have contended with the war on terror and the securitization of Middle Eastern and American Muslim life. Following September 11, 2001, many Middle Eastern Christians had to renegotiate their communal identity within American society, reconfiguring how they identified and whom they identified with. Coptic Christians in Egypt have contended with their own Christian minority status within a predominantly Muslim country, experiencing violent attacks, bombings of religious institutions, and everyday forms of discrimination. As chapter 2 details, these experiences varyingly shape the reasons why Copts immigrate to the United States. Yet the political imaginary of diasporic Copts in the United States builds on these experiences and formations of collective memory in Egypt and transposes them onto a new context of racialization and imperial expansion, in the era of the war on terror. Put another way, Coptic collective memory and cultural trauma as a Christian minority community in Egypt are reimagined in light of US terror rhetoric and new discourses on the threat of radical Islam, and these migrant experiences of securitization and translations of Muslim threat circulate back to Egypt in unique ways. As chapter 4 details, in the post-9/11 New York–New Jersey area, Coptic Christians contended with the optics of security threats by negotiating their racialized positionality and crafting their communal worth in line with national security interests.

Chapter 5, "Diasporic Translations and Global Culture Wars," shows how transnational Coptic Christians have remapped indigenous narratives of persecution and martyrdom, not merely as a form of American political legibility, but also as part of the fight to retain "traditional values." Threading the theopolitical import of the global persecution of Christians (discussed in chapter 1) to a domestic "war on Christians" in the United States has allowed American Christians in/with power to argue that while the blood of Christians does not yet spill into American streets as elsewhere in the world, there are anti-Christian forces working to enact such a plan. In a diasporic context, the weaving of minority victimhood in Egypt (which has included discrimination, violence, and death) and the Christian victimhood of moral injury in the United States appeals to Coptic sensibilities and histories of persecution and martyrdom, and reforms them in translation. Weaving together American Coptic conservative perspectives on religious and cultural life in the United States with new forms of local organizing, the chapter unfolds a distinct form of persecution politics in a diasporic key.

The conclusion, "Wages and Witness," reiterates the thread of class in the duality of martyr and migrant through blood. It briefly zooms in to an alternative site in the American South—Nashville, Tennessee, where Coptic grassroots movements have formed political alliances and migrant networks with other people of color and marginalized communities. These organizations aim to challenge the Christian persecution narrative and instead focus on the suffering of working-class Coptic migrants from Upper Egypt, who are racialized and segregated in Nashville's poorest neighborhoods. Broadly, the conclusion posits unconventional narratives in opposition to the predominant forms of transnational Coptic life as part of a global attack on Christianity. It attends to Coptic "misfits" internal to the transnational community, but also representational misfits within an imperial economy of blood.[111] In these glimpses of otherwise, the conclusion opens the possibility for other strategies of kin-making and solidarity, as well as layers of disappointment and disaster beyond the martyr-migrant binary.

PART I

Scales of Blood

1

Persecution and Power

Every June, the lobbying organization Coptic Solidarity holds a conference in Washington, DC, with the aim of raising awareness about the persecution of Coptic and other Middle Eastern Christians. The Copt-run organization advocates for Coptic minority rights in Egypt among American politicians, religious leaders, and activists for human rights and international religious freedom. When I attended Coptic Solidarity's 2016 conference, entitled "The Future of Egypt's Religious Minorities: Status of Copts after Two Revolutions," attendees were reeling from a recent attack on an elderly Coptic woman in the village of al-Karm, al-Minyā, Upper Egypt. A rumor had spread in the village about a love affair between a Christian man and a Muslim woman. A mob of forty Muslims burned the Christian's home to the ground, beat up the family, and dragged the seventy-year-old matriarch, Suad Thabet, naked through the streets.[1] Former Coptic Solidarity president Alex Shalaby noted at the conference, "The shameful incident in al-Minyā serves as a reminder that Christians in Egypt continue to be the victims of discrimination and violence committed by perpetrators that all too often escape the hands of justice." Republican and Democratic politicians with large Coptic constituencies or strong interest in international religious freedom intermittently cycled into the room between speakers and sessions. Coptic clergy blessed the gathering, and elite figures such as Egyptian Coptic billionaire Naguib Sawiris were the keynote figures of the conference.

During the second panel on the rights of Christians in Muslim-majority polities, Nina Shea, senior fellow at the Hudson Institute, a conservative think tank in Washington, DC, garnered the most attention from her audience of Copts and US congressmen:

> Today is the second anniversary of the ISIS attack on Mosul and from there all of Nineveh (Iraq), in which every last Christian, Yezidi, and non-Sunni Muslim was told to convert or die. There is no Christian

community intact in the so-called Caliphate. There is no religious leader, and there is no church that is functioning throughout all of Nineveh. Instead, those Christians are huddled in seven-foot-wide shipping containers in Kurdistan under the protection of the Kurds. They are basically in a hopeless limbo, waiting that someday they will be allowed to go back to their lands and rebuild their lives. . . . Despite these tragic circumstances in Iraq and Syria, the face of ISIS persecution and the face of Christian faithfulness in the region are the twenty Egyptian Copts and one Ghanaian man beheaded on the shores of Libya last year [2015]. That is the iconic image of ISIS persecution of Christians and the fate of Christians under radical Islam.

Because so many people can't speak in Egypt, we need to use our power here. . . . I'm thinking now of these Christians in Kurdistan and from Iraq and Syria. What can the US do there? I have two basic "next steps": one is to help those who need to leave, to leave, and those who want to stay, stay . . . but yet there is no visa policy in the US to help these Christians. We're ramping up our Syrian refugee policy, and yet half of one percent of those people given visas are Christian, the rest are Sunni Muslim.

An older Coptic man sitting in the front row interjected, "Can you help us get priority for Christians fleeing the Middle East?" Shea responded, "That's what I'm trying to do."

At the conference, think tank fellows interfaced with diasporic activists keen on finding solutions to the plight of Christians in Egypt. Politicians, think tank fellows, and government officials from the State Department, by way of panels and conversation, interpreted Coptic suffering and translated local contexts in Egypt and elsewhere in the Middle East through evangelical imaginaries and US political interests.

Louis Gohmert, former Republican congressman from Texas, took the podium later in the day and elevated the role of the United States in saving Middle Eastern Christians, particularly the Copts. Gohmert wove together a tapestry of American imperial power, calling on the United States to save the world from evil enemies:

"To whom much is given, much is required."[2] The United States has been so richly blessed, and it was Jesus that said to his own disciples, "You're

Figure 1.1. Coptic icon of the twenty-one receiving the crown of martyrdom. Painted by Washington, DC-based iconographer Tony Rezk.

going to suffer for my sake,"[3] and they did. They were blessed beyond measure, but they suffered for his sake. Growing up in the United States, I did not suffer for Christ's sake . . . but Christians are now suffering around the United States, and still nothing like we see of the suffering of Christians in Egypt. If America does not stand up and use the gifts we have been given as a force for good, and a force to stop evil in the world, then we will not get to keep this gift. . . . One of my biggest concerns is that since we have had the power to stand up for Christians across the world and stop their persecution, we have not, and now Christians are being persecuted in greater numbers than any time in history. And I believe it is our obligation as the United States of America that if we don't stop this, where God has given us the ability, then our run will be over and some other nation will be raised as the great nation and it may not be a freedom-loving, caring, compassionate nation. It may be horrible. . . . I believe that we have a role, that we have been blessed with a purpose here in the United States, and I hope God will forgive us for the lack of leadership we have shown in stopping the persecution of Christians. . . . Hopefully we'll get the message across that will allow America to be the best friend Coptics could ever hope to have, short of heaven.

For Gohmert and other American Christians, there is a global war on Christianity, shaped by narratives and representations of persecution. The United States, as global superpower and empire, has taken up the role of protector of the world's suffering. Christians of the Middle East like the Copts have figured prominently in these narratives and have shaped this moral imaginary over the past three decades. Yet American persecution politics—like that exemplified by Gohmert—centers on the idea of an oppressed *majority*, advancing a political praxis of victimhood from a position of religious-racial imperial power. In the latter half of the twentieth century, American evangelicals and their ecumenical counterparts increasingly focused on a vision of Christian victimization in narratives of their own religious identity and also focused on a broader transnational awareness of a global Christian community in peril. During the Cold War, evangelical narratives of persecution were centered on the suffering of Christians under communism, especially in the Soviet Union. As the Cold War ended, this global vision began to break down. While American evangelicals have had religio-political interests in the Middle East since nineteenth-century missions, new opportunities for alliance, kinship, and connection presented themselves in the 1980s, when evangelical leaders and their ecumenical partners along with American politicians began to remap their visions of global Christian kinship in bloody persecution and martyrdom.

While early organizing throughout the 1970s focused on aiding kin in Egypt amid rising incidents of violence against Christians, new connections in the 1980s between Coptic activists and conservative American politicians, religious leaders, and policy makers were formed through a strengthening movement to address *global* Christian persecution. This chapter provides historical analysis on the domestic ascendance of the Christian Right and the rise of global American supremacy and shows how those developments structured how Christian minority migrant communities like the Copts molded (and continue to mold) their communal narratives and political activism into the twenty-first century.

Diasporic Political Praxis

In the 1960s and 1970s, Arab American political action became part of flourishing racial and ethnic minority rights activism, converging on an anti-imperialist ideology.[4] This activism was shaped by Arab Americans' distinctive experiences of injustice and forms of racialization between homeland and diaspora.[5] While more leftist Arab Americans saw their positionality in solidarity with racial-religious others in the United States, different community members focused their attentions on homeland causes and more effective ways to lobby on behalf of kin. Coptic exclusion from these forms of activism and advocacy stemmed from the minority position of Copts in Egypt, a difference and form of marginalization that were rarely acknowledged by such leftist networks. The collective memory of religious persecution in Egypt forged the communal alliances and political futures of diasporic Copts. While Copts, along with Arab Americans, experience anti-Arab stereotyping and discrimination in the United States, such experiences did not form the primary ethos of their diasporic political praxis.[6] While Coptic racialization has been seemingly indistinguishable from Arab American racialization, Coptic political engagement with and activism against such stereotypes have historically been lacking.[7] Primarily, this is because anti-Arab racism has been hinged with anti-Muslim racism. It is here at the intersection of race and religion that Copts are interpellated into the very figures (Islam/Muslims) that they seek to distance themselves from and undo in diaspora; shifting the gaze back onto Islam and Muslims (in Egypt and elsewhere) as the primary sources of their (Coptic as well as global Christian) persecution.[8] This problem space has forged the primary paradox of activism and advocacy among this migrating minority over the past sixty years.

* * *

In November 1972, the city of al-Khanka (twelve miles northeast of Cairo) became a center of intercommunal strife in Egypt. The Holy Bible Society in the city was set ablaze by local Muslims who had learned that the building's facilities were being used as an unlicensed church. The late Coptic pope Shenouda III responded by sending a flock of clergy members to hold prayers outside the damaged building. In response, local Muslims staged their own rally and subsequently burned Coptic-owned shops and homes in retaliation. To quell the tension, then president Anwar al-Sadat ordered an investigation by a special parliamentary commission.[9] While recommendations were made toward better government procedures for church licensing and construction, they were not implemented. Moreover, the Egyptian government did not bring charges against the assailants, and that failure weighed on Copts abroad.

In this context, a growing community in the United States saw an opening to help their kin back in Egypt through the establishment of a political advocacy group.[10] By counteracting the Egyptian state's dismissal of intercommunal violence, diasporic Coptic activists emphasized the sectarian motives of these crimes and sought reparation. Mathematics professor and community organizer Shawky Karas established the American Coptic Association (ACA) to denounce Sadat's positive rhetoric and political orientation toward rising Islamist movements in Egypt and to raise awareness among US policy makers about discrimination against Copts.[11] On Bergen Avenue in Jersey City, New Jersey, down the street from one of the main Coptic Orthodox churches in the tri-state area, Karas secured a headquarters for the organization, a multistoried home that could house a library, meeting rooms, and offices. The space was meant as a multigenerational hub for an emerging group of Coptic professionals to strategize and organize their movement. Part of these organizing efforts for the ACA was the publication of a newsletter entitled *The Copts: Christians of Egypt* that would circulate and curate a global defense of Coptic rights in Egypt.

The newsletter's archive featured original publications as well as reprinted articles and analyses on the Coptic plight from a variety of Western outlets that reported on anti-Christian violence through ecumenical frames and as human rights violations. During the 1970s and 1980s, the newsletter appealed to an Egypt-centric audience, but slowly began to adjust to growing interest in Copts from non-Egyptians. The newsletter was equally divided between English and Arabic, for Coptic immigrants to remain keyed into happenings against kin in Egypt and to advocate on their behalf, but also for American audiences to become acquainted "with the religious suppression and discrimination being perpetrated against Copts (Christians) in Egypt."[12]

Amid these diasporic responses and following a brief respite of intercommunal tension after al-Khanka, the latter part of the decade

Figure 1.2. American Coptic Association demonstrations in front of the United Nations in October 1978. *The Copts*, March 1979.

saw increased strain in the relationship between President Sadat and Pope Shenouda. Rising Islamist influence on Sadat's regime culminated in administrative and legislative outputs. In 1977 the government introduced draft legislation in the People's Assembly for the application of Islamic law in cases of libel, theft, and apostasy. Subsequent social debate on the matter led to an increasing number of clashes between Muslims and Christians, without much government intervention.[13] In response to raised tensions in Egypt and Sadat's governmental response (or lack thereof), the ACA lobbied US government officials and protested in front of the United Nations to voice its concerns. Images of the protests and their messages reached President Sadat, who grew concerned over the growing nuisance of Coptic diasporic advocacy. To counteract these diasporic efforts, the Egyptian government monitored and intimidated activists, and used media to defame the Coptic diaspora (*aqbāṭ al-mahjar*) as disloyal and as traitors to the nation.

Almost a decade after al-Khanka, in June 1981, Cairo's al-Zāwya al-Ḥamra' neighborhood became the site of a bloody incident of intercommunal violence initially over land and church construction that spilled into local clashes resulting in at least seventeen dead and dozens injured. The ACA responded through protests and publications in *The Copts* newsletter demanding accountability. As diasporic action gained greater attention from the Egyptian government during the 1970s, Pope Shenouda feared increasing anti-Christian violence from this transnational call to justice and appealed to them to set aside their demands and to appease calls to national unity, circulating bishops on repeated visits to parishes in New York, Toronto, and Montreal—but to no avail.[14] This minority opposition abroad increased conflict between immigrants and the Coptic Church in diaspora, as well as between church and state in Egypt.

On August 5, 1981, the ACA and the Canadian Coptic Association (CCA) published an open letter to Sadat in preparation for his imminent visit to the United States. Following the Camp David peace accords, Sadat was particularly angered by diasporic protests and political actions against him while abroad. An August 1981 ad in the *Washington Post*, for example, described how the "violation of the civil and human rights of Christians is a daily routine," with churches being "bombed and burned," Coptic men being "burned alive," and Coptic children "thrown off balconies."[15] The ACA, in English, sought to connect Sadat to figures like Muammar al-Qaddafi of Libya and Ayatollah Khomeini of Iran, who promoted "state-sponsored fundamentalism." The August 1981 ad describes such incidents in Egypt as a "Muslim fanatical onslaught on the Christian minority."

Following these events and his return to Egypt, Sadat sought retribution for his embarrassment from the Coptic diasporic pressure regarding the situation in Egypt. In early September 1981, Sadat ordered the mass arrests of over 1,500 state, religious, and public figures in Egypt, including members of the Coptic clerical hierarchy. Days after, the government barricaded Saint Bishoy monastery, in Wādī al-Naṭrūn, and Sadat subsequently announced the suspension of the presidential decree approving Shenouda as pope and supported the creation of a council of five bishops to lead the Church in his absence.[16] By removing Pope Shenouda, Sadat attempted to quell intercommunal tension in Egypt that was ever heightened by increased activism from the diaspora.

In the United States, Coptic activists, including and especially Shawky Karas, sided with Shenouda, splitting the diaspora between the makeshift Church hierarchy newly appointed by Sadat and those imprisoned. Over these tumultuous years, Sadat increasingly became fixated on the threat of the Coptic diaspora. Abdel Latif El-Menawy, who once headed the news division of the Egyptian Radio and Television Organization, catalogues Sadat's moments of frustration with this "small group" from New Jersey and in Washington, DC (referring to the ACA): "Why do these Copts want to turn the Christians of the World against me and Egypt?" Sadat would complain repeatedly.[17]

Karas and other Coptic activists wrote about accusations of treason by the Egyptian government and both Muslim and Christian Egyptians for their diasporic action. Accusations of treason reference the possibility of ulterior motives to diasporic Coptic activism, whether it be agitating for the downfall of Egypt, sowing sectarian strife, or being imperial stooges of the United States. However, these arguments fail to account for the embrace of Coptic difference by those in the diaspora and the shunning of national unity rhetoric, which forces Copts (and the Coptic Orthodox Church) to proclaim intercommunal harmony, even in the face of conflict. When Karas and other activists emerged as voices of dissent outside Egypt, the postcolonial rejection of foreign interference and influence in national affairs made it impossible for Copts outside Egypt, especially in the West, to express their demands without mediation by neocolonial and imperial structures, whether through American political interests, the English language, or Western Christian solidarities.

By imagining Christian identity in Egypt as Coptic-ness, and not through the lens of national unity, diasporic activists like Shawky Karas faced a conundrum: they looked to Western governments and political organizations for support in pressuring the Egyptian government, with the risk of being deemed treasonously "foreign." Yet they still understood that they were themselves specifically Coptic, which made them racial and religious foreigners in the West. With this, they creatively translated their Eastern Christianity to Western Christian audiences increasingly focused on combatting the threat of Islamic terrorism and on highlighting growing global Christian persecution, especially in Muslim-majority contexts.

"Strangers in Their Land"

In a grainy home video from 1991, Elhamy Khalil, one of the first Coptic immigrants to the United States, interviewed Shawky Karas at his Connecticut home. With Khalil behind the camera, Karas sat in a wood-framed chair with a flower-patterned cushion; he wore a tan polo shirt with navy blue slacks, and a large gold ring on his middle finger. Originally from Sūhāj, Karas spoke in a thick Upper Egyptian accent as he laid out his vision for the future of Coptic identity in the diaspora by tracing the history of political activism.[18] In the midst of this varied discussion, which ranged from the role of the Coptic Orthodox Church in the lives of transnational Copts to liturgical language and protest tactics, Karas centered his activist ethos around a particular framing of violence and translation. In his accounts of the attacks against and killings of Copts from the 1970s and into the early 1980s, Coptic collective trauma was reimagined through the idiom of genocide and mass death:

> Silence about these things is very dangerous. The genocide against Armenians in 1915 killed over 1.5 million. It started in 1914, and people were silent about the preceding attacks and threats. That silence encouraged Turkey to continue their genocidal campaign to eliminate around 1.5 million Armenians in 1915. And in 1934, there was the beginnings of attacks against Jews, and the Jews were silent because they were scared of increasing the number of attacks, which encouraged Hitler to ultimately murder over 6 million Jews. It is clear from history that silence about these transgressions [al-taʿdiyat] encourages the aggressor [al-muʿatdi].[19]

Similar connections made to genocide and the Holocaust were reflected in protest signs and in *The Copts* newsletter with reprinted articles such as "Documents of the Christian Holocaust Carried Out by the Muslim Arabs" (July 1988).[20] Karas's book *The Copts since the Arab Invasion: Strangers in Their Land*, published in 1986, emphasizes that the Copts in diaspora must urgently fight for Copts in Egypt to survive. On the back cover, Karas describes the book as "the story of a people who faced many holocausts which far exceed any holocaust in the history of mankind; and still in a continuous fear of annihilation. It is a story of survival under extremely adverse conditions." Coptic identity is sutured to waves of violence, described as "holocausts" and "annihilation." The main aggressor in this narrative is the Arab and the colonizing imposition of Arab cultural identity, limiting the exploration of Coptic histories, sensibilities, and flourishing. More specifically, Karas argues that Copts should also be considered the "living victims of Arab imperialism."

While shaping a discursive, political grammar legible to Western audiences, Karas's book was also published at a crucial time for Christians in Egypt that exceeded the translation of the Coptic plight onto American terrain. Pope Shenouda was released from house arrest under president Hosni Mubarak, and the Church took on a different tone with the Egyptian government. Shenouda and Sadat's relationship was one of strain, given the patriarch's open criticism of the state's handling of violence against the Christian minority in Egypt. Following house arrest, however, Shenouda's tone was one of accommodation. Karas and the ACA aligned with the interests of the earliest era of Shenouda, when confrontation and calls for equality were well established. Toward the mid- to late 1980s, their interests diverged and Karas stood in opposition to the Church's official stance. He criticized the bishops who subsequently came to the United States to receive the Egyptian president, saying,

> Why do these bishops come to America only when the Egyptian president is here? Is the purpose of their presence to mask the Coptic plight [in Egypt] and show clerical support for the fanatical Egyptian government? . . . I suggest buying a house next to the Washington, DC, airport where a Coptic bishop can reside and we can name him the "bishop of the airport" to greet President Mubarak instead of all of the bishops having to travel seven thousand miles.[21]

Karas criticized the Church for distancing itself from any calls for equality and protest against discrimination. The problems of the Coptic people, he suggested, extend beyond the domination of Egypt's Muslims in public life and the discriminatory practices of the Egyptian government. The Coptic Church and Copts themselves are responsible for their plight, as they cooperate with the government that uses them to cover up discrimination and violence against their own communities in Egypt: "The Coptic problem is caused not by the Muslims, but by the lack of courage [*al-rakib al-mūkhlaʿa*] among the Copts to whom the words of Jesus Christ apply: '[But woe to you, scribes and Pharisees, hypocrites! For you shut up the kingdom of heaven against men;] for you neither go in yourselves, nor do you allow those who are entering to go in.'"[22]

According to those who worked with Karas in the ACA during the 1980s and 1990s, Karas's activist fervor stemmed from personal experiences of violence and discrimination in Sūhāj, which translated into what he saw as the collective trauma of the Coptic people, particularly in modern Egypt.[23] While the title *The Copts since the Arab Invasion* suggests that it would discuss Coptic history and tribulation from 641 AD, the book almost exclusively focuses on the twentieth century, when Egypt was under British colonial rule, and concentrates intensely on the postcolonial reign of Egyptian president Gamal Abdel Nasser and the rise of sectarian violence under subsequent president Anwar al-Sadat. Aside from a brief overview of the Coptic Church's practices, theology, and history (parts not written by Karas himself), the majority of the text is divided into two parts, on the political participation of Copts prior to the 1952 Egyptian revolution, and on their suppression thereafter.[24] The year 1952 symbolizes a transition from an era of political influence among the Copts under British colonialism to postcolonial Egypt, where the rights and privileges of the elite—both Coptic and Muslim—were stripped away in favor of a more populist program. The remaining Egyptian government, Karas suggests, was comprised of or influenced by "Muslim fundamentalists."[25]

To explain his position, Karas recounts incidents of violence against the Copts in the lead-up to this new era. He examines what he notes as the "Suez Massacre" of 1952 in detail.[26] At 2:00 pm on January 4, a group of Muslims, after hearing the Friday sermon, went after a group of Christians in the street. They dragged the Christians using butcher hooks and eventually burned them alive by locking them inside Saint Antonious Church. The perpetrators were never brought to justice. The murders were directly connected to the British occupational forces in the city. Rumors had spread that Copts were working with the British against the local militia, and the attacks followed. Karas's and other Copts' retellings of the incident explain that the shared Christianity of the Copts with the British colonizers led the local Muslim community to suspect the Copts of conspiracy.[27] "It is customary in Egypt that any kind of conflict between Christians and Muslims in any part of the world, it will have spillover on the safety of Egypt's Christians," Karas wrote.[28]

At various points throughout the text, Karas remarks that under British colonialism, local Coptic Christians became icons of colonialism; particularly among elites, a Copt became a *khuwāja* (foreigner).[29] In this association, Coptic bodies became the site of resistance to colonial rule, as the widespread influence of Western Christian missionaries placed Copts in a contradiction-laden predicament. The Copt as the indigenous Christian and Copts as the "original inhabitants" of Egypt became at once true and false. Copts as *Christians* varyingly were recognized by Egyptian Muslims as icons of the West; thus, Christianity could not be "indigenous" to the region because it was the religion of the West.[30] In the diasporic context of the late twentieth and early twenty-first centuries, the paradox of Middle Eastern Christian identity, like that of the Copts, is one that is entangled in the expansion of Western imperial power.[31] The figure of the Middle Eastern Christian has become an icon, "a form of relationality that binds the subject to an object or imaginary," whereby a shared imagination is embodied; and a civilizational struggle is performed on the body of the Middle Eastern Christian, where a Christian West meets a Muslim East.[32] In this way, Christianity has come to be understood as inseparable from Western power.

This logic is threaded throughout Karas's discussion of Sadat's speech to the People's Assembly in Cairo on May 14, 1980, where Sadat publicly accused the Coptic Church of committing sedition in its forms of protest against rising sectarian tensions throughout the previous decade. Karas's recounting documents the transnational anxieties of a Coptic civil society organization in diaspora and the increasingly global focus of the Coptic Orthodox Church. In the speech, Sadat asserts that the Church has "pitted the Christians of the world" against him in their protest. The "Christians" here refer to Western leaders, such as then president Jimmy Carter, who voiced sympathy for the Copts.[33]

Diasporic leaders like Shawky Karas were viewed by Sadat and others within Egyptian state security as threats to the stability and national sovereignty of Egypt. Karas insists that the ACA was a necessary organization because Egyptian authorities had not listened to the needs of the Copts, and that encouraged them to "demonstrate [their] religious concerns abroad."[34] He envisioned the ACA not just as an advocacy organization for Copts, but as a bulwark against "the religious fanaticism sweeping the region."[35] In the struggle for equal rights in Egypt, Karas was acutely aware that this activism placed Copts in a precarious position vis-à-vis Western power. The incessant focus on persecution and discrimination through this activism altered Coptic community in the process: "The sad part of it all is that for many individuals who long felt subjugated and oppressed, [they] end up being obsessed with that one issue which totally colors their attitude and feelings towards the oppressors."[36]

As migration to the West persisted throughout this period, Coptic diasporic activism was communicated through and transformed by the demands of American empire. How they relayed their demands to the US government for equal rights in Egypt became increasingly shaped by new vocabularies, new enemies, and securitized discourses on Islam.

In a letter entitled "Doesn't Anybody Care?" published in the *New York Times*, diasporic activists wrote the following in their explanation of Christian conditions in Egypt: "For Moslems in many lands, the crusades have not ended; they are still defending themselves against western invaders. Their overheated, venomous rhetoric about colonialism, Zionism, and the demonic west reflects this eleventh century outlook. The most obvious example is Iran, but the same psychology pervades Egypt as well. And Christians, even Coptic Christians who lived in Egypt for centuries before Islam, are associated with the invading westerners."[37] After emigrating to the United States, Coptic Christians were able to more explicitly voice their grievances against Egyptian Muslims (and critiques against Islam more broadly), but Egyptian contexts were also essentialized and translated through US religious contexts of the Christian Right and policy interests in political Islam (which intensified during the First Gulf War). Closing out the millennium, Coptic diasporic activism derived from Egyptian contexts of violence but was also positioned within an American imperial milieu.

On the Arabic cover of *The Copts* from January 1990, a Coptic cross from Pope Macarius III (1872–1945) centers the page (figure 1.3). On top is a quote from Acts 18:9–10 in Arabic: "Do not be afraid, but speak and do not keep silent; for I am with you." Below the cross, in English, reads the following: "Now is The Triumph of the Cross. The Triumph of the Cross and Freedom in Eastern Europe and The Soviet Union. We pray

Figure 1.3. *The Copts* newsletter cover, January 1990.

for the Triumph of the Cross and Freedom in the Middle East and Other Parts of the World." The cover centers Coptic religious heritage, with a call to action on behalf of transnational kin. Yet it also translates Copticity through a new lens—of Christian persecution whether under communism *or* Islam. The United States' victory over the Soviet Union meant that the world had one remaining superpower, and a new global enemy began to emerge. The positionality of Copts as "living victims" of Islam became the central node of translation into political activism and advocacy in the United States, as Islam and terrorism began to take center stage in America's national security strategy and defensive religious ethos.

Imperial Christian Kinship

All Christians everywhere, the body of Christ, are really one body, so if one part is feeling pain, we should all be feeling pain. . . . The Christian woman raped in Egypt, that is my sister. The guy shot in Pakistan, that is my brother.
—Amy Wierman, "A Rising Movement Cites Persecution Facing Christians"

The US national security and intelligence shift from communism to Islam paralleled a new missionary focus among evangelicals around the globe. In 1989 the Second International Conference on World Evangelization met in Manila, Philippines, where 4,300 evangelicals from 173 countries began to imagine reaching "all the world" for Christ by the year 2000. Argentinian evangelist Luis Bush proposed that the "10/40 window" (an area between 10 degrees and 40 degrees north of the equator, which encompasses the Middle East and much of Asia) demanded particular attention. It is there, Luis Bush said, that Islam, Hinduism, and Buddhism "enslave" the majority of the inhabitants, the "billions of spiritually impoverished souls."[38] The Conference on World Evangelization is part of the Lausanne Movement (also known as the Lausanne Committee for World Evangelization), founded by American evangelical Billy Graham. The movement describes "unreached people" as groups among which there is "no indigenous community of believing Christians with adequate numbers and resources to evangelize."[39]

The Middle East is home to vibrant Orthodox, Catholic, and Protestant Christians (missionized by Europeans and Americans less than a century prior), yet it still fell under the category of the "unreached." For evangelicals like Luis Bush, Islam was and is a social system governing the cultural mores of the Middle East's inhabitants, whether they were Christian or not. To combat Muslim proselytization elsewhere, Bush said, "we must penetrate the heart of Islam with the liberating truth of the gospel."[40] The racialized geography of the Middle East became the renewed target of evangelism and a civilizing mission to enter a new millennium.

Such evangelical moral imaginaries fed into US policy decision making, as information and materials on the Persecuted Church were increasingly produced and disseminated by American and European Christians, as well as Christians throughout the Global South with links to these international networks.[41] The end of the Cold War marked a shift in an evangelical moral mapping of the world and corresponded to the reorientation of US foreign policy. On September 11, 1990, following the expulsion of Iraqi forces from Kuwait, president George H. W. Bush addressed the US Congress. The "New World Order," he said, was one in which the world could be "freer from the threat of terror, stronger in the pursuit of justice and more secure in the quest for peace."[42] This new world order, while purportedly based on cooperation and internationalism, was to be a solely American world order in which "Islam" and "terrorism" were molded as the twin figures of threat.[43] During the latter years of the Cold War, events such as the Iranian hostage crisis (1979–1981), the Beirut barracks bombings (1983), and the First Gulf War (1990–1991) captivated American audiences.[44] For example, nonstop media coverage of the Iranian hostage crisis brought the plight of the hostages and the revolutionary religious fervor of their Iranian captors into the homes of millions of Americans. While each of these contexts had its own politics, American audiences were introduced by news media to new tropes on Islam and terrorism.[45]

American victory in the Cold War aided the narrative of destiny and mission, and affirmed, for evangelicals and politicians alike, the victory of an American model of modernity, endowed with a reinvigorated belief in a universal mission. Moreover, the end of the Cold War coincided with the coalescence of conservative Christianity as a dominant force in America's religio-political landscape. By 1992, for example, the Christian Coalition, founded by Pat Robertson, capitalized on evangelical (and other conservative) Christian feelings that they were quickly becoming a "persecuted" minority.⁴⁶ The domestication of this narrative also coincided with the push by evangelical intellectuals and activists to take up the mantle of human rights as a central paradigm for advocating against Christian persecution in the early 1990s. Key to such advocacy was the juxtaposition of America's advancement of human rights vis-à-vis the Muslim world. Conservatives argued that Islam as a religious tradition was incompatible with the church-state separation that American Christians claimed as a mark of their own commitment to freedom. In tandem with the logic of the 10/40 window, the Muslim world was both a place of "spiritual darkness" (lacking in the salvational light of Western Christianity) and a space where human rights were threatened by the improper mixture of Islam and politics.⁴⁷

From church prayer meetings to lobbying organizations in Washington, DC, Christian persecution was prayed about and translated into networks of witness and testimony as well as advocacy. Engaging frameworks of human rights and religious freedom, the persecuted Christians movement positioned Christian believers as both victims and blessed victors in a "melodrama of steadfastness against evil."⁴⁸ The movement against global Christian persecution brought together religious communities beyond theological difference or denominational distinction. The persecuted could be Protestant, Catholic, or Orthodox Christians, and those most invested in the theopolitical movement tended to be part of a global conservative coalition.

During the Cold War, the scaffolding of popular religious and political support for the Persecuted Church was cultivated through a focus on persecution under communism. Father Keith Roderick, an Episcopal priest of the Diocese of Springfield, Illinois, would become a staunch advocate for Middle Eastern Christians and especially the Copts in Washington, DC, lobbying circles in the 1990s.⁴⁹ Yet his fervor for persecuted Christians began during the Cold War, when he spent about twenty hours a week on various projects connected with Christians under Soviet rule, including writing letters, distributing names of the needy, and editing a newsletter. "There are some people who can't say no in these situations and I'm one of them. . . . Being involved in their suffering and helping, even from a removed standpoint, is rewarding."⁵⁰ Roderick's sentiment of compassion is cultivated within an affective economy of persecution. As Melani McAlister has argued, channeling the work of Elizabeth Spelman, compassion can also be a source of power; "those who feel compassion may attempt to frame the meaning of others' suffering to determine the moral categories and political valences at stake, and in the process mute the sufferer," insisting on making their *suffering* the "object" of compassion.[51] In this movement, suffering solidarity subverts the power asymmetries at play between American Christians and Christians of the Global South and emphasizes a globalism that flattens difference.[52] Solidarity with the suffering for the American Christian, like Roderick, comes from a position not of persecution, but of power; such solidarity with Eastern Christian suffering was not divorced from Roderick's positionality as an American Christian clergyman who focused his energy on political activism in the name of the Persecuted Church.

With the end of the Cold War, Coptic diasporic activists in the United States began to increasingly form new kinds of alliances and audiences with figures like Roderick, and in turn Roderick and many others who were part of the persecuted Christians movement saw Copts as part of a global pattern. As Copts took center stage in this geopolitical battle against Christian persecution, Coptic advocacy "moved with the events, ... with whatever the Middle East Christian topics were at the moment," as one Coptic activist framed it.[53] Coptic diasporic activism was communicated through and transformed by the shifting demands of US empire—where the fight for Coptic rights was also translated through US interest in saving the world from Islamic threat.

Representing Victimhood

Since the 1970s, Copts politically mobilized and translated Egyptian contexts of intercommunal strife and Christian persecution for lobbyists, government officials, and the American public. In this transnational translation, Coptic injury from Egyptian sectarian contexts also lent itself to burgeoning fields of anti-Muslim public discourse. Attending to the translational politics of such minority wounds is important for unpacking the impacts of broader US persecution politics on Middle Eastern Christian identity in diaspora. As discussed by Wendy Brown and Lauren Berlant, "wound culture" curates "the injury of the individual as the grounds not only for an appeal (for compensation or redress), but as an identity claim, such that 'reaction' against the injury forms the very basis of politics, understood as the conflation of truth and injustice." Such critiques should not result in a refusal to listen to painful pasts as histories of injustice (and pain here is understood as the "bodily life of such histories").⁵⁴ More important is listening to the affects and effects of pain as a way of calling into question, rather than assuming, the relationship between collective memory of violence and communal identity.⁵⁵ While the deployment of new vocabularies and discourses on persecution were not wholly shaped within and by US empire, Copts were still compelled to channel their cause and make their plight in Egypt legible to the center of global power. As they did so, histories of social difference in Egypt had to be rendered in translatable form that fundamentally necessitated the transvaluation of local contexts of conflict and violence.⁵⁶

The Copts newsletter showcases this communal transition explicitly by reprinting articles that discuss the Copts as "persecuted" from organizations such as Christian Solidarity International, Voice of the Martyrs, and the Jubilee Campaign (among others), while also using the legitimacy of Western Christian organizations, journalists, politicians, and writers for minority mobilization. Coptic diasporic activists associated with the newsletter utilized grammars, events, and policies that were legible to US policy makers and religious leaders. In the January 1990 issue, for example, the editor notes, "The Egyptian government has been attempting to create new Islamic towns by not allowing the construction of churches. This religious apartheid policy is comparable to the racial policy of South Africa."⁵⁷ Copts adopted and adapted new frameworks to describe their plight and reshaped their Christianity along with changing evangelical politics in the United States.

Along with translating the Coptic plight through American vocabularies of political legitimacy and expediency, Coptic diasporic activists curated an economy of Christian kinship in line with the changing field of the Persecuted Church. In the early 1990s, the newsletter republished open letters on Christian persecution in Egypt, as well as articles on the oppression of Christians in majority-Muslim countries like Sudan, particularly related to issues of forced conversion and punishment for proselytizing. Reprinted in January 1990, "Now Is the Triumph of the Cross" was a speech delivered by Dr. Ernest Gordon, president of the organization Christian Rescue Effort for the Emancipation of Dissidents (CREED) at its 1989 conference, held in Princeton, New Jersey. The speech focused on the memory of communist violence against Christian dissidents and their martyrdom in the face of tyranny, and ended with a call to caution in a postcommunist world to beware of those who compare Christian and communist morality. At the conclusion of the reprint was a comment from the newsletter's editor that read,

> Also, there is no common morality between Christian morality and Islamic morality. Jihad (Holy War) and sexual morality in Islam has nothing in common with Christian morality. The above is a message to the clergy in the Muslim Arab countries who compromise their faith, and even function as propagandists for Muslim Arab dictators who persecute the Christian peoples in the area and suppress their religious freedom.

Issues from the early 1990s saw the proliferation of comparative logics of oppressive regimes. "Will Islamic Socialism Follow Soviet Communism into the Good Night?" read another editorial from 1992.[58]

While maintaining Arabic-language content that focused more specifically on local contexts in Egypt and their transnational translations for the Coptic diaspora, the English-language content of the newsletter evidenced an emerging diasporic imaginary of persecution politics where different incidents became "'linked,' 'amalgamated,' and 'labeled' as one transcendent and value-charged type of thing" that is globally scaled.[59] In this imaginary, Egypt's Christians felt the same experiences as other geopolitically important communities, in such places as Sudan and Pakistan, that were also the focus of US foreign policy and evangelical lobbying efforts. Along with reprinted State Department reports that highlighted killings of Copts and freedom of religion issues, press releases from evangelical organizations such as Voices United for Israel declared, "Severe Persecution of Christians Widespread in Moslem Nations."[60] The conclusion of that press release asks, "How long will Moslem-persecuted Christians be among the forgotten 'friends' of the United States? How long will the United States pursue the policy of rewarding Islamic intolerance?"

In an anonymous editorial from 1992 entitled "Wolves in Sheep's Clothing," a newsletter editor explicitly deals in civilizational language. Writing about the differences between Islam in the Middle East and how Muslim activists in the West politically organize around it, the editorial reads, "They brag about being Americans, and have the American flag cover the background of their program set. This is the same flag Muslims burn in their daily rituals in Iran, calling America 'The great Satan.'" In other newsletters throughout the 1990s, the contrast between Islam and America became even greater. In two editorials from 1995 and 1996, a writer by the name of Victor Mordechai even described the Qur'an as an "Islamic Mein Kampf."[61]

While clearly the work of *The Copts* in the late 1980s and through the 1990s was shaped by several emerging discourses on Islam, fundamentalism, and terrorism, the curation of a Coptic perspective on discrimination against minorities was directly shaped by experiences from the homeland. Although the dangerous consequences of diasporic rhetoric on Islam and Muslims should not be overlooked, Coptic immigrants to the United States also channeled their experiences in Egypt of pervasive discrimination and violence into networks of American empire building.

An Empire of Freedom

In the early 1990s, former Cold War think tanks like the Hudson Institute, Freedom House, and the Institute for Religion and Democracy partnered with religious conservatives in shifting from the fight against godless communism toward the fight against persecution under fundamentalist Islam. In doing so, they began to advocate for religious liberty in new ways, reformulating their Christianity in the process. "Too often people in the West, peering through the selective prism of Christian history in the West, reflexively think of Christians as persecutors, rather than the persecuted," a member of the Southern Baptist Convention commented to a US House of Representatives subcommittee in early 1996 (reprinted in *The Copts* newsletter).[62] The pain of Christian others became the pain of American Christians, an appropriation that transformed and even neutralized non-Western Christian pain into Western Christian compassion. The pain of the persecuted was curated for Western Christian consumption and ultimately political utility with *uneven* effects, and that pain does not produce a homogeneous group of bodies who are together in their pain.[63] As Kleinman, Das, and Lock argue, "Collective suffering is also a core component of the global political economy. There is a market of suffering: victimhood is commodified."[64]

A crystallizing moment for the persecuted Christians movement was at a summit organized in January 1996 in Washington, DC, at the Mayflower Hotel. At the summit, the National Association of Evangelicals, a membership organization of over forty-five thousand congregations, released a "Statement of Conscience" that pushed for the United States to take action to combat religious persecution.[65]

The summit coincided with the creation of a new Coptic organization, US Copts, which tailored its activism to a younger generation of advocates ready to defend international religious freedom in the name of Coptic rights. Michael Meunier, founder of US Copts, represented a new era of activism. Meunier immigrated to the United States in 1990 from the village of Abū Qurqās, al-Minyā, Upper Egypt. After graduating with a degree in mechanical engineering from Virginia Tech, he began to expand his involvement in Coptic politics outside the traditional circles of Shawky Karas and the American Coptic Association (ACA). He described the strategies of the ACA as limiting: "The Copts used to cry to the Copts."[66]

During the 1990s, Karas and others from the ACA collaborated with Father Keith Roderick and Middle Eastern Christian activists such as Walid Phares to move the Coptic issue into the sphere of US foreign policy politics in Washington, DC.[67] Meunier, in his twenties at the time, sought to technologically transform the way the Coptic cause was disseminated in the emerging age of the Internet, capitalizing on his professional career as an IT consultant working for what was then known as Price Waterhouse (now PwC). In 1996 he founded the US Copts Association for the specific purpose of policy advocacy on behalf of the Copts in Egypt and in diaspora, and published Copts.com, the first website to document incidents of violence against Copts in Egypt. The website was updated daily and was able to reach Copts globally.[68] Additionally, Meunier used an email listserv of thousands of Copts, American politicians, and religious leaders to disseminate the *Coptic Digest* between 1996 and 2007.

Meunier's media shift paralleled a broader trend as evangelical activism moved online, making use of the Internet, sending out email alerts, and developing simple but effective sites for telling the "stories of the persecuted."[69] Groups like Open Doors USA, Voice of the Martyrs, Christian Solidarity International, and a host of others raised money and solicited prayers for Christian sufferers in Africa, the Middle East,

China, and elsewhere. All of them trafficked in detailed stories of suffering; many made use of equally dramatic photos of (for example) pained faces, poverty, and imprisonment.

Between 1996 and 1998, discussions around the International Religious Freedom Act (IRFA) took shape, and Copts, according to Meunier, were central to those discussions. In April 1998, Meunier and Roderick wrote op-eds in the *Washington Times* detailing the persecution of Copts and stating support for this legislation.[70] IRFA brought together a constellation of Middle Eastern Christian activists like Meunier, American religious leaders, politicians, and think tank fellows such as Nina Shea (formerly of Freedom House, now of the Hudson Institute), Paul Marshall (formerly of Freedom House, now also of the Hudson Institute), and Michael Horowitz (former advisor to President Ronald Reagan and former senior fellow at the Hudson Institute).[71] IRFA established the Office of International Religious Freedom in the US State Department and a special IRFA advisor to serve on the National Security Council. While IRFA's stated mandate is to censure religious persecution wherever it occurs in the world, it provides a special waiver to important geopolitical allies and economic partners of the US government, such as Saudi Arabia and Israel.[72]

Prior to its final, revised form, IRFA proposed sanctions for countries that violated religious freedom protocols. This presented particular challenges to Copts in Egypt. As documented in a 1998 article in the *New York Times*, Egyptian Copts saw IRFA as a new form of imperial interference that would impact upon Christian-Muslim relations. Edward Ghali Eldahabi, a Coptic member of the Egyptian People's Assembly in Cairo at the time, noted, "Those who are trying to incite foreigners to interfere in Egypt's internal affairs are, in fact, stabbing Copts in the heart." An Egyptian Coptic businessman quoted in the article also said, "Such laws may advance the political agenda of some, but they overlook the harm it could do to all Copts here."[73] The transnational dissonance between Copts here, there, and elsewhere scales the contemporary politics of translating injury globally. In the case of the Copts, emplacing collective memory anew requires adjustment between different registers of the minority condition that continue to be guided by national and imperial forces.[74]

Although the signing of IRFA was neither the beginning nor the end of the story of US activism on religious persecution, it was a high point for conservative activists who wanted to make global issues central to their community. Their success was due in part to good organizing, but it was also the product of a new kind of "common sense" emerging in/ from the evangelical public sphere.[75] This "common sense" on the Copts placed them in the evangelical and international spotlight as Christian victims at the hands of Muslim perpetrators. In doing so, conservative political forces helped to translate Coptic collective memory of persecution to new geopolitical audiences; thus, memory—of violence and subjugation—was remapped onto different imperial theologies of blood and suffering. These religious campaigns and their political affects have placed communities such as the Copts in certain binds of recognition between diaspora and homeland.

A Common Bond of Suffering

We are a part of the international Christian globe now. The
Coptic cause is the global persecuted Christian cause now.
—Michael Meunier

Following the passage of IRFA, politically active American Copts were increasingly being labeled the "bad guys" by members of the Arab American community. In an op-ed for the *Cairo Times* in February 1999, Khaled Elgindy describes how Copts specifically contributed to anti-Muslim hysteria in the United States that has had transnational consequences:

> Pushing their message of "Christian persecution" in Egypt—one that has resonated with a Congress dominated by right-wing zealots, a press that is still loyal to Israel and a popular opinion largely distrustful of Arabs and Muslims—the organized Coptic American community has created all sorts of problems for the Egyptian government, while simultaneously antagonizing Muslims and sowing the seeds of division in the Egyptian and Arab communities in the US.[76]

Key to the separation of Copts from the broader Arab American community were both the demonization of the Egyptian government (by pressure from the imperial power of the United States) and the targeting of Islam and Muslims in diasporic activism, having far-reaching effects for

American Muslims and the figure of Islam in US foreign policy. Yet Elgindy's questioning of "Christian persecution" dismisses Coptic experiences and distances them from the cultural ethos and political itineraries of a collective Arab American community (regardless of religious tradition). While the alignment of Coptic associations with Christian Zionist and pro-Israel organizations understandably stirred the ire of Arab Americans (many of whom are Palestinian and/or have been directly affected by Israel's settler colonial project in the region), the focus on the Copts' Christianity and the discrimination they experienced in Egypt was taken less seriously by members of this community. Elgindy goes on to note the intersections of Coptic demands with the broader agenda of the Christian Right: "The powerful Christian Right, whose cult-like devotion to Israel and profound disdain for Islam are among the pillars of its religious-political doctrine, has also given wide play to Coptic claims of persecution. For evangelical Christians, the litany of 'social ills' these born-again soldiers of God aim to defeat—abortion, homosexuality, pornography, higher taxes, etc.—was added a crusade against Islam and Muslims."[77]

Right-wing attention to Coptic conditions in Egypt has historically placed diaspora communities in a contradiction-laden position. On the one hand, drawing attention to the Coptic plight inevitably sets them apart from the broader concerns of the Arab American (or Middle Eastern) communities that are split along religious lines (mainly Muslim and Christian). This attention enhances the fractures that are internal to the body politic that seeks redress for the forms of discrimination and racialization in diaspora, and specifically anti-Muslim/anti-Arab racism pervasive in US society. On the other hand, Coptic calls for American protection or advocacy set up an unstable synergy between the security this affords and the insecurity it engenders. It places Copts in a contested relationship to other racialized Arab American communities—combatting anti-Arab/anti-Muslim racism—as well as to some Coptic kin in the homeland who vehemently disagree with their political tactics from the diaspora.[78] Coptic dependence on such organizations that emphasize religious (and particularly Christian) difference and the evils of Islam and Muslim-majority rule amplify violence against Copts as a way of showing shared Christian kinship and heartfelt compassion for the persecuted, yet ultimately such compassion is channeled through imperial means and for imperial ends. The focus on Islam and Muslim monstrosity as the root of violence became necessary features of the effort to make Coptic discrimination legible in diaspora with ever-increasing stakes.[79]

After 9/11, the saliency of the Coptic plight in Egypt became more acute as the war on terror furthered a global narrative of Christian persecution at the hands of Muslim terrorists. This period led to a proliferation of diasporic organizations that held competing strategies and goals, given the heightened attention to Islam and radicalization. In 2004 Adly Abadir Youssef convened the First International Coptic Symposium in Zurich, bringing together key Coptic activists both from Egypt and its diasporas, alongside conservative and right-wing figures such as the controversial Daniel Pipes from the Middle East Forum, as well as organizers with the persecuted Christians movement, such as Hansjürg Stückelberger, founder of Christian Solidarity International.[80] In addition to these figures, Father Keith Roderick also presented a talk, entitled "Besieged Christians under Islamic Rule."[81] While the talks focused on the Egyptian contexts of the Coptic plight, in historical and contemporary perspectives, the conference also took the Coptic case as evidence of the broader context of "radical political Islam," the title of the third section of the conference.

Roderick's speech focused specifically on a political theology of Islamic rule that centers the persecution of Christians and other non-Muslims. With comparisons to Nazi Germany and contextualization as far back as the seventh century and the emergence of Islam, Roderick framed the diminishing presence of Christians in the Middle East as an inevitability of Muslim governance. As an American religious leader, Roderick compared the global Christian plight to the legacies of slavery and the perpetuation of anti-Black racism in the United States:

> As African Americans organized resistance to the oppression of the Jim Crow-society following reconstruction by seeking strength in unity and cultural pride, Middle Eastern Christians should devote themselves to forming alliances in solidarity with other suffering communities. They should seek to establish a common identity as dhimmis.[82]

The use of "dhimmi" (or non-Muslim community of either Christians or Jews) is purposeful and references more than its theological bases or historical contexts. "Dhimmitude" emerged as a right-wing idiom to argue that if the global war on Christians is not won, American Christians will resemble Middle Eastern Christians, subjugated under Islam, where their religion is kept private, violent attacks target them and their way of life, and care is taken so public acts do not offend the state religion, that being Islam.[83] Roderick argued in front of conference participants that Copts and other *dhimmī* communities must come together to resist:

> The common bond among non-Muslims in Islamic societies is diminishment, humiliation, and suffering. Then let that common experience of suffering and marginalization be the thing that identifies you.[84]

That marginalization is not based on racialized difference, class discrimination, or asymmetries of global power. Christian difference becomes imbued with a geopolitical aesthetic of suffering, and he implores the Copts in attendance and others to see the persecuted kinship between American Christians and Coptic Christians in the post-9/11 moment of shared Islamic threat. He continues,

> There is a tremendous reservoir of strength in the unity of the larger Christian community. Arabization and Islamization draw their strength from a common identity, but Christians have been fragmented among communities and unable to forge the same kind of cultural force. And in the division of those communities, there is weakness.[85]

While remaining clear in his speech that real change must be "indigenous," emerging organically from within contexts like Egypt, Roderick builds a world of Christian solidarity that is forged in and by resistance to Islamic governance.[86] Following this conference, organizations such as Coptic Solidarity were established to lobby the US Congress for Coptic issues in Egypt, but as indicated previously, it jointly has hosted continued conversations around the paradigmatic role of Middle Eastern Christians, such as the Copts, in a global geography of Christian persecution.

Today, in US think tanks and other advocacy organizations, Copts now hold positions of power, shaping policy through the lens of human rights language and the discourse of Christian persecution. To this conservative coalition, Copts, as both symbols and actors in their own right, have offered a striking portfolio of bloody, convicting narratives and imagery, which reinforces persecution discourse.[87] One Coptic activist noted to me that within current policy-making circles, newer Coptic organizations, Middle Eastern Christian policy platforms, and government interests have utilized such communities to the detriment of their original goals of advancing and guaranteeing rights for their communities back in the region: "These organizations are all businesses. They commercialize the Copts. This is the commercialization of the Coptic cause."[88]

Suffering Bodies

In December 2017, the Third International Archon Conference on Religious Freedom was held at the Trump Hotel in Washington, DC. The Archons of the Ecumenical Patriarchate are a society of laity, chosen by the patriarch of Constantinople for their service to the Greek Orthodox Church and for their respect within the community. Titled "The Persecution of Christians in the Holy Lands and the Middle East: Consequences and Solutions," the conference offered a theologically eclectic schedule, its speakers comprising politicians of evangelical backgrounds, Greek Orthodox influencers, Syriac and Coptic bishops, and upper-middle-class Copts involved in advocacy work in Washington, DC.

At registration, conference volunteers handed out tote bags filled with the typical conference materials, including a folder, schedule, notepad, and engraved pen, as well as a pin with the Arabic letter "noon" (ن), which was painted on the properties of Christians living under ISIS. The tote bag contained the book *Muslim: What You Need to Know about the World's Fastest-Growing Religion* by conference presenter Hank Hanegraaff, a convert from evangelicalism to Greek Orthodoxy, who gained fame through his radio show, *Bible Answer Man*, and his numerous publications on Christianity and American culture. While the book is concerned with the rising global demographic divide between Muslims and Christians, it is equally concerned with connecting global processes and contexts, forming them into an all-encompassing narrative of Islam and terror. "Equally grave is the specter of global Islamic jihadism now exacting mass genocide on Christians in the East and ever-multiplying terrorist attacks throughout the West," he writes in the afterword, citing Coptic diasporic writer and conservative commentator Raymond Ibrahim.[89] Hanegraaff's book and its message for such a conference stand at the crossroads of the defense of Western civilization and the offensive on Brown and Black bodies in the war on terror.⁹⁰ In this imaginary, Islam as a system of governance stands as a threat to Western political, social, and spiritual values. By deploying Copts and other Middle Eastern Christians as exemplary victims of such a system, the audience of evangelical and Greek Orthodox elites (an otherwise unlikely alliance) instrumentalized their victimhood.

Session 2, titled "Persecution of Christians and Possible Solutions," took place at an auditorium on Capitol Hill. The auditorium was dark, except for bright lights focused on a large stage projection of the twenty-one Libya martyrs of the Coptic Church, darkened to black and white, lined up on their knees in front of masked members of ISIS standing ominously behind them. Following opening remarks, clerical leaders from various Middle Eastern churches gave speeches regarding their positions on persecution and Western intervention. Bishop Angaelos of London spoke on behalf of the Coptic Orthodox Church.

Angaelos has explicitly decried the persecution of Copts, appearing on the BBC and numerous other outlets following attacks in Egypt, and has sought the support of evangelicals in the battle against global Christian persecution.⁹¹ For example, in 2016 he addressed board members of the National Association of Evangelicals (NAE) and emphasized ecumenical partnership. The bishop held up images of the twenty-one killed by ISIS on Libya's shore in February 2015, evidencing recent martyrdom but also shared Christian kinship with evangelicals marked through spilt blood: "The body [of Christ] does not have an East and a West. It's one body, one body of Christ." This partnership is a specifically diasporic one, in that evangelicals and other Protestants in Egypt have a contested relationship with the Coptic Orthodox Church, contextualized by a history of Western Christian missions and evangelism targeted at Orthodox Egyptians.⁹² Beyond the Egyptian postcolonial and contemporary national context of denominational tension, an extra-national and global alliance with Western evangelicals (as well as Catholics) has formed in relation to an "ecumenism of blood."⁹³

At the NAE meeting in 2016, Angaelos told board members that he believes that the twenty-one martyrs of Libya, proclaiming their faith to their last breath, were the ones who demonstrated power, rather than the terrorists who held knives to their throats. "The world saw that Christian witness was more powerful," he said. Then NAE president Leith Anderson was among the leaders who welcomed Angaelos to the evangelical board meeting: "Bishop Angaelos powerfully presents the cause of our fellow Christians. We thank God for the amazing faith of Christians in the Middle East who face martyrdom and other persecutions and remain faithful. They bless and challenge us."[94] Angaelos was the first Orthodox Christian to appear at a meeting of the NAE, which speaks to his persistent interest in the contemporary molding of a unified Christianity, built on the shared kinship of martyrical suffering.[95]

At the Archons' panel in December 2017, Angaelos's appearance against the backdrop of the Libya martyrs on their knees was striking. The effectiveness of the image carried the bishop's comments to the audience:

> We come at a time when there are two hundred to five hundred million Christians persecuted around the world. In scores of countries . . . they are suffering at a time when we as humanity are in an era of our development that prides itself on international treaties, international conventions, and a right to life. . . . The Christians of whom we speak are those that deny and reject minority status, for they are indigenous people. If what is happening in the Middle East were to happen to the indigenous people of America or Canada or the Aborigines of Australia, the world would be up in arms. They live the faith that was born in the region.

Speaking to the witness of the twenty-one martyrs, the bishop described how he was compelled by the image to mark his own body:

> The twenty-one martyrs of Libya have changed the world. Typically, the Copts have a cross tattoo on their inner right wrist. Just as a sign of who they are. I grew up in Australia. I didn't have one, I didn't see the need. But when I watch this video and the . . . man in the middle having to mask his face so we would not know who pointed that knife and said, "We are after the nation of the cross," I felt a need to get a cross for them. We hear the stories of the saints and the martyrs in our church every day. Another bombing, another martyr, another saint, it's still happening. It happened on our screens. We saw it before us.

The persecuted body not only marks Christians as under global siege but argues that through the blood of persecuted (Eastern) Christian bodies, all of Western Christendom and its imperial formations are sanctified.[96] The bloody icon of the persecuted body among Christians, across theological, racial, and national lines, has produced new kinds of affiliations defined by its embodiment, its global knowledge, and the marks of shared victimization.[97] The "globalatinization" of the twenty-one martyrs of Libya exceeded a specific Coptic martyrology and became part of a mediatized form of modern Christian witness, consumed as sacred spectacle and revered as bloody martyrdom on a global scale.[98]

Later that evening, in a ballroom at the Trump Hotel just down the street from the White House itself, President Trump's closest associates were the keynote speakers and key figures of the conference dinner. The first remarks came from Jordan Sekulow, executive director of the American Center for Law and Justice (ACLJ). His father, Jay Sekulow, was a frequent commentator on the Christian Broadcasting Network and on Fox News, a Messianic Jew, and one of Trump's personal lawyers. Jordan Sekulow remarked on the persecution of Christians around the world, but especially in the Middle East, as an American problem. By looking to the faith and tragic circumstances of the Copts, America should be inspired to carry the imperial light of religious freedom to all corners of the globe. Sekulow proclaimed,

> We cannot forget that our brothers and sisters in Christ, whether they be of the Orthodox faith or just the Christian faith generally, are facing immense persecution around the world. For all of us, do not forget those Coptic Christians who are in the heart of Egypt, worshipping on Christmas Day, worshipping on Easter, and hundreds are killed. And yet, next Easter, hundreds more show up. And that is a symbolism of their Christian faith, but it is also unacceptable in the world that we live in. . . . Here we are in the United States of America. . . . You have a government that accepts freedom. And we're unique. In the United States, we have to learn in a unique way how to take that understanding that we have been born into and ingrained into us, and take that to parts of the world where that is not ingrained. Where the free exercise of religion is not the first right. We have so much to do for the Persecuted Church.

In this discourse, America is the leader and the savior of the world. America can bring freedom to other parts of the world, where persecution and devastation have prevailed. The Persecuted Church is defined by one feature: Christians who suffer. It is the viscerality of their suffering—the spilt blood broadcast to and for the world—that draws one into the consummation of martyrical witness. Such suffering threads to Christ on the cross. Martyred Copts *are* Christ upon the Cross. Yet this witness to Christ's death and resurrection is also consumed *in* the world and takes place on the altar of US empire, in the use of images of suffering and icons of persecution that exceed the context of their bloody sacrifice.

Blood Circuits

During the modern period, Coptic communal character was represented by Orientalist writers, missionaries, and colonial regimes as part of a broader Christian kinship that drew them into white, imperial powers, while at the same time subjecting them to both racial and religious difference. In this context of imperial encounter, Christians were gathered together through blood, and in particular spilt blood.[99] Without flattening contextual difference, the social (*worldly*) translation of Christian witness in the form of martyrdom has a long history whereby Christians have had to wrestle with the transition from persecution to power. Early Christians, for example, struggled to maintain the stance of the persecuted even when increasingly in hegemonic positions. Protestants, historically, have rejected self-imposed physical pain, such as flagellation or extreme fasting, embraced among some early Christian communities in tandem with remembering the martyrs. Yet Protestants retained the belief at the root of these practices, that martyrs—*through their pain*—had attained a special intimacy with God. A conceptual approach to the historical imagination of martyrdom in relation to ideals of the sanctified life gestures toward some enduring themes in Christian history, such as the spiritual significance of pain and persistent ambivalence toward the exercise of power.[100]

In this way, acts of Christian kinship around martyrdom and blood piety are nothing new to either Western Christian or Coptic traditions. In the context of medieval Christian Europe, Bettina Bildhauer has noted that Christ's bleeding body on the cross was depicted in explicit images and texts that encouraged empathizing with his sacrifice. The Church, the community of all Christians, was/is conceptualized as Christ's body, held together by his blood.[101] Scholars of early Christianity have described the Roman arena, where much martyr blood was spilled, as a public space in which the religio-political imaginary of the society was repeatedly constituted and acted out on bodies Martyrs' blood was part of a "larger ideological drama in which state power and social relations were repeatedly contested, reconstituted, and reinscribed."[102] In a similar way, for the medieval aristocracy, spilling blood was a conduit to gaining power and proving one's worth as a warrior or knight, for example.[103] Western Christianity went furthest in embracing bleeding and the dissolution of the person it entailed, as a chance for opening up to and becoming one with Christ and with a broader community of believers. With the Crucifixion multiply re-enacted by way of miraculous bloodshed events, Christ was kept bleeding multi-locally and trans-historically, and this need for witness through bloody sacrifice in the name of Christ contentiously perpetuates.

During the late twentieth century, a heavenly (and politicized) conceptualization of persecution for Christ formed a new kind of imperial Christian kinship that has continued to mold transnational Coptic life in the process. By unfolding how the Coptic diaspora in the United States began to advocate for Coptic rights back in Egypt and how that initial advocacy morphed into a broader movement for persecuted Christians around the globe, this chapter has traced how transnational Coptic life was remapped by American imperial persecution politics. It also lays the geopolitical foundation to zoom in to the Egyptian social, political, and religious context of the nineteenth and twentieth centuries, where the emergence of a Coptic landowning class under British colonial rule and the breakdown of that class in postcolonial Egypt led to the institutional consolidation of representational power by the Coptic Orthodox Church and a cementing of the sectarian landscape. These national factors led to increasing incidents of intercommunal violence, and broader international attention on them. These mid-twentieth-century revolutionary changes also ushered in generations of Coptic migrants to Western countries, especially the United States, and increased migration over the decade since the 2011 Egyptian revolution has further evidenced the inseparable nature of Copticity between here, there, and elsewhere, as the discourses of activists and advocates have looped back to Egyptian contexts. These circulations and feedback loops, which on the surface render an incommensurable divide, evade the intimacies of everyday life in rural places like Bahjūra where communal accommodations and different kinds of asymmetries engage—but also exceed—the politics of persecution.

2

Sectarian Memory and Migration Forces

Entering Bahjūra, you leave behind agricultural lands and drive between two water projects. On one side of the road, boys and men use one for a refreshing swim on a hot summer day. On the other side, a garbage-laden canal is being packed in by the local government. This is the village's main road, from which you see scattered homes; some are newly built, some are abandoned, and some are magnificent colonial villas from the early twentieth century. Bahjūra's villas—a few occupied and many vacant—are a unique fixture of this small village's local history. The villas stand as a living testament to the Coptic landowning families that once held considerable political and social power, prior to the 1952 revolution and its land reforms. While many of them and their descendants have left the village, settling in Cairo, Alexandria, or abroad in Europe or the United States, their villas remain, as does the memory of their presence in the landscape. Areas are named after a former *'izba* (plantation), stories of their families fill pages of documents at the local libraries, and their family names are on the tips of local tongues who describe their importance to Bahjūra and their broader historical significance to Egypt. Yet the lived memory of this shared landscape has been overshadowed by contemporary anxieties about persecution, sectarian violence, and exodus.

* * *

In June 2017, I woke up in Amin's home on the eastern side of the village. In his late forties, tall with salt and pepper hair, Amin is a dedicated church servant in the community, a math teacher at the local public school, and a father to three children. He is widely known in the community as generous and kind to everyone he encounters. Around 10:30 a.m., after breakfast, Amin and I started walking through the village, heading to the primary school where both he and his wife work, closer to the old canal; Amin wanted to show me a day in his life.

Figure 2.1. Bahjūra from a rooftop, June 2017. Photo by author.

We arrived at the primary school after a fifteen-minute walk, weaving through the narrow and winding dirt streets. The Mounira Takla school was founded in 1906 by Daoud Takla, a Coptic lay leader and landowner.[1] The school is the original home of Daoud and was converted into the primary school. When walking into the building, you enter a large room, with smaller classrooms connected to it. The desks appear quite old, worn by decades of use. The last room to the right is the teachers' lounge. We entered, and I was greeted by three women at separate desks, one of them Amin's sister Marina, whom I was meeting for the first time. Amin knew that I would be interested in speaking with Marina, given my project on migration and narratives of persecution, and explained to the women that I was keen to hear their stories. Marina's daughter, Amin's niece, lives in Bayonne, New Jersey, and attends a Coptic church there. After they shared their kin's migration stories in detail, I asked Amin and the women *why* Copts want to leave Bahjūra, and why most of them from the village end up in the United States.

Even though I noticed that the women wanted to comment first, Amin interjected:

> Look, people travel abroad for two reasons—for the love of money because the economic situation here is . . . the opportunities for work are limited. They go to America for a better standard of living. Also, in America, there's more freedom. So of course, anyone travels there because of freedom. These are the two most important reasons for immigration [*hijra*] to America. Okay, in order to travel, there needs to be an interview at the US embassy [in Cairo]. So I'll go there and say what in front of the consular officer at the embassy? In order to receive sympathy [*'aṭif*] and get the okay to travel to America, we [as Christians] use persecution as a frame [*ash-shamā'a*] for our situation in order to travel to America.[2]

The women nodded in agreement and told me that they would be applying to the Diversity Visa Program again that fall in the hopes of leaving Bahjūra for good.[3]

* * *

Global media networks, Western politicians, and Middle Eastern Christians in diaspora themselves contend that Christians in the region are on the brink of extinction, and are fleeing from mass violence and religious extremism for their existential survival.[4] This chapter sketches the contentious ethnographic texture of transnational migration for a Christian minority community in the Middle East, focusing on the contemporary conditions of Coptic emigration from Egypt to the United States through the Diversity Visa Program, or Green Card Lottery. The ethnographic constellation of this chapter is mainly based in the Upper Egyptian village of Bahjūra, which has had a high number of Lottery recipients, altering the physical and intercommunal landscape of the village and resulting in an ever-increasing number of vacant villas and dilapidated apartment buildings. Despite increased Western attention to violent attacks against the Christian minority in Egypt at the hands of Islamists, the government, and everyday Muslim neighbors, Coptic migration has been predicated on both increasing religious discrimination against Christians and declining socioeconomic conditions for all middle-class, working-class, and poor Egyptians. By attending to the intersectional and institutional dynamics of increasing Coptic migration, this chapter examines how local conditions (and histories) in Egypt interface with the global persecution politics discussed in chapter 1.

While the following pages initially attend to the contemporary dynamics of minority migration, Bahjūra is also a site that evinces the contrasts of shared life among its residents—through traumatic presents and collective memory of intercommunal (and classed) flourishing. As we explore the intricacies of such sectarian histories in the south of Egypt (a novelty in its own right[5]), the seemingly ordinary character of Bahjūra becomes extraordinary as its landscapes tell stories that are both bound by and exceed the politics of persecution. The importance of these histories to the contemporary context of migration and the din of persecution politics lies in imagining Christian identity in Egypt otherwise. With this framing, the chapter homes in on two specific questions: How does the development of an internationalized Coptic identity built around the politics of persecution condition forms of sociality in Egypt? Are there other forms of collective identity that have been subsumed within this framework, and how do those impact everyday relations in Egypt?[6] Instead of concluding that contemporary Coptic migration is either forced or voluntary, the different sections ethnographically and archivally texture how the exigency to decide the validity of such a narrative of flight both shapes sociality in contemporary Egypt and ultimately erases the contentions and care-politics of shared intercommunal life in Egypt's rural parts.

Narratives of Flight

On a February afternoon in 2017, I walked through an embassy row in downtown Cairo, down a labyrinth of streets obstructed by cement blocks from revolutions past. At a café frequented by American embassy officers, I met with two officials who covered visas and public relations. Both organize the Lottery entry each year—answering questions online, recruiting at Egyptian universities, and managing the day-to-day operations of the program. I asked them about the Coptic perception that the Lottery is a conspiracy—to drain Egypt of its Copts. "The Lottery is a lottery, meaning they pull numbers. There is no thumb on the scale," one of the officers said. "People might register everyone in their group, which could later be an issue since it is prone to fraud. We know that organizations do this, but we caution against it." Referring to the Coptic Orthodox Church, the official emphasized the way local dioceses enter Christians into the competition without their knowledge. He explained away conspiratorial framings of the Lottery process:

> Think about the odds, that's what's most important. Instead of thinking that the Lottery itself is choosing people from areas affected by sectarian violence and "draining the Middle East of Christians," more people may very well apply after incidents of sectarian violence happen. . . . If more Christians from a village apply because their church organizes information sessions, that simply increases their odds. Their probability increases.

In *Motherland Lost: The Egyptian and Coptic Quest for Modernity* (2013), Samuel Tadros, former senior fellow at the Hudson Institute's Center for Religious Freedom, describes Coptic immigration to the United States since the 2011 revolution as the only option: "The prospects for Copts in Egypt are, to say the least, bleak. Their options are limited. . . . Unlike the Jewish emigrants escaping Egypt in the '40s and '50s, for Copts driven out of their ancestral homeland, there is no Israel to escape to. . . . The only option in front of them is to pack their bags and leave, putting an end to two thousand years of Christianity in Egypt."[7] Such a perspective on a Coptic exodus does not attend to the particulars of Coptic emigration from Egypt, especially the structural modes by which it is happening. The Church has been a major conduit to migration, increasing the socioeconomic disparity of some of its most precarious communities in Upper Egypt and ensuring its own financial survival through remittances and transnational circulations of charity. To withstand political and economic turbulence in Egypt, the Church has become a source of social services, which the state fails to provide, and the center of Coptic identity, molding its possibilities and futures. To ensure its continued flourishing, diaspora contributions in the form of buildings, complexes, and organizations have aided the expansion of the Church's institutional reach.[8]

As part of the Immigration Act of 1990, the United States instituted the annual Diversity Visa (DV) Lottery, encouraging nationals of countries that historically sent few migrants to the United States to apply for one of fifty thousand legal immigrant visas. Sparked by the advocacy for undocumented Irish migrants in the United States in the late 1980s, policy makers created the Lottery as an instrument for legal migration outside family, employment, and refugee admissions categories.[9] Since the 2011 Egyptian revolution, the number of Coptic immigrants, particularly those on the Diversity Visa, has increased exponentially, with more and more Copts—in areas ranging from cities to the most remote villages—applying for the Lottery.[10] Thereafter, many parishes in the New York-New Jersey area felt the pressure, as dozens of families, especially from areas of Upper Egypt such as al-Minyā, Asyūṭ, and Najʿ Ḥammādī, came to churches directly from John F. Kennedy International Airport each week, seeking shelter and work.

With such a large influx of Copts in such a short period of time, many clergymen of these parishes grew skeptical of the Green Card Lottery, wondering whether there was a hidden plot behind the movement. When we met in his narrow, cluttered office, with pictures, icons, and books strewn across the desk and chairs, Abouna Jacob, a priest in Jersey City, told me that he was concerned about what the influx means for Copts back in Egypt:

> Why does the Green Card Lottery select so many people from Upper Egypt, and especially from such remote villages? It doesn't appear to be random in the least. A bishop told me five years back that he serves a village that has seen its Christian population decrease in half—from eighty thousand to forty thousand, which is quite shocking. All of them have received the Green Card Lottery. It makes sense to a certain extent—if the Christians leave, the Muslims will have the upper hand in these areas. Christians will be forced to sell their lands and Muslims will come and buy it all up.

For those in the United States, the number of Copts who have come through the Green Card Lottery is alarming, and increased Coptic immigration may mean Christian vacancy in Egypt. The concern for Christian vacancy is that it will lead to their extinction and the domination by Muslims of the Egyptian landscape. Abouna Jacob's fear of Coptic erasure in Egypt comes in the context of increased numbers of migrants and their families streaming into his parish on a weekly basis. The Green Card Lottery, first seen as an opportunity for those seeking a better life abroad, has also become a source of conspiracy theories as well as anxiety for transnational Coptic identity.

While clergy in the United States like Abouna Jacob lament the number of Copts coming through the Lottery, the Church in Egypt is itself at the center of its operation, encouraging locals to apply and giving them the tools to do so. "When a whole village in al-Minyā receives the Green Card Lottery, you have to ask, who received this and when? Who brought their family members? Did others migrate by different means?" the other US embassy official noted during our conversation in Cairo. "The reality is much different. It's natural to interpret such instances as conspiratorial, instead of analyzing how there are more organizations to help community members sign up." The Coptic Orthodox Church has helped Copts to migrate, which has led to the emptying of villages like Bahjūra throughout Upper Egypt, where many Copts reside, and where local economies have been decimated by urbanization, decline in the agricultural economy and its labor force, and youth migrating to cities for education since the 1970s. Migration has had a long-lasting impact on the demography of such places and, moreover, has led to a restructuring of sectarian relations.

Chance Migration

Every October, as the Green Card Lottery website opens and applicants start to submit their information, Copts around Egypt flock to their local church computer centers. There, the community gathers to have a church volunteer (*khādim*) take their required photo and submit all their information correctly.[11] Depending on the parish, they usually charge a fee for every applicant, including dependents. While Copts have the option of submitting their applications through a parish center, Egyptian Muslims do not have a similar system in local mosques, and many choose to submit their application at these church computer centers. As they enter, some Muslims face side-eyes and grimaces, but they feel that it is their only legitimate option for ensuring that their application is submitted correctly. Out of suspicion and fear, Copts view Muslim presence in their landscapes as a threat. Increased intercommunal tensions and the frequency of attacks against communities and their places of worship have driven a wedge between Christian and Muslim Egyptians.

Muslim participation in Green Card Lottery entry at churches is also filtered through the Egyptian state security's mandate to maintain an intercommunal gap between Christianity and Islam in Egypt. As Angie Heo has noted, "Sectarianizing the public is one key tactic for governing Christian-Muslim interactions."[12] In addition to these national contexts that have a local impact upon these processes of migration, Middle Eastern Christians like the Copts are also part of a global Christian community, the Persecuted Church, which frames perceptions of their mobility. American politicians have voiced favor for the entry of Middle Eastern Christians rather than their Muslim counterparts, although this has not translated into preferential treatment.[13] The increased migration of Copts through the Green Card Lottery takes place in this context, and many Copts in Bahjūra and neighboring Najʿ Ḥammādī viewed migration to the United States as an answer to their economic woes and social hardships *as* Christians. The Lottery has become central to Coptic life in contemporary Egypt, especially because the Coptic Orthodox Church, in its local parishes, has supported the enterprise and has jointly benefited from it.

To show me the annual Lottery entry firsthand, Amin brought me to the Coptic Center for Computer and Internet Services in Najʿ Ḥammādī on a cooler evening in mid-October. The center is on the second floor of a church. Bola, twenty-six, is the head of the center and the one who submits all the entries for the Lottery. He has never won the Lottery himself but takes pleasure in helping others. His two assistants, Yacoub and Daniel, sixteen and eleven, respectively, helped Bola out by taking photos and assisting the numerous people who walk through their doors. As candidates started to fill the room that evening, I asked Bola how many people applied from Najʿ Ḥammādī last year. He counted each of the files on his desktop and they numbered 333, which does not include dependents (the number could be much larger, maybe into the thousands). It is not just people from this church who apply. Because this particular church has a high success rate, with dozens of people winning the Lottery each year, many from the surrounding villages have flocked there.

Some applicants looked like they had just come from work either in construction, with their clothing and hands covered in dust, or from the fields, wearing *galabayas*, covered in dirt and water.[14] They believe that because this church has had success, percentage-wise, it will continue to have success, with people from neighboring Sūhāj and Qinā coming to Najʻ Ḥammādī to apply, even though they also have computer centers in their respective areas more than capable of entering them into the Lottery. For each of these Lottery entrants, Bola charged twenty Egyptian pounds per family member.[15] Some of the applications that Bola showed me had all the spots for dependents filled, and some even wrote more onto another application.

Bola explained that many people who come in do not understand the idea of the Lottery, thinking that as soon as they apply, they will win. "People come in here and think they are going if they merely apply. Right away they want to know who will help them when they get there, asking who will buy their tickets and provide them with work when they arrive in America."

Of every applicant who entered the center, Bola asked enthusiastically, "Do you want to go to America [*ʻāiyyz trūḥ Amrika*]?" One of the first groups to apply that evening were two women from neighboring Bahjūra with their children. One woman's husband works in Kuwait. She was applying for the family because she said that her chances from Najʻ Ḥammādī were better than if her husband entered for them in Kuwait. I spoke with her about why she wanted to immigrate to the United States. "After all the incidents that have happened here, it's better for us there. Yes, things will be hard, but at least they treat you with dignity [*karāma*]. They treat you like a dignified person." Compounded with attacks, Christians also deal with the current economic conditions that have left all Egyptians without many options. They are subject to government austerity measures and lack of employment opportunities that all Egyptians must face, but they also encounter systemic discrimination as a minority community, experiencing an increased sense of affective exclusion and spatial encroachment.

One example of this encroachment came up over dinner one evening. Amin and I spoke about my day with another local family. His wife was studying with their son in the other room for an exam. I thought that it was the same Arabic exam that the other family's children were studying for that week. The previous night and that day, they showed me their materials for Arabic, which included sections to memorize from the Qurʼan and particular Islamic phrasing. One of the things that they had to repeat for Arabic was the correct phrasing to appropriately name Muhammad as the Messenger of God (*rasūl Allāh*); they must subsequently say "Peace be upon him" (*ṣala Allāh ʿalayhi w salam*). Amin began to laugh, and recounted how at school, every morning, students must say two phrases: "God is Great. God is Great" (*Allāhu akbar, Allāhu ʿāẓm*) and then "Long live the Arab Republic" (*taḥiyā al-jumhūriyyat al-ʿarabiyya*). Amin recounted that there was one principal who observed students mumbling the first part, and reciting the second with a loud voice. She corrected them, telling them that they needed to say the first part with a loud voice as well. Amin described her as "Muslim Brotherhood-esque [*ikhwāniyya shwaya*]," with a chuckle.

In Egypt, Copts are caught in a strange play between visibility and invisibility.[16] They are of course visible in Egypt and in the West during violent attacks, their maimed, bloody Christian bodies on full display in the fight against terrorism and in the production of Muslim enemies. Yet Copts also desire a visibility that takes seriously their everyday *lived* religiosity in an Islamic public sphere. After some pause, Amin looked at the carpet on the dining room floor with misty eyes. He raised his eyes to me after a minute or two and asked, "What is the greatest miracle [*muʿajiza*] you have seen in Egypt?" After a long pause, as I was contemplating the question, Amin responded, "We [Christians] are still living here, in the middle of this society. . . . Every time I think about emigrating, I think about what would happen to Egypt after I left. If we [Christians] all leave, Egypt will be like Saudi Arabia. I can't emigrate and see Egypt like this."

In Bahjūra, many Copts like Amin indicated, by telling stories of forgotten pasts or narrating the layers of the village's Christian landscape, that they did not want to blend into an Egyptian identity that does not integrally involve their Christianity. Continued Christian presence—in the people, landscapes, sensorium—is a bulwark against the breakdown of Egypt as a national (and blessed, extra-national/trans-historical) frame. Christian presence moderates shared belonging beyond religious difference.

Landscapes of Loss

Contemporary Bahjūra is demarcated along religious lines, as are many other rural and urban areas of Egypt. The oldest part of the village—known locally as Shig al-Naṣāra, or the Christian area, by neighboring Muslims—stands next to the canal. On the other side of the canal, former and current agricultural fields of past and present Coptic landowning families have become the poorer areas of the village. 'Ezbet Kamal, 'Ezbet Daoud, 'Ezbet Abu Iskander—names of the contemporary outskirts of Bahjūra—were all former plantations of Coptic landowning families during the early twentieth century. Along the old canal, the villas of the Coptic landowners remain, many vacant, having been abandoned when their owners migrated abroad. One such property was owned by Kamal Bek Takla, whose former *'izba*, 'Ezbet Kamal, lies behind the family property. Today, a wall surrounds the compound, which contains the remarkable villa, the Saint George Church (known locally as Anba Bola), and a four-story center built by the local diocese of Najʿ Ḥammādī, under the auspices of the late Bishop Kyrillos.

The Kamal Takla family left Bahjūra in the early 1950s for Geneva, Switzerland, anticipating that a revolution was imminent and subsequent political and economic reforms along with it. The family left the villa vacant until the early 1980s, when Kamal's first son, George, known as Berty, returned to Bahjūra to officially settle the financial matters of the estate. Many of Bahjūra's Christians, including clergy, describe Berty's return to the village as marking the end of the era when Christians held power in Egypt under British colonial rule; his return made that loss permanent. During a particularly hot summer day, I sat with Abouna Mina of the local church in his office. He grew up in Bahjūra and remembered the family fondly. He recalled, "Coptic families, like the Takla family, held all of the power because of their land, but now they are selling their lands. In the early 1980s, I can remember when a fight broke out between Muslim villagers during Ramadan. One villager hit the other. They went to the Takla villa, to Berty Takla, to settle the dispute." As described by local clergy and villagers alike, Coptic landowning families like the Taklas were looked to as mediators of conflict, even for Muslim neighbors, because of their wealth and social status.

Few of these Coptic landowning families live in Bahjūra today; their villas are vacant or have been sold to other parties. The Takla family is the best-known of these families, and none of the family members reside in the village. Their villas are all that remain. I became acquainted with the Takla villa in early 2017. I participated in a three-week English-language program for youth from Bahjūra and the surrounding villages. We resided in the four-story diocesan center directly next to the Takla villa. Ironically, the laundry was located on the second floor of the villa. During the first week of the program, we entered the villa to wash clothing and discovered a magnificent home still in pristine condition. Next to the grand staircase, bathed in multicolored light from sunlight streaming in through the stained-glass window, stood four large cabinets with glass pane doors. The doors were locked, but I could see through the glass panels stacks of books and documents covered in dust and dirt. I became intrigued and asked the villa's caretaker to open one of the doors for me to look at the documents. He kindly agreed, and I became acquainted with the Kamal Bek Takla family. Through their material remnants and archival artifacts, I pieced together how the close relationship of the Sidarous-Takla family to those in power operated through negotiation, competency, and management.

Illuminating the historical background that contextualizes the Sidarous-Takla story, Egyptian historians Raouf Abbas and Assem al-Dessouky describe the development of private landownership in Egypt during the nineteenth century as a culmination of the advance of a free-market economy. Three institutional changes allowed the growth in large landownership: the improvement of irrigation techniques, the obtainability of land, and the availability of credit.[17] The Coptic elite benefited from this new system. Under Muhammad 'Ali and subsequent regimes, Copts had the ability to become large landowners, with the acquisition of private estates by officials, village notables, and urban merchants. As historian Gabriel Baer notes, however, it was not until the 1880s, under British occupation, that Copts stood out as an important group of large landowners.[18] During British rule, the Copts were placed in contradictory configurations and difficult positions. They were seen both as Christians from whom much about the early church could be learned, and as Christians who were debasing Christianity with their degenerate ways. Likewise, the Copts took care not to appear to be collaborating with the occupying power, in case they endangered relations with their compatriots, but at the same time did take up government and administrative positions. Because of larger structural changes to landholdings, Coptic elites found openings to increase their rank and privilege within Egyptian society, with the help of British colonial forces.

Even before the British occupation of Egypt began in 1882, however, Christians obtained extra privileges from foreign powers. For those Christians who were able to acquire a *berat*, or a license that allowed several tax exemptions and access to European law, navigating imperial regulations became much easier than for their Muslim counterparts. Perhaps even more important than the acquisition of a *berat* was the appointment as a local consular agent. By the middle of the nineteenth century, Western protection of minorities in the Ottoman Empire had greatly widened. Elite Christians had their taxes reduced and utilized separate courts based on Western legal principles to take advantage of these new provisions. At the same time, the Ottoman government was attempting to remove some of the restrictions on non-Muslims. In Egypt, for example, such policies included the abolition of the *jizya* tax for non-Muslims in 1855 (which was often variably enforced).[19] In such imperial efforts at modernization, the regional governments also required local agents, and since non-Muslim minorities like the Copts were perceived as more educated and Westernized, their role in administration and policy making increased in tandem with their socioeconomic status.[20] In particular, the Ottoman Land Code of 1858 and its counterparts in Egypt allowed free transfer of land and made it possible for Christians to accumulate vast holdings through grant, purchase, or foreclosure for debt.[21]

Under the Muhammad ʿAli dynasty, the entrance of European colonial powers into Egypt, and the reformation of agricultural property, Coptic and Muslim elite families alike were able to expand their wealth beyond what it had been previously. Landownership in nineteenth-century Egypt was the basis for a particular class to emerge. The two are inextricably linked. Landownership was a means to attain power, and this power further expanded landownership.[22] Economist Adel Beshai, engaging the work of Charles Issawi, asserts that according to the percentage of taxes paid on agricultural lands in the nineteenth century (16 percent) compared to their percentage of the population (6 percent), Copts owned proportionately more land than Muslims; this was particularly influenced by Western protections for Christian minorities and general colonial influence on the preference of Christians for positions of power.[23] Beshai speculates as to why Muslims were not angered by Coptic wealth and prestige at the time. "Perhaps the reason lies in the marriage of economic and political power," Beshai writes.[24] Despite colonial interference in Christian preference, the political power of Copts at this time was connected to their wealth in a way that traversed religious difference and brought classes together in shared financial control and domination.

When agriculture became profitable during the late nineteenth century, many of the elite shifted their investments, and wealthy Coptic families, like the Sidarous-Takla family of Bahjūra, bought large swaths of land. Elite Copts, especially those who worked as consuls for European countries, knew how to navigate the system that would best serve their financial interests. As Abbas and al-Dessouky note, "These Copts could benefit from landownership as well as from the Capitulations and from other institutions such as the Mixed Courts that looked after the affairs of the Europeans and those affiliated to them. It is not surprising to find that the British occupation saw a considerable increase in investment in agriculture; Copts were among those doing the investing."[25] Under the occupation, Coptic landowning families had wider opportunities to expand their agricultural investments and increase their wealth, with extra privileges and preference given to them because of their Christianity.[26] With this socioeconomic context and because the British army was more advanced than the Ottoman Egyptian army in terms of equipment and organization, many from the elite of Egyptian society—from the Khedive to aristocrats, both Coptic and Muslim—chose to support the British to protect their interests.[27] Economic interests surpassed much else for this elite landowning class.[28] Yet, more than that, there was also a sense of intercommunal care and familial intimacy between the large landowning families, whether Copt or Muslim. Shared life, environment, and priorities between landowning families and ruling elites evidence not simply transaction, but also connection and exchange through common flourishing and class subjugation.

Similarly, historian Ussama Makdisi describes how socioeconomic status rather than religious identity mediated communal relations in rural Mount Lebanon. Makdisi writes, "The great families of Mount Lebanon presented themselves as the intermediaries between religious communities. They drew their pride and their social position from a combination of their religious standing and the respect, tradition, and reciprocity that they enjoyed with other elite families."[29] Makdisi carefully argues that conflict between Druze and Maronites in Mount Lebanon, for example, was described through religious difference, but it was subordinate to and enmeshed in a range of competing discourses of social life and distinction inherent in local contexts. There were shared values and interests held by the political elite, regardless of religious affiliation.

Shared life through material concerns and principles molded relations beyond communal difference. Yet, by imperial and colonial manipulations of the nineteenth century, new concerns were brought to the fore throughout the region. The portrayal of Mount Lebanon, for example, as a Christian sanctuary under threat from Islam was not something that registered to local communities until the onslaught of Western missionary efforts.[30] In the competition between Western colonial powers, Ottoman imperial will, and local elites, villagers of Mount Lebanon (in some parallel ways to Upper Egypt) grappled with competing forces and pulls that drew them out of everyday material concerns. Makdisi constructs how agricultural life in the village may have been experienced by the agricultural classes (peasants, or *fellaḥin*) as follows:

> The villagers centered their lives around various crops and trees. Seasons were described by the produce they brought in their wake, and the all-important mulberry tree's yield made the difference between prosperity and penury. Women unwound and reeled raw silk and participated in battles. Together with the men of the village they struggled to pay a number of taxes, the largest of which was the basic Ottoman land tax known as the *miri*, which amounted to 10 percent of the produce of the cultivated land. Depending on the region, villagers had numerous other obligations: in Kisrawan, they presented their shaykhs with a quantity of soap, coffee, honey, or tobacco at Easter or on the occasion of the marriages of the shaykhs' daughters, sons, or sisters. Villagers could not marry without the permission of their lord, and it would have been unheard of to have a celebration or feast without inviting the clergy. Certain plots of land that the shaykh owned were set aside and not taxed. The produce of this land defrayed the costs of hospitality, but it was the peasants who had to work the land collectively, usually on a Sunday after the local clergymen had exhorted them to do God's bidding.[31]

Comparably, we can surmise that the lives of villagers from Egypt's rural parts were quite different from those living in Cairo. While those in Upper Egypt intermittently interacted with imperial rule, they also maintained their own customs and traditions. This is quite evident in the Orientalist accounts that differentiated Coptic-Muslim relations and mores in the city from the countryside. Edward Lane (1801–1876) wrote that in more urban settings, Copts and Muslims wore distinctively different attire: "In the towns, they [the Copts] are usually careful thus to distinguish themselves from the Muslims; but in the villages, many of them wear the white or red turban [usually reserved for town-dwelling Muslims]."[32] Andrew Watson (1834–1916) of the American mission in Egypt notes the same: "No respectable Copt in the large towns would then allow himself to be mistaken for a Muslim by wearing a white turban, even had he been allowed to do so; but in the villages there are no such distinctly marked lines."[33] It is important to comment that many such descriptions were of *fellaḥin* and not of elite families, who adapted their styles to the imperial, and later colonial, powers they served.

Copts and Muslims of the same social class, even in villages, would have more in common than a Coptic *fellaḥ* and a member of a landowning family. Or, as historian Doris Behrens-Abouseif has argued, "In villages differences between Copts and Muslims were not very prominent, and the traditional Islamic restrictions on the dhimmi not to ride horses or wear white turbans as well as not to carry weapons, were much less respected in villages than in cities. As observed by a longtime European resident in Egypt, a Coptic peasant has much less in common with a Copt from the city than he has with a Muslim peasant."[34] Orientalist historians of modern Egypt even noted that before the British occupation of 1882, they had seen "Coptic churches built by Moslems, and a mosque, built only a year or two before the Occupation, by a Coptic landowner. In the Secular Coptic schools, built by private munificence, in different parts of the country, I have never failed to find Moslem pupils; and no one thinks of excluding Coptic children from similar schools built by the Moslems, especially in the country places."[35]

Laying out these alternative perspectives on the history of intercommunal life does not deny that incidents of violence and discrimination intermittently did and do take place against Christians in Egypt, or that Christians even in Egypt's southern and rural parts were not captured by the imperial influences of Cairo or Constantinople. But, as Makdisi points out, this did not overshadow other ways of identification in local society. "From shariʿa courts, Ottoman decrees, village proverbs . . . it is clear that such a language [of religious discrimination and differentiation] existed, but it was subordinate to and enmeshed in a range of competing discourses of obedience, allegiance, and loyalty inherent in local society. It presented, in other words, no significant barrier to a social order founded on the shared values and interests of a nonsectarian elite."[36] By outlining the history of landownership in early modern and modern Egypt, we can see that the supremacy of religious difference as a marker of sociality is troubled by the interactions of elite families and rulers in southern Egypt. This elite status existed in a shared world with other members of the same social class.

In the lead-up to the 1952 revolution and the rise of president Gamal Abdel Nasser, marches for nationalization and socialist reform affected the rich, both Muslim and Christian. Copts, it can be argued, were affected by these economic shifts more, though not because of religious discrimination or prejudice on the part of the new political leadership. Rather, elite Copts held leading positions in banking, industry, and business.[37] But many Copts continued to hold such positions because of their proximity to British colonial power. This placed them in a contradiction-laden predicament, much of which was articulated through the many debates spawned by the 1919 revolution on the demand for (or opposition to) minority rights. Saba Mahmood outlines the impact of the minority debates in this way:

> Western religious and secular discourses were crucial to the construction of the minority problem in Egypt. The political imaginary of Copts and Muslims alike at the turn of the twentieth century had become saturated with European depictions of Islam and Christianity. Just as the European discourses on race and eugenics undergirded the Coptic claim to racial purity, the Western portrayal of Islam as a barbaric and uncivilized religion was the foil against which declarations of Muslim glory were crafted. Similarly, the fact that the fate of "Eastern Christians" had been indelibly sutured to European beneficence since the eighteenth century was crucial to how Copts articulated their case, how Muslims opposed it, and how Egyptian nationalists critiqued the granting of minority rights. In summary, none of these positions is comprehensible without an adequate appreciation of the power that the British colonial government, the missionaries, and European public opinion exerted in shaping the self-understanding of Egyptians and the field of political action within which they operated.[38]

British rule gave Muslims and Copts the pretext on which to unite—in favor of or opposition to colonial power, depending on their socioeconomic status and political influence. In many cases, the British sowed division between Christians and Muslims in Egypt to maintain their power. Evelyn Baring, first Earl of Cromer, and missionaries working in Egypt advanced the idea that the occupation had saved Copts from a massacre, and used the concern for Coptic safety to justify British rule.[39] While religious difference was a figure of Ottoman rule throughout the empire—whereby Ottomans used existing ecclesiastical structures for their governance—British colonial rule and Euro-American influence in Egypt spurred the development of minority consciousness during the late colonial period (1911–1923), when the Copts' status as a minority was debated publicly.[40] Through such debates, Copts transformed from a community (under the Ottoman imperial system of governance) to a minority.[41] While there were certainly majority/minority dynamics under the Ottoman Empire, the introduction of the minority concept into Egyptian public discourses reimagined political form and intercommunal links. Citizenship (*al-muwāṭana*) and equality became the measurements of Muslim-Christian relations that shaped the constitutional debates of 1923.[42]

Decades later, following the 1952 revolution, Nasser created an administrative structure that did not draw upon the political elites of the nationalist movement at the forefront of the anticolonial struggle. Instead, Nasser's political apparatus consisted of a different cadre of loyalists and supporters. In his push to quell civil society, Nasser undermined the authority of the Coptic laity—for example, economic elites such as the Sidarous-Takla family—and the Coptic Communal Council, or lay council (*al-majlis al-milli*), which had sought to democratize the ecclesiastical structure of the Coptic Orthodox Church.[43] While Nasser's reforms created a strong sense of national identity by giving all Egyptians access to public goods and resources, they also weakened the power of Coptic elites, who held authority over the Coptic Church and had broad influence in regional societies, such as Qinā (Bahjūra's wider province).

By weakening Coptic elites, as well as Parliament and the Coptic Communal Council (run by Coptic landowners and elites), Nasser groomed the Coptic Orthodox Church as a national institution to represent and consolidate "Coptic" interests, regardless of class difference. As a result of an intense political crackdown and the Agrarian Reform

Act of 1952, the Coptic landowning aristocracy was decimated.[44] By destroying the economic power of Coptic elites, the reform destroyed their political power and influence, as well.

Following Nasser's death in 1970 and shifts in economic conditions, the state could no longer provide the same kinds of services it had under the socialist programming of the 1950s and 1960s. Instead, under the Open Door, or *infitaḥ*, policy (1974), president Anwar al-Sadat initiated the privatization of the economy and public goods, and the Church acquired further power and prestige by alleviating the state in matters of social welfare—providing employment, educational opportunities, and healthcare within the community. In return, the Church received further recognition from the state as the spokesman for the Copts.[45] Under Nasser, state institutions had been strengthened, creating a new middle class and destroying the former landowning elite. Sadat, through his Open Door economic policies, privatized the Egyptian economy and spurred increased migration, which then became a significant facet of Egyptian identity. The 1970s and 1980s became an era of mass migration, when Egyptians sought work in Arab states of the Persian Gulf, such as Saudi Arabia and Kuwait. As the old agricultural system, decimated under Nasser, became nearly extinct, *fellaḥin* in Upper Egypt sought opportunities abroad, reshaping the economy and culture for decades to come.

As detailed above, Coptic identity over the past century remolded itself away from lived class identities in which class structures provided more of an occasion for commonality, community, and perhaps even solidarity rather than strict associations of religion/ethnicity (i.e., Coptic Christians versus Egyptian Muslims).[46] Tracing the emergence of this genealogy and its mid-century transformation opens up space for thinking about its social and material remnants in the lived environment, landscape, and memory of Bahjūra and among the village's Copts.

Minority Contentions

Just as historian Kenneth Cuno argues for the era of Muhammad 'Ali, the 1952 revolution was not a complete rupture.[47] Despite land reform, some Coptic landowning families remained. While the landscape of the village has changed over decades, it remains interconnected through the memory of what once was, under the power and prestige of the landowning families and the economy of the '*izba*. In her family memoir, *The Cotton Plantation Remembered*, Mona Abaza conceded that the village of her family in twenty-first-century Egypt is no longer what it was even in the 1970s and 1980s. That village no longer exists.[48] Back then, homes were not made from red brick like they are today. Old mud-brick dwellings are now used as storage, or as secondary homes. Some homes remain empty because their owners live in Cairo. Bahjūra, like many other villages throughout Egypt, has physically, socially, and soulfully changed.

* * *

On a summer evening in 2017, Amin picked me up from Shig al-Naṣāra. We walked a short distance to the decorated gate of the Ayoub household, one of the last remaining Coptic landowning families in Bahjūra that still receive most of their income from agriculture.[49] We entered the grounds through a small turquoise door. Nader, the grandson and heir of the Ayoub name, had kept the original design. We sat on wood-carved furniture beneath an ornate chandelier. Before us hung an enormous portrait of his grandfather, who had lived in the same home nearly a century earlier. The similarities between the two men were quite striking, especially their large, solemn eyes. "Tell me about your family," I started. Nader began:

> Before the 1952 revolution, we had power through our land. I remember my father telling me stories about my grandfather. In the summer, they would water the ground [*yrashhu maya*] in front of our house and take a couple of chairs and sit outside. Anyone who would pass got off their donkey and walked in front of them as a sign of respect, and many of them even worked for our family.

The Ayoub family still owns considerable landholdings in the surrounding agricultural areas, which keeps Nader in Bahjūra. His nuclear family consists of his wife, Jackleen, and their children, Christina and Danyal. Nader's mother also lives with them. Nader, in his late forties, was the first to marry someone outside the predominant Coptic landowning families. Jackleen comes from a middle-class family in nearby Naj' Ḥammādī.

Another evening later that week, Nader picked up me, Jackleen, and Christina from a youth meeting at a church in Naj' Ḥammādī. He pulled up in a 1970s baby blue Fiat. We twisted and turned through the winding

Figure 2.2. The small mosque next door, Bahjūra, Upper Egypt, June 2017. Photo by author.

backroads and finally arrived at the Ayoub home. We sat in the villa's garden, and Nader started to grill burgers for dinner. As I conversed with Jackleen, a man wearing a brown-grey *galabaya* and white turban, or *'amma*, approached. The family needed some water from the nearby market, so Jackleen asked him whether it would be possible to grab some for us. After the man left, Jackleen turned toward me and said, "That's Ahmed. His entire family has worked for us in agriculture. His grandfather, father, himself, and now his children work tending our fields. He's Muslim, but I swear to you, he has gone to the Virgin Mary Church nearby and brought blessed bread [*orban*] back for us. No one at the church looks at him strangely because they know he is a part of our family. He even enjoys eating *orban* with us."

The next evening, we had dinner together again. This time, we grilled chicken. Ahmed stopped by again, right before the breaking of the fast [*iftar*] for Ramadan. "Do you need anything?" he asked Jackleen. "No, thank you, Ahmed," Jackleen replied. She turned toward me after this. "He checks on us every night because he just wants to make sure we're okay. He's an educated Muslim and knows the faith well. He's even a *mu'adhin* who rotates throughout Bahjūra.⁵⁰ His sons are also set to enter one of the Al-Azhar schools in the future."⁵¹

An hour later, around Maghrib (at dusk), the call to prayer, or *adhān*, started loudly from the small mosque next door to signal the breaking of the fast. Jackleen held her hands over her ears and looked disgusted.

* * *

In Bahjūra, there is a mixture of intercommunal closeness and distance. Jackleen relates to Ahmed as caregiver, employee, and family. He inquires each night about what he can provide for the Ayoub family. Jackleen relates Ahmed's Muslim character to his openness to entering Coptic religious spaces and traversing spatial lines of communal separation. Moreover, he is "educated," and Jackleen admires this pursuit for himself and his children's future. Ahmed and Jackleen relate to one another through shared life and flourishing—in a transactional relationship, but also one imbued with familial closeness. The *adhān* from the mosque next door lacks this relationality. It is a nuisance, a reminder of Islamic imposition, rather than openness, as with Ahmed's entrance into Bahjūra's Christian spaces.

Jackleen reads and experiences the *adhān* through sonic interference, also enmeshed in contemporary contexts of violence against Copts. Bombings, shootings, and stabbings occurred throughout 2017, during my fieldwork, in which assailants associated with ISIS killed dozens of Copts in attacks throughout Egypt. A sense of embattlement was voiced by Jackleen in many of our conversations, where she demarcated between those "violent" Muslims, Islamists, and terrorists and "educated" Muslims like Ahmed. Here there is distance from those who have set out to harm Copts. In semiotic determinations of "those people," religious signs mark possibilities of danger and disgust. The *adhān* is a marker of threat; the presence of Ahmed, a source of comfort.

Sectarian divides guided who could and who could not become my interlocutors in the village. Because of these spatial and relational constraints, I experienced Bahjūra through the Copts. Bahjūra's Muslims were those members of the community I passed in the streets or who briefly visited Coptic families. In these meetings, it was clear that new traditions of sociality still loosely maintain those of old. Ahmed's ancestors worked for the Ayoubs on their plantations. Copts and Muslims interact with one another in shops, on the road, and at the local *feseekh* dealer on the side street near the old canal.[52] Yet what was lost in the breakdown of the plantation and what its lifeworld meant to Coptic landowners and their economies have been consolidated by and are now interpreted through oppositional logics of sectarianism, which govern intercommunal life in contemporary Egypt.

Intercommunal and intra-communal sociality have been reconfigured in its wake. For example, the marriage of Jackleen and Nader would have been impossible a century prior. Even though they are both Coptic, the differences in social class and family background would have made their union untenable. In pre-1952 Egypt, class differences and status decided many relations, even within religious communities. The Ayoub family would not have allowed one of their own to marry someone outside their social status, of same or greater wealth and landholdings. Today, the legacy of the Ayoub and Sidarous-Takla families is a form of shared heritage for all strata of the Coptic community of Bahjūra—from the street children who play on the grounds of the Takla villa to the clergy members of Bahjūra.

While the reforms under Nasser raised the living standards of many Egyptians, it was also an era when the Coptic elite were politically and socially marginalized, which had adverse consequences for all Copts in subsequent decades. Where class differences may have affected the possibility of a cohesive Coptic identity in the pre-1952 era, shared religious identity became a primary marker of Copticity in post-1952 Egypt. Thus, the memory of the Coptic landowning families, even though they may have oppressed Coptic (and Muslim) *fellaḥin* on their plantations, is now a source of pride for most Copts in Bahjūra. Shared religious identity as collective memory and ethos has subtly encroached upon other forms of intercommunal identity and belonging, where at one time social rank or status may have connected more readily than religious affiliation. And migration has scaled and exacerbated these logics. The classed reconfiguration of Copts and homogenization of a "Coptic community" during the mid-twentieth century by the Church and the Egyptian state were contextualized by the paradoxical relationship between the emergent postcolonial nation's majoritarian values and the communal differences of its minorities. Internal transformations within the Coptic community worked in tandem with the postcolonial retraction of European colonial rule. Yet, by the late twentieth century, the politics of religious difference in the postcolonial moment was re-attuned to a new transnational resonance as Copts migrated and circulated ideas of minor injury made geopolitically significant by the emergence of the persecuted Christians movement, as detailed in chapter 1. This paradigmatic shift has affected how these memories are interpreted under national, postcolonial dynamics and transnational political conditions.

Class and Kin

Edward worked for the Sidarous-Takla family, as his father and grandfather before him had. They were the secretarial staff of the Coptic landowning elite. Edward eventually moved from Bahjūra and worked for the government. In his Alexandria apartment, he explained to me, with his wife listening, why there was so much disdain among the families and those associated with them for the 1952 revolution:

> The 1952 revolution was centered around class difference [*mufāriq bayn al-ṭabaqāt*] in Egypt. The workers who tilled the land became the fathers of the revolution, when Nasser formed the Socialist Union, saying, "Raise your head, my brother, servitude has come to an end, colonialism has come to an end." Those peasants who had the courage to rise up felt that they were protected, and they then began to enter politics, elections, and things like that. So, for example, a member of Parliament . . . this is so dangerous to say . . . his name is Musa, who was the president of the Committee on Youth.[53] His father was the head camel jockey of the Kamal Takla household, and his nephew now is the secretary of the Human Rights Committee! This is a family that lives in a world of animals! Animals that are not civilized! These are people who have nothing in their brains, except

a million evil and corrupt things! The problem now is that people are not concerned with principles or the person, they are more interested in "this guy is from our group," "that guy is from this family," "he's Muslim." If I brought the most elegant and learned Christian, like Boutros-Ghali, and ran him as a candidate against Musa, Musa would win. Why? Because Musa is Muslim and Musa is from a big family in today's Egypt.

Where the Sidarous-Takla family in pre-1952 Egypt held economic power, and thus political power, Musa and his kin are a "big family" today not because of their elite rank through their economic success and, subsequently, political prowess. According to Edward, they are a big family, first and foremost, because they are Muslim, and through their religious identity, they have traversed the authoritarian regimes of power and have learned to be ruthless in their economic and political dealings. The Sidarous-Takla family surely had to make similar dealings in its era. Yet sectarian presents have reconfigured the lens of legibility between Egyptian Muslims and Christians by which to understand a family's level of education, prestige, and refinement; all of these have become shaped by religious difference as a reconfiguration of class. In Bahjūra, as Edward describes, a Muslim (Musa's father) worked for a Christian (Kamal Bek Takla), and this was considered part and parcel of the socioeconomic structure. In contemporary Egypt, the descendent of that Muslim (Musa) became a political representative in Parliament, which was impossible prior to the 1952 revolution simply because of class difference. Religious kinship has gradually (and at times varyingly) taken precedence in the affectual ties of relatedness in Egypt, reducing the possibility of other forms of solidarity nurturing themselves forth.

For this reason, the impact of economic transformation under Sadat's Open Door policy on Coptic communities was less spoken of among my interlocutors. Farming and agricultural development had been the main sources of wealth for these Coptic landowning families. With the liberalization of the Egyptian economy, these traditional economies began to wholly break down. The connection between economic transformation and downturn, on the one hand, and the rise of intercommunal conflict and violence on the other should not be overlooked. Collective memory recalls a time when landowning Copts employed Muslims and held both economic and social capital. And despite the historical realities, whereby that economic success was limited to a select number of Coptic families, the memory of that influence is what has made Coptic residents of Bahjūra remember and reflect. They reflect on the order and security of a past that, for many, was *not* their ancestors' history. But they still reflect, given the disintegration—yet continued presence—of Coptic life in Bahjūra.

* * *

On a summer day, I had lunch in neighboring Najʿ Ḥammādī with local historian Khalil al-Bahjuri. We looked over some documents that I had photographed from another Coptic family in the village. Flipping through the pictures on my laptop, he stopped at a land rental contract from 1924 between Ibrahim Takla and a handful of Muslim *fellaḥin*. "This is significant," said Khalil. "Pre-1950s land reforms, Copts held power [*al-quwwa*]. Members of these Coptic families were the ones to mediate conflict, even between Muslims, because of their social status. They were extremely respected. That kept Christians connected to authority. Now, since those families have either traveled abroad or many of them have passed away, Copts have been lowered in social stature within the village; they have less clout." He paused for a moment before solemnly saying, "After the 1960s, Muslims made more money abroad, in places like Saudi Arabia and Libya, and then they bought our lands."

Following my meeting with Khalil, I returned to Bahjūra and the Ayoub household. After I elaborated on our conversation, Nader recounted a time when he took a position at a bank in Najʿ Ḥammādī that provided him with a stable salary and a nine-to-five workday. His father scolded him then, for lowering himself to the position of a worker rather than an owner like the rest of his family; his superiors did not hold his family's social stature or historical position. Nader then lamented the current state of his family and Christian life more broadly in Egypt: "In the early twentieth century, my family and others like us owned the land, had influence as Christians, and provided jobs for many generations of farmers, especially Muslims. Now, where once my family held much wealth, descendants of my workers own more than I do after traveling abroad to work in Kuwait and Saudi Arabia. They have come back with more wealth than we have now."

His father's picture overlooked the table where we sat. I could not help but think about the ways in which their house serves as a mu-

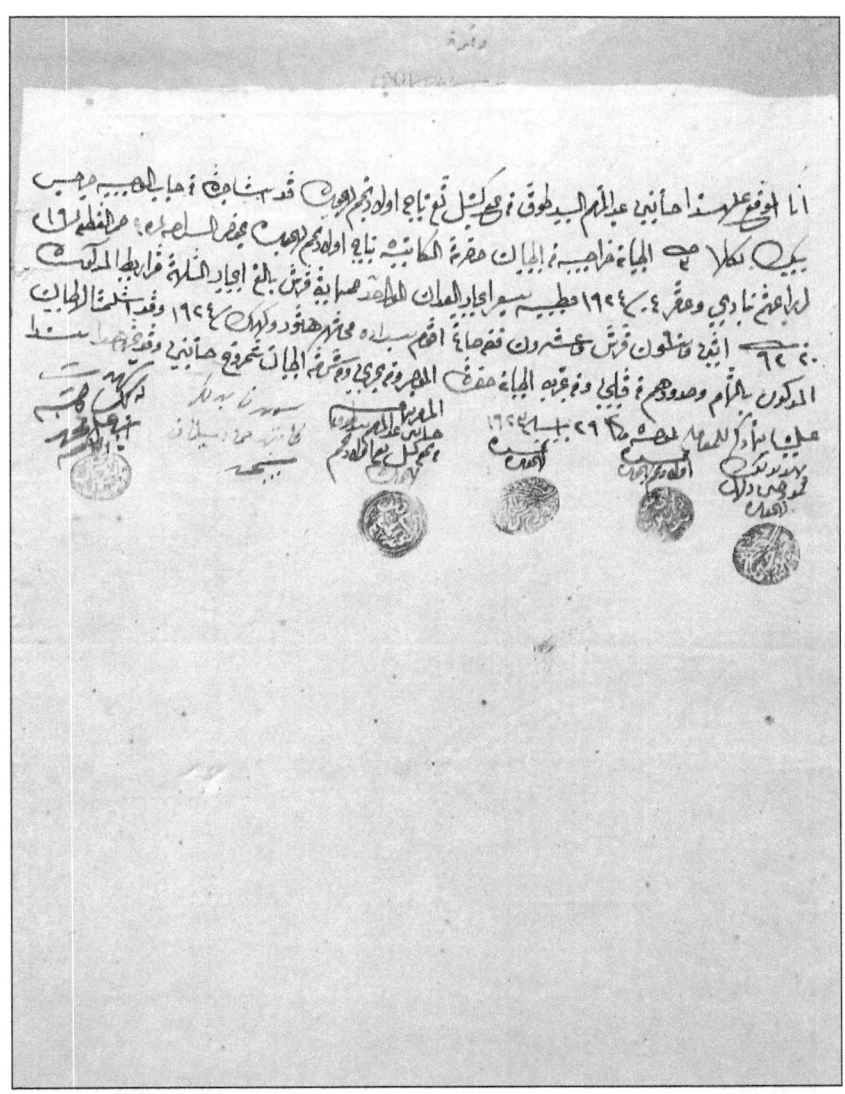

Figure 2.3. A 1924 land contract. Photo by author.

Figure 2.4. A room in Bayt Ayoub. Photo by author.

seum to their family's heritage, a legacy now mostly preserved and lived through the moving memory of that past. Throughout the estate, portraits of family members adorn the walls, and murals of a bygone era in Egypt cover the ceilings. On one ceiling, there is a *felucca* traveling the Nile on a hot sunny day.[54] Unlike the ground floor, for dignitaries and guests, the tiles on the residential floor squeak and crackle underneath the Persian carpet strewn across it. The room shakes if you walk too quickly. This home, with its baby blue exteriors and beautiful woodwork balconies and terraces, stands in the middle of what for many Egyptians in the north is a no-name town in the middle of Upper Egypt.

Nader admitted that he has tried to emigrate from Egypt through the US Diversity Visa Program, or Green Card Lottery. I asked him why he would apply for such a thing, especially when he remains so attached to Bahjūra and to his family's history. "You just never know where this country is going economically, and especially as Christians, I want to be prepared." While Nader and his mother washed dishes, I asked Nader's wife, Jackleen, "What do you think about what Nader said?" She grimaced and responded, "It's sad that such a great family lost this prestige [*hayba*]. The way that Nader describes it to me, I feel that loss too. They have blocked us in, here [*sidūna hina*]. Look at what happened in al-Minyā. Look at how influential Coptic families like the Ayoubs were at one point in time.[55] To see Copts in this state today, especially in fear of being the targets of terrorist attacks, it's unthinkable."

Violence and Shared Life

On May 26, 2017, masked gunmen opened fire on a bus filled with Coptic pilgrims traveling from Maghāgha, al-Minyā, Upper Egypt, to the Monastery of Saint Samuel the Confessor. At least twenty-eight were murdered/martyred and at least twenty-two were injured/witnessed. I arrived in Bahjūra an hour after the attack hit Egyptian news cycles and international media. The family I was staying with gathered in the living room, with solemn faces, for tea. Coverage of CTV, a popular Coptic broadcasting network, played in the background. The women of the household had to start getting ready for the wedding we were all set to attend that evening. Churches in the area had immediately sent WhatsApp messages to their congregations informing them that upcoming monastery trips were postponed until further notice. During the wedding, the martyrs of al-Minyā were on the lips of many, and some questioned whether to even allow dancing or music, in honor of the dead. Many of the men drank and danced throughout the night. An older man was visibly intoxicated. One of the sisters whispered in my ear, "People are sad tonight because of al-Minyā." Later that night, after we returned home, a cousin of the family sat in the living room scrolling through his Facebook. In his late twenties, Ishak expressed his frustration about the way Muslims were relating to the al-Minyā events; he desired a more direct acknowledgment of their martyrical suffering and death. On Facebook, his Muslim friends would comment, "al-baqā' lillāh" or "innā lillāhi wa inna ilayhi rāji'ūn"—both phrases of consolation. Ishak said sternly, "These phrases are used when someone dies from sickness or gets in a car accident, not for when people are murdered. It's like you're adding insult to injury!"

For a nightcap, we made our way to the rooftop of the building. The conversation centered around al-Minyā, and one of the women interjected: "I think the problem is connected to the pope and his support for the president [Sisi]. When he came out on July 3rd [2013] with Sheikh al-Azhar and Sisi, he was sending a message in support of the deposal of Morsi."[56] Her sister-in-law replied, "But I think he [the pope] had to do so. The message of July 3rd was that Muslims and Christians are both supporting the deposal of Morsi." Another family member responded, "But this is why it is so dangerous, because the Islamists use this as a reason to kill Copts." An uncle retorted, "We've been here for 2,017 years, and they've only been here for 1,400 years. Who are the original inhabitants of this country [mīn aṣl al-balad]?" The following day, a friend and I made our way to a local church to meet with a priest. Sitting in his office, he asked us, "Did you see what happened?" Abouna was referring to the al-Minyā incident. He continued, "Of course, many people are emigrating, with the state of the country and this persecution [iḍṭhād]!"

Yet other Copts from Bahjūra insisted that the narrative of persecution does not encompass all aspects of life. Even despite the horrors of the al-Minyā incident, Coptic interlocutors in Bahjūra emphasized that discrimination [tamyīz] was not only directed against Christians by Muslims in Egypt. Rather, discrimination also occurred between Chris-

Figure 2.5. Funeral prayers for the martyrs, televised on the *In the Light* program on CTV, May 26, 2017. Photo by author.

tians, based on class divisions [*ṭabaqāt*]. "It's not just Christians and Muslims," a young pharmacist insisted. "Al-Minyā is a political incident, and it will continue to occur because those terrorists [*irhābyīn*] attacking are hitting Sisi's weak spot—Christians. They have supported him. So targeting them is like targeting Sisi." Muslim-Christian relations in Egypt are not solely demarcated by persecution politics, or the framing of sectarian relations by conflict and cooperation (as a perpetual waiting for the next incident of violence to erupt). Rather, the ambiguities of intercommunal tension and shared life offer a different way to think about the politics of migration beyond a binary of socioeconomic factors and forced displacement and dispossession.

The oscillation between a politics of friendship and conflict defines Muslim-Christian relations in an Upper Egyptian village like Bahjūra, where in one instance a Muslim mother might tell her child, "Don't eat in the Christian area [*Shig al-Naṣāra*] because they'll poison you," and in another she might take her child to the church for the Saint George festival every November to receive blessings, or *baraka*.[57]

In June 2017, I was walking through Bahjūra, again, with Amin (who opened this chapter). As we began to walk, I noticed that a falafel restaurant at the end of the street was open and serving food. I peeked inside and saw that there was a "There is no god except Allah, and Muhammad is his messenger" decorative portrait, indicating that the place was most likely owned by Muslims. I was perplexed, given that it was Ramadan and in places like Cairo, cafés open during the day have been forcibly shut down by Egyptian police.[58] As we walked further, I noticed that, on the predominantly Muslim street, there was also a sheesha shop open for business, with customers drinking tea and smoking cigarettes. I became even more perplexed. I inquired about these scenes to Amin. "Things are different here in the village," he said. "I would say only about 50 percent of Muslims fast during Ramadan." I then noted to Amin that in Cairo, the police would come and shut down these businesses themselves if they were open. He responded, "We don't have anything of the sort [ma'andinash al-kalām da]. We have a shared life together [al-hayat al-mushtarika]. We decide what is permissible and what is not."

What are some practical implications for an ethics within the framework of local difference as a classed communalism?[59] Shared life entails a collective frame of the everyday—in its common conditions of electrical outages, road (dis)repair, sweltering weather in the summer months and frost on the dirt pathways in winter, and in the affective communion of landscape and historical presence.[60] Minority experiences of discrimination and violence are also part of this collective frame, but they are negotiated intercommunally (although the state intervenes in such negotiations as well[61]) for a common flourishing in a place like Bahjūra.

There are intersecting scales in the above scene with Amin. Class difference—as channeled through geographic difference from the centrality of the Egyptian state in Cairo—unfolds how locality molds relationality with the other, which also can spill over into disagreement as well as violence. In violent spillover, those forms of negative relationality scale upwards to national, transnational, and imperial frames, when violence against "the Copts" melts the Christians of Bahjūra away from their Muslim neighbors, those they depend on (like the relationship between Jackleen and Ahmed) and those they despise.

Migration circuits have exacerbated this dynamic, straining the continuation of a collective frame, as Christians leave and return to/

from the United States with new frames of religious difference. In the summer of 2021, I returned to Bahjūra and had lunch one July afternoon with Jackleen and the rest of the Ayoub family. Over post-lunch tea, Jackleen described how, when her mother visited London, she rode a taxi with a Pakistani driver. Along the way, the driver asked her whether she was Muslim. Her mother responded with an emphatic "No!" After recounting the short anecdote, she asked me, "Why do they allow all of these Muslims into England and America? My sister in Florida says that they are taking over whole neighborhoods near her. You think that you'd be able to escape them after leaving Egypt!" The abstraction of "Muslims" from Jackleen's everyday encounters and friendships with Muslims—at the local school, shopping with colleagues in Najʿ Ḥammādī, or calling old classmates on the phone and talking for hours about family life and death—in this retelling gestures to imagining the outside of Egypt through the reconfiguration of religious difference.

Shared life for someone like Amin is upended in its translations in migration enabled by empire (determining the flows of people to where and by what means). Amin voiced his frustrations with these flows during one of our many post-dinner conversations: "Coptic people in the diaspora don't understand everyday life in Egypt, and especially Upper Egypt. They have their own image in their minds as to what life is like here, especially in the village—that there is religious persecution nonstop. But the reality is that here, in Egypt, Copts have to deal with the messiness and the humiliation [*bahdala*] of the everyday, living in poverty, without jobs or a future." Although religious difference and sectarian violence condition intercommunal relations even in places like Bahjūra, other factors such as class also shape persecuted positionalities and (im)possibilities of repair. An "ethical thematization" of religious difference in Egypt includes an intersectional approach to precarity.[62] Put simply, Coptic precarity is also dependent upon class and economic difference, and contextualized by geographic difference. As economic opportunities dwindle in Egypt, especially in the south, migration to places like the United States, where relatives speak of Christian flourishing and the American Dream, often becomes the solution to broader structural disparities at the intersection of religious identity and poverty.

Figure 2.6. The streets of Bahjūra's old district, June 2017. Photo by author.

Emigration of Roots

"Emigration does not worry me. It is the emigration of Copts within themselves that does; the culture of fear."[63] Egyptian-Christian columnist Soliman Shafik argues that it is not the physical movement of Copts that is a concern, but rather the movement of Coptic communal life from the everyday to the event—the bombing, the incident [ḥādth], the attack. Since the 2011 revolution, Copts have emigrated—temporarily and permanently—to the United States in fear of the political future of Egypt. The Coptic Orthodox Church's facilitation of the Lottery has helped to further this narrative of exodus. As one US embassy official mentioned to me regarding the involvement of the Church in the Lottery, "For the long term, though, and this is less clear as to if the Church is actually thinking about this out loud, but maybe, just maybe, they are thinking about their future existence in Egypt."

The recent immigration of Copts to the United States has produced new sites of concern in the places they leave behind and the places they reside in the lands of immigration. As this chapter has illuminated, one of the major effects of this migration has been on everyday relations. The loss of a moral universe, in which, for example, Coptic landowning families held power and prestige, is remembered today in its remaining artifacts in Bahjūra—mainly homes, documents, photos, and neighborhoods. The remembrance is reflected in and interpreted through the contemporary conditions of Coptic life—mainly demarcated by incidents of sectarian violence and events of terrorism, which have targeted the Copts as a symbol of the state and as connected to the West/Christianity.[64] Terrorism and incidents of sectarian violence are the paradigms by which "the Copts" have been constructed and narrated, with the Church as the central representative, moderator, and mediator in the wake of these attacks.[65]

Following the 1952 revolution, Copts became connected to one another, as national citizens, through (primarily) Coptic Orthodoxy, above intersectional identifiers. They are now both symbols of national unity and international representatives of Christianity, as a *persecuted* Christian community. In many ways, violence has come to shape a *global* Coptic kinship. Yet this chapter has described how

Coptic community has varied historically, and how violence was not always the main form that relationality took.

The American push for greater policy attention on the plight of Middle Eastern Christians has intensified this particular narration and representation of the Copts. In *Religious Difference in a Secular Age*, Saba Mahmood describes the predicament in this way:

> Copts are no different than other minorities in that any attempt to draw attention to their plight inevitably sets them apart from the identity of the nation. The postcolonial nature of their predicament is apparent in that their call for Euro-American protection sets up an unstable synergy between the security this affords and the insecurity it engenders with respect to their relationship to the nation. Their dependence on supranational forms of support requires them to amplify their difference to a certain degree. This is not simply a case of the victim's hyperbole, but a necessary feature of making their discrimination legible in terms of Euro-American geopolitical interests.[66]

The suturing of Copts to persecution politics does not merely operate in the political theater of Washington, DC. In the everyday lives of those in the Coptic diaspora in the United States, this framing of their collective identity is institutionally mediated by the Coptic Church and has set them apart from Middle Eastern Muslim communities. One Coptic interlocutor in New York suggested the following to me over tea:

> The Church would do itself good if it defined a Copt as having a broad interest with Coptic persecution in Egypt . . . (a) because the situation is going to change very slowly, so there will always be points of concern, and (b) because it gives you a lot of power and inclusive reach.

Forging the Coptic diaspora around Christian persecution and Islamic violence has far-reaching consequences for the ways Copts define themselves and are narrated in/by the United States, especially after 9/11. Since the 2011 Egyptian revolution, new Coptic migrants have filled churches throughout North America. While most of these migrants have arrived through the Green Card Lottery or family reunification, still others have stayed in the United States by applying for asylum.

These asylum seekers have sought refuge as geopolitical interest in their plight has sharply increased, and this has had a direct impact on how they frame their stories (or rather, their identity) around the law and its grammars of persecution. The following chapter follows these Coptic asylum seekers during the legal process, unfolding how the politics of persecution operates through the logics of persecution in US courtrooms.

3

Religious Difference and Asylum Law

"BULLETS IN THE HEART OF THE COPTS." The July 1997 issue of *The Copts* newsletter, a publication by Coptic diasporic activists in the United States, opened with the image of a young boy ominously holding the casing of a bullet that had killed his father. His piercing look expressed the tragic aftermath of bloody, wanton violence in Bahjūra and surrounding areas. As described by other digital diaspora publications, members of the Islamist organization al-Gamaʿa al-Islamiyya attempted to target the Egyptian security detail at the Saint Shenouda Church and failed, so they decided to shoot into the nearby neighborhood of ʿEzbet Daoud.[1] As neighbors walked to the local store or sat in front of their homes, the assailants fired randomly, killing twelve Christians and Muslims—their bodies strewn across the street, their blood mixing and flowing into the crevices of the dirt road. The English caption of the image of the boy gripping the bullet between his fingers in *The Copts* newsletter read, "Holding the bullet with which [a] Muslim extremist killed his father in front of him," and grouped it with other incidents elsewhere in Egypt to show patterns of Christian devastation.

In June 2017, I was driving with Mina and his brother-in-law Kyrillos on the outskirts of Bahjūra. Mina works in sugarcane extraction, which produces black honey—a delicacy of Upper Egypt—or *muʿassil*, used for smoking tobacco. After a tour of the extraction process, Mina showed me a warehouse far outside the village that contained two million Egyptian pounds' worth of product. Winding through the side streets back to the village center, we crossed into ʿEzbet Daoud, known for its mixed Muslim and Christian population. Mina recalled the area as the location of the 1997 attack. I asked Mina whether the attack was meant to specifically target Christians, given that several Muslims also died in the incident. He responded,

> No, Muslims live here as well. They [the attackers] wanted to give the appearance that this place is not secured [*mafish amn*].

Yet the image and its explanation—published in *The Copts* newsletter in a mix of Arabic and English—associated the attack with the specific targeting of Copts as Christians. As noted in chapter 1, the newsletter's readership was a mixture of diasporic Copts and Western Christian audiences interested in the contemporary condition of Egypt's Christian minority. The narrative of Muslim violence against Christian victims framed the incident for the newsletter's transnational readers rather than highlighting the local ambiguous character of security's absence. As described by Mina in present-day Bahjūra, the attackers sought to sow chaos and to specifically target the Egyptian state through the infliction of disorder. Yet neither of these conceptualizations of violence—sectarianism or insurgency—attend to the scaled translation of the 1997 attack or of any other. Such scaled translations flow back and forth/up and down multiple dialectical sites in migration to the United States—from diasporic activism and advocacy to legal typologies of injury and refuge.

* * *

In July 2013, the first democratically elected Egyptian president, Mohamed Morsi, was deposed from power by the military. Following the coup, 3,407 Egyptians were granted asylum in the United States—14 percent of all individuals granted asylum—up from 536 in 2010.[2] In Coptic asylum cases in the New York–New Jersey area after 2011, many decisions have been made based on "pattern or practice of persecution"—that is, being part of a social group with a well-founded fear of future persecution. This chapter primarily shows how logics of persecution in US asylum law are translated through the politics of persecution that positions Copts as victims of bloody, wanton violence like the 1997 shooting described above. It also demonstrates how asylum distinguishes Copts religiously (as persecuted Christians) yet obscures how they are recognized and targeted *differently* as racialized figures in everyday American life. Weaving together legal, geopolitical, and theological perspectives on persecution, the chapter examines how Copts have been discursively sutured to *religious* persecution (as victims and martyrs) in ways that have marginalized them from other precarious communities between the New York–New Jersey area and Bahjūra.

Media narratives of exodus and polemical discursive formations that position Christian victims and Muslim monsters have impacted the adjudication of Coptic asylum cases in the United States.[3] Persecution is a particular legal category within asylum law around the world associated with refugee status. What I note as "commonsense legality," also described to me as "judge-made law," has shifted in identifying Copts as "persecuted" rather than discriminated against, especially after the 2011 revolution and the influx of Coptic migrants to the United States. The idea of "commonsense legality" gestures to the fact that judges are aware or made aware by the asylum seeker's lawyer of these media narratives, and this leads to a "commonsense" notion of Coptic persecution, which impacts how judges adjudicate asylum cases. Shifts in legal rationalization have altered how Coptic cases have been made to be persuasive. The shift from discriminated against to persecuted in American legal parlance has far-reaching consequences.

While persecution has framed Coptic identity for centuries in Egypt, at the hands of Roman and Byzantine imperial rulers and Islamic empires, the social imaginary of Copts and Muslims alike at the turn on the twentieth century was also layered by European perspectives on Islam and Christianity over centuries of missionary circuits and decades of colonial rule. Western portrayals of Islam as barbaric, and Muslims as a "monstrous race" and "frightening figures" have impacted Coptic framings of suffering, most especially in diasporic contexts through their political translations into advocacy and activism.[4] Over the course of the twentieth century, the fate of "Eastern Christians" was given political attention and religious translation through shared spiritual kinship by European and American humanitarian efforts.[5] The longue durée of the Western gaze on Eastern Christians has been consequential to how Copts have articulated their cause, transnationally, in the contemporary contexts of the war on terror and the configuration of the global Muslim terrorist.[6] As outlined in chapter 1, in defining *Islamic* terrorism as a threat to national security, US policy makers and religious leaders positioned Christians as simultaneously victims and witnesses to Christ. In making persecution a political concern during the late twentieth and early twenty-first centuries, evangelicals and ecumenical allies (including Middle Eastern Christians themselves) have carved out a special place for Eastern Christians and their plight in the broader image of Islam as barbarous and Muslims as terrorists. A theopolitics of persecution—as spearheaded by American evangelicals through the persecuted Christians movement—has formed the conceptual landscape for thinking about the figure of the Middle Eastern Christian today and has altered the ways Copts are made and make themselves legally legible within the US "asylum game."[7]

Other studies of asylum elsewhere have examined the relationship of legal and administrative procedures in adjudication,[8] the constitution of asylum seekers between biological life and full social citizenship,[9] and the paradoxes of refugees as a category of transgressive mobility and as a form of life.[10] In France, for example, the asylum cases of the 1970s from Chile and Vietnam rapidly declined and were increasingly replaced by applicants from sub-Saharan Africa, as well as Kurds, Afghans, and Kosovars. Feelings of solidarity and compassion to such groups seeded into suspicion of the racialized other. Although most refugees live in Asia and Africa, asylum became the central issue in European, and more recently American, debates on the presence of such migrants and the possibilities of threat to the demographic homeostasis of white supremacy and heightened fear of stolen economic opportunity. The desire to parse the worthy from the unworthy migrant has charged processes of managing asylum. The narrative for asylum seekers—which until the 1970s in France had been the cornerstone of proof—no longer sufficed. Physical and psychological marks became the embodiment of truth to uphold declarations of persecution.[11]

In one of the last interviews he gave before his death, Michel Foucault contended that the "ethos" of a time articulates "games of power" and "games of truth."[12] Through the intersection of practices of the self and technologies of power, Foucault asks, How are free individuals constructed through these technologies, and how do they play truth games? How do asylum applicants navigate a system, a game if you will, that rewards them based on familiarity with legal bureaucracy and its inner workings?[13] In the case of Coptic asylum seekers since the 2011 Egyptian revolution, the game of power and truth has been centered on the shift in legal legibility—Copts as persecuted rather than discriminated against—which has dually affected the everyday understanding of Coptic life and intercommunal conflict both in Egypt and in the United States.

Put differently, increasing American imperial interest in the precarity of Coptic Christians since 2011 has contributed to the legal transformation of Coptic Christians into a persecuted social group rather than individual asylum seekers facing discrimination. The *coherence* of this transformation into a logic (or common sense) is what makes its social and legal effect powerful. In *Philosophical Investigations*, Ludwig Wittgenstein speaks of the conditions for establishing the truth of a confession as lying not in the correct *description* of a process, but rather, in the special criteria of *truthfulness*: adherence to the logics of a particular game. Coptic testimony at asylum trials is carefully curated by a lawyer versed in the specific legal logic required of the asylum system. The system requires that applicants recognize the right way to answer questions—a "dangerous game of truth management."[14] The commonsense understanding of Copts as a persecuted people matters in these cases. Most judges I interacted with during fieldwork *knew* about the Copts and their plight. The common sense of the US asylum system as it pertains to the Copts has positioned their persecution as a given. Their persecution is depicted as "inherent in the situation, intrinsic aspects of reality, the way things go."[15] The idea of commonsense legality outlines how the plight of certain groups is made more recognizable through the institutional performance of judges and lawyers who argue for and decide persecuted matter-of-factness.[16]

Commonsense Legality

Persecution is rather vague within US asylum law, yet it determines whether an asylum case is worthy of approval.[17] The legal parameters of the "fear of future persecution," a nomenclature needed to secure group status, persuades the applicants to efface specifics and attend to "countrywide conditions." The suffering of specific Coptic individuals and the intentions of particular perpetrators of persecution melt into the background, in favor of listing countrywide events—this bombing here, that ISIS attack there. Within this legal space, the processes of determining Coptic eligibility for asylum are left to classification—that the person before the judge is a Christian from Egypt—and their fear of *future* suffering or persecution is prioritized for approval. In modern Egypt, Christian-Muslim conflict has historically been weaponized under colonial and postcolonial authoritarian regimes for political gain. Egyptian sectarianism is remapped and reconfigured by Western legal regimes such as asylum, translating events for coherence—to make plain how "the Copts" are a persecuted people for matters of judicial adjudication. While such events are already sectarian within the national context of Egypt, attorneys and judges in the United States bring together incidents of violence—this shooting with that stabbing and this fight between a Christian shop owner and a Muslim customer—that end up further entrenching practices of structural separation between Muslim and Christian Egyptians in diaspora.

By translating thick political problems into thin legal representations like "persecution," US asylum law flattens Coptic life and struggles for equality in Egypt into a civilizational rift between barbaric Muslims and civilized Christians. Exemplified within academic literature, news media, and policy discourse, Copts have been discussed and framed as passive victims and not actors in their own right.[18] In post-revolutionary US asylum proceedings, Copts are incited to stress their graphic and bloody victimhood, in order to preserve their claims to persecution. To secure this position, lawyers emphasize immediate Coptic suffering through the listing of particular events rather than through an engagement with the broader political and economic processes that produce the infliction of violence.[19] In many ways, these events must keep up with the pace of the trial, ensuring that there "was a shooting at a church *just last week*," as one lawyer argued in their debate with a government attorney. The urgency is vital. The need to continue the documentation of suffering apace with the American legal system consigns Coptic life to its death, limiting other ways of being even in diaspora. America is a place of salvation, a place of freedom from Egyptian Muslim barbarism. From this perspective, asylum language simplifies complex and ambiguous situations, erasing important differences among both victims and perpetrators.[20] Within the forging of a story, legal actors rationalize persecuted personhood within the limits of commonsense legality. It is here that transnational Coptic subjectivity is reshaped by the legal transformation from person discriminated against to persecuted social group.

Probabilities of Violence

In an office covered in Egyptian pharaonic memorabilia, Gabriel, an immigration attorney in his late fifties, explained that the approval rate of Coptic asylum applicants is upwards of 95 percent, particularly since

Egyptian president Abdel Fattah al-Sisi took power in 2013.[21] Why did the approval rate change so drastically after 2013? Gabriel explained that the consistent nature of attacks against Copts in Egypt, or at least greater international focus on them, paradoxically transitioned Coptic cases away from what they used to require, something he calls "having a story." In most asylum cases, the applicant must include a declaration, considered a supplementary document, which narrates the events that led to a person's migration or forced displacement. The declaration constitutes the sworn testimony of an asylum seeker's version of the facts and explains their personal history. The document is important, as the asylum officer will draw questions from it during the interview that will seek to prove or disprove a person's account.[22] Since 2013, Coptic declarations have become less about the cohesive presentation of personal circumstances and more focused on the immediacy and severity of structural conditions. As Gabriel explained,

> It's easier to win an asylum claim [in the Coptic case] if you don't have a story. That's counterintuitive, but it makes sense if you understand the dynamics of how the law works. It works because first of all you don't have a credibility issue.... If you are making a claim that X and Y and Z happened, you need first corroboration, which is not always easier to get. But even if you have it, it's questionable if it's legitimate, and the asylum officer is always dubious if they're familiar with how corrupt the system is. And then there's the credibility. Is it true, is it not true? So if you start your story by saying, "I have never been persecuted. Certainly, never threatened. And never violently attacked. But I don't want to live in my country because of the patterns, because of the possibility [of violence]." That's called the reasonable possibility test or the well-founded fear of future persecution.... This is the bible on asylum law.... It's a black letter law, membership in a particular social group. And as long as it's not half of the population, meaning females or whatever, as long as it's reasonably small—but not two or three!—you have a group, and then the question is, Is this group being targeted?

Prior Coptic asylum cases mostly relied on the issue of credibility. Do you have a credible *story*?[23] The story was personal and specific, and documented a chronological narrative of events.[24] Persecution was not determined to be systemic, at least under US immigration proceedings, and instead such cases relied on their cohesiveness, believability, and authenticity. Subsequent political upheaval following the Egyptian revolution of 2011 placed Copts in a precarious position. Various stages of the revolution and the transition back to authoritarian rule following the 2013 coup resulted in a shift in commonsense legality. The Egyptian revolution and its collapse were on the evening news in the United States, and the Obama and subsequent Trump administrations were both keen on continuing political relations in the form of consistent military aid and security collaboration. These geopolitical shifts also impacted Gabriel's work. Coptic cases were increasingly understood through the legal lexicon of persecution, whereby as a *religious community* there is a *reasonable possibility* that, in the future, they may experience persecution in the form of violent attack. The politics of probability centered on the scaling of suffering from the level of the person or individual incident to the level of the community:

CANDACE: But even before the revolution, in the '70s, '80s, '90s, and early 2000s, you had major incidents that happened . . .

GABRIEL: But it was localized, to some extent. I don't think you would say it's countrywide, and the United States government came out with reports each year, so did Amnesty [International], and they often had this refrain that "the majority of Coptic Christians remain unaffected and live normal lives." And that may have been politically motivated too. You didn't have the same kind of evidence then. . . . You had pockets. The question would always come up: Why couldn't you relocate? You see, asylum is country-specific, it's not city-specific. Clients will often like to tell me, "There was this attack that happened on my block and there's a mosque across the street from me and every time I would walk out, they would call me names and threaten me." The first question the asylum officer would ask is, Why don't you move? Now, things are relatively consistent. There's not a week that goes by somewhere in Egypt, from Port Said to Luxor, where there's not something going on somewhere. And that makes it easier to convince the court that this is a pattern and practice that is countrywide, and that there is nowhere they can reasonably resettle without fear.

Within the US asylum system, incidents prior to 2011 were understood to be isolated, and cases were decided accordingly.[25] Localized incidents involving Muslims attacking their Christian neighbors or church attacks not covered by Egyptian national media were unable to rise to the level of commonsense legality used to decide such cases based on persecution. Within the logic of this system, daily discrimination is constructed as localized, and cannot be elevated to the level of *persecution*. Asylum officers between 2011 and 2013 increasingly began to understand Copts as persecuted, *countrywide*. Countrywide is the antithesis of the local. The local is probed and questioned for details of the event and of the chronology narrated on the applicant's declaration. In this legal rationality, maps are rewritten and the character of Christian-Muslim relations in Egyptian localities is scaled upward.

Measuring Persecution

Back in his office, Gabriel explained how the legal system has measured persecution since the late 1980s:

> GABRIEL: And do you know what the standard, the burden of proof is? The burden of proof in a landmark case, a Supreme Court case, *INS v. Cardoza-Fonseca*, is that a well-founded fear is a reasonable possibility that one will be subjected to persecution, and in a footnote in *Cardoza-Fonseca*, the court said even a 10 percent possibility is enough to establish the burden of proof. That constitutes the reasonable fear. And if you flip that, if there is a 90 percent [chance] that nothing happens, you win asylum in America because of the 10 percent chance that there could be something. It is an incredibly, incredibly low burden of proof. When you talk to other lawyers about this, in criminal law, it's beyond a reasonable doubt, which is an extremely high burden of proof. It's hard to get that. And in civil proceedings, it's a preponderance of the evidence, which still is relatively high. But for asylum law, it's only a reasonable possibility. And that quote in *Cardoza-Fonseca* is a 10 percent chance.
> CANDACE: How do you measure that 10 percent?
> GABRIEL: It's hard to do that. The way I put it to clients is that if it's reasonable and documented, you're probably going to show it's a legitimate claim, that it's countrywide.

In *INS v. Cardoza-Fonseca* (1987), the court rejected the government's contention that section 243(h) of the Immigration and Nationality Act of 1952—which requires an undocumented person to show that he or she is more likely than not to be subject to persecution—is also the section that governs applications for asylum. Justice Stevens argued that Congress used different, broader language to define the term "refugee" as used in section 208(a) on asylum in the Immigration and Nationality Act.[26] The Refugee Act of 1980, an amendment to the Immigration and Nationality Act and the Migration and Refugee Assistance Act of 1962, was created to provide a systematic procedure for refugees of special humanitarian concern. The US Congress's purpose in enacting the Refugee Act of 1980 was to give the United States flexibility to respond to situations involving political or religious dissidents around the world; the Court's decision in *Cardoza-Fonseca* would further Congress's purpose by increasing that flexibility.[27] As a result of *Cardoza-Fonseca*, if a person establishes a "well-founded fear," even if less than a 50 percent chance, then an immigration judge can grant asylum at their discretion.

This has had far-reaching consequences that have directly impacted Coptic cases. Deborah Anker and Carolyn Patty Blum have outlined how and why the Board of Immigration Appeals shifted its focus away from personal credibility determination in asylum cases. Rather than discretion or credibility, the board utilized another basis for denying many asylum claims—namely, "a narrowing conception of persecution and political opinion under the statute."[28] After *Cardoza-Fonseca*, the board focused specifically on the claim of persecution itself, rather than on personal credibility and testimony. Thus, cases have focused on specific country contexts of violence in assessing the merits of applicants' claims.[29] In the case of Coptic asylum applicants, their actual beliefs as Christians have lessened in relevance. There is no line of questioning in which the applicant is asked to recite the Nicene Creed or recount Oriental Orthodox Christology. Rather, Copts are legally reasoned as an *ethnos*, where their Christian bodies are interpreted as distinct from their Egyptian Muslim counterparts.

Since Copts are now defined as an ethnic, persecuted body, violent attacks against Coptic Christians are reasoned to be imminent by the US asylum system. In his opinion in *Cardoza-Fonseca*, Justice Stevens notes,

There is simply no room in the United Nations' definition [of persecution] for concluding that because an applicant only has a ten percent chance of being shot, tortured, or otherwise persecuted, that he or she has no "well-founded fear" of the event happening. As we [the Court] pointed out in *[INS v.] Stevic* (1984), a moderate interpretation of the "well-founded fear" standard would indicate "that so long as an objective situation is established by the evidence, it need not be shown that the situation will probably result in persecution, but it is enough that persecution is a reasonable possibility."[30]

The "objective situation" is determined by the observer (in asylum cases, this is either the immigration officer or the judge at trial), demarcating the fine line between persecution and discrimination. For example, in the *Matter of Mogharrabi* (1987), the Board of Immigration Appeals upheld an Iranian's asylum claim where there was minimal evidence of any individual political activity by the applicant. The board also required little, if any, affirmative proof of the Iranian government's persecution of persons in circumstances like Mogharrabi. The board simply stated, "The Service does not dispute that opponents of the Ayatollah Khomeini are often persecuted for their opposition."[31] At the time, negative perceptions of the Iranian Revolution were pervasive, particularly in Western media, and it can be argued that such images possibly influenced the board's decisions.

In Coptic cases, commonsense legality is contextualized by images circulating globally of their maimed and bloodied bodies, through mainstream media, and social media shares. Judges, lawyers, and bureaucrats engage this common sense in the adjudication of their cases. Gabriel explained how increased perceptions of Copts as *persecuted*, by way of media and policy focus, have influenced the decisions of immigration officers and judges at trial:

GABRIEL: Since Sisi's ascension to power, the situation got demonstrably worse for the Coptic community there. As a consequence, with the evidence we present . . . our claims were in the upward range of about 95 percent success at the asylum level, and therefore we had very, very few cases to take to court. . . .

CANDACE: Are you saying before 2013 cases were easier?

GABRIEL: No, to the contrary, beginning with the first revolution, with Mubarak and then once the al-Ikhwan [Muslim Brotherhood] assumed control in 2012 . . . when Morsi was elected . . . it was all speculative, but it became much, much easier to win claims. It dramatically shifted. We were winning 50 percent on the first level, and then it went up significantly after the second revolution when Sisi assumed control through this coup d'état, then it got violent. We had more empirical evidence to present to the courts and to the immigration service . . . and then Daesh [ISIS]. This is only over the last year [since 2016], literally once they started a series of horrific attacks in Cairo then Tanta and Alexandria and in al-Minya. In court, it became unprecedentedly easier.

Through the transnational reverberations of such attacks, Gabriel persuades his clients that their communal affiliation to such murdered and martyred Copts satisfies the burden of proof necessary to grant them asylum. Thus, the granting of asylum is not determined by each Coptic applicant's specific memory of personal events, but rather whether their application adheres to the logics of what is legally recognizable. Where the authority over the legitimacy of representations of suffering is left solely to the asylum officer or judge's discretion, applicants must fit the *legal* understanding of what the causes and effects of violence and persecution are, even if they are not familiar with them.[32]

GABRIEL: I spend most of my initial consultations with the client trying to convince them that their story is fabricated. In most cases, they are. Very, very rarely will a client maintain, "No, this really, really happened and it's true." But they're usually not.
CANDACE: So they think that their personal circumstances are what is going to drive the case?
GABRIEL: They think that. That's the underlying assumption. That doesn't mean that Christians are not being persecuted. It's just that the people who are getting out are not usually the ones who are suffering. The people that are winning their claims here are basically riding on the backs of the people that are really suffering in Egypt, because those people can't get out. People in Upper Egypt. The small farmers. Or the people that have hardly enough to eat. They are the

ones not getting the visas, and they are the ones who are being pressured and persecuted. And the people who are living in Cairo, or not even in Cairo! I have a lot of clients who lived in the Gulf, Qatar, Dubai. Their fingernails never get dirty. They travel first-class and they come to the United States and they file for asylum and they win because their membership in a particular social group is a legitimate and enumerated basis for asylum. . . . They are here because of those people back there.[33]

Persecution is legally reasoned as "pattern or practice," where there is nowhere to go inside the country of origin without feeling fear. Thus, much of what determines successful asylum cases is awareness of this condition by the immigration officer or the judge. Specific political discourses mobilize or direct the behavior of the legal system. This functions in similar ways in other asylum courts. For example, Didier Fassin observes of the French asylum system,

In 2010 . . . quite unexpectedly, the country for which the portion of favorable decisions was highest, 75 percent, is Mali, which was then considered as peaceful and democratic, without a recent history of persecuting ethnic groups, religious minorities, or political opponents. By contrast, among asylum seekers, Russians, who are Chechens in a proportion of 80 percent, had a 14 percent rate of asylum granting; citizens of the Democratic Republic of the Congo, where the lives of civilians are probably the most exposed to violence worldwide, culminated at 12 percent; and applicants from Haiti, where a natural disaster in 2010 added its toll to chronic political insecurity, did not exceed 10 percent. The reason why Mali is an exception to this general severity resides in the recognition in 2001 by the National Court of Asylum of a "social group," according to the official terminology, composed of "women who fear the reason to be submitted to a genital mutilation against their will" . . . were they to return to their country—and this protection was extended to parents who oppose traditional circumcision for their daughters and thereby invoke for themselves the risk of persecution. As this jurisprudence came to be known, a growing number of couples, often in France for years as undocumented, sought asylum, arguing that were they to be deported, their daughter would have to submit to the ritual cutting.[34]

The reconfiguration of the perimeter of persecution to include female genital mutilation in France shows how the category is quite an ambiguous one, and dependent upon the intersection of knowledge production and translation—how a particular group is made legible to Western legal systems.[35] The group, now legally defined, conforms itself to definitions that exceed the matrices of self-understanding for the purposes of migration and legal status. Of course, it cannot be overstated that there are asymmetrical tendencies and pressures that bind asylum seekers to mold their communities into the languages of the dominant society they have submitted applications to. Processes of translation into the registers of asylum law define and limit the possibilities of legal legibility and existence. Those asylum seekers who know how to navigate these proceedings and be shaped by the state's representations of their social existence are the ones who succeed. Cases are adjudicated on the political economy of suffering made legible by way of commonsense legality of the immigration officer or judge making the decisions as well as proper legal rationalization by lawyer and applicant. The messiness and ambiguity of such a system lace themselves through the transnational lives of Copts between Egypt and the United States, reordering traditional ways of sociality and creating barriers to shared life.

Establishing Distance

Legalized sectarian separations have manifested themselves within the Coptic diaspora in the United States and are reconfigured by US imperial racial and religious formations, and these intersections are illuminated by the asylum process. Yet these reconfigurations do not end within the United States, but circulate back to Egypt, creating new modalities of difference and separation.

In October 2017, I sat with Andrew and our mutual friend John at a café close to the train station in Najʿ Ḥammādī. Andrew had moved to Boston after temporarily residing in the United Arab Emirates (UAE) for work. In the UAE, he obtained a tourist visa to visit the United States, and returned from the UAE to Egypt around 2012 to mull over a decision to immigrate. During that time, he decided that he wanted to permanently move to the United States and heard from others in Najʿ Ḥammādī and the neighboring village of Bahjūra that he could claim asylum (*liguw' dīniyy*) there. In 2013 he left for New York and stayed with a friend, originally from Bahjūra, who had immigrated to Queens. Andrew approached an asylum lawyer for help. From 2013 until 2017, he waited patiently for a decision in his case. After finally receiving his green card, he was able to return to Egypt after four long years to see his family. He sat with me on a warm summer-like night sipping Nescafé as the Egyptian Railway train heading for Aswan sped by us.

Andrew's case never went to trial, but during his interview, the asylum officer asked him specific questions to measure and prove his persecution. His lawyer prepared him thoroughly with scripted answers prior to the appointment. "They [the lawyer] know that you need to say specific things," Andrew said in English "I told the officer that the Ikhwan [Muslim Brotherhood] was attacking us, and now ISIS is attacking us.[36] The lawyer told me to say this." The collective Christian "us" brings together Copts from different socioeconomic classes, regions, and connectedness to the Coptic Orthodox Church. Although Andrew has never personally experienced an attack orchestrated by the Muslim Brotherhood or ISIS affiliates, the Coptic "us" has. That "us" is brought together through discursive reinforcement at the national, Egyptian level, where the Coptic Church is the representative of all Copts (even all Christians, to one degree or another) in Egypt, and at the geopolitical level, where Copts are collectively framed as all awaiting a martyr's death, waiting for the next bomb to go off or the next shooting to take place. Copts are collectivized as an "us" through the legal parameters of US asylum procedure, as well, which continue and reinforce an Egyptian national process of Coptic consolidation into a religious communal formation that flattens class dynamics and difference.

Continuing our conversation, I asked Andrew whether the officer had asked him about specific things that happened to him, like they had with other asylees I had spoken with. Andrew responded in the affirmative and elaborated the following story that endorsed the officer's desire for narratives of collective persecution: "I told him about an experience I had in high school. Once, a Muslim teacher slapped my Christian friend in the face. Abuse from teachers happens a lot in Egypt, but the officer wanted to know if this was something more than that. So I explained that my Christian friend then slapped the Muslim teacher back. All the Muslim students in the class would not accept that a Christian student slapped the Muslim teacher, so they decided to fight all of us [Christians]." It is not uncommon to hear of teacher abuse against students in Egypt, whether they are Muslim or Christian.[37] Yet the officer's inquiry incites the asylum seeker to religiously demarcate these incidents—that his friend was slapped in the face only because he was Christian, not because of wider systemic abuses in Egypt's education sector. The inquiry forces the respondent to separate Muslim from Christian. However, these intercommunal distances as translated by diasporic legal and administrative procedures are not dissimilar from embodied Coptic partitions from Muslim neighbors in Egypt.

In Bahjūra, as discussed in the previous chapter, there is a collective frame of intercommunal life in everyday interactions and exchanges. Yet such shared life does not encompass the totality of religious difference in the local landscape, which is also shaped by sectarian distinction. For example, an interlocutor in Bahjūra would switch to English to describe Muslim clients: "They are un-Christian," they noted on a car ride. Other scholars working in Cairo have described how Copts lower their voices when saying the word "Islam," sometimes rephrasing to say "other religion" or mouthing the word "Muslim" instead of voicing it aloud.[38] Communal boundaries are marked to stay in affective indexes of sectarian separation, cataloguing social values of moral difference. Separation also operates in many other ways—university organizations based on religious identity, demarcated neighborhoods, as well as language. In the summer of 2015, I attended courses on Church history, political participation, and theology at the Coptic cathedral in Cairo. A course administrator asked why I had not attended the previous week, and I told them that I had been sick. They looked shocked that an illness had gripped me for so long in the summer, and I replied, "wallāhi" (I swear to God). Taken aback, the administrator responded, "We, Christians, do not say such things. Say 'ṣada'iyni' or 'bimāna.'" Both roughly translate to "I swear," "Believe me, by my faith." Yet Copts argue that *wallāhi* denotes an emphasis on God (I swear by "my God"), whereas *ṣada'iyni* or *bimāna* emphasizes one's own self or one's own faith—a way of positioning moral and theological humility and at the same time superiority. Such linguistic separations also operate by way of daily greetings. From my first trip to Cairo in 2007, I was told by a member of my Coptic host family that you could tell who a Christian was if they said "ṣabāḥ al-khayr" (good morning) instead of "as-salamu 'alaykum" (peace be upon you), an Islamic greeting.

Different linguistic registers such as these have long manifested through the sectarian logics of postcolonial Egypt, which intensified during the presidency of Anwar al-Sadat (1970–1981).[39] Those committed to religious revival among Egyptians since the 1970s have been intent on making differences apparent. In her seminal work, *Politics of Piety*, Saba Mahmood recounts a lesson of a *dā'iya* (preacher) who implores her Muslim listeners to make themselves distinct from their Christian neighbors:

> Look around in our society and ask yourselves: who do we emulate? We emulate the Westerners [*gharbiyyin*], the secularists ['*almāniyyin*], and the Christians: we smoke like they do, we eat like they do, our books and media are full of pictures that are obscene [*faḥḥāsh*]. When you enter the homes of Muslims, you are surprised: you can't tell whether it is the house of a Christian or a Muslim. We are Muslims in name, but our acts are not those of Muslims. Our sight, dress, drink, and food should also be for God and out of love for Him.[40]

Muslim distance from the non-Muslim other and Christian distance from the non-Christian other have equated to spatial distance as well as linguistic and cultural difference. In the case of Mahmood's interlocutors, this meant the cultivation of bodily aptitudes, virtues, habits, and desires that serve to ground Islamic principles within the practices of everyday living and that are juxtaposed with what this *dā'iya* understands to be the secularization and/or Westernization (the Christianization?) of Egyptian society, where visible demarcations between Muslim and non-Muslim have become less apparent.[41] Coptic Christians in Egypt have also been incited to socially distance from their Muslim Egyptian neighbors. Anthropologist Anthony Shenoda recounts how he frequently heard Coptic Sunday school teachers imploring their pupils to act in the world in a way that highlights them as different, that shows them to be Christian.[42] This difference takes on semiotic form in the way Muslims and Christians in Egypt decipher one another through speech, expression, and ethos.

Such semiotic ideologies of intercommunal determination and differentiation in Egypt developed in the latter half of the twentieth century, when postcolonial transformations and religious revival among Muslims and Christians took root. These revivals cultivated new forms of religious embodiment, inscribing tradition onto the sartorial practices of the self. For example, the beard did not become symbolic of Islamic counterpublics in Egypt until the 1970s, when certain Muslims began to embody the Islamic revival by marking themselves with facial hair.[43] Before that, the beard had been a marker of distinction or dignity in some circles.[44] In the national erection of partitions and establishment of distance, sectarian logic has led to a more simplified and enclosed world. These scaled narratives and translations of intercommunal violence elaborate prejudices and eliminate ambiguities and are exacerbated by new imperial logics of religious difference.

Andrew was mindful of his new legal status, as an asylee, after nearly four years of his absence from Bahjūra's landscape. Asylum, as a recent semiotic-sectarian mode of separation, has circulated even in Egypt's rural South. On our way to the café in October 2017, I softly spoke with Andrew about his new status and how his recent return to Bahjūra has impacted him. I used the Arabic term for religious asylum: *liguw' dīniyy*. He hushed me further and responded, in English, "Don't mention this term out loud in Egypt, just in case other Muslims hear. Say 'asylum' in English instead." Becoming a Christian asylee performs the work of affirming that "those" Muslims are categorically considered a collective whole as well; they are the ones the asylee has sought shelter from in their country of resettlement. It at once affirms Christian difference from Muslim others and further inscribes their connection to the West, in particular the United States, which recognizes Coptic identity through the paradigm of persecution at the hands of the Muslim collective.

Bodily Hermeneutics

During the asylum process, applicants must affirm Christian difference from Muslim others in Egypt through the recitation of sectarian incidents and the performance of Coptic victimhood for a Western gaze. In the interview, the immigration officer incites the Coptic applicant to identify incidents, marks, and scars as evidence of the barbarity of their Muslim persecutors. The hermeneutics of the Coptic body becomes woven into commonsense legality, whereby the body must reinscribe persecution; as a persecuted people, Coptic bodies must produce evidence of suffering. But such a hermeneutics also presupposes that what appears on the surface is not the entire truth. Through bureaucratic interpretation, "it converts absences into signs."[45]

Abanoub is a Coptic man in his early thirties, tall, with dark eyes. While staying with his mom and sister in Alexandria, Egypt, in the summer of 2015, I heard about Abanoub's work in the North African desert as a petroleum engineer. His mother would point to items in the house—this television, that top-of-the-line fan—and let me know that her son was taking care of her. By the time I started fieldwork, Abanoub had been in the United States for a year or so, trying to forge a new path for himself outside the grueling and lonely labor of the desert. Over a buffet meal in Belleville, New Jersey, we talked about his asylum application process. He has a large scar across his left cheek and some on his hands from his engineering work. During his interview, the immigration officer asked him to identify his scars as signifiers of persecution:

> "Did you experience any physical harm ['*atada' gasady*/physical assault] from Muslims?" she asked. I told her, "No." [She replied] "But I see you have marks on your face and hands." I laughed, "No, these are from accidents [*ḥawādith*]." The only thing I said in my case was that I was nervous about what could happen in the coming period [in Egypt]; that the situation will not turn out well [*al-waḍa' ma yba'sh kwaiys*].

Many times, asylum officers will incite the applicant to form their stories around certain concepts, such as genocide.[46] Abanoub's officer read his body, interpreting his scars to confirm legally legible and acceptable claims of conflict and persecution. But Abanoub tells the officer that the interpretation is incorrect; it is more mundane, more ambiguous, and outside the purview of asylum proceedings that perform the maintenance of acceptable narratives of proof.

Didier Fassin and Estelle d'Halluin have argued that the great majority of persecution accounts are perceived as untrue, at least within the French asylum system.[47] This has led asylum seekers, lawyers, and officers to look for new evidence of alleged persecutions on the body. Where testimony has proven insincere or simply not quite enough, the body has become the object of scrutiny in search of scars attesting to violence.

While Copts are part of a persecuted group, making it easier for them to apply and win asylum since the 2011 revolution (according to Gabriel), the applicant must still establish such suffering in their declaration. Because applications must fit the definitions of persecution established by law and interpreted as such by officers, the information therein must be set up to emphasize elements in people's accounts that make them eligible as asylum seekers. So, during the asylum interview, their approval or forwarding to trial is left up to the asylum officer's discretion. Applicants must fit the officer's understanding of persecution. In other words, to successfully be a victim of persecution, they must remember a specific argumentation around Coptic identity and violence in post-revolutionary Egypt, to make it intelligible to the asylum officer and not necessarily correct in terms of the applicant's personal experience. Abanoub's body became both the place of an inscription of power, as the figuration of persecution in Egypt, and an inscription of truth, insofar as the body bears witness to persecution for the US asylum system.[48]

While all asylum cases are predicated on some form of evidence—regarding credibility or countrywide conditions—legal procedures molded by newly accepted knowledge of Copts as a persecuted people have bound applicants to reinterpret intercommunal relations and translate interactions, relationships, and forms of violence and prejudice into essentially religious encounters predicated upon a (persecuting) majority and a (persecuted) minority. This discursive form contradicts the politics of national unity within the Egyptian context, in which the Coptic Church, as a body of Coptic faithful, is an active part. National unity rhetoric understands sound Muslim-Christian relations in Egypt as an essential part of the national fabric. Advocates of this discourse deny the existence of a Coptic minority within Egyptian borders, conceiving of Copts as so fully and harmoniously integrated into Egyptian society as to be indistinguishable from Muslims.[49] For the Coptic Church, the promotion of this rhetoric has meant the downplaying of sectarian violence and attacks against Coptic places of worship and Coptic bodies, to maintain its alliance with the Egyptian state. And these institutional dynamics have consequences for individual Coptic asylum seekers regarding how they argue and prove their cases.

Since 2014, under the rule of Egyptian president Abdel Fattah al-Sisi, church bombings, shootings, and stabbings have resulted in dozens of

Figure 3.1. Bus from Jersey City to bring Coptic and Muslim Egyptians into Manhattan during the UN General Assembly, September 2017. Photo by author.

Coptic deaths. This has produced a structural problem for the alliance between the Coptic Church and the Egyptian state. As greater numbers of Copts have protested against al-Sisi's lack of protection for the community, the clerical hierarchy has found it more difficult to rally Copts across the Atlantic in support of the Egyptian president.[50] Several Septembers since 2014, bishop after bishop visited the New York–New Jersey area for circulations of *iftiqād,* or pastoral visitation, as well as to garner support for al-Sisi during his appearances at the United Nations General Assembly. In September 2016, Pope Tawadros sent Anba Yu'anis, the bishop of Asyūṭ, and Anba Bieman, the bishop of Naqāda and Qūṣ (two Upper Egyptian dioceses), to the New York–New Jersey area to gather Copts for the welcoming delegation for al-Sisi.

On the first Thursday of their visit, the bishops attended the weekly meeting of Anba David, bishop of New York and New England, in Staten Island. Following the spiritual lecture, written questions from local Copts from Staten Island and the surrounding areas were collected by an archdeacon and delivered to the table where the three bishops sat. Anba Yu'anis opened a piece of paper and read aloud the question, "Why should Copts in the United States care about welcoming the Egyptian president?" After a short pause, the bishop looked up to the crowd and responded, "Don't forget the days of the Muslim Brotherhood [*ma tinsūsh ayam al-Ikhwān*]." He repeated this statement three separate times looking at each corner of the church. "We are living our best days [*eḥna naʿiysh aḥsan ayāmna*]. I've been the bishop of Asyūṭ for two years now and I haven't dealt with a [sectarian] problem in those two years, and we're next to al-Minyā.... [*We* haven't dealt with a single problem] because we have strong relations with everyone. Listen, once there was an issue with a church in the diocese and the security forces [*al-amn*] wanted to close it. I spoke with the head of the Security Directorate [*mudariya al-amn*] by telephone and we finished the problem in a minute and a half, and no one was harmed!"

Bishop Yu'anis references the personal relationship between the clerical hierarchy and the Egyptian security state to "finish problems" through individual contact. Under the al-Sisi regime, the Church-state relationship has been likened to the personal relationship between former Egyptian president Gamal Abdel Nasser and Pope Kyrillos VI of the 1950s and 1960s. The relationship's pinnacle came with the consecration of the Grand Cathedral of St. Mark in ʿAbbāsiyya, Cairo, on June 25, 1968, and was very important for the emergence of an "informal entente" between church and state, one that entailed the state offering concessions to Church leadership in return for its political support.[51] The concessions included approval of and financial support for the cathedral, dispensing half a million Egyptian pounds from the government's budget for its construction, and participating in its inaugural festivities. Because the security apparatus granted (difficult to obtain) church-building permits, Nasser's relationship with the pope facilitated the process more easily. With the elevation of the patriarch to a semiformal state position as representative of the Copts, he was empowered with important political concessions regarding Coptic representation in public life. Through this process, the Coptic Church became an essential part of the nation's administrative body.

On January 6, 2019, al-Sisi inaugurated a new cathedral in New Cairo, one that is said to be the largest Christian church in the Middle East.[52]

Commentators noted that the Nasser-Kyrillos covenant was renewed through a holding of hands, as al-Sisi called for national unity between Christians and Muslims, echoing the words often used by Nasser in his public speeches. Yet despite the Church's official statements praising the government for its protection, incidents of violence and the imprisonment of Coptic activists led many in the community to criticize the Church's unwavering loyalty to the Egyptian president.[53] However, the official stance of the Coptic Orthodox Church has been one of support because symbolic gestures like the building of the cathedral and the attendance of al-Sisi at the yearly Christmas liturgy represent strong *institutional* relations between church and state. Bishop Yu'anis's emphasis on this during the meeting in Staten Island is indicative of this logic.

The Church's transnational institutional authority as administrative body and spiritual protector is channeled through the visitation of Pope Tawadros II and the circulations of bishops between Egypt and the United States for political meetings and fundraising efforts. These visitations and circulations are opportunities to give authority to the Church's supportive institutional stance vis-à-vis the Egyptian state, where such a stance is perceived as a bulwark against further bloodshed, bloodshed that many in the Coptic diaspora see as imbued with long-lasting communal effects.[54] From this perspective, the Church in Egypt, as spiritual mother, is both injured and strengthened through each attack because members of the body are targeted and martyred, but also "the Blood of the martyrs is the seed of the Church." This body—which consists of its clerical hierarchy—is a spiritual one in the sense that the Church is the minister of the Body of Christ, and thus, the body makes decisions for the preservation of its parts, its people. But as part of the Egyptian state, the contemporary Coptic Church also operates through the *regulation* of transnational religious life. Coptic religious life is not carved out and compartmentalized by rituals, education, and liturgy; the "spiritual" and the "bureaucratic" are not necessarily distinct. Rather, Coptic (religious) life entails the totality of Copts' communal formations, which the Church has continued to define through its allegiance to the Egyptian state even beyond its borders.

Ministerial Measures

For asylum seekers who are not active in church life—liturgical or otherwise—obtaining proper documentation for their cases can prove a challenge. Despite migration, the transnational reach of the Coptic Orthodox Church continues to operate through the administrative maintenance of its people. To prove the Christianity of the Copts, they must prove their *presence* in a local Coptic church by obtaining a certificate affirming their faith. During my fieldwork, Copts noted that there was a fear among priests that a person claiming to be a Copt may really be a Muslim. One Copt recalled that a person who described themselves as a Christian approached the American Coptic Association (ACA) in Jersey City for help obtaining a letter from the Church to prove their Christianity for their asylum case. After some initial conversations, it was revealed that the individual was a Muslim. Such stories of suspicion also have the possibility of adding to applicant difficulties in obtaining a letter from a local Coptic church affirming their Christianity, especially when they are not well known in the community because of their employment schedules or deeper issues with clerical politics. The difficulty, then, for any Coptic asylum seeker is that they must look to the Church to authorize their Christian identity and guarantee their position within the Coptic group (as a persecuted community in Egypt). While manifesting itself anew in diaspora, the Church has historically authorized Christian identity in Egypt, and those "homeland" conditions continue to frame clerical/lay contentions in the diaspora.

In the 1960s and 1970s, the Coptic revival movement in Egypt spatially reoriented communal life around the Church—from social gatherings to religious services, and even employment. The clericalization of the Coptic community bolstered the Coptic Orthodox Church as a state institution that represents *the* Coptic people.[55] The Egyptian state defines its citizens based on religious affiliation and regulates religion through bureaucratic agencies, administrative courts, and ecclesiastical institutions.[56] These mechanisms set the terms of Coptic relationships to themselves, to the community, and to the state. The administrative significance of Coptic identity meant that its religious status would be subject to verification by the state. The linking of religion with citizenship was intended to ensure communal integrity and internal coherence.

As Hussein Agrama has argued, the state's power to determine religious and secular domains helps to "consolidate and expand the state's sovereign authority to decide what counts as religious and what scope it should have in social life."⁵⁷ Egyptian identification cards label someone either Christian or Muslim, and that person is understood to be that wherever they go. Even in negated spaces like bars, sheesha cafés, and prisons, Copts are still Copts, despite the belief that such spaces separate one from God.⁵⁸ Unorthodox spaces mark Coptic otherness in Egypt, and the Church disciplines its people into understanding such spaces as outside *proper* Coptic identity.

Similarly, Coptic churches in the United States also regulate Coptic life, and particularly determine whether a Copt can claim asylum or not. While structurally similar to church-communal relations in Egypt, migrant Copts, in escaping the legal, social, and political constraints of the Coptic Orthodox Church's institutional force in Egyptian society, are pulled back into its authoritative structure, as they secure their documented livelihood—whether immigration status, job, or marriage—in the United States. This similar movement, transnationally, speaks to how the secular state and its institutions (whether in Egypt or the United States) regulate religion in modern life, regardless of the degree to which certain countries are understood as improperly, or incompletely, secular.⁵⁹ Despite this formulation, secularism has a globally shared form of religious regulation, and the secular state has sovereign power to stipulate what religion is, assign its proper content, and disseminate related subjectivities.⁶⁰ While the state claims to maintain the separation of church and state, modern governmentality involves the state's intervention and regulation into many aspects of socio-religious and political life.⁶¹ And the Coptic Church operates as an Egyptian state institution, transnationally. Its regulative authority follows Copts in migration.

The administrative power of this construction binds Copts outside the geographical confines of Egypt's borders to spaces, places, and identifications that are normative to religious authority and geopolitical interests. If the applicant's argumentation is not legible to the asylum officer's understanding of persecution, then the applicant is referred to trial. It is at the asylum trial where judges take up the mantle from asylum officers to give the final answer, whether countrywide Coptic persecution is legible to them or not. In lines of questioning and legal deliberation, the Coptic

B/body is bound by Copts' Christianity and persecution by Muslims/ Islam, and narrated through the identification of victims and monsters.

Trial Performance

The trial of Abanoub, the Coptic asylum seeker from Alexandria, took place on a Monday. Before the trial, Gabriel, Abanoub's attorney, and I met to discuss what to expect. "They might ask whether he [Abanoub] is really a Christian or not," Gabriel noted. Knowledge of faith would not evidence Abanoub's Christianity. There needed to be *proof*, in addition to a Church certificate. During trial, the line of questioning would provide the evidence. Underlying such bureaucratic measures are what Hussein Agrama terms "legalized suspicion." Suspicion of the applicant is directed toward their potential motives of material interest—that they are not "persecuted," but rather only desire better economic opportunities in the United States. As Agrama argues, in the context of the freedom of religious belief, it becomes imperative to determine whether acts or expressions of belief are *genuinely* religiously motivated.[62] Legalized suspicion presumes the power to probe and determine one's character. When an asylum seeker claims persecution based on religious affiliation, a distinct form of suspicion is performed during the trial.

Together, we sat in the waiting room mulling over potential questions from the government's attorney and the judge. "The main focus needs to be on issues of identity," Gabriel told me. During our rehearsal, the government's attorney came into the waiting room; Gabriel recognized him. He approached us and began fielding potential arguments he would make in the courtroom. "But the [Egyptian] government isn't doing anything about this?" he asked. After a short interaction with Gabriel on the question, he left. "We might be in trouble if he wants to fight this," Gabriel said nervously. "If he pushes that the Egyptian government is doing things to prevent this persecution, then there couldn't be a totality of fear crippling the Copts."

As we entered the courtroom, Abanoub was visibly nervous. The past three years had been in anticipation of this trial determining whether he would stay in the United States or go back to Egypt—determining whether he is "persecuted" or not. The judge entered the courtroom and asked the two sides whether they would like to converse without her present before the proceedings began. They agreed. Gabriel turned to the government's attorney as the judge left the courtroom. "This is an easy case," he said. "It is based on a well-founded fear claim." The government attorney responded, "What has the [Egyptian] government response been?" "Their efforts have been ineffective," Gabriel answered. "Look at what recently happened in Helwan.[63] Videos have surfaced evidencing the complete lack of security around the perimeter of the church complex."

The judge returned a few minutes later, and the trial began. Gabriel gestured to stacks of papers on his desk that contained a plethora of news items on violent attacks. "Would you like to hear from our expert witness?" he asked the judge. Gabriel's expert witness was one of the chief architects of the International Religious Freedom Act (IRFA), and helped galvanize American churches to get it passed in the US Congress (discussed in chapter 1). Expertise within this policy community does matter, not because a single expert on Christians in the Middle East helps shape a single policy response, but rather because of the collective power these experts wield in shaping and reshaping the "conventional wisdom" in DC.[64] Through it the underlying assumptions, values, and ideas then drive US policy decisions as well as shape commonsense legality that determines asylum cases and guides judgments during trial.[65]

Expertise demands a simplification of context, whereby violence at the level of persecution can be confirmed and translated through legal bureaucracy. Incidents presented as evidence in interviews and at trial are surmised to constitute the danger *each* Copt faces in Egypt, regardless of class (or regional) differences. Incidents in al-Minyā or even the twenty-one martyrs of Libya, however, are class-specific, meaning that those targeted were already some of the most vulnerable of society.[66] As Gabriel emphasized in his office during one of our conversations, the Copts sitting in courtrooms and interviews for asylum throughout the United States (until 2023) were not of the same socioeconomic group as those experiencing the brunt of sectarian violence documented by Coptic organizations, NGOs, and international networks; it is "because of those people back there" that the Copts in asylum courts in New York and New Jersey are here. For many Copts who make it to the United States on tourist visas, who then claim asylum, their personal stories matter little. Instead, the stories of the twenty-one martyrs of Libya, the martyrs of al-Buṭrusiyya, of Ṭanṭā, of Alexandria (among so many other incidents of violence) provide the evidence necessary to grant Copts asylum in the United States.[67]

Gabriel's expert witness's services were not necessary during Abanoub's trial or any of the other trials I sat in on; his expert affidavit was sufficient. The judge rifled through the papers in the file, noting, "I have no issue with country conditions." Gabriel began his line of questioning with Abanoub:

GABRIEL: How famous is your name?
ABANOUB: It's a Christian name in Egypt.
GABRIEL: So, it reflects your identity? People would know you are Christian from your name?
ABANOUB: Yes.
GABRIEL: How else would they know you're a Christian?
ABANOUB: I have a cross tattoo on my right wrist [*holds up his tattoo for the court*].
GABRIEL: When is the last time you attended church and why?
ABANOUB: Last week. For Christmas.
GABRIEL: What groups are specifically targeting the Copts?
ABANOUB: ISIS, the Muslim Brotherhood.
GABRIEL: That's all. Thank you, Abanoub.

Gabriel's line of questioning aims to mark Abanoub as a particular Christian subject. The name, tattoo, religious observance, and most importantly, the perpetrators of violence against the Copts all come to define Abanoub in US asylum law and contextualize him as a part of the Coptic community, a community defined as a "particular social group." They are brought forth as a collective community under persecution; they are sutured, in their collective trauma, to Muslims; they are defined as objects of violent attack by Islamist organizations like ISIS and the Muslim Brotherhood. A Copt is not simply a Christian from Egypt. They are a part of a broader community of persecuted peoples constructed and narrated by asylum officers, judges, experts in Washington, DC, American politicians, and news media.

That day, Abanoub was granted asylum. Following the decision, I approached the bench to speak with the judge. "When did you start presiding over Coptic asylum cases?" I asked. "Since 2011, Coptic asylum cases have become pretty regular," she noted. "However, it's only been recent changes where most of the cases were decided based on well-founded fear claims. Prior to this, cases were based on a personal story." The judge's response exactly matched Gabriel's description during our interview and subsequent discussions. Individual Coptic applicants have been interpellated into a group, whereby the Coptic community has been constructed by and imagined through frames of persecution. Since their cases are no longer decided by personal stories of discrimination and violence, Copts rely on the stories of other Copts to frame their cases. Instead of actors in their own right, they are legally understood as icons, metonyms of a persecuted people.[68] Fleshy and descriptive markers bring Copts together, beyond class and regional divides, and the Church stands as the transnational, institutional gateway that authorizes their inclusion into the community.

* * *

After the trial, Abanoub gave me a ride back home. Sitting in wintry traffic, I jokingly asked him whether it was difficult to answer questions related to church attendance, knowing full well his disinterest. He said, laughing, "I haven't been to church in a while. I feel like everything is about politics. Nothing the Church does is for the people. The bishops all just show off for Sisi, and could care less about the people. That's why if I do go to Church, I'll go and stand in back and leave right after." Amidst the snow falling around us as we sat in the car, Abanoub voiced his disagreement with the Church's political stances—its official support for Egyptian president al-Sisi and general denial of Coptic rights outside the confines of church walls. Yet it is a gateway institution, both in Egypt and now in the United States through which Abanoub networked to find housing, a job working at a gas station, and most importantly that letter *verifying* that he was a Christian. He is tied to it by necessity, but also stands in opposition to its political practices. For many Copts in Egypt and in diaspora, the Church is an institution that has structured its politics in parallel with the authoritarian regimes of Egypt (in many ways mirroring their practices) as well as the conservative politics of the United States.[69] For asylum seekers like Abanoub, the Church authorizes and defines Coptic identity, even in diaspora.

Stories and Suspicion

I observed several other asylum trials, including some that lasted no more than a few minutes. "Much of this has nothing to do with the law," Gabriel would tell me. "And more to do with circumstance. Most cases are a sham." Gabriel's description should not indicate that there are cases that are "merited" or "unmerited." Rather, it sheds light on the importance of performance, a legal game of truth telling that determines those who are "worthy" of asylum and those who are not. Indeed, successful applicants are distinguished by their ability to navigate legal proceedings and language with the aid of a well-networked lawyer, who knows the judges and the government attorneys they will face at any given trial. Successful applicants are those with the ability to seek out legal counsel that can manage and shape the state's representations of Coptic existence, cater to the political economy of suffering upon which their specific case is based, and contribute evidence to solidify commonsense legality of a persecuted group.[70]

During one trial, a judge stopped Gabriel's elaborations mid-sentence and said, "I know the Copts, I'm aware of what they have experienced over the past several years with increasing attacks from Islamist terrorists." Quick approval times have shocked other asylum seekers I came into contact with in the courtroom waiting areas. After a rather speedy trial, a Nepalese man who had been an asylee since 2010 waited for a decision in his brother's case, and said that he had "never seen anything like that"—that the speediness of Coptic asylum trials was jarring. The assuredness of Coptic asylum cases operates off the argument that, while there was no past persecution, there is a fear of future persecution. This gesture toward the future frees the Coptic asylum seeker from wading through the sludge of suspicion.

Proof of group membership and country conditions are all that seem to matter—in most cases. However, if past persecution does come up (if a Coptic applicant submits a declaration with a personal story or slips up during testimony), the government's ethos regarding such asylum claims becomes dominated by suspicion. Applicant case histories are questioned, facts are challenged, and evidence is disqualified. The story of the past must be verified by others. The value of the story is present in the documents of corroboration, which hold legal value.[71] Filled with content to parse, Coptic trials are turned into interrogations, where legalized suspicion seeks to systematically determine ulterior motives from genuine intentions, to find out whether the applicant's motives are genuine and religiously motivated—that they are fleeing because they are Christians and not for material interest or worldly power.

* * *

Monica is a woman in her mid-thirties from Luxor, Upper Egypt. There, she worked as a nurse at a government hospital. In 2015 Monica traveled for the second time to the United States and filed for asylum. Her case bounced around between states, as she switched lawyers trying to find one best-suited to guarantee her approval. I sat in a private space in the waiting room area of the court with Monica's extended family—her brother, who had come to the United States on the Green Card Lottery nearly two decades ago, her parents, who had come through the family reunification process, and her son, born in the United States. In cramped quarters, Gabriel told Monica that he was not comfortable with her current case. Prior to Gabriel's representation, Monica had filed for asylum and initially submitted a statement testifying to past persecution along with it. The original statement said that, after she had exited church following Palm Sunday liturgy, a boy on a motorcycle stole her purse, and she argued that he stole it because she was Christian. "This is not a reason for asylum," Gabriel told her. "There are so many holes in your story. How do you know he was a Muslim? Maybe he was just hungry!" Monica's mother interjected, "We know he was [Muslim] [*eḥna 'arfīn bṣiraḥa*]."

Gabriel encouraged Monica to de-emphasize past persecution, and instead focus on a future fear or possibility of attack:

> You want to say, "Look, I'm a Christian. I'm willing to suffer discrimination to some extent, but look, my family is here, my church is here, my community is here, I have a lot of things to live for. I was very active in church." You can tell them it was a meaningful life. There are rich traditions, the community you're involved with there. You didn't actually want to come to America! . . . But at some point when your life really became not personally threatened, but when you felt like you couldn't walk the streets without being afraid, you couldn't go to church without

being afraid, without fearing you could be blown up—that's it! I came. There was no specific event, in other words, that triggered your decision to leave. It was a cumulative effect of all of these attacks that were occurring on a week-by-week basis. It's very intimidating knowing ISIS, and what they represent and what they did in Syria and Iraq, [is] threatening the Christians in Egypt.

Like American fears of recurring terror following September 11, legal logics of persecution look to possible events that may or may not happen. Fear of future persecution operates on the possible; it could happen *anywhere, anytime*. Yet during her questioning, Monica not only pointed to incidents of personal attack because of her identity as a Christian, but specifically stated how her Christianity heightened sexual harassment—something she had not mentioned in her official declaration. Gabriel's initial line of questioning (abridged below) focused on identity, as it had in Abanoub's case before:

> GABRIEL: You have a long name, Monica Mankarious Karas, is that correct?
> MONICA: Yes.
> GABRIEL: Is this name a Christian name?
> MONICA: Yes.
> GABRIEL: Do you have any symbols on your body that might reflect your identity as a Christian?
> MONICA: [*Holds up right wrist.*] I have the cross on my hand. I've had it since I was a child.
> GABRIEL: When's the last time you went to church?
> MONICA: Today, for Jonah's fast.
> GABRIEL: Why did you leave Egypt in 2015?
> MONICA: Persecution; because there was no security, I was very scared of what was happening in Egypt [*'ashān mkānsh fi amn ana kunt khāyfa gidan min eih illi byḥṣal fi maṣr*].
> GABRIEL: Can you be more specific?
> MONICA: Attacks, sexual harassment.
> GABRIEL: Who was perpetrating this persecution?
> MONICA: Muslims.
> GABRIEL: All Muslims?

MONICA: The Muslim Brotherhood, the extremists [al-muta'ṣibiyyn].
GABRIEL: Are there any other extremist groups that would target Christians?
MONICA: ISIS.
GABRIEL: How do you know all this information?
MONICA: From the news.
GABRIEL: Were you ever targeted in Egypt?
MONICA: Yes.
GABRIEL: How?
MONICA: Not bodily, but psychologically.
GABRIEL: What kind of psychological abuse?
MONICA: Persecution [idṭhāa]; the feeling that you are persecuted just because you are Christian.

After Gabriel's questioning, the government attorney focused their intervention on Monica's testimony about sexual harassment as a form of persecution. The indication of past experience with such persecution was the main route of suspicion.

GOVERNMENT ATTORNEY: Was your husband aware of the persecution or harassment you experienced, as outlined in your written statement?
GABRIEL: Objection. The respondent testified that she feared persecution, not that she is a victim of persecution.

* * *

GOVERNMENT ATTORNEY: You testified that in Egypt you suffered psychological harm and abuse. Since being in the US, have you sought any counseling?

* * *

GOVERNMENT ATTORNEY: Can you explain what you meant by sexual harassment in your statement?
MONICA: We would be walking on the street and people on motorcycles would come by, grab my hair or hit my back.
GOVERNMENT ATTORNEY: How many times did this happen?
MONICA: Many times.

GOVERNMENT ATTORNEY: Is this the only type of thing that happened?

MONICA: No, also cursing.

GOVERNMENT ATTORNEY: Let's stick with the touching first. You were harassed physically by having your hair pulled, is that correct?
And that happened often?
Did you ever need medical attention?
Did you ever go to the police for help?
How long did this harassment last?
How many times were you harassed physically?
More than ten, more than twenty?
Did your husband or sister witness any of these incidents?
Why didn't you talk about this type of harassment in your asylum claim?

MONICA: Because I thought when I'm talking about persecution, you understand that it's happening to all the Christians; that's what's happening to all of the Christian girls.

GOVERNMENT ATTORNEY: I understand that, but you were asked if you ever experienced physical harm, and the statement I have says you haven't, but you just testified that you were physically pushed and your hair was pulled. So how come you didn't mention any of those things in your statement?

MONICA: I mentioned a few things to my lawyer. I mentioned that someone stole my purse from me, this was one of the incidents I considered to be persecution because I was exiting my church at the time.

GOVERNMENT ATTORNEY: We're talking about the things that happened to you. You just testified to me that you actually had your hair pulled, you were actually pushed from behind on many occasions.

GOVERNMENT ATTORNEY: How come we don't have that listed in support of your application?

MONICA: The basis of my case is persecution. It is known everywhere; those details are known everywhere. This is how Christians in Egypt are persecuted.

GOVERNMENT ATTORNEY: I understand that, but you just mentioned things that specifically happened to you.
Ma'am, you also testified that you were verbally harassed.

> Were you specifically verbally harassed?
> Can I have some examples?
>
> MONICA: Yes, I would walk on the street, and people would say infidel [*kāfira*] and Christian [*naṣrāniyya*].
> GOVERNMENT ATTORNEY: You're testifying that these [statements] are [from] Muslims threatening the Christians?
> MONICA: Yes.

The judge interjects:

> JUDGE: What I'm trying to understand, ma'am, is that all the Coptic Christians in Egypt—to the extremist groups, ISIS, the Muslim Brotherhood, and others—do they discriminate in their killing between men and women?
> MONICA: They kill the Christians.
> JUDGE: So, it doesn't matter, right? They're both infidels in their eyes.
> MONICA: Yes.
>
> JUDGE: When did you begin having the fear you claim you have now? When did that fear begin in Egypt?
> MONICA: Since the explosions, the attacks, and the persecution started, when Morsi was deposed from power. The Brotherhood felt that the cause was because of Christians.
> JUDGE: When you came in 2012, did you have this same fear?
> MONICA: When Sisi promised we would have safety and stability, I had hope, but these were empty promises.

At issue for the judge and the American government was the lack of signed affidavits attesting to Monica's claims under oath, and the fact that Monica had visited the United States in 2012 yet did not claim asylum at that time. While Gabriel hoped that the case would solely focus on fear of future persecution, Monica described the cases of physical and psychological intimidation she experienced back in Luxor, Upper Egypt, whether work discrimination or social harassment, like men shouting inflammatory words at her on the street. Because of her description of such incidents, the government's lawyer seized the opportunity to scrutinize them and evaluate them under normal asylum proceedings—to assume suspicion rather than truth.

> GABRIEL: We appreciate the court's offer to give us time to obtain the affidavits, and we will certainly take that opportunity, if that will satisfy the court and the government. Our theory of this was that this case should be predicated primarily, if not exclusively, on a future fear of persecution. Although the respondent used the term "persecution" to describe her experiences, it appeared later that what she had meant by that was more along the lines of discrimination.

During the proceedings, Monica had mentioned a lack of promotions at work and Muslim patients preferring a Muslim nurse over a Christian nurse.

> JUDGE: Even though the respondent used the word "persecution," based on questioning by the government and by the court, it was clear that was not persecution the way we understand it. But it was certainly discrimination, harassment. This is the type of case where I believe country conditions speak for themselves. Country conditions are also fairly fluid. There was also a shift in country conditions, categorized as a worsening of conditions between her two trips (2012–2015), which troubles the court as to why she didn't seek asylum in 2012, but there was the whole election, Morsi's deposal, the coming of Sisi, etc. There was a change in country conditions. Nonetheless, I do think it's important for her to corroborate her claims to the extent that it is possible.

The court adjourned for a master calendar hearing at a later date.[72] Outside the courtroom, Gabriel explained how the debate between himself, the government's lawyer, and the judge was centered on legal logics of truthfulness—of the correct deployment of the state's representation of Coptic existence and suffering rather than a "correct description" of the personal story of the applicant. Success revolves around the elimination of legalized suspicion and the accurate navigation of particular words and concepts. In the lobby of the courthouse following the trial,

Gabriel was frustrated with Monica's deviation from pattern or practice of persecution to past persecution corroboration.

> GABRIEL: These letters are total nonsense because there is nothing to corroborate. The judge wants to grant this case; he just needs to sound like he's doing his duty. He's basically giving you an opportunity to corroborate with these letters that explain they pulled your hair, to corroborate what you testified to. Once he gets his *pound of flesh*, he's going to grant this case. He knows about the problems in Egypt you're facing. He knows there has been an increase in violence against Christians. This case was not based on past persecution until you started talking about it. If you stuck to the script—it's just verbal, it's just verbal—there would be nothing to corroborate. The judge is going to look at these letters. Say thank you. Ninety-nine percent chance he [is] just going to say, "Okay, see, I made her squirm, I made her cry, I got my star." Then he's just going to grant it. He didn't want to hear from [the expert witness] and that's the key. He knows the country conditions.

Suspicion around Monica's testimony—her lack of understanding of the legal difference between discrimination and persecution—is not simply an ahistorical phenomenon. More broadly, in Europe and North America, "asylum" is becoming less legible as a legitimate category justifying the protection of the international community—a result of an increasing "logic of xenophobic suspicion."[73]

Anthropologist Liisa Malkki has argued that the technologies of controlling the movement of people into the (wealthy) Global North are driven by the continuous search for "impostors," "fakers," "inauthentic refugees," by deliberations of trickery.[74] This begs a geo/politically complicated and contested question: Who, then, might be classified as "the tricksters"? Those working on behalf of and even scholars advocating for asylum seekers have been understandably reluctant to raise this question, but it is useful to think about it critically for the sake of clarifying how certain cases and populations become legible over others and why these logics of communal comprehension and narrow compassion perpetuate. Gabriel described such technologies of power and games of truth through the metaphor of the "pound of flesh," as a legal rationality whereby the applicant must exhibit mastery of the game that rewards correct navigation.[75] Each Coptic asylum seeker must show their cross tattoo, produce the letter from a clerical official "proving" their religious affiliation (despite the fact that they might not even be consistent parishioners), and affirm their second-class, persecuted status in Egypt. In cases like Monica's that oscillated between country conditions and the "story," asylum seekers must perform worry on their faces, and in some cases tears, to prove their "worthiness"; they must show their sincerity to ward off suspicion of motives of material interest or worldly power. They must prove in every case their belonging to the persecuted body. A theology of the persecuted body draws from biblical interpretation: *That is why, for Christ's sake, I delight in weaknesses, in insults, in hardships, in persecutions, in difficulties. For when I am weak, then I am strong.*[76] Coptic asylum seekers are granted asylum for their weakness, and in their success, they are strong.

Transnational discourses on persecution have become central nodes of contemporary Coptic identity. Asylum cases since 2011 have sutured persecution to Coptic legal status in the United States. More recently, Gabriel noted that he has developed a new theory in addition to his employment of "pattern or practice of persecution":

> It's a theory that psychologists refer to as "vicarious trauma," which means you don't have to be a percipient witness to a violent crime or church burning in order to be traumatized. You can watch it through live streaming or the media. It's so real when you see it online. If you use the analogy—if you were to see a close relative being shot (even if it were not in real time, even if you were not actually present), just seeing it on a video clip or live stream, it would be just as traumatizing. This is what we are encouraging—I mean, the theory I am presenting. These people are coming here not because they are percipient witnesses or [have] been exposed to actual violence, but *they have seen it, they have seen lots of it*, readily accessible through the Internet. And then watching it, you can become completely traumatized. It's called PTSD. And that's how we are winning these cases. I haven't had to bring in doctors because they [my clients] are able to graphically describe what they see. In some cases, if it's a church burning or bombing, it's body parts. Literally, body parts! In Qudisiyyn, in Buṭrusiyya. Literally they had these things that were live streamed, and coupled with expert testimony, we win these cases.

Legal legibilities of persecution have bound Copts in diaspora—for purposes of immigration or political advocacy—to particular narratives of their dispossession, displacement, and suffering. This is not to say that such narratives are not felt and experienced, but of note are the ways they are mediated by imperial formations of power. The increase in the number of Copts who applied for asylum after 2011 has effected new separations between Christians and Muslims in contemporary Egypt and has aided in the policy-oriented knowledge production on Middle Eastern Christians that helps to mold the criteria of interpretation for conflict. These mechanisms of power have placed Copts back in Egypt in precarious circumstances.

During British colonial rule, some Copts and other Christian minorities (of elite socioeconomic status) were segregated, privileged, and elevated at the expense of their Muslim counterparts. By the influence of colonial and Western missionary projects, communities were categorized and separated on the basis of religion. The persistence of these colonial borders and divisions has led to permanent difficulties for Christians like the Copts in Egypt. Copts are stuck in the postcolonial allegiance to a nationalist vision of community, whereby diversion from such a vision (of bringing grievances to the majority) is translated as a neo-imperial threat. Thus, advocacy in the Coptic diaspora—free from the everyday constraints of interaction, conflict, and cooperation—places Coptic communities in Egypt in precarious circumstances. Egyptian Copts must pledge allegiance to the nation, and also answer queries about their loyalty, given the specters of imperial referees who mediate proper forms of community, deprioritize local forms of knowledge, and standardize value systems of their own making. Despite these constraints, there remain forms of friendship, relationality, and ambiguity between Christians and Muslims in Egypt that defy the neat logics of empire, be they articulated through the US asylum system, Washington, DC, experts and policy makers, or the everyday forms of racialization and politicization in diaspora.

"Here in Our Village, They Know Us"

Since 2015, Copts in Egypt began telling me that the US embassy in Cairo was denying their applications for tourist visas because they were

Christians. Even for temporary trips, Copts regardless of region or class were being denied. In 2017 I met with an embassy official affiliated with non-immigrant and immigrant visas, and asked about this accusation. "How can I frame this without getting in trouble?" they responded. "We take everything into account during our decision-making process, which includes the personal condition of the applicant, as well as the social and political conditions in the place they are applying from. I think that's all I can say on that." The official's response indicated that they were in fact taking the increased numbers of asylum cases in the United States into account in the decision-making process. "We are in communication with DHS. If they tell us, 'Hey, we've seen an increased number of asylum cases among this group of people,' we're going to respond." During the conversation, another official sitting with us chimed in, "If a young man comes to me, I see he doesn't have a job, but has a brother who lives in Revere, Massachusetts, I'm going to have to deny him because of the possibility that he would stay in the United States. There's too great of a risk."[77]

The politics of asylum in the United States have been mainly marked by class difference since 2011, and privilege one narrative of the Coptic experience in Egypt. While conflict and violence characterize some intercommunal experiences, everyday life is much more ambiguous. One of the main issues in Coptic asylum cases has been the shift to the legal determination of persecution as "countrywide." Shifting away from local dynamics in such logic cements a kind of deterritorialization from the space of human relations. The lines between the "realistic" and the fictional landscapes depicted are blurred; the further away audiences are from the direct experiences of local life, the more likely they are to construct "worlds" of persecution.[78] As a result of this shift away from local dynamics, the nuance and ambiguity of intercommunal relations are lost in a geopolitical sea of war, violence, and conflict that the United States has significant material and cultural investment in maintaining. The local dynamics in a place like Bahjūra, as discussed in the previous chapter, offer a different way to consider the legal rigidity of asylum determinations in the United States, which reinscribe passive victimhood onto Coptic identity.

* * *

On another hot summer morning, Mina, Kyrillos, and I made our way from Bahjūra into Najʿ Ḥammādī. The transition between Bahjūra and

Najʿ Ḥammādī is a gradual one. After you drive over the canal, you encounter sugarcane agricultural lands to your right and the small marketplace to your left. As you continue driving, the town starts to take shape with newer buildings and even government-commissioned artistry (at the entrance to Najʿ Ḥammādī, there is a tiled depiction of Upper Egyptian men playing musical instruments). We entered March 30th Street, the main street of Najʿ Ḥammādī, and parked the car in front of a gold shop, owned by one of Mina's family members. I sat down on one of the tattered black leather chairs lining the wall of the shop. After we drank the required Pepsi of hospitality, two women in *niqāb* from a neighboring village entered, carrying twin girls. The sisters wanted to sell some of their gold and get the twins' ears pierced. Mina told me after they left that they were from a nearby village where a feud between two families of villagers had intensified as of late. However, he emphasized that the violence was only between the villagers themselves: "If I came to the village looking for a particular person from one of the families, and I asked a member of the opposing family for directions, not knowing of the feud, any villager would lead me directly to the person I requested without harm."

Mina explained that there was a difference between the internal dynamics of a village—including both conflict and cooperation—and relationships between villagers and outsiders, even if they were Christians like himself. Local issues between Muslims and Christians do not lie in matters of theology, but rather are dependent upon the interactions, the comradery, and the strength of exchange (*tabādul*) between Muslims and Christians in any given locale. Mina clarified further, saying that, for example, in Bahjūra there are many Christian landowners who hire Muslim workers, and since they are giving them a salary, there are really no issues because there is *tabādul*. Yet the exchange here is also between an owner and a worker in an asymmetrical relationship of socioeconomic power. Mina also suggested exchange to mean a general relationship of accountability and presence, rather than a scaled imaginary of communal oppositions. Exchange is channeled through uneven encounters, but those encounters are part of a localized collective, which can be expressed in violent interaction as well as in shared laughter and frustration at prices, electricity issues, and transformations in the lived environment."[9]

After the gold shop, we traveled to the Bahjūra hamlet of ʿEzbet Kamal for a lunch of *hawawshi*, rice, and baked chicken with Mina's extended family.[80] Mina's mother, Vivian, spoke of the al-Minyā bus attack that had taken place earlier that week. "The terrorists came from [neighboring] Qinā, not Libya. They were helped by the neighboring Arab tribes because those tribes want the land of the monastery. When you ride the metro in Cairo, you take the women's car, don't you? But even [Muslim] women will harm you, even in the most ordinary of times. These terrorists are from this country itself. They live among us [*yaʿishu ḥuwalina*]." Her daughter, Rola, sitting next to her, nodded in agreement. But Vivian was also quick to dismiss the idea that all incidents and negative interactions that occur between Muslims and Christians are "sectarian" in nature.

When speaking about the kidnapping of youth in Bahjūra and Najʿ Ḥammādī, especially after the 2011 revolution, Vivian noted that these were not sectarian acts. "They kidnap anyone who may be rich. That is why they kidnapped the children of some rich Coptic families here, not because they're Coptic. If they were kidnapping all Copts, no matter what their class, then it would be a sectarian matter, but they are not." Vivian's older brother, Karas, interjected, "You know, it was [poor] Copts who directed those Muslim thieves to the rich Copts." Vivian replied, "The economy is the reason for all of this nonsense [*al-iqtiṣad howa al-sabab likul al-bilawi di*]."

I asked Vivian and Karas about relations with their Muslim neighbors in Bahjūra. "They know their limits with us," Vivian replied. "But if we left Bahjūra for another area, people would question who we were and where we came from. Here in our village, they know us." Shared life in the village produces bonds of friendship and familiarity that build forms of social responsibility to the other. Sectarian difference does manifest within Bahjūra —in spatial separations between Christian and Muslim neighborhoods and the boundaries of relationality and sexual separation (to avoid intercommunal, romantic entanglements).[81] Yet there are Christian-Muslim social bonds that exceed the rigidity of such instruments as American legal frameworks. While in some cases such bonds burst into conflict, in the most mundane ways they also offer comradery in economic and social hardship, and intimacy with Bahjūra's dirt roads, the local corner store, the gold

Figure 3.2. 'Ezbet Kamal at dusk, May 2017. Photo by author.

shop, and the sunset over the agricultural fields. Yet, in migration to the United States, intercommunal comradery is eschewed and intercommunal conflict from Egypt takes on distinct logics of interpretation, especially in a post-9/11 landscape that has heightened Muslim difference and Islamic threat. Such imperial enclosures frame the new minority binds among American Coptic communities.

PART II

Communities of Blood

4

Affective Bodies and Security Praxis

On September 11, 2010, prominent anti-Muslim activists Pamela Geller and Robert Spencer and their organization, Stop Islamization of America (SIOA), staged a protest against the Cordoba Initiative at 51 Park Place next to the site of the World Trade Center.[1] That day, along with speakers ranging from Jordan Sekulow to Andrew Breitbart and John Bolton to Geert Wilders, Joseph Nasrallah Abdel-Masih also took the stage. Nasrallah is a Copt and the founder of a California-based Christian satellite television station called The Way TV, as well as Media for Christ, a conservative Christian production company responsible for producing *Innocence of Muslims* (2012), an Islamophobic short film denigrating the Prophet Muhammad. In a letter addressed to Pamela Geller and Robert Spencer following an earlier rally, in June 2010, Nasrallah had described himself as a refugee from "the oppression of Islam" and said that he seeks to "expose to the American public what kind of instigation [of violence] we [Coptic Christians] suffered at the hands of hateful Muslim preachers." He approached the microphone wearing an American flag tie and started his speech with an impassioned wail: "God bless America!" The crowd roared. He continued,

> I come from Egypt. Egypt was Coptic; it was Christian until 1,400 years ago when Muslims conquered our country with their lies.... They [think they can just] lie just to build this mosque ... [over] my dead body! Do you know why? Because I escaped from Egypt for freedom here.

Nasrallah held a white cardboard poster depicting a blood-drenched man from the Najʿ Ḥammādī Christmas massacre of January 2010. Below the image, it read, "Stop killing the Christians of Egypt." He held the placard up toward the audience: "This is one of our dear friends in Egypt [killed] . . . in the name of Islam. They said, 'Allāhu akbar' and they killed them in front of the church. Three thousand persons burned here," as he pointed back toward the site of the World Trade Center.

> And in the same area they need to build a mosque! Can you imagine that? . . . I know the truth because I'm from Egypt. I know the truth because our country [was] conquered [by them]. The same way they need to conquer America. . . . That's why I'm saying to you now. I'm coming all the way from California, on behalf of all the Coptic Egyptians and Christians and even [on behalf of] human rights. I'm saying to you, Wake up, America! America, you don't need to be like this picture. Stop [the] Islamization of America![2]

After delivering his passionate speech to the crowd of ten thousand, he was later escorted off the premises by police. According to some media reports, Nasrallah and a friend were speaking Arabic to one another, which inflamed members of the rally.[3] Even if his testimony was cheered on stage in front of the crowd, off-stage, his audible difference (speaking Arabic) stoked fear among the crowd. The contradictions at the rally and Nasrallah's ambiguous position of solidarity for his American audience speak to a larger social transformation. Since 9/11, the racialization of Copts in the United States as Middle Eastern/Arab/Muslim, non-white others intensified through governing practices and everyday experiences in the context of war on terror securitization.[4] Coptic racialization is a dual process oscillating between Christian kinship with white America and a sensorium (including audition) of non-white suspicion. Yet, like other racially minoritized migrant communities, Copts have varyingly sought inclusion into the American body politic by claiming a Christian kinship forged in persecution. This inclusion is conditioned both by religious marginalization in Egypt and by the supremacy of Christianity in the United States.

* * *

Following September 11, 2001, Middle Eastern Christian communities in the United States encountered renewed racialized logics on terrorism and emerging apparatuses of securitization along with their Arab and Muslim neighbors. In Egypt, Copts have faced challenges as a Christian minority in a Muslim-majority context, encountering violent assaults, attacks on churches, and everyday discrimination. Chapter 2 delved into how diverse experiences of minor feelings and injury influence the motivations of migration to the United States.[5] However, once Copts are in the United States, their political narratives draw on these Egyptian events and formations of collective memory, and adapt them to new procedures of racial-religious evasion during the war on terror era. To put it differently, the cultural trauma and collective experiences of Coptic Christians as a minority in Egypt are reinterpreted in light of US terror discourse and emerging discussions on the perceived threat of radical Islam. These migrant experiences of securitization and the translations of Muslim threat have also reverberated back to Egypt in distinct ways. In the post-9/11 New York-New Jersey area, Coptic Christians grappled with the optics of suspicion by negotiating their racialized positionality and crafting their communal worth in line with national security interests.

Thinking with Barbara Fields and Karen Fields's notion of "racecraft," we can think of the racialization of Coptic Christians in American society as pieced together in the ordinary and extraordinary course of everyday doing, mediated through discursive forces of terrorist threat and suspicion of the Middle Eastern other, racial infrastructures of securitization (through profiling programs), and the cultural logics that have proliferated after the event. The dominance of racial difference—a difference that makes one recognized as a dangerous other—lies in the dense set of prior representations and practices on which they build in US empire. The Muslim, the "illegal," the Catholic, the immigrant, the Black person—the histories of these threats to American freedom and democratic stability interweave with one another.[6] Coptic Christians integrate into the shifting gaze of racecraft in the United States in the way their visibility—as martyrs—is veiled by their positionality as non-white migrants from the Middle East, a geography racialized as Muslim and therefore incommensurable with Western, American values.[7]

To mitigate this integration, Coptic Christians have also contributed to and participated in the racial infrastructures of securitization that proliferated following September 11 through the FBI, the New York Police Department, and other law enforcement branches in New Jersey (and throughout the United States). Describing these contributions as part of white supremacy is not an assertion of phenotypical indifference or avoidance of discrimination. Rather, by participating in literal or discursive structures of the security state, Copts displace the gaze of racial difference and participate in its dispersion onto others—and sometimes even marginalized members of their own community. Scholarship on whiteness and immigration has emphasized the unmitigated benefits that being identified as white or white-adjacent confers on the holder: power, social status, and financial rewards that are attained primarily by the exclusion of others. Yet the assertion of agency in "choosing whiteness"—participating in the structures of power that seek to oppress, differentiate, and ultimately control non-white others for the state—does little to highlight how a transnational minority community like the Copts negotiate themselves into US racial logics while at the same time transposing Egyptian contexts of religious difference onto American terrain.[8] Scenes in this chapter—from Copts as targets of post-9/11 security measures in the New York-New Jersey area to Copts as part of the security force and contributors to counterterrorism infrastructures, and back to Bahjūra for local translations of American racial difference—weave together a story of participation and constraint that connects the US context to minority memory and sectarian logics from the Egyptian context. Ultimately, the chapter attends to how the ruin of 9/11 has reconfigured transnational Coptic life, and thinks through how Copts themselves negotiated with their racialized difference through participation, critique, and refusal.

Suspicious Bodies

On the morning of September 11, 2001, Daoud was driving back from university on the New Jersey Turnpike. To his left, he saw the World Trade Center engulfed in flames; he swerved and nearly crashed his car. The rest of the day was mired in confusion, grief, and anger. Later that evening, as a way to process it all, he met up with Coptic friends at the local 7-Eleven in Bayonne, New Jersey. Standing in the parking lot around their cars, a group of men, whom Daoud describes as "Hispanic-looking," approached the group and began threatening them. "You f——ing terrorists," they shouted. "Look what you did. We're going to get you!" Frightened, Daoud and the others quickly got back into their cars and sped away, in fear of an oncoming assault. Daoud recalled the incident in a joking manner on a cold winter night in Staten Island some seventeen years later. "We had the wrong complexion. [After 9/11], you felt like you were a target and it wasn't your fault."

After 9/11, anti-Muslim assaults and intimidation rose significantly in the United States, with the number of hate crimes jumping from 28 incidents in 2000 to 481 by the end of 2001.[9] Heightened in post-9/11 America, the racialization of Muslims meant that certain bodies were made suspicious.[10] One of the early victims of this violence was the Egyptian-born Coptic Christian Adel Karas, who was shot dead inside his grocery store in San Gabriel, California on September 15, 2001.[11] American Copts, non-Muslim Arabs, non-Arab Middle Eastern communities (including Armenians, Assyrians, Chaldeans, and Kurds), Sikhs and other people of South Asian descent, and many other racialized bodies were also the targets of Islamophobia and anti-Muslim rhetoric, as well as the targets of securitization.[12]

* * *

Magdy Beshara was the Coptic owner of the St. George's Shell gas station in Bayville, New Jersey. He immigrated to the United States in the early 1980s and was known locally as "Max." Shortly after 9/11, the FBI came to the family's home in the middle of the night, questioning Magdy about whether Marwan al-Shehhi, one of the 9/11 hijackers, had worked at the gas station. Because of Magdy's stable business, he employed relatives who also stayed with the family. Neighbors grew suspicious that the family was part of a "terrorist cell" and told FBI agents that they had seen someone who looked like al-Shehhi working at the gas station. A man at a nearby pizzeria said he had served al-Shehhi two slices a day, and the owner of a local deli said they had sold him and other members of the "cell" phone cards. "I'm positive it's him," a local hairstylist recounted, saying she had bought cigarettes from al-Shehhi at the gas station.[13]

Cultural means of discrimination, in the form of identification and recognition—*feelings* of difference—are channeled through institutional forms of discrimination by way of the security state. These two layers—everyday life and state regulation—intersect with one another to shape a complex social system of racialized targeting. Yet the process of racialization is never a complete one. It must always reproduce itself through suspicion and sensing similarity.[14] As Magdy Beshara himself commented to a reporter, "Middle Eastern people, we all look alike, you know what I mean." The FBI later acknowledged that it had pursued the wrong man, admitting that "it might be a look alike." Magdy even made copies of a letter from the Justice Department indicating his innocence and handed them out to customers to clear his name. But the damage had already been done.[15]

Michael, Magdy's stepson, described the aftermath of the initial FBI raid: "People would drive by and say, 'We're going to kill you terrorists' and throw a big liquor bottle at me and my sister."[16] During their investigation, the government confiscated anything it desired from the gas station and the family's home. Their mail was opened and phones tapped, and Michael was followed to school by federal agents. The family faced death threats. Despite pleas to the police to intervene, the police refused. Michael described how the incident forced him to differentiate. "It made me feel weird to say aloud, but I always thought to myself, 'I'm not a Muslim, I'm a Christian.' I felt like I was putting them down to say, 'Hey, look, I'm the good guy.' I felt like we had to do anything to defend ourselves."[17] At school, Michael was bullied and physically assaulted on dozens of occasions. At one point in the months following the raid, an unknown assailant set the family's house on fire while Michael and his little sister were sleeping. All of this took place even after the FBI notified Magdy Beshara that he was no longer a subject of investigation. Many American Copts (and other Middle Eastern Christians in the United States and elsewhere) have tried to combat such suspicion by emphasizing their Christian faith as a way to assert racial-religious misrecognition.[18]

The attempt to correct misrecognition relies on multiple premises: that the viewer is assumed to be white (despite the proliferation of these attacks by people of color) and is open to and willing to discern the visual differences between Middle Eastern communities—*that differences within difference matter* and that violent backlash toward Copts is a displacement of hostility from the rightful object, the "real" Muslims.[19] The displacement of suspicion onto the "actual" Muslim body, then, does not just reinforce the gaze—that there is a real danger, just not on/in *my* body. Rather, it also makes it correct—that the Muslim body *is* a threat and worthy of securitization. This has far-reaching implications for all bodies of difference caught in the grip of state violence and social persecution. In her examination of the Rodney King case, Judith Butler notes that "the visual field is not neutral to the question of race; it is itself a racial formation, an episteme, hegemonic, and forceful."[20] The racial production of the visible and the audible is saturated by the "inverted projections of white paranoia"; evidence and correction ("I'm not a Muslim, I'm a Christian") "will always and only refute the conclusions based on it."[21] Jasbir Puar argues that fear and anxiety over the impossibility of the containment of feared bodies ultimately end up binding such bodies together, "creating pools of their suspicious bodies."[22] Coptic attempts to disentangle from the affective economies of fear have only reinscribed their bodies as other; their salvation only in their ability to be recognized in glimpses of their persecuted Christianity (i.e., their humanity in martyrical suffering and death).

Immediately after 9/11, a local priest in the New York–New Jersey area was said to have been placed under house arrest because of his supposed resemblance to Osama bin Laden.[23] Copts changed their attire to sartorially distance themselves from Arabs/Muslims, and some even changed their names to elude the potential of acoustic threat. Coptic clergy in New Jersey recounted that Pope Shenouda III allowed priests to wear a wooden cross similar to Catholic clergy and to trim their beards in the hopes that they would not be the targets of backlash or hate crimes. And in Los Angeles since 9/11, Coptic Orthodox metropolitan Serapion allowed clergy to forgo their traditional head covering (*'amma*)—an informal requirement throughout the Coptic Church—because, according to one priest, "they look like Islamic turbans."[24] In various incidents, Copts have reformed their religious practices (such as priestly garb) to reconcile with post-9/11 racial infrastructures that code such aesthetics as threatening. Yet, in tandem with these security reformations, Copts have also become part of the apparatus itself—to participate in surveillance and displace the gaze away from Coptic communities.

Security Bodies

Abram moved from Egypt to New Jersey in 1976 when he was eleven years old. Sitting in the back of his cop car while on break in May 2017, I asked Abram about his entry into law enforcement. "When I entered into the force, the idea of an 'Egyptian police officer' here was not something accepted in the Coptic community." After serving as a corrections officer for three years, he took the academy test. "I put my letter on the altar of Saint George, who was also a soldier, and said 'I want to be just like you.'" Abram entered law enforcement shortly after 9/11 and quickly realized he had to explain his identity to his colleagues. "When I became a cop, the first thing people would say, 'Oh, you're from Egypt! As-salamu 'alaykum.' I had to explain that not everyone in Egypt or in an Arab country is Muslim. And this was the perspective of all my colleagues—Black, Hispanic, Asian, too."

Part of Abram's job was educating his colleagues about the Copts and differentiating them from Muslims. Yet this was something he had long experienced. Following the First Gulf War, he was bullied in high school:

> They said to us, "Oh, you guys are Saddam Hussein." My main concern was correcting them: "Guys, I'm not from Iraq, I'm Egyptian." After 9/11, you got blamed for it because the whole world said you're Muslim. The whole world said you did it. They don't care, [they didn't say] "Oh, they're Christians. They don't even believe in jihad. They don't believe in this or that." You still got blamed for it except you didn't get the protection. While there was a lot of biased incidents and a lot of hate crimes against Coptic people, there was zero protection. The world looked at Coptics like, "Oh, you blew up our World Trade Center. You horrible Muslims. You terrorists or whatever." You try to explain. The same thing that I told you in high school about the kid who bullied me saying, "Oh, you're Saddam" or whatever. It was the same thing again, except on a much bigger scale. A lot of people assume it was just Caucasians. No, it was from everybody—Blacks, Hispanics. [They thought] we were all terrorists. We were all horrible.

From the latter half of the twentieth century and into the twenty-first, the Coptic population of New York and New Jersey has grown exponentially, and along with it, Coptic members of law enforcement.[25] "People know who we are by virtue of our numbers. I brag to my colleagues, we're the lowest percentage of criminals in New Jersey," Abram noted. Part of the drive for Coptic participation in law enforcement has been the desire to have "insiders" in these departments, as native informants of the community. "If you work in any police department and interact with, for instance, Copts in your everyday work, [if there is something going on that involves Copts], it's not just 'those guys' or whatever anymore.... You have to ask your colleague what's going on over there, and they can explain it to you." With more Copts on the force, the politics of displacement and misrecognition are institutionalized within and translated by the racial logics of securitization. Coptic cops are made to differentiate: these people are my people/those people are not my people. They are made to show how American Copts are upstanding, successful members of society. "I brag about our community—we have the most doctors, lawyers, and the least inmates, criminals." These movements are meant to displace suspicion and surveillance onto others: *We are not the ones you're looking for*. While racialization is an externally imposed process (which sets the criteria of white acceptance and American success), it is also clearly a reflexive one in which minority communities like American Copts shape their occupational choices, political praxis, and affective connection to security infrastructures themselves.[26]

In this way, many Copts (clergy or otherwise) have understood their targeting not simply as misrecognition, but also as necessary for the strengthening of global American power. Following liturgy one afternoon in the late spring of 2017, just down the block from where I met Abram, I made my way to the clergy office to greet a bishop from South America visiting the parish. We sat around a table in the center of a cluttered room adjoining the main priest's office. As we joked with one another over a post-liturgy meal (also known as *aghāby*), the bishop explained to us in Arabic what he had to endure to enter the United States. The day prior, he had arrived at customs in John F. Kennedy International Airport, and for hours, security officers interrogated the bishop, asking about his beard, his black robe, and his purpose in the United States. He explained to them that he was a bishop of the Coptic Orthodox Church, which puzzled the immigration officers; they had never heard of the Church, let alone that there were Christians in/from Egypt. After nearly three hours of detention, he was released. As he recounted the incident to us, his fellow clergy were sympathetic, having experienced similar instances of confusion and misrecognition, from walking down the street to enduring airport security. Pausing for a few moments following the retelling of the incident, the bishop began lauding then president Donald Trump for his policies on immigration and security measures against immigrants from the Middle East. "He's keeping extremists out of America, and if my interrogation is necessary to do that, so be it!"

The bishop does not read himself as the enemy of the United States; the Arab/the Muslim is the enemy, and the bishop is neither.[27] This political paradox of (mis)recognition—in its longue durée of religious-racial unfoldings in the figurations of European civilization and Western Christendom—molds certain affective stances toward security, law, and order among contemporary Copts in migration. But correction exceeds visual displacement into the realm of affect. Affect takes us from "a frame of misrecognition, contingent upon the visual to discern the mistake . . . to the notion of resemblance, a broader . . . frame where the reason for the alikeness may be vague"—where a body vaguely resembles "one of them."[28] Resemblance is mired in an affective space that pushes toward the conviction of radical difference—that this body before me is illegible. But the bishop from South America was not concerned with either misrecognition or resemblance in the matrix of the security gaze. Instead, the bishop's sacrifice in the moment of interrogation is funneled toward a larger, more subliminal configuration of Christian power.

Trump famously said to an audience on the 2016 campaign trail that "Christianity will have power."[29] For Copts who have experienced sectarian violence and discrimination back in Egypt or inhabit a collective memory of persecution in the many diasporas, this is a welcome message. And in the aftermath of 9/11, many American Copts sought to engage that power through deployment of their Christianity as a means to safeguard them from suspicion and threat. In the case of the bishop and other Copts in the United States, they also sacrificed their safety for the American security apparatus. They were sure that America was fighting for freedom (particularly from Islamic hegemony and Islamist violence). Since 2001, this has also meant a realignment of their political affiliations and strengthening of their numbers within the security networks of the United States

While Copts' religious difference in Egypt remaps onto racial difference in the United States, Copts' Christianity is also the source of migratory suspicion back in Egypt. The tangle of potential connections in the flows and circulations of Copts between Egypt and the United States reveals how suspicious bodies shift in focus according to the imperatives of the globalized US security state. One priest interlocutor from an Upper Egyptian village, for example, applied to the Green Card Lottery as well as for a tourist visa on several occasions. Year after year he tried to obtain a visa in the hopes of seeking a better life for him and his wife. In January 2017, he called me while I was waiting for sandwiches in a friend's car in Najʿ Ḥammādī on our way back to Bahjūra. Donald Trump had just been inaugurated, and Copt after Copt I met in Upper Egypt would express a message of hope for a more favorable policy of support for Middle Eastern Christians than under Obama. The priest told me as much: "Trump . . . I see him as a good person. Better than Obama. Obama didn't like Christians. I was at the American embassy in Cairo for an interview and they rejected me right away."

The rejection of Copts at the US embassy in Cairo may seem disconnected from the interrogation of the Coptic bishop at John F. Kennedy International Airport or even the choice of Abram to join New Jersey law enforcement, but they share a similar node within the racial infrastructure of US empire. The Coptic body has been transvalued as a martyrical allegory of persecution politics, but within the United States and extending to the US embassy in Cairo, it also varyingly becomes a threat, as a migrant body, seeking refuge and potentially inflicting demographic harm.[30] The threat of resemblance, then, once Copts are in the United States, disciplines them into compliance with an American racial regime, and more sharply, with the itineraries of the national security state. This oscillation of the economy of blood (between martyr and migrant) has shaped the racial-religious belonging of Coptic Christian politics in the United States as well as the processes of communal formation and the foreclosure of solidarities with other marginalized minority communities. Coptic support for Trump (between 2016 and 2020) and American conservative politics more broadly has been grounded in minority experiences in Egypt (as well as the theopolitical positioning of the Coptic Orthodox Church and Coptic Orthodox Christianity within Egyptian society). Yet such support is also constructed within an American racial landscape of white supremacy. American Christianity and white supremacy are enmeshed with one another.[31] In this view, whiteness is a perspective of sociopolitical power, where belonging is produced through narratives of persecution, powerlessness, and enduring threat. The Christianity of the Copts grants them entry into white power, insofar as Coptic blood is translated as martyrdom and not as racial difference in need of securitization—from within or without.

Remapping Injury

The minority Christianity of the Copts allows for a kind of religious inclusion in the United States as it shapes the contours of their activism, advocacy, and everyday interactions. Their racial difference and the discrimination they experience in white America are imagined by progressive and leftist academics and organizers as a motivation for solidarity with other marginalized groups, but this presumption displaces the main communal thread of transnational Coptic life—Christianity. While Coptic Christianity, like other Eastern/Orthodox Christian traditions, has historically been theologically and socially marginalized within a broader ecumenical Christian project, it is the Christianity of the Copts that is relevant not only to Western religio-political interests, but also to Copts who are discriminated against on the basis of that religious difference in Egypt. These transnational nodes of legibility impact upon how transnational Copts translate Islam and how translations of injury from Egypt produce new forms of harm in the United States.

* * *

In March 2017, I drove back to Jersey City from a church meeting with Marie, Carol, and Justina, three Coptic women in their twenties. Carol asked me about my research, particularly in sheesha lounges frequented by Copts and among Coptic street vendors. Speaking about the recent influx of immigrants, I mentioned that many of them work for Muslim street vendors in Manhattan. Justina became agitated: "That just doesn't make sense to me. I thought all the vendors were MB [Muslim Brotherhood]." Carol replied, "Okay, so that means the MB wouldn't hire them? How does that make any sense?" Justina asked, "Why would they hire Christians? Why would they want them to succeed? Giving these Copts jobs means you're helping their future. Why would they want that?" Carol refuted this argumentation as Justina continued, "Have you heard of the one-hundred-year plan? That's the MB's plan to become the demographic majority. They're already on course to be the world's largest religion because they have more babies." While the fear of the

Muslim Brotherhood and its takeover of America has roots in Egypt, Justina's specific rhetoric on secretive plans and demographics and her conflation of Islamists with all Muslims are widely shared among the far right in the United States.[32]

Justina is a second-generation Copt, born and raised in New Jersey, yet her parents are still very much connected to Egyptian political contexts, whether through TV, social media, or communications on Viber, WhatsApp, and other media. In Egypt, the Muslim Brotherhood's rise to political power after 2011 was of major concern to religious minorities like the Copts. Historically, some of the political discourses of the organization and other Islamist organizations have varyingly led to increased violence against Copts. Those very real contexts in Egypt follow Coptic migrants to the United States and intermix with far-right rhetoric on the Muslim Brotherhood and other Islamist organizations—infused with images of a post–Cold War battle for the future of Western civilization and the threat of radical Islam. Such broader geopolitical contexts of US empire and the global reach of American conservatism intersect with national and local Egyptian contexts in the thinking of an American Copt like Justina. Hearing about Egyptian contexts from her parents, following Egyptian news, and thinking about the Muslim Brotherhood through an Egyptian lens contribute to her understanding of them—and everyday Muslims—within US society. The transnational layering of these moves shows how diasporic Copts draw on sectarian memory from the homeland to shape their political orientations and religious solidarities in migration.

Memory (Re)Construction

On a cold winter evening in Staten Island, I sat across from Abouna Girgis in the kitchen of the administrative center of the local Coptic diocese. In his late thirties and recently elevated to the priesthood, Abouna grew up in Bayonne, New Jersey, and has strong ties to his clergy-filled family back in Luxor, Upper Egypt, visiting them regularly. We talked about protests that had stalled zoning board approval of Bayonne's first mosque. (The same board had approved the expansion of a Coptic church in 2011.) After local Muslim community members purchased the property in 2015, their proposal was denied in early 2017, citing traffic and parking issues. The property was picketed and even vandalized with crude phrases such as "Fuck Muslims" and "Fuck Arabs," in the name of Donald Trump, then Republican nominee for president.

Bayonne is a working-class neighborhood where historically many Italian, Polish, and Irish immigrant communities took up residence. More recently, Bayonne has become home to many Middle Eastern communities, including and especially Egyptians, both Muslim and Coptic Christian. When Abouna was growing up, though, his family was one of a few Middle Eastern families. "You could tell, even at that age, that people weren't used to your complexion. They weren't comfortable with having people of your complexion around," he said. Now, the community has two Coptic Orthodox churches and is expanding with a new influx of Coptic immigrants from Egypt. Though the community also faces its own share of discrimination, Copts joined in the protests against the Bayonne mosque. Protestors held signs that said, "Stop the mosque!," "If the mosque comes, the mayor goes!," and "No mosque, remember 9/11!" I asked Abouna Girgis what he thought about the protests in his hometown. "Look" he answered, "if you're Coptic, you're going to protest Islam. When you've seen and gone through the harassment, the persecution in Egypt and everything, can you blame them?"

Coptic protest against mosques in the United States partly reflects communal trauma manifesting itself in diaspora, but reaches through the experiences of marginalization in Egypt and punches new holes of religious-racial exclusion for Muslim minorities into the landscape of the United States. While the paradoxical character of these protests—as also impacting upon non-Muslim Brown bodies such as the Copts themselves—reflects scenes that have preceded this one, such protests and their infusion of a collective memory of Coptic persecution in Egypt require attention to the ways diasporic lenticularity—of seeing through multidimensional framings—factors into community separation.[33] It is at this juncture that concerns over Coptic infrastructure and the maintenance of Coptic presence are as important in Bayonne, New Jersey, as they are in Bahjūra, Upper Egypt.

Until today, depending on local political conditions, Copts continue to deal with issues of church construction and repair in Egypt.[34] Despite recent government efforts to streamline the process, Christians varyingly face official and social restrictions on building their houses of worship: officials are slow to issue permits, security agencies fail to protect churches from attack, and violence from Muslim neighbors has succeeded in preventing church construction in communities throughout Egypt.[35] Beyond this, church burnings and government negligence in Egypt shape how transnational Copts see threat and destruction and affect their everyday interactions with Egyptian Muslims in New Jersey and beyond.[36]

* * *

In early 2017, I sat in a packed room of parents and other parishioners in Jersey City. Abouna Lazarus was explaining a multimillion-dollar new church project. The current church building, unchanged since the 1970s, was far too small for the influx of immigrants from Egypt and the growth of the second generation. With a map of the area on the television screen next to an icon of Christ, Abouna outlined how much of the land had already been purchased. However, there was a stumbling block: a key piece of land was yet to be acquired for the property because it was owned by a "non-Christian, but Egyptian man [*howa ghiyr masiḥy bas maṣry*]. I won't say more than this [*mish ha'ūl aktar min kida*]." He smiled at the congregation, almost with a wink, sharing an unspoken recognition of who this was (an Egyptian Muslim) and why the refusal occurred.

After the meeting, parishioners clamored to see the priest and ask for favors, blessings, and a quick exchange of greetings. I finally reached the front of the line and asked to speak with him on the side. "What did you mean by what you said earlier—that the piece of land was owned by a 'non-Christian, but Egyptian man'?" I asked. "He simply will not sell this to us. What would that look like? A Muslim Egyptian selling a piece of land in the United States for the purpose of building a church? How would this news be received in Egypt by Muslims there?" While the exchange remains local—on the subject of a church construction project in New Jersey—it has far-reaching consequences for Copts, most especially between Egypt and the United States. Sectarian politics from Egypt are mapped onto new American terrain, soaked with possibility for Coptic expansion, a kind of manifest destiny unavailable in Egypt. The expansion of the church measures the expansion of the community in diaspora, yet dwindling in Egypt. Diaspora plays kinship in and across migration, where Coptic *Christian* difference offers opportunity for transfiguration—to be made anew, through institutional expansion amid remnants of sectarian threat.

In rural Pennsylvania, a general bishop of the Coptic Orthodox Church has also entered into the American real estate market. On various trips to the United States, the bishop has purchased properties, sometimes sold through eBay. "He's a COO. He knows a good deal and he knows how to get things done," Samir, a servant close to the bishop, said of him. During the era of former Coptic pope Shenouda III, the bishop was entrusted with the purchasing of different properties throughout the United States and Canada on behalf of the Coptic Orthodox Church. One such purchase was that of a convent in the Midwest. Two older Eastern Orthodox nuns were the remaining servants left on the property, and they knew that they needed to sell, initially setting the price at a little over one million dollars. One day, the bishop asked Samir to drive with him for nearly eight hours to see the property and place an offer. Prior to the drive, Samir had no idea where they were going, but followed the directions provided by the bishop. After they arrived and toured the property, the bishop turned to him and said, "I'm tired from the journey. Tell them I'll give them $750,000." The nuns refused the price, and the bishop grew frustrated. The bishop rebutted in Arabic, "Do you want Muslims to buy it, or do you want us to buy it?" Samir translated for them, explaining the importance of selling to Christians instead of Muslims. The nuns acquiesced.

This retold exchange between the Coptic bishop and the Eastern Orthodox nuns is not only connected to the threat of sectarian scarcity in Egypt playing itself out in another place. Infused in the motto "We buy. We don't sell" (noted by one North American bishop) is the vision of Coptic opportunity in diaspora—one shaped by the idea of the United States as a Christian land, filled with possibilities for expansion and exclusion. Toward the end of our conversation on the Egyptian bishop, Samir commented on the Bayonne mosque controversy. He suggested that the zoning argument—to prevent Muslim expansion—was particularly effective, and that this was a good thing. "They should always just say it's a zoning issue. We need to do anything to prevent a mosque from being built, even if the city has to pay out." In contemporary Egyptian history, Copts have struggled to legalize and construct churches and Christian youth centers in a majority-Muslim society. In diaspora, the pain of that struggle at times manifests in vengeance, retribution, and distance, but it is also shaped by the pervasive Islamophobia of US empire.[37] The experiences of marginalization and anti-Christian violence in Egypt map onto this new imperial terrain and transform Coptic communal life and relationality, and have also framed participation in the post-9/11 counterterrorism apparatuses of the New York-New Jersey area.

Islam and Coptic Securitization

After liturgy one Sunday in New Jersey, I sat in the cafeteria owned and operated by the church. Over the window facing the main street, there is a photo of Pope Shenouda III laughing; an Egyptian flag hangs next to his photo, almost as if he was the Coptic president of the area. Older, first-generation Copts gather there habitually to catch up on politics and news from Egypt while drinking sugary Lipton tea out of flimsy Styrofoam cups and eating food made by community elders. This particular Sunday afternoon, Moheb, a man in his mid-fifties who immigrated in the late 1980s, introduced me to the table. I had made it a weekly postliturgy ritual of having a tea at the café, but that day, there was someone at the table I had never seen before. The mystery man had jet-black hair, and oddly wore dark sunglasses inside the cafeteria. Moheb explained to members of the group whom I had seen, but never formally interacted with that I was researching Coptic migration, and they nodded in acknowledgment. After some time, the man with the sunglasses asked to speak with me privately outside. As we stood in the doorway of the café, other congregants walked by us, heading for the Egyptian supermarket down the street or making their way with children in tow to the Sunday school lessons. "Your Arabic is excellent, and it seems like you know our community well. Have you considered working for the FBI?" He reached for his pocket and pulled out a business card. It only said, "Special Agent Mark," with the FBI crest. I politely declined and quickly excused myself from the cafeteria. After that day, I never saw "Mark" at the church or café again.

* * *

Since 9/11, American Copts have increasingly joined law enforcement as a way to aid US efforts in the war on terror, and to enlighten such institutions about Coptic difference from Egyptian Muslims. On a crisp November evening in 2017, I met up with Hany, a Copt from Long Island and law enforcement officer working between the FBI and the New York Police Department, for dinner at the base of One World Trade Center.[38] Hany immigrated from Cairo to the United States in 1992 to reunite with a sister already living in the New York–New Jersey area. On October 31, 1999, EgyptAir Flight 990—on its way from John F. Kennedy International Airport to Cairo, with 217 people aboard—crashed into the Atlantic Ocean shortly after takeoff. After retrieving the black boxes, investigators tried to piece together what happened. Shortly before the flight crashed, the "cruise" co-pilot calmly repeated, "tawakkaltu 'ala Allāh" (I put my trust in God). News media ran with stories hinting at the possibility of this being a suicide attack, and debate swirled around the proper translation of the Arabic words he uttered prior to the crash.[39] Hany was particularly frustrated by the incident. "I actually knew the pilot, and I know he wouldn't do that." From that moment, he wanted to join law enforcement, to bring cultural sensitivity to the force—to correct and to target "actual" terrorists.

"You can tailor any part of the [Islamic] tradition to the way you want. If you want to be a peaceful person, I can point you to the passages that explain that." After 9/11, Hany joined the Joint Terrorism Task Force (JTTF), applying his Arabic skills and connections within the community to investigate terrorism in the New York City metropolitan area and around the world. Besides correcting cultural misunderstandings on the force, he was particularly concerned with the breakdown in official communication between the United States and Egypt during the investigation. As an Egyptian immigrant, Hany became a central node linking the NYPD and the Egyptian consulate in New York. Yet Hany's entry into law enforcement post-9/11 was also framed by his transnational experiences as a Copt.

In Egypt during the 1980s, Hany had a Muslim friend, Ahmed, who used to attend church celebrations with him. At one point, however, Hany went to temporarily work in the Sinai Peninsula. Ahmed was left alone in the neighborhood. A fellow neighbor had begun organizing with the Muslim Brotherhood and brought Ahmed under his wing. Ahmed's mother contacted Hany, troubled by the changes in her son's behavior. "Please save my son!" she begged Hany. "He's wearing a *gala-*

baya now and telling his sister and me that we're *kufār* [infidels] because we don't wear *ḥijāb*. He's always at the mosque. Do something!" Hany rushed back home to visit with his friend. In the past, both would share a cigarette together as a way of relaxing and bonding. During the visit, Hany offered him a cigarette. Ahmed refused, explaining that he had quit and, more importantly, it wasn't permitted in Islam. "Ahmed was a normal kid. After that, I really began to ask myself how those people were able to brainwash kids like him."

Hany's career path was shaped by a desire to protect the United States from the radicalization he had heard about and experienced in Egypt. He explained that he had met Farag Foda, a prominent Egyptian writer and human rights activist who was later assassinated by al-Gama'a al-Islamiyya after being accused of blasphemy, during his final trip to the United States before his death; after hearing Foda speak, Hany began reading more critically on Islam.[40] He was devastated by Foda's assassination: "You and I know that the first chance they get, they would come to this country and destroy it, just like *they* did Egypt." "They" does not refer to actual people, but rather the pervasiveness of a particular form of conservative Islam. In this way, Coptic securitization in the diaspora—the participation of people like Hany in the security apparatus—also works in tandem with Coptic racialization and subjugation by that very security apparatus.[41] Part of the appeal in participation is the impetus to correct cultural errors—to become experts and officials in differentiation. For example, the NYPD's Demographics Unit (renamed the Zone Assessment Unit and now disbanded) mapped neighborhoods predominantly occupied by twenty-eight so-called "ancestries of interest"—that is, national origin associated with Muslim populations as well as "American Black Muslims." The NYPD expressly excluded from its surveillance and mapping activities non-Muslims such as Coptic Christians (as well as Iranian Jews).[42] Yet, even surveillance was home inside the force. As Muslims joined security agencies as part of a growing infrastructure, they also became targets of internal investigation.

In September 2017, the *New Yorker* published a story about Bobby Farid Hadid, an Algerian immigrant who decided to join the security apparatus after 9/11. In 2007 he became a member of the Joint Terrorism Task Force (JTTF), and eventually aided in the NYPD Muslim Surveillance Program, but grew uncomfortable with its tactics. The NYPD opened an internal investigation into Hadid, as it had done with other Muslim police officers. Hadid was transferred out of the Intelligence Division in May 2009 after failing to file reports in the division's database system. He eventually was pushed out of the NYPD and cited religious discrimination.[43]

In the years after 9/11, Muslim officers were promoted to prestigious units because of their Arabic-language skills and cultural knowledge. In 2005 the NYPD publicly said that it was "reaching out to immigrants" who want to take "Islam back from terrorist groups."[44] But their new visibility also brought them under surveillance. In a 2008 lawsuit, an Egyptian Muslim officer in the Intelligence Division's Cyber Unit complained that his colleagues told him that Muslims had no place in law enforcement, that they should be operating food carts instead. In a different lawsuit in 2016, another officer described to the *New Yorker* how he often received "this disgusted look" from his supervisors and colleagues because he had a beard. "They seem to be asking, 'Why can't you assimilate? Assimilate or quit,'" he said.[45]

The day the Bobby Hadid *New Yorker* article was published, Sam—a Coptic cop with the NYPD—picked me up for my flight to Cairo. During the car ride from Staten Island, I asked Sam about Bobby and the allegations in the article. "They always play this card, but it's not true. My experience in the department proves otherwise." Disgusted by the article's narrative of bias in the NYPD, Sam called a superior to ask him about Bobby (whom he did not know personally). They bantered back and forth and focused on the accusation of Bobby's intimate relations with a witness while in Paris as part of the JTTF. Over speakerphone as we drove, Sam asked pointed questions to his colleague, wanting to dispel (for me) any idea that the force discriminated against Muslim officers.

After he hung up the phone we were waiting on the Belt Parkway to John F. Kennedy International Airport as traffic was at a standstill, and Sam lamented his own experiences of discrimination in the NYPD as a Christian from the Middle East. Some of his Muslim colleagues have joked with him about converting, and others have shunned him after finding out that he is not Muslim. He recounted how a Turkish colleague showed him a picture of his wife's sister. "Isn't she pretty?" the colleague asked him. "Wouldn't you want to convert to Islam for her?" Sam was offended: "Even if we speak the same language and share the same culture, we are not the same religion, and that matters!"

Religious difference matters to a Coptic cop like Sam, whether in his everyday interactions with colleagues or in the systems of surveillance blanketed across migrant communities in the New York–New Jersey area after 2001. The *Christian* part of Coptic Christian opens to forms of acceptance and solidarity with the powerful. And even in the background of Sam's comments, it is also connected to persecuted pasts in Egypt, where Coptic difference mattered with regard to governing communal administration and distinction for centuries. Leaving those conditions of securitization, which did not allow for participation, has opened onto new opportunities in the United States, where Christianity produces new forms of relationality with power.

Persecution and Policing

Sam had mentioned to me on a few occasions his desire for a Coptic union in the NYPD to distinguish him from his fellow officers of Arab and Turkish Muslim backgrounds (they have their own union in the NYPD—the Middle East and Turkic Society). In early 2020 St. Mark's Coptic Law Enforcement Officer Society was founded, and more recently (especially after the COVID-19 pandemic), the group has held and appeared at several events in New York City. In August 2021, the society held a banquet in support of the Police Benevolent Association of the City of New York at Saint George's Coptic Orthodox Church in Brooklyn. On social media, the society emphasized its support for police forces across the United States, as well as its Egyptian patriotism. In many ways, the society is not only a response to American social unrest regarding police brutality and violence against Black people. It also connects its support for law and order back to an Egyptian national context.

At the banquet, speeches and commentary were in a mixture of Arabic and English. One man commented, "The police are the most important thing for the economy. They are the people who support businessmen and protect women and children in the streets." During another speech, a board member of the (now defunct) Egyptian Christians for Trump organization connected support for American police to revolutionary trauma in Egypt: "Today, we're dealing with a very critical period like what happened with the police during the days of the revolution. People didn't respect the law, and these days it's the same story in New York. We support the police . . . and we say Blue Lives Matter, too."[46]

The audience was an eclectic mixture of law enforcement, Egyptian community members—both Christians and Muslims—and Coptic clergy. Bishop David of the New York and New England Diocese of the Coptic Orthodox Church connected the American context back to Egypt as well. Speaking to the audience, he noted, "Remember during the first revolution in Egypt in 2011 when people lost trust in the police? That was the worst time in Egypt because there was no security, safety in the streets. All the looting. People had to protect their whole families." Then the bishop recited from chapter 13, verses 1–3 of Saint Paul's Epistle to the Romans:

> Let every soul be subject to the governing authorities. For there is no authority except from God, and the authorities that exist are appointed by God. Therefore, whoever resists the authority resists the ordinance of God, and those who resist will bring judgment on themselves. For rules are not a terror to good works, but to evil. Do you want to be unafraid of the authority? Do what is good, and you will have praise from the same.[47]

Melani McAlister has discussed the importance of Romans 13 in bolstering both evangelical support for and evangelical opposition to apartheid South Africa, arguing that those verses "exert power on believers who take them seriously, even as their meaning is shifting and negotiated."[48] International evangelicals understood themselves quite differently vis-à-vis the state depending on their minoritized status or entrance into positions of cultural and political power over the course of the 1970s and 1980s. And these different positions cultivated their own scriptural reading practices. Similarly, the reading of Romans 13 varies between Egypt and the United States among transnational Coptic Orthodox Christians. Its reading in Egypt might be understood as a means of protecting the authority of the Coptic Orthodox Church and staving off state violence against the Coptic minority. In the United States, Coptic readings of Romans 13 might be caught between migrant status (the adherence to the rule of law as part of a model minority framework) and ascendance to Christian majoritarianism. Thus, in its recitation, an enactment of Christian supremacy comes forth—shining through both Coptic social obedience and political engagement.

Behind the bishop flew the Egyptian and American flags. Dressed all in black, wearing a shiny clerical headdress, or *'amma*, he connected his service to those of the officers. "We are not only God's ministers, but you as police officers in uniform are also God's ministers. . . . You are our angels who protect us." With over two hundred Coptic officers in the New York City and New Jersey police departments, Bishop David has a broad constituency that includes members of law enforcement as well as supporters of the force, and given their experiences in Egypt, many such Copts in America desire cooperation with the police. "Remember the 'See something, say something.' These little things we remember. We need to talk more about how we can cooperate together," he concluded.

The willingness of US law enforcement to welcome Copts shifts Coptic perception of belonging in American society. Coptic Christians in Egypt feel alienated from the security state, a sector from which they are almost wholly excluded. The exclusion of Christians from the security sector is a critical example of a much broader phenomenon of Coptic underrepresentation within the Egyptian state and bureaucracy. In this way, the state has fueled social segregation through such religious differentiation in everyday life, which is stratified through the security apparatus. Beyond arguments for repair through diversity, this form of minority separation in security makes such communities dependent on the state for protection and in doing so, partitions them from political power.[49]

This relegation is magnified in the Egyptian context because of the outsized role of the military and the broader security apparatus in the economy, politics, and social networks. Thus, stating the overall exclusion of Copts from such centers of power and authority is not to suggest that they also be *included* in the repressive infrastructure that undergirds authoritarian stability and sustainability in a similar kind of imperial multiculturalism.[50] Instead, it is to note that exclusion from state institutions of power—most especially the security apparatus—"limits the kinds of power that can be attained by Christians [in Egypt], and informs popular perceptions regarding the nature of [their] citizenship."[51] "It pushes you to feel disengaged from your country," a young Copt told a *Guardian* journalist in 2015, a pithy description of the affect of exclusion.⁵² "How could someone maintain his love for his country—and be passionate about building it—while at the same time he can't be whatever he wants to be, whether a military commander or a police commander?" Minor feelings of exclusion in Egyptian society refract onto their political orientations and forms of social solidarity that extend transnationally. The circulations and feedback loops of this affective marginalization—from parliament to the police—have far-reaching impacts for how Copts imagine belonging as a majority/minority in migration and deliberate on "the outside."⁵³

Becoming the Majority

Over different conversations with Amin (a teacher) and Nader (a landowner) back in Bahjūra between 2017 and 2022, both would voice their frustrations to me over Coptic activism—from Egypt to the United States. During a lively 2021 conversation about Coptic youth movements in post-revolutionary Egypt, Nader noted in a frustrated tone, "It's like this everywhere in the world. The majority dominates the minority. Don't whites discriminate against Black people in the US? It's inevitable for this to happen everywhere!" Only a few days after this debate, Amin would voice similar concerns over the exceptional focus on violence against Copts, when they see—via social media—spikes in gun violence in places like Chicago, for instance. These specific concerns over representations of Copts as victims and martyrs by Western "foreigners" (of which they included younger generations of the Coptic diaspora themselves) eventually became part of a broader and ongoing conceptual conversation on the binds of the nation-state and majority/minority dynamics. "Muslims are the majority here!" Amin contentiously debated in his living room during a power outage on a stifling July afternoon. "But they are also the minority there [in the United States], and it's possible for the majority Christians—and as Copts we are part of that majority in America!—to persecute them [Muslims], too." Amin and Nader—even from different socioeconomic classes in Bahjūra—shared a similar frame in understanding the binds of majority-minority dynamics here and there. In the case of Coptic participation in the US security apparatus then, layers of homeland contexts of violence and collective memory of martyrdom have intersected with a new diasporic and imperial reshaping of racial-religious threat (especially after 9/11); such a reshaping is juxtaposed with previous model minority frames that reproduce among immigrant communities in an anti-Black America.

* * *

Back at the banquet, Lieutenant Mariana Zakhary, founder of the St. Mark's Coptic Law Enforcement Officers Society, noted that the society promotes "the unique Coptic identity" and preserves "rich Egyptian history and heritage while celebrating being part of this great country, the USA."[54] The aura of celebration is also connected to the possibilities of civic participation in the United States disallowed in Egypt. And the NYPD and other law enforcement institutions frame Coptic inclusion through a narrative of shared persecution and promise in America.

Toward the end of the event, the former president of the Police Benevolent Association of the City of New York, Officer Patrick Lynch, spoke to the crowd. "We're going through a difficult time as NYC police officers. . . . Many folks may see the shield on our police officers' chests and try to demonize it." In the wake of the murder of George Floyd in May 2020, Coptic cops also had to hold the line for the police in the streets and on the Internet. Dioceses from around the United States released statements of condemnation. The Southern Diocese of the United States condemned the murder, but also released a statement that circulated on social media noting, "We must remember that most of law enforcement is on the side of the people and are protecting us from much harm. . . . Now is the time to help our nation heal. The rioting and looting must stop so the voices of reason can be heard and justice can prevail."[55]

Lynch echoed such sentiments during his speech, imploring Copts to correct community members who defame the police. "When they try to act like we're from the outside, when they try to say we don't belong, remind them that NYC police officers may be sitting in the same pew in the church, the synagogues, and mosques of this city."[56] This pluralistic view of security is nothing new in American society. By the 1890s, for example, first- and second-generation Irish Americans made up a disproportionately high percentage of policemen.[57] From 1880 through 1920, new white immigrant communities made up the majority of police in northern states. In prior generations, Irish had been understood as undisciplined and dangerous. Yet, by the mid-twentieth century, they increased their representation in police departments and surveilled Black populations, displacing suspicion. As historians have shown, European working-class immigrants embraced whiteness, not as a marker of phenotype, but as a means of distinguishing themselves from Black people, whom they associated with slavery and dependency, and from newer immigrants, whom they perceived as strange and inferior races.[58] Therefore, whiteness can be better understood as a political project that forges a sense of American belonging (of privilege and acceptance) through violence and the exclusion of others.[59] This was particularly true for the Irish, a group that had long occupied the bottom ranks of the social hierarchy and whose own whiteness was often called into question.[60]

Historian Noel Ignatiev expands upon the processes of Irish inclusion into whiteness through their participation in securitization, particularly by targeting Black bodies in Progressive Era Philadelphia: "The Irish cop is more than a quaint symbol. His appearance on the city police marked a turning point in Philadelphia in the struggle of the Irish to gain the rights of white men. It meant that thereafter the Irish would be officially empowered (armed) to defend themselves against the nativist mobs, and at the same time to carry out their agenda against black people."[61] As Toni Morrison has aptly written, "Although US history is awash in labor battles, political fights and property wars among all religious and ethnic groups, their struggles are persistently framed as struggles between recent arrivals and blacks. In race talk the move into mainstream America always means buying into the notion of American blacks as the real aliens."[62] In this way, policing and prejudice are not surgically separated from histories of slavery and anti-Blackness in America; the security state, its contemporary racial infrastructure, and the politics of social belonging in the United States have developed from those histories.

Ascension into whiteness (as a form of belonging, a right to indifference[63]) is both a participation in the exclusion of the forever Black other of America and a kinship of migration and persecution. To that end, Lynch invoked his Irish Catholic heritage in front of the Coptic crowd:

> Many of us come from countries where we were persecuted . . . and many of our people . . . strive to come to America to be protected, to believe what they want, to worship where they choose. . . . Remind those that try to demonize NYC police officers that the reason they can do it in safety

is because, yes, they are willing to protect us on the streets, but they are also willing to stand up and protect us when we pledge allegiance to a flag. They are willing to stand up and protect us when we stand outside our church, when we go to worship, to make sure no one comes through those doors and tries to stop us.[64]

* * *

The tapestry of the scenes woven throughout this chapter shows how Copts have been the targets of FBI raids, racial profiling, and violence as part of a matrix of suspicion—and they have also been those doing the profiling, conducting raids, and seeing others as threats to national security. For Lynch, inclusion of the Copts into an American civic consciousness means allegiance to securitization, as well as an affective connection across immigration stories of shared persecuted (Christian) pasts. Yet this formulation circles back, yet again, to a central paradox of this book—that Copts are caught between their racialized migration and the theopoliticization of their bloody martyrdom. The recognition of Coptic collective pain in Egypt lends itself to an unceasing investment in it, eliding possibilities of other forms of relationality that upend bloody persecution, as well as alternative translations across scales of memory. Communal memory of persecution in Egypt aligns Copts with different polities around security, and Coptic processes of racialization in diaspora interface with transnational translations of Christian persecution, showing how new formations of racial-religious legibility impact upon diasporic political connections on the basis of persecution even beyond the remapping of Egyptian contexts of Christian death. Discourse around rising Christian persecution in America includes Copts in the United States—as *Christians*.[65] In these diasporic and transnational renderings of long-standing and reinvigorated US culture wars, Coptic Christians have reimagined their Christianity, not just in opposition to Islam and Muslims, but also under new itineraries of secular threat.

5

Diasporic Translations and Global Culture Wars

Every Labor Day weekend for over a decade, Abouna Bavly James, a popular priest from Cairo with a major following in the diaspora, holds seminars on family, social issues, and evangelism.[1] With the largest program of missionary activities in Egypt and throughout the African continent, James has made a reputation speaking on cross-cultural communication, ethics, and relationships. The parking lot of the upstate New York hotel in September 2017, where the seminars were to take place, was packed to the brim with cars from the tristate area.

The hall of the seminars held five screens that surrounded the priest—two for projecting presentations to each of his sides, two others for translation to each side of the hall, and yet another behind him projecting a picture of Christ with a lamb, as the Shepherd. It was positioned so that Christ was directly behind the priest in the camera shot. There were several other cameras broadcasting, one from the Christian Youth Channel (CYC), a television and Internet-based station that operates in English. Before beginning the first lecture, Abouna answered questions from the audience, brought to him on pieces of paper. One question that caught my attention asked how youth in America should approach issues such as same-sex marriage. He began, "In my opinion, you have persecution here more [as Christians] than we do in Egypt. Here, you have a secular society that imposes demands on you as Christians that are against your faith. In Egypt, we may have a terrorist come and blow up a church, but it doesn't affect our faith. You all are more of a minority [here, than we are there]." He continued to clarify, "We cannot say that homosexuality is natural. It is a sin, but we must not judge others. I am also a sinful person. Just because we are in a secular society and this is accepted, we don't let go of our faith and deny our Christ."

The attacks on Christians in Egypt, for Abouna, do not affect the faith, but only strengthen it. Yet in the United States, Copts have been subjected to a liberal politics of pluralism, where ethical choices must be made in the everyday to maintain the sanctity of one's faith. In Egypt, minority politics of separation, repression, and resistance are reconfigured within the current US culture wars, where Copts share in common with evangelical and conservative others' feelings of threat to Christian values and persecution by the larger society for their belief in Christ. The global protection of "traditional values" has traversed theological divides and has appealed to many Copts in the United States as well as in Egypt. While Copts are a minority in both Egypt and the United States, in the United States Copts have had to reckon their values in a public sphere that is dominated both by pluralism and by pervasive evangelical politics that shape their social positionings and apologetic strategies.

Transnational Coptic Christians have remapped indigenous narratives of persecution and martyrdom, not merely as a form of American political legibility, but also as part of *their own* fight to retain Coptic "traditional values" in the United States. While Egyptian Coptic reformers have historically emphasized that Protestantism must be expunged from contemporary religious life, Coptic Christians in the United States have continued to collaborate with Protestants (and Catholics) on matters pertaining to the threat of Islam to US national security and cultural life, as well as the threat of secularism in the form of progressive politics, which are placed into tension with the conservatism of the Coptic Orthodox religious tradition between Egypt and the United States.[2] This new kind of conservative ecumenism is part of a broader frame of what can be described as an American persecution complex.[3] Elizabeth Castelli has argued that the contemporary US context unfolds a story of Christian martyrdom from two threads of ever-present threat and identity politics, "promoting a utopian vision of looming danger and moral injury, collective struggle and perseverance, and holding out the promise of redemption—whether it be spiritual, moral, or political."[4]

Connecting the imperial theopolitics of the Persecuted Church (as discussed in chapter 1) to the discourse on persecution against/the war on Christians in the United States has allowed American Christians in/with power to argue that while the blood of Christians does not yet spill into American streets as it does elsewhere in the world, there are anti-Christian forces working to make that happen soon enough.[5] Within this movement, "Christians" emerge as members of an identifiable and homogeneous group, targeted and victimized for their faith, and it is here that the language of rights "loses its anchoring in the historical narratives of the dispossessed and disenfranchised."[6] In this diasporic context, the intersection of minority victimhood in Egypt (which has included discrimination, violence, and death) and the Christian victimhood of moral injury in the United States both appeals to Coptic sensibilities and histories of persecution and martyrdom, and reforms them in translation.

War on Christians, War on America

Following a liturgy one Sunday in August 2020, I sat with Amir and Verina, who had just dropped off their youngest son at college. The upcoming elections and Black Lives Matter protests had consumed news media, and the conversation naturally directed itself there. Amir explained that he was concerned about where American society is going, even hinting that if protests continue (reminiscent of the 2011 Egyptian revolution and the downfall of former Egyptian president Hosni Mubarak), he will move back to Egypt. "Trump is a Christian, and he's trying to keep America a Christian nation," he said. "Obama supported the Muslim Brotherhood in Egypt. The Muslim Brotherhood was against the Copts, leading to more violence. With Trump, he supports the Christians back there." Verina chimed into the conversation, "Under Obama, it was 'Happy Holidays'! Now, we can say 'Merry Christmas' again. We came to the US to escape discrimination in Egypt. We don't want to be stripped of our rights again as Christians here."

Support for the reelection of Donald Trump in 2020 was structured through the "war on Christians," but also through specific Coptic migrant translations of Islam and the American Dream. Two months after meeting Amir and Verina, I visited the new home of a Coptic family in Jersey City who had previously lived in a small apartment closer to their church for more than a decade. Ramy immigrated to the United States in the late 1990s on the Green Card Lottery from Najʿ Ḥammādī. He later married Marina in Egypt and brought her to Jersey City, where they had two sons. Ramy shares his conservative views on his Facebook page— from images of Donald Trump referencing the "stolen election" of 2020 to photos of Fox News stills or Hillary Clinton and Joe Biden, interspersed with commentary on New Jersey state politics and an LGBTQ curriculum, and news from Egypt.

Since the beginning of the COVID-19 pandemic, Ramy had been unemployed, relying on Marina's salary as a teacher's aide. Both Ramy and Marina are vocal supporters of Trump, weaving their understanding of Trump's political movement through their own anxieties about the status of Christians in Egypt and the pressures of being a new immigrant (from the Middle East) in the United States. "So many people don't want to work here. They take money from the system and don't want to give back," Marina grumbled over lunch. "I think they should do a merit-based immigration system. We don't know who they are letting in!" Peculiarly, the family's presence in the United States was only made possible by the Lottery system. But now that they are in the United States, changing immigration law to filter out those deemed unworthy or a threat to American society became a recurring theme in many of the conversations we had together.

As we finished lunch, we made our way to the living room for tea; the conversation shifted to the dangers of Egyptian Muslim migration to the United States. "Look at France! We don't want those extremists to come here. They need to be able to assimilate. They come here and demand that people conform to their perspective. They want America to be Islamic!" As detailed in chapters 1 and 4, Coptic perspectives of Islam are a refraction of personal experiences or the experiences of kin in Egypt that are then filtered through a new national politics of belonging in the United States (a transvaluation in the service of US empire at home and abroad). But they are also a reflection of anxieties about the perceived transformations of American society away from its Christian character and toward a more progressive framework that would allow (paradoxically) an Islamic *and/or* secular takeover of the United States.

Lenticular sentiment such as this conditioned broad public support for Trump's 2020 reelection among the Coptic community of New York and New Jersey. "God bless America and Egypt" was the motto highlighted on the now defunct Egyptian Christians for Trump website. Board members appeared on the Coptic Sat TV show *Ask with Mira* on October 23, 2020, to garner support for the advocacy group and to discuss why Egyptian Christian support for Trump was so crucial to the community in diaspora.[7] One particular viewer, a second-generation American Copt, called in to express his support for the organization:

I don't think it's any coincidence that in the new capital city that [Egyptian] President Sisi has built, the biggest Coptic cathedral in the Middle East is built there, and President Sisi is very excited to highlight this to the world and to show this to President Trump—[implicitly saying] "Look at what I'm doing for the Coptics!" and that's what we want, we're happy with that. I'm glad President Sisi did that. We want him to continue . . . and the way we're going to get there is by supporting our great President Trump and letting him know, "Hey! The Coptic community supports you and we expect you to support our brothers and sisters back home."

American Coptic support for Trump was woven into a political imaginary of diasporic advocacy, but more pervasively it coalesced around the idea that Copts in the United States belong to a broader constellation of the Christian Right. While this framing does not preclude other alternative communal perspectives, Coptic conservatism in the United States draws on concerns similar to those expressed by Christian Right and conservative, evangelical activists and advocates, including and especially on abortion and LGBTQ issues as well as the threat of Islam to American society and social welfare reform.[8]

With a framed picture of Trump on the desk behind him, the vice president of the organization, a financial advisor, connected support for Trump to support for Egypt's al-Sisi, but also encouraged Coptic immigrants to become model minorities.[9] "If you stay on welfare and Medicaid and wait for social services . . . this is what happened to the Blacks [*as-suwd*] and Hispanics [*espan*] here. They vote for Democrats so they can get food stamps. To all our family who immigrate from Egypt, please don't get stuck on Medicare and food stamps. Go achieve your dream, work hard, and don't wait for people to give you money." Concern for the persecution of Egyptian Copts interweaves with the *limits* of that concern once those very Copts leave Egypt. They must achieve economic success in the United States, so as to avoid association with "failed minorities"—Blacks and Hispanics. This returns to what Toni Morrison has argued: "Only when the lesson of racial estrangement [from the native-born Black population] is learned is assimilation complete."[10]

Coptic Christians imagine themselves in relation to the Christian Right as kin—in their shared concerns about the future of (Christian) religious life in the United States, but also, more implicitly, in the

Figure 5.1. Screenshot from the now defunct Egyptian Christians for Trump website, October 2020.

evangelical-capitalist theological underpinnings that frame conservative American Christianity.[11] Conversely, the extension of kinship from conservative American Christians to Coptic Christians is a relation of persecuted blood. Therefore, American Copts see their ties with the Christian Right in terms of shared persecuted blood rather than as a racial formation. While appropriating the model of Black struggle against racial discrimination and their ongoing claims for justice, the "war on Christians" movement legitimates and routinizes a new, Christian identity politics. Conservative American Christians—beyond the Trump administration—emerge as the singular exemplars of innocent victims.[12] Copts refashion this double movement by demanding both a right to indifference—to be seen as any other successful (white) American (Christian)—and a reformation of their minority condition between Egypt and the United States.

Minority Conditions and National Belonging

While migration remaps Coptic collective memory onto American polemics of persecution, this transnational translation does not exceed the original contexts of minority injury and pain. In Egypt, Copts also draw on Orthodox religious symbols and concepts to negotiate and practically shape an Egyptian Christian citizenship.[13] In February 2017, while in Bahjūra for a volunteer program with diasporic Copts and others to teach English (mentioned in the introduction), my partner, Sarah, and I organized mock elections in each of our classes to build stronger communication skills between classmates. Students who ran for office developed their own political parties and platform to better Egypt. Visiting each of the students as they drew their logos and wrote their statements, we noticed how most of the party names related to Christianity: the Party of Christ (*Ḥizb al-Masiḥ*), the Party of the Saints (*Ḥizb al-Qudisiyyn*), even a party named simply "Jesus." One of the student candidates approached the front of the classroom, platform in hand. "We need to increase access to clean drinking water, increase access to medical treatment, improve our education system, and protect our churches." As they said this, they made the sign of the cross and said aloud, "In the name of the Father, the Son, and the Holy Spirit, one God, Amen." Qur'anic recitation was blasting into the classroom from the nearby mosque as the children clapped loudly. In later reflection that day, I rhetorically asked myself in fieldnotes, *If Copts became the majority, what would they want Egypt to look like?*

* * *

When we consider the import of "Christian nationalism" for Coptic migrants to the United States, we can see that legacies of and trauma from their minority condition in Egypt shape how they interpret a new landscape of Christian supremacy in the United States.[14] The post-2011 Egyptian political landscape offers some key considerations. During the 2011 revolution, Coptic political groups emerged to make visible Coptic identity and problems in the Egyptian public sphere. Following the Maspero Massacre in October 2011, where over two dozen Coptic Christians were killed by the Egyptian military aiming to disperse a march and sit-in at the Maspero state television building, such groups were both galvanized and splintered along differing political orientations. One of the most popular groups among them was the Maspero Youth Union (MYU), which promoted political secularism, or the separation of religion from politics, as a solution to intercommunal strife and as a remedy to intra-communal conflict over the position of the Coptic Orthodox Church as sole representative of the community. At the same time, the group emphasized its Coptic identity through religious symbols and imagery at protest events. While the MYU officially endorsed secular governance to overcome sectarianism, its actions also made visible internal conflicts over the representation of Coptic identity in contemporary Egyptian society.

While the MYU engaged the citizenship principle—insisting that religious difference did not impact equal citizenship rights—it also proclaimed itself a Coptic group working on the "Coptic issue" to fight for the freedom and equality of all Copts. This paradox—the need both to accept and to refuse religious difference in political organizing—is not specific to the Coptic or the Egyptian case but is a broader issue of difference within political modernity and its sociolegal execution through the modern nation-state.[15] Among Egyptian Copts, there was varied support for these groups that openly displayed Christian imagery at their protests. One Coptic politician described how "fanatic" Copts, many associated with the MYU, found a window via the revolution to communicate their experience of discrimination with other marginalized groups in Egypt as well as abroad. Conversely, a prominent Coptic political analyst and politician emphasized the importance of Coptic groups like the MYU in promoting Christian visibility: "This new generation is playing a very important role in fighting for citizenship rights and equality. They are not fanatics; they are proud of their Christianity."[16]

Anthony Shenoda has argued that what was desirable for Copts in post-2011 Egypt was a visibility that took seriously their religiosity.[17] With continued calls for national unity and a flattening of communal identities and conflict, what was at stake for Copts, such as those youth in the MYU, was their everyday lived experiences, where their Christianity structures forms of discrimination and difference. For many Copts in Egypt, their identity as Egyptians is enmeshed with their identity as Christians—seeing Egyptian streets, landscapes, and the built environment through a sociohistorical lens of Coptic presence and absence. Because many Copts are uncomfortable with their positioning in the Egyptian nation-state (as a community administered by the Church) or Islamist imaginations of Egypt (where, in some framings, Copts are characterized by a *dhimmī* status), they engage with what they believe to be alternative strategies to ensure their emplacement.[18]

As one self-identified Coptic liberal described during a personal interview in 2012, everything in Egypt is focused on the projection of a particular religiosity, and for Copts, this has been centered on building churches, Christian schools and hospitals, or other institutional buildings (as visible, concrete embodiments of Coptic religiosity). "All of the churches have to be as big as the mosques in order to show off," he said. Thus, many Copts have developed, and continue to stress, their own time (for example, through the Coptic calendar and fasting periods) and space (churches, monasteries, and other building projects), which form a landscape of Christian Egypt.[19] A Coptic world, as separated from a Muslim one, has been imagined through sacred space and time, having roots in pre-Islamic Egypt, before Muslim influence and domination. Markers of Copticity contain a separate body of literature, movies, and videos that are circulated through the Church and independently run Coptic television channels, such as Aghaby, CTV, and MESAT.[20] Pilgrimages to monasteries, youth community service trips, sports programming inside church walls, and specialized courses (from Church history to political participation in some dioceses) form pieces of an all-encompassing Coptic life in Egypt.

Coptic groups like the MYU redefined social boundaries and made publicly visible what was left invisible in Egyptian politics. Many Copts desire to be recognized as *Christian* Egyptians. One illustration of this is the symbols, language, and hymns used during the MYU's demonstrations, which were fused with calls for equal citizenship as well as chants invoking Church leaders, and Coptic theology and history.[21] As part of the paradox of political modernity—wherein emancipation is imagined through abstraction in the particularity of the national citizen—the idea of secular equality through citizenship rights also eludes the social manifestations of difference that perpetuate everyday inequalities. In response to these binds, Copts sought to reshape a citizenship that allowed for the expression of Christian identity—a kind of citizenship with various possibilities.[22] Anthony Shenoda outlines this predicament clearly: "Many Copts want to be *seen* as being an important part of the fabric of Egyptian history and society, and not simply as members of Egyptian society, but as Christian members of Egyptian society.... They seek a visibility that finds valuable their religiosity without subordinating it to a meta-narrative of a national unity that pretends acceptance of Coptic religious difference while incessantly seeking to homogenize and incorporate it."[23]

The national unity paradigm in Egypt has generally argued that Christians and Muslims are citizen-kin and that the origins of any bouts of violence come from the outside—foreign hands and conspiratorial/imperial forces. Yet such visceral violence discounts other forms of difference-making in the everyday—the call to prayer openly broadcast throughout the streets by megaphones in Heliopolis, a suburb of Cairo, while a Coptic Christian in his jewelry shop must keep the Coptic hymns he plays in the background on low volume so as not to disturb any customers; or the utterance "bismillah al-raḥman al-raḥim" (In the name of God, the Most Gracious, the Most Merciful) by a Muslim politician before a speech at any public event in Egypt, when if the same speech started with "bism al-ab w al-ibn w al-ruwḥ al-quddus (ilayhi wāḥid, amin)" (In the name of the Father, the Son, and the Holy Spirit [one God, Amen]), the Christian politician giving the speech would be charged with endangering national unity. A list of everyday snapshots of (in)visibility would be limitless, but what is important to infer from these examples is how Copts are treated and represented not only as inherently religious (as *Christian* Egyptians), but also as inherently a threat to the nation-state. They must disprove suspicion of allegiance to their religious tradition over the nation and disconnect from "Coptic" issues to be accepted into non-Christian (read: Muslim, Egyptian) circles. The Muslim citizen within Egyptian society is the ideal citizen, as Islam and Muslim life mold the basis of majoritarian norms that form the background of political, legal, and social thought. Coptic Christians are compelled to publicly reinforce their *invisibility* as Christian citizens and *visibility* as Egyptian citizens.

In migration to the United States, Copts can make public their Christianity in a Christian-majority society. The translation of that Christianity, though, is predicated not only on its social function in everyday life, but also on its charged and contested political power and supremacy in an American landscape.

Translating the Culture Wars into Coptic

During the hearing on the Supreme Court nomination of Amy Coney Barrett in September 2020, Copts took to social media to voice their support and express concern over the encroachment of their Christian values from secular political forces. In October 2020, a Coptic youth meeting was held in New Jersey to discuss the confirmation hearings and the questioning of Barrett's Catholic faith. At the meeting, entitled "A Successful PATRIOT: Because of Faith, NOT In-Spite Of," those in attendance grappled with their Coptic positionality in American Christianity. "Sometimes you feel like you're the minority, and now we're less than the minority," a Coptic mother and doctor in attendance commented during the discussion. While the priest and organizer of the event framed the discussion around culture war politics and the decline of Christianity in America, he noted that much of this decline stemmed from evangelical influence:

> By us staying silent, by us not living our faith and demanding our right to voice our love, to voice the right, balanced message of Christ, we are

Figure 5.2. Youth meeting flyer, New Jersey, October 2020.

allowing the incorrect view of Christianity to prevail. . . . I think that we get so embarrassed and so intimidated because of the backlash, because of what this misrepresentation of Christianity has caused, that we ourselves get intimidated. And it has made the non-Christians or those who do have a strong opinion on the bigoted vision or version of Christianity to come out to the extent that at a Senate hearing, publicly on television, somebody's faith can be attacked or at the very least criticized.

Bishoy, a youth attendee, chimed in: "We have to recognize that the definition of the word 'Christian' in American society is far from what our Middle Eastern Brown background understands this word to be." Gesturing toward a politics of translation and a clash of (Western/ Eastern) Christian traditions, Bishoy conveyed to the priest that not everything described as "Christian" is reconcilable or even compatible with Coptic Orthodox histories, sensibilities, and pedagogies. Beyond this, Coptic, and more broadly, Oriental Orthodox racial difference (including Armenian and Ethiopian experiential distinctions) from white, evangelical America lends itself to divergent experiences of being Christian in American society. American Coptic politics are remapped by these US culture wars, which chart religious public life onto a left-right spectrum and are conditioned by identifying racial others and ultimately structured by white supremacy, which binds Copts to varyingly adopt positions that diverge from their own theology and religious traditions. The priest grimaced at the comment and sought a more pragmatic political angle: "We have power in numbers, though!" Bishoy replied, "If you're with the wrong numbers, you have the wrong power."

* * *

American Coptic contestations over the culture wars are enmeshed in the community's new positioning as a minority in the United States. Yet scales of the US culture wars stretch far beyond the confines of official American borders. As was discussed in chapter 1, American evangelicals have operated as part of a larger transnational coalition of conservative religious communities, bringing together Orthodox, Catholics, Mormons, and other Protestants, as well as Jews and Muslims (among others).[24] Tracing the globalization of this conservative coalition spearheaded by American evangelical politics and political affects requires recognizing that evangelical visions were never rigidly focused on domestic issues and have gradually entailed a more global ecumenical approach on social issues around family values—among Christians and other religious conservatives more broadly.[25] During the Cold War, Catholics and Protestants were both involved in international anti-communist religious freedom crusades that were the foundation for the persecuted Christians movement. And domestically, an emerging alliance specifically between conservative Catholics and evangelicals on the issue of abortion began to reorganize the Christian Right beyond theological difference.[26] These theopolitical transformations at home, among many others, fed into an already globalized American mission structure that not only spread the Gospel and ideas of the divine good, but also *American* perspectives on political advocacy and activism to put into action a reimagination of the world for Christ.[27]

Since the late twentieth century, this conservative coalition consisting of a wide range of ecumenical partners has crafted a shared understanding of social politics and conservative values, focused on religious freedom at home and abroad, abortion, and most especially LGBTQ rights issues such as same-sex marriage.[28] An explicit example of this coalition is the 2009 Manhattan Declaration, a manifesto signed by more than 150 religious leaders, among them prominent evangelicals, Catholics, and Eastern Orthodox Christians.[29] The inclusion of Orthodox Christians as signatories is significant and gestures toward increasing American and transnational Orthodox participation and leadership in the global culture wars.[30] The Manhattan Declaration is split into three sections—"Life," "Marriage," and "Religious Liberty"—and is focused on Christian perspectives of human dignity, which commands opposition to abortion as well as same-sex marriage. It insists that "the impulse to redefine marriage" to include same-sex couples is just one symptom of the larger, more insidious "erosion of marriage culture" and declares that Christians should use their religious liberty to be clear on their traditional message in an increasingly liberal (and ungodly) society.[31] Positioning religious communities that counter these broader social movements of liberal progress as persecuted or witnesses for one's faith, the declaration notes the willingness of American Christians to defy the state when it demands that Christians support social behavior that contradict their sincerely held beliefs: "We will fully and ungrudgingly render to Caesar what is Caesar's. But under no circumstances will we render to Caesar what is God's."[32]

The United Nations Family Rights Caucus also consists of a conservative coalition beyond theological difference focused on the family and concerns over the influence of LGBTQ activism and advocacy. The caucus is composed of individual and member organizations from around the world and is sponsored by Family Watch International, led by Sharon Slater (a Mormon), and mainly focuses its efforts abroad, especially throughout the continent of Africa. Many of its forums concentrate on spreading traditional family values and condemning homosexuality, offering testimonials from people who have undergone "conversion therapy."[33] The efforts of this caucus and a global focus on the family was partially realized in 2015 when the UN Human Rights Council adopted a resolution (29/22) on the protection of the family, "through its role in poverty eradication and achieving sustainable development" that was initiated by some of the members of the UN Group of the Friends of the Family, which includes Uganda, Bangladesh, the Russian Federation, and Qatar, as well as Egypt.[34]

Egypt's endorsement is indicative of not only the government's stance, but also the official position of the Coptic Orthodox Church. Over the past several decades, LGBTQ Egyptians have been the target of government prosecution and discrimination.[35] Amid this rising crackdown on the LGBTQ community in Egypt, American religious and political actors—who themselves have promoted pro-family/anti-LGBTQ policies—have also aligned with the Egyptian government, most particularly for their concern over Christian persecution in Egypt.[36] Along with the government's initiatives, the Coptic Orthodox Church has sought to combat what it considers to be immoral behavior.

Since the late 1990s and early 2000s, representatives from all Christian churches in Egypt have held meetings officially opposing attempts by other Christian churches outside Egypt to legalize same-sex marriage.[37] In 2003, during its annual clergy convention, the leaders of the Coptic Orthodox Church discussed recent issues related to homosexuality. The convention was presided by the late Pope Shenouda III. In attendance were twelve bishops from North America, Egypt, Australia, and Europe, and 180 priests from the United States, Canada, and Australia. The issues discussed included the legalization of same-sex marriage, the ordination of a homosexual bishop in the Episcopal Diocese of New Hampshire, and the vote of the Uniting Church in Australia to allow the ordination of any homosexual clergy.[38] Since the early 2000s, the Coptic Orthodox Church between Egypt and the United States has reiterated its position on same-sex marriage as well as homosexuality.[39] In November 2019, the Synodal Committee for Mental Health and Anti-Addiction of the Coptic Orthodox Church held a conference in Egypt entitled "Homosexuality: Preservation and Recovery," which centered around raising awareness on "how to achieve a 'speedy recovery' from homosexuality."[40] Defining homosexuality through the framework of mental illness and addiction stirred controversy among transnational Copts, particularly in its connections to "conversion therapy," a method illegal in regions of the United States and throughout Canada.[41]

In Egypt, Dr. Awsam Wasfy has been a leading proponent of "conversion therapy," and while he is Coptic Protestant, he has also been utilized by Coptic Orthodox clergy.[42] He has appeared on Egyptian television promoting his views and is highly popular on social media sites, including and especially Facebook.[43] On his (now defunct) YouTube channel, he outlined much of his source material, which mainly derives from American psychiatrists, including the controversial Dr. Paul R. McHugh, University Distinguished Service Professor of Psychiatry at the Johns Hopkins University School of Medicine.[44] Wasfy's viewpoints on homosexuality and concern for the cultural acceptance of LGBTQ practices are prominent among Coptic Christians in and beyond Egypt. For example, a video from Philip Wissa (a popular Coptic Protestant musician living in Europe) widely circulated on Facebook in June 2022. In it, he defends Wasfy's work and recounts a conversation with a government official in Europe who frankly stated to him that he had some concerns with the influx of refugees and their potentially extremist views. However, he notes in the video how he cannot state these opinions publicly for fear of reprimand. "There are many members of ISIS who entered with those refugees," Wissa proclaims. Such government censorship, he argues, is not limited to the migrant crisis in Europe, but also carries over into discussion on the topics of homosexuality and gender identity—from school curriculums to the Disney backlash as a result of the Parental Rights in Education bill, also known as the so-called "Don't Say Gay" bill, signed by Florida governor Ron DeSantis in March 2022.[45] "This is terrorism on free speech [al-irhāb 'ala hurriyat al-kalām]," he notes in the video, and continues, "This is a new kind of terrorism, worse than any terrorism we have seen in the world." While Wissa lives in an undisclosed location in Europe, his video was also watched by American Copts. One comment on the video read, "As an Egyptian living in a majority-Democrat state, I have lived every word you have spoken, and I feel the same sense of fear and danger that encroaches more and more everyday. All Egyptians must know that this is the anti-Christ agenda that is being implemented in most countries of the world, including Egypt."

Discourses on LGBTQ rights and the impending threat of global moral breakdown span national borders and are also enlivened by US foreign policy and through transnational religious influence. The US culture wars are exported and appropriated in local ways from Egypt to Russia but are still infused with episodes and contexts originating in the United States (as well as Canada, Europe, and Australia—all of which have large Coptic diasporic communities).[46] Sophie Bjork-James has examined how white evangelical perspectives on the family form the majoritarian norms—racially and religiously—of the contemporary United States.[47] As such, their concern over the demise of Western civilization or fears of Islamic peril or secular conquest are premised on the idea of themselves as a "persecuted majority," a feeling of encroachment even despite their power. In reaction to this encroachment, conservative evangelicals and their ecumenical partners have politically organized to fight against what they deem to be pro-LGBTQ stances that, for example, school curriculums are beginning to reflect. Members of the movement (which include American Copts) have become part of school boards and other local structures of political power to overturn the rising tide of progressive, secular threat.

Focusing on the Coptic Family in New Jersey

In January 2019, New Jersey governor Phil Murphy signed a law requiring schools to teach middle school and high school students about the political, economic, and social contributions of LGBTQ people. Coptic Christians (as well as Egyptian Muslims) came out against the curriculum, with clergy and other members of the community attending town hall meetings to express their views. One Coptic priest proclaimed during one such meeting, "You want our children to learn something that is against our values, freedom, and our faith." While the curriculum was implemented during the 2020-2021 pandemic school year, Copts and other religious communities continued to fight it, calling on New Jersey to offer them vouchers for private schooling if they cannot opt their children out of the curriculum.

After a 2021 Palm Sunday liturgy in Jersey City, a petition was circulated for signatures on the voucher proposal. It read that "Jews, Muslims, and Christians" of New Jersey are coming together against the curriculum, and "the environment is toxic and intolerant of [our] families' deeply held religious beliefs." They asked parishioners to sign the petition and mail it to their representatives. Over the course of 2021, op-

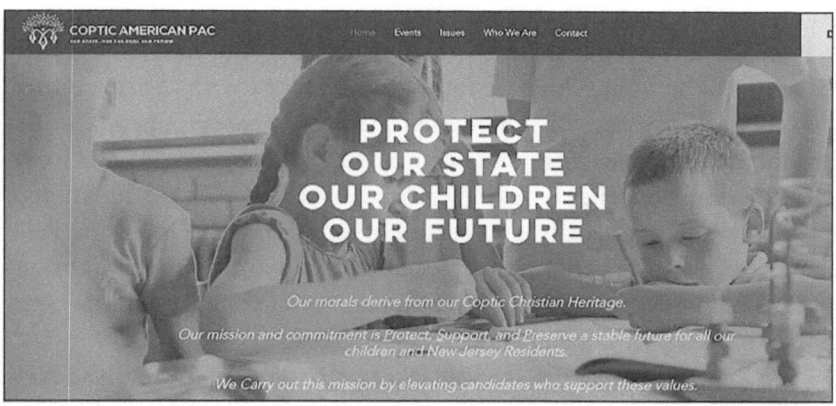

Figure 5.3. Screenshot of the Coptic American PAC's website, launched August 2021.

position to the curriculum gained steam as the region began to open up post-vaccination. Between early 2020 and 2021, Copts and other New Jersey residents took to Facebook groups to share their concerns and to think about possible solutions to the crisis. In July 2021, the Coptic American Political Action Committee launched its (now defunct) website and social media platforms with the slogan, "Our state. Our children. Our future." The website outlined the goals of the group—to help conservative American Copts run for political office, to determine their own futures, and to challenge the liberal tilt of the state's administration. Its stated goal is to promote "Christian family values," which "derive from our Coptic Christian Heritage."

In early August 2021, the PAC hosted its first event to support three candidates for state senate and assembly. Bringing together clergy and laity from the community, the fundraiser emphasized the importance of Coptic organizing for Christian values in the lands of immigration. One woman involved in the pushback against the curriculum approached the stage and described her father's immigration story in relation to moral difference. Her father had immigrated in 1968 during the Vietnam War. She recalled him seeing people kissing in public parks and signs that said, "Make Love, Not War." Her father was appalled, she recounted: "'How am I going to raise my children in this culture?' [he would ask]. That was the counterculture of the 1960s. My Dad left the frying pan, Egypt, and walked right into the fire." His solution was to place his children in Catholic schools, and the woman related this experience to her own today with her son, who had recently entered public high school. "I found myself faced with cancel culture, 'woke,' and focus on various sexual ideologies and an agenda in the school that wasn't solely focused on academics and sports." With Coptic clergy looking on, she expressed embarrassment at even the mention of sexuality, gender identity, and sexual orientation. "Has inclusion been narrowed down to meaning the acceptance of particular sexual orientations or gender identities, but not including anyone who doesn't embrace that lifestyle choice?"

To close the event, Bishop David, the current papal exarch of New Jersey (as well as the bishop of New York and New England), addressed the crowd. As opposed to the St. Mark's Coptic Law Enforcement Officers Society event (discussed in chapter 4), there was no Egyptian flag displayed, only an American one. The bishop lamented the fact that the Church has limitations on its earthly influence: "As a religious organization, we are limited in what we can do. We need someone to do what we cannot do." Drawing from the words of the late Coptic patriarch Pope Shenouda III, Bishop David encouraged his flock to not be "the silent majority" amid "the vocal minority." While the term "silent majority" harkens back to the Nixon era, in recent political discourse, supporters of Donald Trump have also deployed it.[48] "The LGBTQ community are some 3.5 percent in the US. How can we allow 3.5 percent to decide our fate? Because there are 96.5 percent silent. We cannot be silent. We cannot allow the government to impose things on us that we don't agree with." The bishop then historically contextualized this contemporary political position as one of endurance through persecution: "We have to get our point across because when our Fathers, the Apostles, were faced with persecution, they said they ought to obey God rather than men. We're not going to let men impose on us something that our conscience does not accept."

At the end of his remarks, the bishop smiled at the audience and said,

> I cannot leave you before I tell you about Egypt. Because I love Egypt. Egyptians went through two revolutions because they said, "We will decide what our future will be like." . . . You have the brain of the pharaohs; the Coptic people are the pure descendants of the pharaohs. We have the

best brains in the whole world. That's why we have the best doctors, the best everything. The new Egypt of President Sisi is something else that you need to be very proud of. As much as you are proud to be Americans, the greatest nation in the world, but we should not forget our roots. In Egypt, we went through difficulties and persecutions, but . . . we should be proud of Egypt and being Egyptian.

Egypt is both a geography and a metaphor of legibility for many American Copts. Matthew Hanna, one of the first candidates to run through the Coptic American PAC, was present at the event.[49] In the early 1980s, his father was an electrical engineer who went from Algeria to Spain, then to Russia, and on to Japan. In 1992 he decided to move his family to the United States. Matthew frames his story around the promise of the American Dream—that if you work hard, you will be successful. The American Dream is not universal for all Egyptians, Matthew noted to me, but it has offered him career success as a lawyer and an entrepreneur, and personal security as a husband and father.[50] While he has an economic advantage over many other Egyptian immigrants in the New York–New Jersey area, he also shares their values, and feels he can connect with them (and other immigrants) on levels that old, white conservatives cannot.

In the early fall of 2021, in the lead-up to the election, he had a meeting at the home of the two Coptic heads of the Republican committee in East Brunswick, New Jersey. (At the time, they had been in leadership for nearly twenty years.) Leaving their home, he hopped in his car and realized that he did not have enough gas to get home and his usual gas station was closed for maintenance. He pulled into another gas station, nearly running out. Matthew quickly realized that the person who approached the pump was Coptic. The man spoke to him in Arabic and Matthew replied in English. With his campaign posters in the backseat, he took it as an opportunity to solicit the attendant's vote. Matthew tried to relay to the man that he was running for state senate, but nothing clicked until he said "curriculum." The man pulled Matthew out of his car into the gas station store and asked him whether he had the Viber communication application. Matthew had not used it in years. The man immediately added him to three groups with over five hundred community members sharing posts and articles on the curriculum as well as their fears.

The incident made Matthew rethink his political strategy, knowing that immigrant communities beyond the Copts were also concerned about the curriculum changes. "This is our Pearl Harbor moment," he said. The persecuted pasts in Egypt transmit themselves to this political moment on curriculum change. "I'm sure you heard a couple years ago when the church blew up and all those kids died. That night, they were buried in the same church. In the United States, Christianity is also under attack, but in a different way. The Coptic community comes here a bit more emboldened. They're not afraid to share their religion now that they can."

During the 2011 Egyptian revolution, many Copts in the New York–New Jersey area championed the changes in Egypt, changing their Facebook backgrounds to the Egyptian flag, among other forms of solidarity. However, in the midst of this diasporic fervor, Matthew grew frustrated with the community's lack of concern for domestic US issues. "My wife was my girlfriend at the time, and I was arguing with her brother, who was very much out there every day celebrating the whole movement, and I said, 'You know, we need you guys to care this much about the problems here.' I told him something that my father told me growing up: 'You're not Egyptian, you're American.'" He recalled how his father emphasized this regularly, and made it known that Egypt was no longer their country—America was. "And who really put this issue front and center? Donald Trump."

Trump's supremacy on the Christian Right spoke to the desires of many Coptic immigrants to the United States leaving their religious *minority* status in Egypt. Despite racial difference from white America, many American Copts also overwhelmingly see their ties to the Christian Right in terms of religious kinship rather than racial difference. Copts are a racial minority in the United States, but they are also part of the Christian *majority*. This shift in communal positionality has produced new kinds of political orientations and affective concerns.

In September 2020, Bishop Youssef of the Coptic Orthodox Diocese of the Southern United States delivered a lecture on Zoom to Coptic Orthodox youth entitled "The Future of Orthodoxy in America." During his lecture, he described the threat of secularization and progressive politics on the diaspora, recalling how shocked he was to discover that an airline was asking customers for their gender—with boxes marked "male," "female," "unspecified," or "undisclosed":

For seven thousand years, we know that genders are male and female. If you Google now, you will find more than fifty-eight different genders. How can this be imposed on me? What does this mean for me? ... This is the culture that unfortunately we are living in it. We should have a voice as Christians, as Orthodox Christians.... We need to speak up.[51]

Coptic translations of the US culture wars are not a mere mimicking of dominant discourse. Concerns over "secularization," from Coptic bishops to everyday American Copts, are connected to legacies of minoritization in Egypt rethought anew in lands of immigration. Bishop Youssef continued, "America was founded on Christian principles, but now they are removing the Christian principles and they are secularizing America.... The culture in America became anti-Christian." Anti-Christian discrimination and violence in Egypt are remembered and (re)constructed by new translations of threat to Christian life and flourishing in the United States. While Islam continues to varyingly remain a threat to those on the right, such a threat is transmitted and molded onto the risk of Christian decimation in secular America.

Sectarian Legacies and Conservative Alliances

During Matthew's campaign, he visited a New Jersey hookah café with a mutual friend he partnered with in real estate. At the café, he met a man named Abdallah. "I'm usually good at identifying which religion someone is by their name." They struck up a lively conversation and he eventually steered it toward the LGBTQ curriculum. Abdallah wholeheartedly agreed with Matthew's fervor on the curriculum and in passing, noted that such discussions were also happening at his mosque. "I said to him, 'Wait a minute, you're not Coptic?'" Matthew recounted. Abdallah looked back, puzzled, and replied, "So what?" To Matthew's surprise, Abdallah, even as an Egyptian Muslim in New Jersey, shared much of the same perspectives on family and social values that he did as a Copt. "When you grow up in a Coptic household, you know there is a line between Coptic and Muslim. I realized sitting there talking [to Abdallah], that *there is no line*."[52]

* * *

Sectarian lines have been ambiguously upended by Coptic culture war crusaders in the United States. Yet, despite shared political conservatism, legacies of religious difference from Egypt, as Matthew admits, continue to frame intercommunal imaginaries among American Copts and foment division.[53] Collective memory of Christian persecution from Egypt fuses other forms of colonial devastation under its banner. The reverberating effects of British colonial rule and Euro-American missionary efforts are at once admitted and eschewed, as the ultimate trauma of Islamic oppression takes precedence.

At a swanky Manhattan restaurant owned by a New York Copt, I sat in a booth with two priests in May 2017. I had just returned from a seminar in Washington, DC, on Orthodox theology and the Coptic tradition—meant as a corrective to a heretic in the United States.[54] During the seminar, a participant asked, "Why do we use Protestant materials in our Sunday school curriculum?" and I recounted the exchange in the restaurant. One of the priests retorted, "And we were also using Catholic theology under Pope Shenouda too. We essentially used Catholic books and materials and made them Orthodox." After a moment of realizing what he had said, the priest became frustrated with his own critique and exclaimed, "God, we were raped for 1,400 years! Jesus Christ, it's a miracle we're still existing! Every new sultan that came to power in Egypt would steal all the treasures of the Church, and we would have to rebuild. We dealt with that for centuries! Our history is different from theirs!"

The priest's vibrant response to the Coptic effects of Catholic and Protestant missionary reordering and continued influence on the tradition is directed toward the nature of the comparison. According to him, Copts have dealt with other circumstances and should not be blamed for their pedagogical mix-and-matching. Instead of addressing the Protestant and Catholic missionary contexts that produced such a criterion of credibility, he points to the role of Muslim rule as the site of corruption. Yet the idea that the Coptic Church had been "raped for 1,400 years" is also not a new assertion. It is one that Protestant missionaries made during their time in Egypt.

One such British missionary who lived in Cairo wrote, "Torn with dissensions and political intrigue in the fifth and sixth centuries, [the Copts] offered themselves as an easy prey to the lusty Moslem invaders, swelled with the pride of unbroken victories further East. . . . [Coptic] beliefs are in many respects corrupt, and among the poorer Copts great ignorance prevails and strange superstitions."[55] The image of the Church being raped by Muslims resonated with foreign audiences, who interpreted the Coptic Church as a helpless, ignorant, and feminized institution in need of strong, Western (masculine) leadership and education. These colonial discourses continue to resonate among transnational Copts and impact American Coptic politics, as seen in conservative organizing efforts discussed in this chapter and the diasporic activism in chapter 1. However, while such civilizational discourses could indicate a unidirectional flow, an ever-growing campaign for conservative solidarity is building, especially among the younger generations of American Copts like Matthew, creating new forms of diasporic political subjectivity and social connection.

* * *

In the fall of 2021, the New Jersey governor race was firing up. Republican candidate Jack Ciattarelli became an immediate favorite in the Coptic community, visiting churches from East Brunswick to Cedar Grove. After such appearances, he posted the following to his Facebook: "25 years ago, the Coptic community only had two churches in the state of New Jersey. Today, they have 27 and counting. Coptic values are Republican values; family, faith, lower taxes, opportunity, and security." American Copts enthusiastically shared the post, voicing their support and pride in Republican recognition. Comments from other white community members shaped their alignment with the Copts in relation to their place within the matrix of persecution and family values:

> The Coptic Christians are a courageous and noble people who've faced extreme persecution and tribulation as a minority in the Middle East—yet, they don't play the victim, they build their own prosperity, protect and nurture their own families, and set the example for us to follow.

> Coptic Christians have suffered so much, and their sufferings have been totally ignored by the UN. Coptic Christians are overflowing with love for God, Family and Country!

This underlying kind of "Christian nationalism"—shared between white Christians and American Copts (and many non-white others)—stands in tension with a rising need to form intercommunal alliances to fend off liberal, secular America. Recounting his late-night sheesha lounge meet-up with Abdallah, Matthew expressed regret about the face-off between sectarian legacies from the homeland and conservative alliance formation in diaspora. "We are fighting the same fight. . . . We do have the same values. It doesn't just come down to religion or culture. It comes down to values. . . . There are liberal values and there are conservative values. . . . We actually share common goals here. We're parents. We're religious people. Whatever we are, whatever brings us together, we must really emphasize that instead of just realizing it by happenstance. Me realizing it at a hookah bar at 11 o'clock at night, 'Oh God, we have the same values!'—that is not something I should just realize in passing. . . . How do we combine our efforts to make this a stronger movement?"

"We Live in the Ruins of Christendom"

One afternoon, at a Coptic convent in the New York–New Jersey area, I sat at the kitchen table with Tasoni Makrina, a *mukarasa* (female consecrated servant), and Michelle her colleague at university, a strawberry blonde-haired woman in her late thirties. Michelle had come to visit the convent and the retreat center, formerly owned by Dominican monks and recently purchased by the Coptic Orthodox Church, as a possible meeting location for members of her Episcopal church. Before touring the facilities, we sat around the kitchen and talked about the class they both attended on theology and evangelism. Michelle described how important the class was for her because of the different perspectives that classmates brought to the space. Classmates included a rabbi and an Eritrean Orthodox priest, among others. I asked the two women why knowing theology is so important in contemporary American society. Michelle cited Pew Research's 2014 study on the religious landscape in America.[56] From the study, she recounted that the vast majority of millennials cannot describe their church's perspectives on, for instance, hell or atonement. They have lost this kind of vocabulary or way of thinking in their everyday grammar and form of life. Michelle thought aloud whether it would be better for youth to *know* their theology better (to be able to answer such questions) or, instead, to cultivate religious sensibilities (no matter how those sensibilities are theologically expressed), even if it is a "theistic morality" of sorts.

Tasoni glared at Michelle. "What sensibilities, though, are you talking about?" she asked. She seemed uneasy with the assumption that, for instance, even if Coptic youth become Muslim, at least they retain some orientation to a divine order. Instead of addressing Tasoni's underlying concern about *Truth*, Michelle continued by detailing how different youth are today from what they were a few decades prior. "Unlike older generations, many youth don't engage in the words of atonement, for example. In the future, they will probably instead identify as 'mystics' rather than as Christians." To Michelle, this seemed like a fine proposal. Tasoni's reaction veered between confusion and complete disapproval. Michelle grew up in a small town in the South. She explained that when she was growing up, everyone knew who the bad and good people were. The people who went to church were the ones who were good—they were respectful and of good character. The people who didn't go to church were the ones who were not so good. The difference between these two groups of people, for Michelle, was their attendance at church. However, when she moved to New York City and met people of different religious backgrounds who were good and "holy," her perspective began to change. "I met the most holy Muslims and atheists, and the worst Christians. My perspectives flipped." Tasoni interjected, "What do you mean by 'holy'?" Michelle didn't directly answer the question, only to say that after moving north, she stopped equating "holiness" with churchgoing.

* * *

Transnational Coptic translations of conservatism reflect the changing conditions of religious life and political orientations in the United States, writ large. While Islamic danger and Muslim difference in the lands of immigration looms large for Copts, secular threat continues to pose an even greater concern for the community. "We live in the ruins of Christendom," a Coptic priest from Southern California argued in a webinar for youth in early 2021 entitled "Church vs. State: Godly Citizen under a Secular Master."[57] The absence of (a Christian) God or godly presence in secular institutions concerns evangelicals and Coptic Orthodox alike in the contemporary United States. After recounting the debate over LGBTQ rights and the Equality Act in Congress, the priest connected the absence of God in such proceedings to a new kind of persecution faced by all Christians. Mentioning the twenty-one martyrs of Libya as well as the martyrdom of "millions of Orthodox believers in Russia under the communists, in Greece and Armenia under Turkish fanatics," he directly channeled the exclusion of biblical logic in a secular public sphere into bloody, violent death at the hands of governing authorities:

> Our secular society today continues to betray Christ by denying his divinity and carrying on as though he does not exist. Our secular society is completely lacking that element of personal holiness, that element of seeking God first and offering him the praise and glory that befits him.... You know, brothers and sisters, the days are coming when we may be called upon to witness for Christ. Maybe not through death, but rather perhaps by being cancelled or losing our job or stripped of our degrees because we said something that the current authorities and idealogues don't agree with.

While Coptic translations of the US culture wars are not conscriptions of an imperial retelling (they have Egyptian roots), such translations are shaped by Christian hegemony in the United States, a hegemony that many Coptic migrants are fighting for against secular threat.

Throughout this book, the binds of persecution politics—diasporic activism, migratory possibilities, legal translations, racialized in/exclusions, and conservative intersections—do not exceed other possibilities of representation and narration, beyond blood bond or boundary. The conclusion turns toward other perspectives of witness, unfolding forms of diasporic difference that elucidate Coptic wages in migration.

Conclusion

Wages and Witness

> ... the sanguification of rhetoric has yet to produce
> a world of oceans without shores,
> power without borders,
> blood without walls.
> — Gil Anidjar, *Blood: A Critique of Christianity*

On a warm August afternoon, I sat on a crate as Samuel served customers at his food cart in downtown Manhattan. Samuel came to the United States after 2011 on the Lottery, working nonstop since then, seven days a week, eight hours or more a day. After selling a couple of hot dogs to tourists, he spoke to me of his dissatisfaction with Egyptian Muslims in the United States, even mentioning how one of his close friends from Jersey City was murdered in Atlantic City, allegedly by an Egyptian Muslim. "It's dangerous for us, even in America. There was an entire [Coptic] family murdered in Jersey City back in 2005," he said.

Samuel was referring to the brutal murders of Hossam (age forty-seven), Amal (thirty-seven), Sylvia (fifteen), and Monica (eight) of the Armanious family in Jersey City, which sent shock waves throughout the Coptic community locally and globally, through online chat rooms and diaspora publications. The family had migrated to the United States from Luxor, Upper Egypt, in 1997. On January 11, 2005, family members were found bound and gagged, with their throats slashed and heads stabbed repeatedly. The Armanious family murders lit a spark between Copts and their Egyptian Muslim neighbors in Jersey City. Rumors swarmed that the murders were a hate crime, directly connected to Hossam Armanious's angry exchanges with Muslims in Paltalk messenger chat rooms on Islam. Armanious's Paltalk name was "I Love Jesus," and he said he received death threats from someone in the chat room during an argument

Figure c.1. El Saraya sheesha café, Jersey City, winter 2018. Photo by author.

about Christianity and Islam.¹ Rumors also swirled that a Coptic cross tattoo on fifteen-year-old Sylvia's wrist had been deliberately stabbed.²

The funeral for the family in Jersey City erupted in chaos after local Muslims, clergy and laity, came to pay their respects. Bishop David embraced Sheikh Tarek Yousof Saleh of Bay Ridge, Brooklyn, and Coptic men began shouting at the bishop, berating him for inviting Muslims to attend the service. The bishop and the sheikh were taken away by local police officers into a nearby garage, as the group of Copts continued screaming and waving wooden crosses at the two religious leaders.³

During the somber funeral, Coptic protestors also carried signs reading, "American Family Beheaded on American Soil. Welcome Bin Laden," with a photograph of the smiling family. Other Coptic mourners clashed with the protestors. "Muslims as a group kill people. Nobody else slaughters people. If it was a robbery, why tie their hands and cut their heads?" one Coptic protestor said. Another shouted, "Islam is not a religion!"⁴ "We don't need any talk about Sept. 11 or Muslims!" a Coptic mourner retorted. Inside the church, screams and wails filled the space, which was packed with nearly two thousand people. One man inside the church screamed, "Muslim is the killer! Muslim is the killer!" before he was dragged away by police. Mounir Dawood, then president of the American Coptic Association (ACA), said to reporters that "Muslim terrorists" were to blame.⁵

In March 2005, two suspects were arrested for the murders. They were neither Egyptian nor Muslim. Instead, one was the upstairs neighbor, Edward McDonald, and the other was his friend, Hamilton Sanchez. In 2011 McDonald was sentenced to three hundred years in prison; all charges were dropped against Sanchez in 2009.⁶ Yet in Jersey City even now, suspicions still linger that a Muslim was involved. The murder split Muslim and Christian Egyptians in the diaspora. The El Saraya sheesha café is owned by Copts and caters to local Muslim and Christian Egyptians. It also happens to be right next to the local church's second building for liturgical services. For a time following the murders, the sense of comradery experienced between Copts and Muslims went stagnant, with less frequent interactions between community members at places like El Saraya. Both communities had bonded from a shared immigrant experience; Samuel, for example, works with many Egyptian Muslim immigrants as a food vendor.

* * *

Reverberations from Egyptian contexts of violence have threaded through the translation of Coptic experiences in the United States, where they map such contexts onto new geographies of empire. As a Middle Eastern Christian migrant population in the United States following 9/11, Copts translated the murder of the Armanious family through both collective memory of Christian harm in Egypt and war on terror discourses of Muslim violence. A *New York Times* article published a week after the killing described the tensions this way: "The murder case, while tragic on its own, has opened a wound and produced an outpouring of emotion that even Egyptian Christians and Muslims struggle to explain. The answer is layered: there are old-world grievances, a largely unspoken anger toward Egyptian Muslims after 9/11, and a newfound immigrant power that has left the Egyptian Christians—a repressed minority in Egypt—unafraid to assert their voice here."[7]

Yet the blood of Christian martyrs also *exceeds* these secular framings of migrant translations of religious tradition. The blood of the Armanious family was commemorated as martyrdom; they were described as four "icons from Thebes"—"the city of martyrs" (*madinat al-shuhada'*)—who transfigured in New Jersey.[8] While secular courts found the perpetrator guilty, some Copts refocused the brutal violence against this family—their martyrdom—on their witness to Christ, as renewed icons of Abel. *The voice of your brother's blood cries out to Me from the ground.*[9] While the circumstances of their murder appeared vague to some, Christian witness in their daily lives reframes their murder as martyrdom:

> How can Satan not be hostile to a family that immigrated from Thebes (the city of martyrs) in 1997, not for the pleasure of the flesh, nor to exalt one's life, but rather to testify to Jesus Christ, even if such witness leads to blood[y death]? Is this witness (with the courage of faith, acceptance of the challenge, and the cry of blood) not martyrdom?[10]

*　*　*

As this book has elaborated, Christian tradition and theology of martyrdom, and Coptic collective memory and contemporary experiences of persecution and violence in Egypt have all informed Coptic translations onto diasporic terrain. Yet the Copts are not a diaspora like any other.

Since they are Middle Eastern Christians, their personal experiences and the collective construction of their victimhood under Islamic rule have been utilized by American political, social, legal, as well as economic power structures for imperial expansion—to "save" persecuted Christians both at home and abroad. Transnational Copts—between Egypt and the United States—interface with these discursive constructions of their community in the ways they migrate and the theopolitical forms they inhabit.

To reiterate, transnational Copts are not simply conscripts of empire. Rather, an agential account of empire—of conscripts and resistors—misses its more pervasive and elusive forces. Empire is immanent, not a distant web of power. Therefore, manifestations of empire "are less likely to look like spectacular power plays and more likely to take the form of assimilative exercises structured around affect, attachment, and humanization."[11] These "assimilative exercises" are connected to how contemporary problems are framed and how potential solutions are made possible. In the case of marginalized, minority migrants like Copts, their contemporary problems in Egypt are charged with colonial legacies of subjugation that perpetuate in authoritarian modes of governmentality and ongoing social conditions of anti-Christian violence and sectarian strife. While such problems are shaped by national imperatives and local conditions, they are both transvalued and instrumentalized by Christian conservatives in the United States and beyond and extend through a long history of an economy of blood, where the persecution and martyrdom of Christians are never complete but are part of the very essence of the tradition. The interrelation between this long arc of Christianity and its present manifestation in the United States layers affective conditions and sociopolitical forces at play.

While at times exacerbating national and local problems of violence and death, the United States has also offered refuge from them—for example, in the form of migration from their minority condition in Egypt to the potentiality of being part of a Christian majority in the United States[12]—and refuge through the absorption of their difference into a "hegemonic episteme."[13] While many Copts during my own transnational fieldwork have argued for the benevolence of the United States—in saving Christians and improving socioeconomic life for those in and outside the United States—the subtle ways in which diasporic

Coptic suffering in the form of working-class labor and racial discrimination is sidelined in favor of US hegemony as protector of Christians around the globe speak to how empire can be both the sickness and the remedy. These asymmetries of suffering determine martyrdom—or what is accepted both institutionally and socially as Christian witness (most especially in the form of spilt blood).

As Elizabeth Castelli has argued, focusing on "martyrs"—socially recognized, institutionally sanctioned, or theopolitically expedient—as those who willingly give up their lives keeps attention converged on the narrowest category of victimhood and directs it away from other forms of witness—whether as spilt blood or bloodless sacrifice—"in the ordinary and terrible violence that both characterizes the lives of so much of the world and overwhelms our capacity to apprehend and assimilate its scope and its depth."[14] Recent scholarship has focused on the idea of "Coptic misfits," "those who do not seek to negotiate aspects of the perfect visible image of a Coptic Christian in Egypt today neither as victims nor agents of their identity and faith."[15] While the negotiation of martyrdom within the Coptic community and in relation to the Coptic Orthodox Church is an aspect of the conclusion of this book, the example of the Armanious family or the other examples to follow exceed the idea of "willing" involvement or negotiation into the discursive and geo/theopolitical force of Christian martyrdom, of which Coptic martyrs are one group among many others. Instead, in the final pages of this book, I offer alternative sites of martyrdom in migration to think about Coptic suffering through working-class labor and disappointment from Nashville, Tennessee, a burgeoning Coptic hub of migration from Egypt's rural parts to Jersey City and back to Bahjūra to contemplate the translations of American persecution politics in Egypt's South.

Coptic Southern

"We need 1,000 people."
"I can get you 2,000!"
—John Milad, interviewed by author

In the mid-1990s, Opryland Resorts was building an extension of its Nashville empire around the same time that Coptic immigration increased to New York and New Jersey through the Green Card Lottery. John Milad first settled in New Jersey and then left for Nashville, but kept close ties to his home church in Jersey City. As a supervisor at Opryland, John knew that management was having issues with guest workers. For the expansion, they were looking for cheap laborers with permanent residency. John knew where to go.

In 1995 he contacted his former priest in Jersey City and scheduled job interviews in the basement of the church with Opryland administrators. In between visits, he even produced a video to be played on loop in the basement of the church, advertising the new hotel and water show. The video showcased images of the new development and footage of John himself in a suit and tie. In February 2018, John described to me how he wanted to present himself to the Coptic immigrants and now potential employees: "I told them in the video, 'I started as a waiter, and now I'm a manager. I have a company car. I have a credit card.' I even showed the credit card [on the video]. I wanted to show them that this is the real deal; not a gimmick." But he was also sure to note that images of the dish washing rooms they would ultimately be working in were on display in the advertisement as well.

John curated a new life for migrant Copts, some of whom only found out about the opportunity when they arrived at the Jersey City church from John F. Kennedy International Airport. With suitcases in hand, they slept on the floor of the church basement, waiting for a bus to Nashville the next day. "When they came here [to Nashville], it was like heaven," John exclaimed. "The majority of these people were from Upper Egypt. . . . We rescued these people from squalor to a big, open land." He listed the things these families acquired after starting their jobs: a car, an education, a home. This heaven is the American Dream with ideas of financial success and the promise of Christian belonging.

In Nashville, Copts are estimated to number between ten and twenty thousand, a population that continues to grow.[16] The presence of Copts in Nashville is felt in its thirteen churches and counting, but also in everyday life: Copts work as gas station clerks, airport cleaners, mechanics, bakers, teachers, and sellers of beer and tobacco. They now also make up most of the serving staff at Opryland; Coptic students are the majority at some local schools; and nonprofits focus on directing their efforts to the Coptic community through Arabic translations of materials and advocacy on their behalf at the state level.[17] Copt-owned stores line Murfreesboro Road, which leads from downtown Nashville to downtown Murfreesboro, another large Tennessee city. Such stores advertise Ramadan specials and sell halal meat and fresh produce. L&E Market sees a steady daily stream of Coptic workers utilize its Western Union kiosk to send millions of dollars per year back to their families in al-Minyā and elsewhere in Egypt's South.[18] From factory workers and government employees to even some of the unhoused, Copts are integral to Nashville's working-class landscape.[19]

Within this socioeconomic frame, Nashville's Copts also imagine themselves as a majority compared to Muslim populations, and the imagining of majority speaks to the American dream of Christian supremacy. As in New York and New Jersey, Nashville's Copts are also configured in this tension between their religious belonging (as Christians) and racial difference tinged by class marginalization. The focus on Copts' Christianity and attuning political orientations to the right has left many working-class Copts in peril.

In June 2019, the Elmahaba Center was established to better serve a community caught in the middle—between a conservative Christian culture and Church hierarchy, and working-class needs unfulfilled.[20] Using a unique mixture of social media, archiving, and service, the center has focused on community building across a myriad of intersectional obstacles. Over the years, Copts have become a sizable worker population, for example, in the Tyson Foods factories throughout Tennessee. In particular, the factory in Goodlettsville, Tennessee, has faced sharp criticism for its neglect of Coptic workers and others during the COVID-19 pandemic. Copts in Antioch had been favored employees with the support of the local church, after the mostly Somali workforce at another Tyson factory plant in Shelbyville started unionizing. Even though Coptic workers also complained about working conditions, intercommunal division prevented them and Somali workers from organizing together. When the pandemic hit, Tyson covered up that workers had contracted the virus and forced them to work without protection.[21]

A month after the first Tyson factory case, dozens of Copts from the community contracted the virus. Yet the Church did not step in to advocate for Coptic workers. The Coptic Orthodox Church has typically been the main representative of Copts in Egypt and abroad. But as new generations of Copts grow up in diaspora, there is even greater potential for the flourishing of diverse approaches to Copticity.[22] As has been documented in other discussions among ethnic studies scholars around identity and diaspora, Coptic communities in the United States and elsewhere have refused a singular core (focused on religion, language, or race) that legitimizes a unified Coptic politics—even despite the pervasive imperial force of persecution politics outlined in the chapters of this book.[23] Coptic community contains and engages with multiple political possibilities and can be the site of ongoing contestation as new forms of life emerge in the diasporic imagination.[24]

* * *

I met Lydia Yousief, founder of the Elmahaba Center, in early 2021 at a strip plaza in South Nashville.[25] As we sat on a bench, a weekly festival was taking place around us, with vibrant music and children playing in the background of our conversation on Elmahaba and the future of Coptic Nashville. In Nashville, the nonprofit sector has struggled to recognize the Copts and has not had a vested interest in Arabic-speaking peoples, especially those not part of Arab Muslim communities. On the other end, the Coptic Church steered Copts away from engaging in or donating to organizations outside the clerical confines of the community. At issue for Coptic organizers like Lydia has been the lack of accountability and transparency to help the working class: "The Church spent over a million dollars on land and buildings during a pandemic when thousands of Coptic people were on unemployment and couldn't feed their kids."

Beyond the clerical push for more land and property, Lydia's main concern has been the Church's desire to be the diasporic liaison between the Copts and white people, as if recycling a civilizing mission from colonial Egypt. "You can see this dynamic in the language they [Church officials] use—'these people are uneducated, backward. They come from southern Egypt; they don't even know how to clean a carpet. We're not able to help all these people because they are ignorant.'" The Church administers the community among the major government institutions of Nashville, from the police to the mayor's office. The lack of accountability from the Church to the most precarious Copts originates in its monopoly on Coptic identity and its supremacy to decide what community concerns *should* be. This dynamic of social isolation is something Elmahaba seeks to challenge through the establishment of new forms of communal solidarity with other marginalized people.

During our conversation Lydia noted that nonprofits in Nashville have been more interested in Kurds from Iraq, for example, because they organize around Muslim identity, which involves other racially and religiously marginalized Muslim communities in the area and beyond it, and many of them are from the middle-upper classes of Nashville's suburbs, allowing for greater intra-communal socioeconomic solidarity. Many Copts, by contrast, are caught in the middle, as Christian immigrants from the Middle East, religiously similar to conservative regional forces yet racially marginalized along with other Middle Eastern and Muslim migrants, *and* as working-class poor. The idea of the model minority for the American Coptic community has produced a fraught predicament. Upper-class Copts shy away from Coptic working-class communities to distance themselves from minority failure. "I didn't think there were people who slept on the floor, but these are children and parents. They are going into debt to get their first car and then you have these upper-class people in Nashville who think they're going to save themselves and this community by saying, 'We're rich. We don't need help.'"

The Church has eschewed efforts to build intercommunal solidarities beyond the white Christian upper class. Because of this, working-class Copts who have the same interests as other working-class poor (which disproportionately include Black and Brown communities) in Nashville—from unionization efforts to housing—are isolated. The Church has also exacerbated this isolation, especially regarding unionization. "Priests will say in a sermon, 'Don't cooperate [with other communities]. You have to be distinct.' They might not say it explicitly, but everyone knows who they are talking about—Muslims." This is not to say that the Coptic working classes passively engage this rhetoric. It structures their immigration story, echoing what Matthew, the Coptic American PAC candidate in New Jersey, described in chapter 5. "A lot of Coptic people in Nashville feel emboldened; they feel like 'We are part of the majority here, so I can now say bad things about Muslims very openly and not have any fear of retaliation.' For them, *that* is freedom. So, the more I can say I'm not unionizing with Muslims—*that's* freedom, because they feel disdain, and this is something the employer plays on."

At the Tyson Factory in Goodlettsville, owners directly relayed their recruitment efforts to the Coptic clerical hierarchy. They specifically targeted the Coptic community, knowing that it would be difficult for them to organize with their Somali co-workers. In the Shelbyville plant, Hispanic and Somali workers had come together to unionize, and Tyson factory owners wanted to prevent this in other locations across the region. Owners and management at Tyson Foods played on Coptic trauma by, for example, wishing them a blessed Ramadan or confusing Coptic names with Muslim ones.[26] Coptic workers are placed in a bind by the clerical hierarchy and upper-class Copts, who both perpetuate a model minority narrative and utilize persecution politics for their own socioeconomic gains.

Elmahaba has tried to combat this bind through a new idea of power. "We don't believe that power is given or derived, but rather power is shared, and power is at its greatest when the many hold it."[27] It is through community engagement on street corners, in homes, and through mutual aid that power is built and shared by the many. This has jointly meant working beyond the Coptic community to build working-class migrant solidarities. In 2021 Elmahaba began organizing with Spanish-speaking and Somali communities who have intersecting issues with Arabic-speaking neighbors like the Copts. On issues ranging from workers' rights, school resources in South Nashville, and affordable healthcare to dignified housing, the organization is creating a vision for a future in tension with the politics of persecution outlined in this book that have sutured Copts into certain narratives and representations between Egypt and the United States.

Elmahaba has connected transnational modes of power to remap community onto new terrains of legibility. The organization has argued that sectarianism, while a term usually associated with Egypt and the Middle East more broadly, is a "divide-and-conquer" strategy also deployed in the United States as well. Both Muslims and Christians are subjected to figurations of racialization—whether within security infrastructures or in everyday life—and set in opposition to one another to earn full social citizenship. And government bodies and nonprofit organizations tend to lean on religious leaders for the allocation of resources and services, showing preferences for one identity over the other. In light of these dynamics, how does Elmahaba address and counteract such reimagined sectarian logics in Nashville? By empowering community leaders who are not "identity-driven, but rather community-driven," by not participating in "religious in-fighting, Islamophobic, or anti-Christian rhetoric," and by helping "anyone who approaches us—Orthodox, Protestant, Catholic, Sunni, Shia from Egypt or Iraq or Mexico or Somalia. Sectarianism is a symptom of imperial powers and exploitation. We are fighting back."[28]

In February 2021, Elmahaba wrote the following on its Instagram page: "Coptic people do suffer in the US. They are the working class who put food on the tables in the US, but can hardly feed their own children. They are the ones without healthcare. They are the ones the bank won't give a loan to. They are racialized, segregated, isolated in Nashville, and those narratives will not be erased for the sake of the MODEL CHRISTIAN narrative."[29]

In *Black Reconstruction in America*, W. E. B. Du Bois contended that whiteness operated as a "public and psychological wage," bestowing upon impoverished whites in the nineteenth and early twentieth centuries a valuable social status derived from their opposition to "Black" classification.[30] The central assertions within this thesis include the idea that whiteness offers meaningful "compensation" (as termed by Du Bois) to individuals otherwise exploited by the structures of capitalism; that the worth of whiteness relies on the devaluation of Black existence; and that the advantages experienced by whites extend beyond mere monetary gains. This layered problem space has significantly influenced subsequent attempts to conceptualize white identity and to comprehend the (non)formation of radical political coalitions in the United States.[31] Coptic wages in Nashville's context have meant that some working-class members of the community have focused on the evasion of exploitation rather than its confrontation. Yet, through Elmahaba and other grassroots organizations and networks in and outside Nashville, Copts are contesting the politics of persecution through new forms of labor solidarity and radical kin formations and coalitions in opposition to racialized marginalization and capitalist hegemony.

Promise and Peril

Shenoda came to the United States from Alexandria in 2013 on the Green Card Lottery. In Alexandria, he owned a law firm and taught at the Faculty of Law at Alexandria University in his spare time. He applied for the Green Card Lottery seeking better education and job opportunities for his two children, and won. Upon arrival in New Jersey, though, he fell into a deep depression at the difficulty of finding work and did not leave his home for six months until he eventually began working as a taxi driver. A local Coptic store owner selling religious goods—from liturgical vestments to icons—offered Shenoda a job as a stocker in his store. In late 2020, I visited the store to purchase a few things with a local priest. With masks on due to the COVID-19 pandemic, we stood at a distance while we spoke. Shenoda had plastic bags tied around his jeans' belt loops from unpacking the merchandise. Sensing his pride in his children's success in the United States, yet alienation (*ghurba*) from the isolation that his life had become, I asked him about his time in Alexandria practicing and teaching law.[32] His eyes welled up in sadness, and mine did as well. Before we could continue our conversation, the store manager called to Shenoda to ask him a question, and he went off to work.

* * *

Many Copts, like many other Egyptians, dream of immigrating abroad, and many act on such dreams.[33] Their desire to migrate may only seem like a response to Copts' religious positioning and persecution in a Muslim-majority society—that is, a desire to escape religious persecution and government corruption by emigrating from Egypt. However, Copts across Egypt also layer their desire to permanently migrate to places like the United States with the hope of economic and social success abroad—something Egypt cannot offer them, most especially as Copts. Socioeconomic despair is compounded by the social disparities Copts structurally experience in Egypt. Imagining the United States as a promise of religious (Christian) freedom and economic progress circulates through Coptic kin networks over social media and everyday communication with those in the United States or visiting from it for summer vacations. It is in these flows of information among transnational Coptic communities that the possibilities offered in immigration to the United States are channeled through the corruption of the Egyptian state, but also by the dissemination of US imperial power in the form of economic aspiration and in the reshaping of religious life and sectarian relations at home and abroad in the most subtle ways.

* * *

In August 2021, I returned to Bahjūra after an extended absence due to the COVID-19 pandemic. Walking along the winding dirt pathways of Shig al-Naṣāra, I arrived at the local church with two teenage girls, Julia and Maria, to reunite with Lottery administrators, clergy members, and the local church librarian. I walked up to the second floor of the church and through the door of the small room that was the administration headquarters of the Lottery. Maurice was not expecting me and had an enormous smile of surprise on his face. He was eager to show me all the applications he had completed the previous fall, arranged by family name on his desktop. "This person won last year, and this one, and this one too!" he announced enthusiastically. One of the clergy members was notified of my arrival and picked me up from Maurice's office. Abouna Luka was eager to tell me of his recent return from South Carolina. In 2018 I had met Abouna Luka in Jersey City during another visit of his to the United States to search for a way to have his sons immigrate for high school, and he has petitioned church administration on many occasions to offer him a position there.

After nearly an hour sitting in Abouna Luka's office drinking orange Fanta and observing the cycle of parishioners coming in to ask for prayers and blessings for upcoming travel, whether to Cairo, Kuwait, or the United States, I departed for the library and church archive on the second floor. Gamil greeted me at the entrance, and was just as surprised to see me as Maurice had been. He immediately showed me around the new acquisitions and lamented the lack of funds to preserve new periodicals he had acquired. Although I had visited the library several times before, I had only just noticed a closed bookcase toward the front of the room with a sign notifying visitors that they could not check out those books. I inquired why. Gamil opened the cabinet and retrieved one of the books, an Arabic translation of the second edition of *By Their Blood: Christian Martyrs of the Twentieth Century* by James and Marti Hefley from 1996.³⁴ "We need to be careful. A book like this could start *fitna* [civil strife or violent conflict] against Christians in Bahjūra. So we keep it safe in the library and are careful with who reads such books."

The book cover shows two hands holding the world with the Arabic translation of the title *By Their Blood* (*Bidamā'hum*), dripping red droplets onto the world. In the epilogue of the second edition, the authors write, "Whatever the political changes, repression of Christianity will continue. Martyrdoms may even occur in America where a cultural and moral war is now raging between biblical morality and hedonistic immorality. Whatever comes, believers will be heartened by God's promises in Holy Scripture that His kingdom will prevail."³⁵

* * *

This book has argued that local and national considerations of violence and memory are already scaled by transnational and global translations of religious difference. By rethinking Christianity and US empire through Coptic minority migration, this book has sought a new understanding of how contemporary religious life is uncontainable in either local or national frames within a globalized world of asymmetrical power circuits. Among Copts, the geopolitical refractions of American hegemony through pathways of migration as well as globally mediatized understandings of Christian suffering unfold in the ordinary affects of imperial persecution politics. With the focus of Western Christians, policy makers, and Coptic diasporic communities themselves on the varied experiences of violence against Egyptian Copts, some of those very Copts question the uneven attention on narratives of bloodshed in Egypt.

Back in Bahjūra, Amin asked me over breakfast in the summer of 2021, "Why do they say things are violent here? There are of course incidents that are happening—kidnappings, church burnings—but what about in America in places like Chicago? There is more violence there than here." Amin and other Copts in Bahjūra voiced their frustration at the constant focus of the diaspora and Western politicians on violence against Copts that perpetuated narratives of instability and intercommunal intolerance in regions like Upper Egypt. They pointed to wanton gun violence in the United States and anti-Black racism as examples of cracks in the veneer of America's promise of a better life.³⁶ What is absent from the entrenched politics of persecution and martyrologies of Christian suffering are the wages and witness of migration that exceed such narratives and representations of perennial religious violence. While both acknowledging and attending to the pervasive discriminations that Christians face in Egypt, many of those Christians also know the dangers—both lethal and less-than-lethal—that lie ahead for them in the United States.[37] While awaiting the hope of showcasing migrant resistance to these imperial formations or the openings up to possibility and production in diaspora is a worthy endeavor, its preference displaces the gaze from the structural flows of blood, destruction, and despair that shape the lifeworlds of so many migrants.[38] This book has traced the destructive forces of migration, attending to how violence and sacrifice translate across national and imperial formations, from Egypt to the United States and back again. Copts in migration evince how movement into the abyss both evokes promise and peril. While offering the promise of freedom, justice, and witness, migration also wages exile and alienation, a white (bloodless) martyrdom for uncertain futures of prosperity and possibility.

ACKNOWLEDGMENTS

This book is the end of a very long and winding chapter, which I would not have concluded without the combined care and support of the people mentioned in the following pages. I would be remiss not to thank those who initially inspired the questions I pursued between Egypt and the United States, beginning in Heliopolis, Cairo, almost two decades ago. Mina, Ikram, Nadi, and Mariam, thank you for laying the spiritual foundations of this book. In 2012 I met the people who would sharpen my focus and enliven my heart toward social justice. Abouna Mattias, Ramy, Beshoy, Tony, Mina, Armia, Mariam, and Vivian, your revolutionary courage and strength inspired me to be bold enough to travel with the questions I pursue here.

The specific research for this book would not have been possible without the people of Bahjūra past and present. There, I met the kindest people who challenged my preconceptions of Christian-Muslim relations in Egypt and pushed me to believe in the power of miracles and hope in a world yet to be realized. To the families who opened their homes to me, thank you for sharing meals, laughs, and your histories. I await the years to come, watching your children grow and your lives flourish—there or elsewhere.

I am also indebted to the Coptic communities of New York and New Jersey, and especially the Coptic Diocese of New York and New England. To Bishop David and so many clergy throughout the region, without you much of this work would not have been possible. I am particularly thankful to Jersey City's clergy, recent immigrants, and so many others who welcomed me into their community with open arms. Research in New York and New Jersey would not have been the same without close friends to share hours of conversation over food, tea, and sheesha—thank you, Essam, Basma, and Kerollos. I am also thankful to the clergy of the Diocese of Los Angeles, Southern California, and Hawaii, Coptic activists, and members of the community there who spoke candidly with me, offering helpful comparisons to my primary work in New York and New Jersey.

Many thanks to the Coptic community of Nashville, Tennessee, as well, for offering honest insights into the geographical differences of Coptic belonging in the United States; I am especially grateful to Lydia Yousief, Sue, and Bassam. Elhamy Khalil offered his entire archive of photos, video, and notes on early Coptic immigration to North America. The St. Shenouda Society of North America, and specifically Hany Takla, provided me with a significant number of *The Copts* newsletters used in this book, especially for chapter 1. Cornelius Hulsman completed my archive of the newsletter, as well as other archival documents that contributed to the historical analysis that frames several chapters.

The intellectual development of this book originated in the Department of Anthropology at the University of California, Berkeley, initially under the supervision of Saba Mahmood and later Charles Hirschkind. There is much to say on what Saba taught me about religious difference, the minority concept, and secularism. But it was/is her sharp lens of critique that continues to challenge me more than anything. Her memory has left a haunting presence in everything I write, every argument I piece together. Her insight and unwavering critiques propel me to go deeper, work harder. There will never be adequate words to describe my ongoing heartbreak. After Saba's passing, Charles Hirschkind showed me what an advisor could be under the hardest of circumstances; I learned sincere and dedicated mentorship from him. Through his close reading, I was able to highlight the broader conditions of power that underlie this work. At Charles's home, our writing group with Brent Eng, Ashwak Hauter, Mohamad Jarada, Patricia Kubala, Rosa Norton, and Ian Steele aided in writing the early versions of this book from start to finish. I am grateful for the evenings spent reminiscing on fieldwork in Egypt, the insightful comments on different chapter stages, and the consistency that such a space provided over years of writing.

At Berkeley, Stefania Pandolfo and Bill Hanks encouraged me to think about trauma and language. Samera Esmeir and Jonathan Sheehan provided careful interventions to better frame questions about Christianity and colonialism. Maria Mavroudi sharpened my understandings of religious institutions, knowledge production, and power. Beyond this, Maria has always been a beloved mentor, opening her home to conversation and laughter. Mayanthi Fernando offered new perspectives on religion, secularism, and migration that inspired how this book came together. Suad Joseph's writing group in Davis, California provided me with insightful feedback on this book's research.

Sultan Doughan and Hannah Waits have been thoughtful and supportive voices throughout many different stages of life at Berkeley and beyond it. Brittany Birberick is a friend, confidant, and honest critic, who aided my thinking about the paradoxicality of the martyr and the migrant. I was and have been equally sustained by the friendship and engagement of Lana Salman and Deellan Khanaka. From the Bay Area to Chicago, Callie Maidhof has been a companion and guiding spirit, challenging me to think about religion and secularism in new ways.

During my time at Berkeley, I was first introduced to the subfield of the anthropology of Christianity. Andreas Bandak, Matthew Engelke, and Joel Robbins were generous with their time. Special thanks to Jon Bialecki, James Bielo, Naomi Haynes, and Hillary Kaell for including me in the Anthropology of Christianity Bibliographic blog as a co-curator, where I was able to open new horizons of inquiry into the asymmetries of global Christianity. Before Berkeley, my interest in anthropology was sparked by Christopher Lee at Canisius College in Buffalo, New York, who shaped my ethnographic sensibility that channeled itself into the Department of Middle Eastern, South Asian, and African Studies (MESAAS) at Columbia University, with support from Timothy Mitchell and Hamid Dabashi. I am also grateful for conversations with and encouragement from Lila Abu-Lughod. Although we did not work together at Columbia, Gil Anidjar has been a formidable interlocutor in conversations on religion, Christianization, and empire.

In the development of my initial research questions for this book, Paul Sedra and Febe Armanios shared ideas, suggestions, and critiques. Anthony Shenoda provided spiritual guidance, intellectual engagement, and honesty. Within the field of Coptic studies, I would be remiss not to thank Saad Michael Saad, Hany Takla, Mary Ghattas, Nelly van Doorn-Harder, Magdi Guirguis, Samuel Kaldas, Bishop Suriel, Maged Mikhail, Carolyn Ramzy, Joseph Youssef, and Gaétan du Roy for varyingly engaging my work. Emmanuel Gergis has held me accountable to its theological aspects.

Mina Ibrahim has offered sharp insights on this project. For his intellectual comradery, I am grateful. Weston Bland has been a long-term conversation partner from my earlier research on Coptic political movements and our shared experiences in the labyrinth of Dar al-Kutub. During fieldwork, Mirna Wasef and Miray Philips helped me think through and challenge typical narratives and representations of Copts. Adjacent to Coptic studies, Heather Sharkey has been a generous mentor for thinking about Christianity in the Middle East. I am particularly grateful to the Orthodox Christian Studies Center at Fordham University for offering a space to develop my interest in the intersection of Orthodox Christian studies and anthropology. George Demacopoulos and Aristotle "Telly" Papanikolaou have encouraged more rigorous study of Oriental Orthodox Christianity and have generously included me in projects and conversations within the center, for which I am most appreciative.

Simon Coleman has been sharp in his interventions and always kind in his approach, making surprising connections, suggesting unexpected literature, and being a dependable interlocutor. Michael Allan, Noah Salomon, and Kabir Tambar have helped me think through aspects of this project and refine the book's central thread around blood and martyrdom. During the COVID-19 lockdown, I connected with Jason Bruner and learned enormously from his work on Christianity, power, and persecution. I am grateful to Jason for introducing me to David Kirkpatrick and for their support of this project. Zainab Saleh has offered care and insight into the larger stakes of the book, and she has also exhibited thoughtful mentorship for more broadly considering the connections between US empire and diaspora.

At the John C. Danforth Center on Religion and Politics at Washington University in St. Louis, R. Marie Griffith and Leigh Eric Schmidt were incredibly supportive and encouraging as I navigated revisions and rethought this project in the middle of a pandemic. The center's faculty and staff were a beacon of light during a dark time. I am grateful to David Warren and especially Tazeen Ali for welcoming me to St. Louis with love and being a sounding board for various aspects of this project. I would be remiss not to mention my incredible friends and cohort members—Christina Davidson, Andrew Walker-Cornetta, and Alexia Williams—who provided me with a much-needed support system. I will greatly cherish those two years in St. Louis.

My friends and colleagues in other institutions have provided me with valuable comments on the book and its arguments, invited me to talks, and offered support, especially Lloyd Barba, Jennifer Brinkerhoff, Sargon Donabed, Reyhan Durmaz, Nada El-Kouny, Nicholas Denysenko, Clayton Goodgame, Susan Harding, Hsain Ilahiane, Pantelis Kalaitzidis, Frederick Klaits, Nicholas Lackenby, Ussama Makdisi, Leonard Cornell McKinnis II, Diego Maria Malara, Valentina Napolitano, Joshua Ralston, Aaron Rock-Singer, Elizabeth Shakman Hurd, Adam Stern, Mariz Tadros, Stanley Thangaraj, Sonja Thomas, and Joshua Urich. I am especially grateful to Angie Heo for her sharp suggestions and comments on this project over the years.

I would like to thank Jennifer Hammer, who saw the potential in my work in 2019 and was dedicated to this project's development. I am also very grateful to Laura Levitt, who introduced me to Jennifer and started this project on its journey to publication. I would also like to thank the anonymous reviewers for their valuable feedback. Deborah Thomas left her mark on this book by guiding its central argument by way of my 2021 *American Anthropologist* article. I am grateful to Hallie Wells, who has been a thorough editor.

My colleagues in the Departments of Philosophy and Religion, as well as Anthropology and Middle Eastern Cultures, at Mississippi State University have offered laughter and kindness during transitions and the trenches of revision. The American Examples program and faculty in the Department of Religious Studies at the University of Alabama have also been generous with their feedback and support. There are various colleagues who have generously read through sections of this book, including Carole McGranahan and Aaron Michka, who both pushed me to think more deeply about the interventions of this project on empire, and martyrdom, blood, and Christianity, respectively. Christopher Sheklian and Sarah Bakker Kellogg have read the entirety of the manuscript and several revised sections many times over the years, and I am indebted to their sharp analysis and connections between kinship, transnationalism, and the minority concept. Melani McAlister has long been a supporter of this project, but more than that, much of this work would not have been possible without her own groundbreaking scholarship on American evangelicals, power, and persecution.

I am especially indebted to the work of Michael Akladios. As a friend and co-researcher, he has been a central part of telling this story and laying out the stakes. Amy Fallas has been a dear friend in this project and beyond it. Milad Odabaei and Jean-Michel Landry have continued to be sharp readers of my work. Aaron Eldridge has been consistent spiritual kin and a generous reader. Thank you for your honesty in all things and for pushing the red thread of blood in this book. Basit Iqbal, words fail me in describing how much your friendship has meant to me. Always a levelheaded and patient interlocutor, you have been there when I needed a laugh or encouragement. Sarah Riccardi-Swartz has been my Orthodox studies partner for several years. In her, I have found a lifelong colleague, and more than this, a friend to share in the highs and lows of life.

Finally, I thank my family for their continued support in every twist and turn my life has taken. I would specifically like to thank my mother, Donna, my heart. To my grandmother Janet, you have been a home in the middle of many storms. And to my grandfather, Joseph, who was always my biggest champion. My final expression of gratitude is to my husband, Mina. You have guided this project over many years as friend and partner—in countless ways, I cannot imagine having written this book without you.

* * *

Research for this project was funded by the Henry R. Luce Initiative on Religion and International Affairs, the Social Science Research Council, the Andrew W. Mellon Foundation, the American Academy of Religion, the Berkeley Center for the Study of Religion, the Center for Middle East Studies, the Institute of International Studies, and the Department of Anthropology at the University of California, Berkeley. My writing was enabled by the Louisville Institute, the Research Fellowship in Coptic Orthodox Studies from Fordham University's Orthodox Christian Studies Center, the John C. Danforth Center on Religion and Politics at Washington University in St. Louis, and the Social Science Research Council's Religion, Spirituality, and Democratic Renewal Fellowship in partnership with the Fetzer Institute. This book was also supported by my participation as a Senior Fellow in the "Orthodoxy and Human Rights" project, sponsored by Fordham University's Orthodox Christian Studies Center, and generously funded by the Henry R. Luce Foundation and Leadership 100. My final steps to publication were supported by the American Association of University Women and the Department of Philosophy and Religion at Mississippi State University.

Adapted and revised materials from this book appear in a variety of academic publications (including *American Anthropologist* and the *International Journal of Middle East Studies*) and public scholarship pieces, which are included in the bibliography for ease of reference.

NOTES

INTRODUCTION

Portions of this chapter are derived from Candace Lukasik, "Economy of Blood: The Persecuted Church and the Racialization of American Copts," *American Anthropologist* 123, no. 3 (2021): 565–77.

1. Counting Copts in Egypt is a matter of ongoing debate. The Coptic Orthodox Church has estimates as high as 15 percent, with yet other sources noting figures as low as 6 percent of the population. See Hackett 2011 for an analysis.
2. Throughout this book, I use the term "evangelical" as a political construction, and one connected to institutional power. Conservative white Protestants, led by Christian Right organizations, have been key players in cultivating the Persecuted Church moral imaginary, especially as it pertains to Muslims and Middle Eastern Christians. Within the broader framework of American evangelicalism, Catholics, Jews, Eastern Orthodox Christians, Episcopalians, and other Protestants have also participated in such a coalition of the faithful guided by evangelical aesthetics, sensibilities, passions, and politics.
3. In 1854 American Presbyterian missionaries arrived in Egypt as part of a larger Anglo-American Protestant movement for global evangelization. Scaffolded by British colonial power and subsequent American imperial influence, the missionary movement flourished in Egypt. After initially targeting Muslims for conversion, American missionaries set their sights on Egypt's Copts for reform as well as conversion. See Sharkey 2008; as well as Sedra 2011. See also McAlister 2018, 10.
4. Marzouki 2016.
5. Throughout this book I employ "economy" as metaphor, not as a theological concept. I articulate economy as circulation with a full set of parameters, interchanges, and interworkings, and that also structures a theological consideration of blood as martyrdom. Economy is a methodological way to consider martyrdom as the activity of the divine in the world, as a "touch event" between the divine and the worldly (see Napolitano 2020). This book's formulation of economy can certainly be related to a theological conception of economy as the divine in the world and in history. As Orthodox theologian John D. Zizioulas in *Being as Communion* writes, "The fact that man in the Church is the 'image of God' is due to the *economy* of the Holy Trinity, that is, the work of Christ and the Spirit in *history*" (19). Yet this book does not address economy as Christ's salvific activity in the world through the Holy Spirit and enacted in history. For more on the divine economy, see especially Mondzain 2005, 20–66. "The economy is the

historical modality of the configuration of truth for fallen souls, and that until the end of time" (48).

6 Communion, for the Christian, refers to the eucharistic bread and wine that become the Body and Blood of Jesus Christ, precisely at the heart of the economy discussed above. It also refers to the idea that certain churches and denominations are "in communion" with each other, an ecclesial extension of the eucharist. This idea of communion has been one of the main metaphors of Christian kinship throughout the ages, defining relationships between different church hierarchies. As with economy, these theological ideas about communion are *not* the main way that I explore ideas of kinship. I thank Christopher Sheklian for suggesting I draw the distinction between "economy" as metaphor and as theological concept, as well as "communion" in the context of this book.

7 1 Corinthians 15:54 (New King James Version). See Rogers 2021, 10.

8 Rogers 2021, 75.

9 This book argues that blood should be understood as an analytical device and ethnographic artifact that has a polysemy—a slippage between the theological importance of Christ's Blood in salvation, material blood in actual veins, and the importance of Blood as spiritual kinship among my Coptic interlocutors observed across different sites. In turn, I have deployed blood as a conceptual tool that has enabled an analysis of the various scales of transnational connection and translation. I thank Sarah Bakker Kellogg for encouraging this clarification on "blood" as the through-line in this book.

10 Anidjar 2014, 53–58.

11 Steinmetz-Jenkins 2014.

12 Anidjar 2015.

13 For another, adjacent context of the idea of transvaluation, see Dulin 2017. In conversation with the work of Stanley Tambiah (1996), Dulin argues that "'transvaluation refers to the parallel process of assimilating particulars to a larger, collective, more enduring, and therefore less context-bound cause or interest.' . . . In short, transvaluation consists of an uptick in imaginative scale" (786).

14 There are other formations of Coptic community in diaspora that think about persecution and oppression in relation with other minoritized peoples in the United States (and Canada). See Morsi 2021; M. Ramzy 2023. This is briefly explored in the conclusion but is *not* the central focus of this book.

15 For a similar formulation in the context of a geopolitics of concern for LGBT rights in Iran, see Franke 2012.

16 For more on these narratives of collective memory, see Heo 2018; C. Ramzy 2015; A. Shenoda 2012; J. Youssef 2013.

17 Castelli 2006.

18 As cited in Bayne 2021, 11.

19 As cited in Bayne 2021, 12.

20 Oliphant 2021, 588.

21 See the following Coptic perspective on the theological importance of the martyr: "The red and bloody fruit of the Vine, which once ran down the wood of the cross, now runs down our stiff and wooden hearts, making them flow with life once more. When, in weakness, our minds overlook this, the ever-spilling blood of the Christian martyrs serves to remind us of Christ's inconceivable sacrifice, which was offered to vivify His creation. His blood, shed for the sake of love, gave us life; their blood, shed for the sake of Love Himself, encourages us to live out lives of heartening renewal." Marcos 2021, 9.
22 Tert. Apolog. 50.15–16.
23 As evidenced through the Donatist controversy, where elements of this movement centered around the will to martyrdom, of seeing martyrdom as the supreme Christian virtue. I thank Aaron Michka for drawing me to the contentions around martyrdom in the early Church.
24 Saint Ignatius of Antioch channels this ambiguity in his desire for martyrdom that balances between a profound sign of holiness or self-glory. "Wherefore he rejoiced over the tranquil state of the Church, when the persecution ceased for a little time, but was grieved as to himself, that he had not yet attained to a true love to Christ, nor reached the perfect rank of a disciple. For he inwardly reflected, that the confession which is made by martyrdom, would bring him into a yet more intimate relation to the Lord." See "The Martyrdom of Ignatius" in *Early Church Fathers: Ante-Nicene Fathers*, vol. 1, n.d., www.tertullian.org. Again, I thank Aaron Michka for these helpful insights.
25 This question pertains to the idea of white martyrdom—or monasticism and strict asceticism—as well as dying for Christ without the shedding of blood, in everyday life. I turn again to a Coptic perspective on bloodless martyrdom from Anthony Marcos's *A Spring in the Sinai*: "If not chosen for literal bloodshed, a Christian is called to be metaphorically slaughtered, engaging in an on-going war with the world. Only then does he merit wearing the crown encrusted with the precious stones of his struggles" (2021, 10).
26 McAllister and Napolitano 2021, 110. See also Furani 2019; Lemons 2018; and Robbins 2020.
27 McAllister and Napolitano 2021, 110.
28 McAllister and Napolitano 2020, 7.
29 Instead of uncovering the "myth" of persecution or the "invention" of martyrdom (from the early Church to the contemporary moment), this book thinks about both concepts as many Christians do and contends with their theopolitical presence and asymmetrical contestations on earth. For an opposing framework to this, see Moss 2013, whose introduction inaccurately deploys the example of Coptic Christian retaliation after the bombing of the al-Qudisiyyn Church in Alexandria, Egypt, on New Year's Eve 2011 to unveil how *all* Christians—from contemporary Egypt to the early Church and back to the United States—"invent" their marginalization and "imagine" martyrdom.
30 McAllister and Napolitano 2020, 2. See also Agamben 2013; and Kotsko 2018.

31 McAllister and Napolitano 2020, 13.
32 This is unlike religious concerns with death among Muslims, "thought to be indicative of social morbidity leading to destructive and self-destructive behavior." For a different reading on Islamic theologies of martyrdom, see Hirschkind 2008.
33 Asad 2007, 87, quoted in Gamble 2003, 153.
34 Bynum 2007.
35 Anidjar 2014, 145.
36 Bynum 2007, 81.
37 Bynum 2007, 192.
38 McKinnon and Cannell 2017, esp. 28–36.
39 Schneider 1984.
40 Thomas, Malik, and Wellman 2017, viii. Major examples include Carsten 1995; Strathern 1985; McKinnon 1991; and Weston 1991.
41 Wellman 2021, 6.
42 Burton 2021.
43 For more on blood as a lens for thinking about paradoxical entanglement, see Carsten 2019, 6–16.
44 Heo 2018, 39.
45 As discussed by Geertz 1973, 104–6.
46 T. Thomas 2021, 104–5, drawing from Carsten 2000.
47 Sahlins 2013, 28.
48 For example, see Ikeuchi 2019; and S. Thomas 2019.
49 C. Ramzy 2015.
50 Papaconstantinou 2006.
51 Armanios 2011, 132, as cited in C. Ramzy 2015, 658.
52 Heo 2018, 107–41.
53 A. Shenoda 2010, 256.
54 Burton 2021.
55 Reid 2002.
56 Dowell 2015.
57 All interlocutor names throughout this book are pseudonyms, unless otherwise indicated or unless they are public figures.
58 B. Carter 1986, 96.
59 B. Carter 1986, 119n38.
60 B. Carter 1986, 96.
61 Quoted in Jacobson 1999, 145.
62 B. Fields 1990. For more on the idea of the "heathen," see Lum 2022.
63 Earl of Cromer 1908, 202.
64 Earl of Cromer 1908, 203.
65 Earl of Cromer 1908, 203, 206; the secondary quote is from Klunzinger 1878, 89.
66 Horbury 2003, 156–57.
67 Mikhail 1911, viii, x.

68 For an example from Orientalist writing in Egypt during the late nineteenth and early twentieth centuries, see Leeder 1918.
69 *Egypt*, April 11, 1911, 11, as cited in Horbury 2003.
70 "Maven Developments' Cali Coasts" 2022; Erol 2023; Salomon 2021, 300.
71 See Gillem 2007; Khalidi 2005; and Roy 2004. More recently, ethnographic inquiry has begun to fill this void; see Simpson 2014; Vine 2015; and Dewachi 2017.
72 Thinking about US empire through militarization and specifically the figure of the American solider and PTSD after return, Nadia Abu El-Haj has shown how focus on the trauma suffered by American troops displaces crucial political conversations on the other *visible* wounds of war—in mass death and dispersion by war. See Abu El-Haj 2022.
73 See Rubaii 2018; as well as Saleh 2021.
74 Stone 2022, 15.
75 There is a body of scholarship that cautions against the deployment of "empire" to describe the United States. Generally, this scholarship argues that use of "empire" will blur the specificity of American power in this moment and eschew the contemporary and historical impacts of other imperial formations (Ottoman, Chinese, or otherwise) and modern biopolitical governance in its difference from the projections of imperial power under British or Russian empires. Yet this book argues that it is helpful to think about the United States as an empire by showing the specificity of American imperial power in how it shapes bodies in mobility and immobility; and to counteract the script that disconnects and disassembles geographies and communal formations from America's imperial grasp. Empire should also be understood beyond the spectacular and visibly extractive, but also in the molding of perceptions and making (im)possible certain forms of life. For a counterargument, see Stoler 2016, 173–204; and Kelly 2006. For a concise version of this debate, see the critical conversation between Ann Laura Stoler and Carole McGranahan in McGranahan and Collins 2018.
76 As cited and elaborated by Abul-Magd 2013, 150–51.
77 Saleh 2021, 7.
78 Stewart 2007, 4.
79 For more on how anthropologists have recently examined US empire, see McGranahan and Collins 2018. A. Goldstein 2014 also draws on similar genealogies to examine present-day iterations of US settler colonialism in North America and its overseas imperialism in the Caribbean and the Pacific. Anthropologists and scholars in ethnic studies have increasingly incorporated these analytics into their work. See Maira 2009; and Imada 2012. The field of American religion has taken up this interest in empire as well; see Wenger and Johnson 2022. For a more detailed lens on US empire and evangelical internationalism, see Corrigan, McAlister, and Schäfer 2022.
80 Wenger and Johnson 2022, 3.
81 Abouna is the Arabic term for Father, or priest.

82 For more on this concept of colonial trauma in the context of Algeria, see Lazali 2021.
83 Gualtieri 2001, 31.
84 Gualtieri 2001, 49.
85 Gualtieri 2001, 48.
86 Gualtieri 2001, 51.
87 In transliterating Arabic words throughout this book, I have used a simplified version of the system outlined in the *International Journal of Middle East Studies* (IJMES).
88 The Coptic community in the United States is estimated to be the largest community to permanently settle outside the Middle East. Yet official statistics for the actual number of Copts in the United States are unreliable. The advocacy group Coptic Solidarity notes, "According to the 2010 US Religion Census, just over 92,000 Copts reside in the US—a remarkably low number considering that the US Coptic population now exceeds half a million." Coptic Solidarity 2020. The 2020 US census results show that 313,720 marked "Egyptian" as their race/ethnicity (www.census.gov) and the 2020 US Religion Census noted that out of the 292 Coptic Orthodox congregations, there were 179,155 adherents. Grammich et al. 2023. However, the US census does not differentiate based on religious affiliation and other studies have been unreliable in accurately documenting the number of Copts in the United States. For example, according to Pew Research, 62 percent of Egyptian immigrants to the United States identify as Christian, per the New Immigrant Survey (NIS). Pew Research Center 2012. Yet only fifty-two main adult respondents were interviewed for the survey.
89 Part of that research has been published. See Lukasik 2022e, 2016.
90 Demographics of migration have also influenced this wedge. Many Christians have permanently emigrated to Western countries, including the United States, Canada, Australia, and throughout Europe (especially Italy, France, Germany, and the United Kingdom), depending on the availability of worker visas and opportunities like the Green Card Lottery. However, the majority of Egyptian migration has been within the Arab world, to countries such as Saudi Arabia, Jordan, and the United Arab Emirates, with more than six million Egyptian emigrants. Many more Egyptians, both Muslim and Christian, out of economic necessity are seasonal laborers in the Persian Gulf. As noted in Pew Research Center 2012 regarding intra-regional migration, "There has been a rough balance . . . between Muslim emigration and immigration in the Middle East-North Africa region as a whole. About a third of Muslim migrants have come from the Middle East-North Africa, and a similar percentage have ended up there, including many who have moved from one country to another within the region." For more information on Egyptian Muslim migration, see Tsourapas 2018; and Schielke 2020.
91 Coptic Solidarity is an advocacy organization that holds annual conferences in Washington, DC. See chapter 1.
92 Abul-Magd 2013, 3.

93   Rieker 1997, as cited in Abul-Magd 2013, 7.
94   Gran 2004, as cited in Abul-Magd 2013, 7.
95   Piot 1999, 178.
96   Elliot 2021.
97   Migration studies has traditionally focused on processes of immigration rather than emigration (exceptions include Brettell 1986; Cohen 2004; and Gardner 1995). In anthropology, though, recent studies have focused on "sending communities"; see Chu 2010; Gaibazzi 2015; and Piot and Batema 2019, as cited in Elliot 2021, 6.
98   Exceptional studies have oscillated between transnational scales. For example, Pedersen 2012.
99   Tsing 2005, 58; Elliot 2021, 9.
100 On transhumant ethnography, see Rubaii 2018.
101 Participant observation and individual interviews in the United States were conducted in both English and Egyptian Arabic, in which I am fluent. Fieldwork in Egypt was conducted all in Egyptian Arabic. No research assistants were used for any stage of this project.
102 Historian Melani McAlister has thoroughly traced the contours of this form of what I term "geopolitical kinship" through the perspective of American evangelicals. See McAlister 2019; as well as Bruner 2021. Also see Castelli 2005; and Elisha 2016.
103 Hage 2021, 5.
104 For a comparative context on the Sikh diaspora and how collective memory of violence molds formations of temporality, affect, and corporeality, see Axel 2001; and Hothi 2024.
105 For a comparable context among the Palestinian diaspora, see Schwabe 2023. Geography and the geopolitics of the imperial encounter impact which (Coptic) Christian ways of knowing and being become normative and dominant or marginalized and diminished. The "accumulated history" of Coptic difference and suffering informs how Copts—as martyrs and migrants—"make sense of social relations, how they know one another across and through difference, and how they practice living in proximity. . . . Yet, these same accumulated histories also bear the weight of new histories, peoples, and ideas that simultaneously are made possible by the histories that they obscure and negate." Kashani 2023, 21–22. For thinking about a transnational Muslim moral geography in tension with the imperial encounter, see Grewal 2014.
106 "The diaspora of contemporary US Empire means that one lives one's homeland differently, as part of a transnational diaspora." Naber 2014, 1113.
107 Stewart 2007.
108 Stewart 2007, 3.
109 Engaging the work of Leiba Faier and Lisa Rofel (2014, 363), Zainab Saleh employs the concept of "imperial encounter" to show how the United States and Iraq are "entangled in an unequal power relation that has reconfigured the lives of Iraqis"

(2021, 7). I follow Saleh's conceptualization in the transnational Coptic context to think about how American discourses of persecution and their attendant regimes (re)shape Coptic identity and community in and through transnational migration.
110 Stewart 2007, 4.
111 On "misfits," see M. Ibrahim 2023.

CHAPTER 1. PERSECUTION AND POWER

Portions of this chapter are derived from Candace Lukasik, "Economy of Blood: The Persecuted Church and the Racialization of American Copts," *American Anthropologist* 123, no. 3 (2021): 565–77.

1 Arraf 2017.
2 Adapted from Luke 12:48 (New King James Version).
3 Adapted from Acts 9:16 (New King James Version).
4 Most Copts do not ethnically identify as Arabs, whether in Egypt or the United States. In the United States, however, their distance from Arab identification is connected to histories of the Arab conquest in Egypt as well as Orientalist and racializing discourses in diaspora of Arabs as terrorists. See Alsultany 2012.
5 Pennock 2017, 6.
6 Pennock argues, "Ironically, when disparate groupings of Arabs in America encountered the larger culture's scrutiny and homogenization of them, they were increasingly brought together in solidarity as Arab Americans to contest the dominant paradigm" (10–11).
7 More recently, there have been Coptic coalitions and diasporic organizations that have sought to challenge anti-Arab/Muslim racism, including Progressive Copts, Egypt Migrations, and the Elmahaba Center of Nashville, Tennessee. For more on this emerging movement, see Mark Ramzy's (2023) interview with Marcus Zacharia, the co-creator of Progressive Copts. "We have been going through multiple layers of oppression and there are many nuances that we are missing. Especially in the diaspora, in the present, it has been constantly used by right-wing entities that have been tokenizing our oppression. They were the ones who have been constantly marketing the word 'persecution' over 'religion-based oppression' or 'discrimination' to prevent us from connecting with other communities. We could be connecting to Muslims who are facing religion-based discrimination in North America or we can be connecting with Bahá'ís or Shia Muslims in Egypt. By centering our own persecution, we are prioritizing our struggle over other people's struggle which doesn't serve us in the diaspora in building bridges and connecting with other minorities."
8 On the comparative context of Middle Eastern Christian misrecognition in Europe, see Hunter and Guiney 2023.
9 "New Church Strife" 1972.
10 For more on the historical contexts of and competing factions among Coptic diasporic activists, see Akladios 2020b, chap. 7, "'Politics Is a Dirty Word': Diasporic Activism in Multipolar Perspective." See also Akladios 2022.

11 Karas (1928–2003) immigrated to the United States in 1959 as part of a government-sponsored student exchange with his wife, Leila Karas, and their two children. In 1967 the family moved to New Haven, Connecticut, where Karas secured a position as a professor of mathematics at Southern Connecticut University. Karas recounted incidents of discrimination when he was growing up in Sūhāj, Upper Egypt, from verbal assaults on Coptic kin to preferential treatment of Muslim students, as discussed by Shawky Karas in a video recorded interview conducted by Elhamy Khalil at Karas's home in New Haven, August 1991 (access courtesy of Elhamy Khalil).
12 *The Copts* 9, nos. 2–3 (July 1982): 12.
13 For more on such incidents throughout 1977, see Pennington 1982, 171–72.
14 Akladios 2020b, 359–60.
15 Led by the then sole Coptic Orthodox church in Queens, New York, churches throughout the United States and Canada sponsored a counter-ad in the *Washington Post* refuting the ACA and CCA's ad days prior. The ad states, "The clergy and congregations of the Coptic Orthodox Churches in the USA and Canada strongly denounce any false claims coming from persons or organizations, especially those who call themselves the 'American Coptic Association.'" It goes on to say that "the Copts are united with their Moslem brothers for the security, peace, welfare and progress of Egypt to fulfill the aims and policy of President Sadat whom we support wholeheartedly."
16 Heikal 1983, 233, as cited in Akladios 2020b, 82–83.
17 As cited in M. Atiya 2018.
18 In this context, the ACA, with Karas at the helm, formed new alliances with US congressmen to advance *al-qaḍiyya al-qibṭiyya* (the Coptic cause). Karas's efforts to tell American politicians and religious leaders about the Coptic plight in Egypt were not necessarily new. In his book *A Lonely Minority* (1963), journalist Edward Wakin notes that even under Egyptian king Farouk, Copts were writing articles expressing outrage over their discrimination and subjugation in Egyptian society. So much so that a selection of said articles was published (most likely translated as well) in pamphlet form under the title "The Cry of Egypt's Copts," by an "interested group" in New York in 1951 (Wakin 1963, 19). Such journals that published articles on violence and discrimination against the Copts prior to the 1952 revolution, like the "Orator of the 1919 revolution" Qumuṣ Sergius's *al-Manāra al-Misriyya*, were suppressed in the early years of Nasser's regime, as were many other news media and commentary. Karas's renewed efforts in the diaspora engaged these older arguments, yet in a new diasporic and imperial context.
19 Video recording of Shawky Karas, interviewed by Elhamy Khalil, 1991, from the private collection of Elhamy Khalil. All translations from Arabic unless otherwise noted are mine. The comparison to the silence on the Armenian genocide and most especially the Holocaust enables the articulation and recognition of other histories of victimization such as that of the Copts in Egypt in a postcolonial age. Michael Rothberg argues that "pursuing memory's multidirectionality encour-

ages us to think of the public sphere as a malleable discursive space in which groups do not simply articulate established positions but actually come into being through their dialogical interactions with others." Rothberg 2009, 5. In the case of Karas and other Coptic diasporic activists, Coptic memory has also been layered onto US geo/theopolitical interests in Islam and Muslim-majority contexts like the Middle East during the latter half of the twentieth century, most especially after the Cold War and increased policy attention to international religious freedom and the persecuted Christians movement.

20 Essay reproduced from Ye'or 1985.
21 *The Copts*, July 1989, as cited in Khalil 1999, 79.
22 *The Copts*, December 1995, as cited in Khalil 1999, 79.
23 Based on interviews I conducted between California and the New York-New Jersey area between 2016 and 2018.
24 Karas notes that Copts, prior to the 1952 revolution, comprised 20 percent of Parliament and were 40 percent of the teaching staff at different institutions of higher learning. Additionally, he states that Copts constituted 80 percent of the staff of foreign banks and companies prior to nationalization. In commerce, he affirms, "Most observers agreed that the Egyptian economy was run by the Copts during the first half of the twentieth century" (Karas 1986, 83). Karas does not discuss the role of the British colonial regime in placing Copts, as well as other minority communities, in positions of power in Egypt. He continues his listing of Coptic accomplishments by emphasizing that "Muslim regimes have tried to minimize or ignore [the impact of the Copts]'" (84).
25 Karas 1986, 96.
26 Karas 1986, 86.
27 "Al-yūm 'aiyydat shuhada' al-aqbāṭ al-Suwīs 1952" 2019 argues that the deadly incident was orchestrated by the Muslim Brotherhood.
28 Karas 1986, 86.
29 This formulation of the icon parallels the work of anthropologist Sarah Bakker Kellogg. While Bakker Kellogg deploys the concept of the icon in relation to Syriac Christians and their racialization by Dutch in the Netherlands, the concept of the icon is also quite useful for thinking about how (Western) Christianity becomes a colonizing force and how Christianity as a polemical concept subsumes Eastern Christians like the Copts within it (see Anidjar 2009). As Bakker Kellogg writes, "An icon is a communicative sign in which a signifier resembles what it represents (e.g., a road sign with an image of a bicycle indicating the bicycle lane). Unlike symbolic and indexical signs, an iconic sign's meaning depends on connections among form, experience, context, and memory." See Bakker Kellogg 2021, 621–22.
30 For more on the translation of Christianity into a colonial force (which transformed Egypt's intercommunal relations with it), see Baron 2014.
31 For example, many scholars have argued that the sectarian divisions now evident in parts of the contemporary Middle East are the result not of long-standing

communal hostilities, but of an aggressive British and French colonial occupation that categorized subjects by religion for its own purposes. For example, Ussama Makdisi (2021) has explored the "ecumenical frame" of coexistence in the Middle East amid Ottoman reformation, European colonialism, and the emergence of nationalism, and Laura Robson's (2011) work has examined British efforts in mandate Palestine to construct religion as a legal and political category in specifically colonial ways.

32 Mahmood 2009, 68.
33 In his 1985 memoir, *The Blood of Abraham: Insights into the Middle East*, Carter documents his encounter with Copts during a liturgical service in Cairo. He voices his concern for their then interned patriarch and notes, "Since the Iranian revolution, however, Moslem groups have become more militant, and the leaders of Egypt and other Arab nations have sometimes responded to these religious pressures with the uncharacteristic persecution of non-Moslems. Throughout Islam, one can detect a growing anti-Western feeling" (148). This passage is also reprinted in *The Copts*. July 1988, 8.
34 Karas 1986, 174.
35 Karas 1986, 177.
36 Karas 1986, 178.
37 Egyptian Christian Organization and Dr. Raef Marcus, "Doesn't Anybody Care?," letter to the editor, *New York Times*, February 15, 1984, as reprinted in Karas 1986, 276.
38 As cited in McAlister 2012, 144.
39 Parks and Scott 2010.
40 L. Bush 1996.
41 McAlister 2012, 153.
42 G. H. W. Bush 1990.
43 McAlister 2001, 42.
44 McAlister 2001, 216–17.
45 These American audiences also included communities of the Coptic diaspora in the United States. For example, in addressing changes to the Egyptian constitution in 1980 in his prepared statement before the then termed Subcommittee on International Organizations, Human Rights, and Oversight under the Committee on Foreign Affairs at the US House of Representatives, Shawky Karas noted that such changes—making the Qur'an the main source of Egyptian law—are "the basis of a Khomeini-type of government in Egypt." Reprinted in *The Copts*, April 1983.
46 Williams 2010, 219.
47 McAlister 2018, 162. See also Hertzke 2004. For a focus on an earlier era of human rights politics among ecumenical Protestants, see Zubovich 2022.
48 McAlister 2023, 155, drawing on the political work of melodrama as a genre from Anker 2014.
49 Roderick's advocacy on behalf of Christians ranged from the Soviet Union to Sudan and South Sudan. He was Christian Solidarity International's Washington,

DC, representative and co-director of the Sudan campaign, and leader of the Coalition for the Defense of Human Rights (CDHR), of which he had been secretary general (1992–2014). In the early years of his advocacy for the Persecuted Church, he founded the Society of St. Stephen for religious prisoners of conscience and their families in the Soviet Union in 1982 and was the co-director of the International Task Force on Soviet Jewry. Walton 2014.

50 As quoted in Keating 1990.
51 Spelman 1997, as cited in McAlister 2008, 883–84.
52 McAlister describes this as an evangelical "enchanted internationalism," of which I argue Father Keith Roderick was a part, even despite his ecclesiastical distinction and theological difference.
53 Zoom interview by author, April 2020.
54 W. Brown 1995, 73, as cited in S. Ahmed 2014, 58.
55 S. Ahmed 2014, 59.
56 For more on the politics of transvaluation as it pertains to quantification, see Merry 2016.
57 *The Copts*, January 1990, 31.
58 *The Copts*, July 1992, 19.
59 Tambiah 1996, 192, as cited in Dulin 2017, 786.
60 *The Copts*, July 1992, 12; July–December 1995, 18.
61 *The Copts*, October 1996, 11.
62 *The Copts*, October 1996, 17.
63 S. Ahmed 2014, 31.
64 Kleinman, Das, and Lock 1997, xi. Anthropologist Joel Robbins (2013) has argued that from the early 1990s, the discipline's primary object of attention became what he calls the "suffering subject": "The subject living in pain, in poverty, or under conditions of violence or oppression now very often stands at the centre of anthropological work" (448). Through engagement with the work of Didier Fassin and Richard Rechtman (2009), Robbins argues that trauma as suffering has embodied a common humanity during the late twentieth century. Thus, in this "market of suffering," American religio-political interest in violence against Copts in Egypt became part of a broader constellation of emerging thought on injury and deprivation.
65 Shea 2008. The statement was reprinted in the October 1996 issue of *The Copts*.
66 Zoom interview by author, April 2020. Michael Meunier is not a pseudonym; his real name is shared with permission.
67 Coptic Solidarity 2014. Phares is a Lebanese-Christian conservative who would later serve as advisor to Mitt Romney's and Donald Trump's presidential campaigns. He was also a director for the Future of Terrorism Project at the Foundation for Defense of Democracies. See Bridge Initiative Team 2019.

In June 2000, Karas along with Michael Meunier and Walid Phares officially established the Middle East Christian Committee (MECHRIC) to advocate for Middle Eastern Christian causes. See "MECHRIC Warns" 2001. However, this coalition informally began as early as June 1992, when Karas and Phares released a statement along with Sargon Dadesho of the Assyrian National Congress entitled "Mashrek 'Eastern' Declaration," outlining the shared interests of the World Lebanese Organization, American Coptic Association, and Assyrian National Congress. The statement went on to note that the goal of the group was to "build up political coalitions between the communities to pressure the Administration to change the policy in the Middle East." As reprinted in *The Copts*, January 1993, 17.

68 According to Meunier, the founding of Copts.com was significant since Egyptian media had a "total blackout on sectarian violence against the Copts and abuses were never reported." Email correspondence, May 26, 2024.

69 As noted in our Zoom interview, April 2020.

70 Roderick 1998; Meunier 1998. Roderick's op-ed framed the importance of IRFA and the legitimacy of Coptic concerns through publicity by organizations associated with the persecuted Christians movement: "Such a high-level campaign to deflect criticism of Egypt's human rights record indicates a real fear—that the Egyptian government may be held accountable to a higher standard of conduct than it has shown toward a vulnerable minority. The international Coptic associations have been accused of precipitating an anti-Egypt campaign. This is untrue. Numerous non-Coptic organizations such as Jubilee Campaign, Human Rights Watch, Christian Solidarity International and the Coalition for the Defense of Human Rights have issued well-documented reports of not only widespread acts of violence, rape and extortion by radical Islamists, but also established policies of the government to intimidate and weaken the Christian minority."

71 Freedom House is one of the oldest think tanks (founded in 1941) and was prominent during the Cold War. The Hudson Institute (founded in 1961) is one of the most prominent conservative think tanks in Washington, DC, today.

72 Mahmood 2015, 95.

73 Y. Ibrahim 1998.

74 Transnational contentions around the politics of diasporic activism precede the 1990s, as has been indicated in this chapter. Another example, though, occurred during a November 1986 meeting at the Monastery of Saint Bishoy in Wādī al-Naṭrūn, Egypt (following the release of the Coptic pope). In response to a question on Shawky Karas and the work of the American Coptic Association, Pope Shenouda said, "Karas is not in Egypt and therefore does not know of developments firsthand. I do not want to discuss his intentions, but the results of his screaming are extremely harmful. He has however no influence in the USA." Later in the meeting, Pope Shenouda stated, "The USA is not a Christian country. They supported the Iran of Khomeiny. There is no interest of the US in Christian minorities if it does not serve their policy. What did the US do for Christians in Africa? They supported El Azhar to increase anti USSR feelings." From the private collection of Cornelius Hulsman, with his permission.

75 McAlister 2018, 160.

76 Elgindy 1999. Such comments resonate with those of Pope Shenouda noted earlier.
77 Elgindy 1999.
78 As noted above on the transnational disagreements over IRFA, Copts in Egypt who adhere to an anti-imperialist frame of national unity have disagreed with diasporic activism tactics, especially those that pit the US government against Egypt. Moreover, those Copts in Egypt also fear retribution from Muslims who see the actions of diasporic Copts as increasing tensions between Muslims and Christians in Egyptian daily life. For more on this transnational dissonance from the perspective of the diaspora, see Akladios 2022; and for varied, classed perspectives in Egypt, see Lukasik 2023.
79 Mahmood 2015, 102.
80 Youssef was born into a prominent Coptic landowning family in Dayr Mawās, al-Minyā, Upper Egypt. In the mid-1960s he left for Zurich, Switzerland, and was an activist most of his life, eventually launching the Copts-United website, which focuses on publicizing Coptic concerns and demands for Arabic- and English-language audiences. For more, see Shukry 2011. According to Michael Meunier, he aided Youssef in his efforts to establish the website (given his own experience with Copts.com) and helped organize the 2004 conference in Zurich. Email correspondence, May 26, 2024.
81 Thomas et al. 2006.
82 Thomas et al. 2006, 98.
83 One of the main thinkers of this discourse is Bat Ye'or (Gisèle Littman), an Egyptian-born Jew who fled Egypt during the 1956 Suez Crisis. A publication that exemplifies this is her 2002 book *Islam and Dhimmitude: Where Civilizations Collide*.
84 Thomas et al. 2006, 99.
85 Thomas et al. 2006, 99.
86 Thomas et al. 2006, 100.
87 Sedra 2009.
88 Interview by author, June 2018, Washington, DC.
89 Hanegraaff 2017, 181. According to his website, Ibrahim is a fellow at the Gatestone Institute and the Middle East Forum, two conservative think tanks, and has authored several books, including *Sword and Scimitar: Fourteen Centuries of War between Islam and the West* (2018) and *Crucified Again: Exposing Islam's New War on Christians* (2013), among others. See his website, www.raymondibrahim.com.
90 Huntington 1996.
91 Banks 2016.
92 As discussed in Armanios 2016, 3–4.
93 As noted in the introduction, Pope Francis has described this Christian kinship as an "ecumenism of blood" that gathers around the persecuted: "In this moment of prayer for unity, I would also like to remember our martyrs, the martyrs of today. They are witnesses to Jesus Christ, and they are persecuted and killed because they are Christians. Those who persecute them make no distinction between the religious communities to which they belong. They are Christians and for that they

are persecuted. This, brothers and sisters, is the ecumenism of blood." Francis 2015. For more on the theological significance of this sermon, see Knapman 2018.
94 Banks 2016.
95 For example, Angaelos also heads the Lausanne-Orthodox Initiative, formed after the 2010 Lausanne Congress on World Evangelization, where he heard an evangelical leader refer to the "unreached" as those in majority-Orthodox countries of Eastern Europe. Per the organization's website, "The goal of the Lausanne-Orthodox Initiative is to reflect constructively on the history of relationships between Orthodox and Evangelicals in order to work towards better understanding and encourage reconciliation and healing where wounds exist. Through this process Evangelicals and Orthodox are mutually enriched and strengthened in the work of mission, working towards mutual respect, support and cooperation in the spirit of our Lord's prayer for His Church in John 17." See its website, www.loimission.net.
96 McAlister 2008a.
97 My earlier discussion of the idea of the "icon of colonialism" focused on how Coptic corporeality became a site of colonial rule. As Christians, Copts exceeded their indigenous character to the land of Egypt and were captured by the religious difference of imperial authorities. This asymmetrical Christian kinship impacted intercommunal relations during the colonial period and in migration. In my reading, the icon concept in the "bloody icon" of this passage takes on different dynamics of power, focused on media representations rather than corporeality and everyday intercommunal relations. In her thinking about relics, apparitions, and icons in the mediation of Christian-Muslim relations in Egypt, anthropologist Angie Heo argues that "the circulation of . . . icons activates multiple 'social imaginaries,' or the ways in which people imagine their belonging to a collective whole" (2018, 19–20). The "bloody icon" of the persecuted body includes the images of Coptic martyrs that are "subject to the social epistemologies" of American networks of global power (20). The holy images of the Coptic martyrs unfold a divine Christian kinship in blood yet are also subject to the imperial institutions that manage the geo/theopolitics of Christian belonging on earth; they exemplify the "economy of blood" that threads this book.
98 On "globalatinization," see Derrida 2002.
99 On imperial encounter, see Saleh 2021, 3.
100 Weimer 2011, 145.
101 Bildhauer 2013, S58.
102 Castelli 2004, 107–8.
103 Bildhauer 2013, S58.

CHAPTER 2. SECTARIAN MEMORY AND MIGRATION FORCES
1 The Sidarous-Takla family name cited throughout this chapter is not a pseudonym. It is used with permission from the family. No remaining members of the Sidarous-Takla family live in present-day Bahjūra.

2. Amin uses the term *ash-shamāʿa* (clothes hanger) as a metaphor for the totality of Coptic contexts being channeled through persecution politics.
3. While Amin has contemplated applying for the Lottery, he has not done so. His retelling of the emigration process here is based on his perception rather than personal experience.
4. One of many examples is Wallace 2013.
5. One other anthropological example of this work includes Aaron Michka's 2021 dissertation "House, Church, Cave: Coptic Landscapes and the Demands of Pluralism in Upper Egypt."
6. I am grateful to one of the reviewers for suggesting these questions.
7. S. Tadros 2013, 211–12.
8. Per the Coptic Diaspora Survey (2012), respondents in the Coptic diaspora preferred the Coptic Church—whether in the United States/Canada/Australia/the UK or in Egypt—as an intermediary organization for their philanthropy.
9. See Goodman 2023, chaps. 1–5. Anthropologist Charles Piot and Kodjo Nicolas Batema's *The Fixer* (2019) unpacks the experience of the Lottery in West Africa, specifically Togo, in ethnographic detail.
10. Between 2020 and 2023, Egypt consistently ranked first in Green Card Lottery winners. See US Department of State, Bureau of Consular Affairs n.d. for official statistics.
11. Church service (or *khidma*) is an integral part of the modern Coptic Orthodox Church. As anthropologist Mina Ibrahim defines it, "*Khidma* is a significant theological and sociopolitical language that embraces a comprehensive network of material and spiritual services in the lives of the Coptic Christian minority in Egypt." See M. Ibrahim 2019a.
12. Heo 2018, 204.
13. For just one example, see Collins 2015. Also see De Luce and Ainsley 2018.
14. A *galabaya* is a flowing, long-sleeved, loose-fitting garment worn by men and women.
15. In 2017 this was a little over one US dollar.
16. A. Shenoda 2011.
17. Abbas and al-Dessouky 2011, 32. I am grateful to Paul Sedra for suggesting this material.
18. Baer 1962, 64.
19. See Magdi Guirguis's introduction to Guirguis and van Doorn-Harder 2011.
20. Issawi 1982, 274.
21. Issawi 1982, 276.
22. Abbas and al-Dessouky 2011, 212.
23. Beshai 1998, 192.
24. Beshai 1998, 192.
25. Abbas and al-Dessouky 2011, 74. For more on the effect of Capitulations and Mixed Courts in Egypt, see N. Brown 2009. For an earlier resource on Mixed Courts in Egypt, see Brinton 1926.

26 This argument is very specific to Coptic elites, not all Copts. Coptic Christians come from a variety of socioeconomic backgrounds past and present.
27 Importantly, Abbas and al-Dessouky (2011) note that not all Egyptians were in support of the occupation. Rather, it was the large landowning class that sought to maintain its status.
28 For a different perspective on the time period, and especially the origins of the 'Urabi Revolt (1879–1882), see Abu-Lughod 1967.
29 Makdisi 2000, 35.
30 Makdisi 2000, 41.
31 Makdisi 2000, 43.
32 Lane 1871, 537.
33 Watson 1904, 54.
34 Behrens-Abouseif 1982, 186.
35 Assyriologist Archibald Henry Sayce quoted in Leeder 1918, 332. These Orientalist and missionary accounts should *not* be held as absolute truth in comparison to indigenous perspectives, yet they do independently evidence similar phenomena.
36 Makdisi 2000, 36.
37 Beshai 1998, 194.
38 Mahmood 2015, 72.
39 B. L. Carter 1986, 66.
40 See Bayly 2012; and Seteney 2009.
41 I use the term "community" and caution deploying the term "millet" especially in the Egyptian context, given that what constituted a millet even outside Egypt has been the subject of decades of scholarship in Ottoman studies. This argument parallels Henry Clements's groundbreaking work on the negotiation of communal recognition among Syriac Christians in the Late Ottoman Empire. See especially Clements 2019; as well as Braude and Lewis 1982; and Deringil 2012.
42 Mahmood 2015, 73–80.
43 For more on the importance of the Coptic Communal Council, see Bland 2019.
44 Hasan 2003, 103.
45 Hasan 2003, 103–35; see also El Khawaga 1998.
46 For more on how the reconfiguration of class in Egypt transformed Coptic community and politics during the twentieth century, see Sedra 1999.
47 Cuno 1993, as cited in Abaza 2013, 122.
48 Abaza 2013, 261.
49 The family name and family member names are pseudonyms.
50 A *mu'adhin* is a Muslim man who performs the call to prayer.
51 Al-Azhar University is known as one of Sunni Islam's most prestigious educational institutions; it has established local branches throughout Egypt.
52 *Feseekh* is a traditional celebratory Egyptian fish dish, fermented, salted, and dried.
53 Musa is a pseudonym.

54 A *felucca* is a wooden sailing boat.
55 According to sociologist Saad Eddin Ibrahim, Copts owned 22.5 percent of all the private investment companies that were founded between 1974 and 1993. Indeed, by 1961, Copts owned 34 percent of agricultural land, which slowly eroded and in subsequent decades took the form of private investment companies. See Ibrahim and Ibn Khaldoun Center 1996.
56 In July 2013, religious and political leaders joined then General al-Sisi in a broadcast announcement of the removal of president Mohamed Morsi from power.
57 For a comparative context in post–Armenian genocide Turkey, see Tambar 2019.
58 "Egyptian Police Raid Cafes" 2016.
59 This question connects to work on sectarianism in Lebanon through the lens of infrastructure and geography, as well as class and gender. See Nucho 2016.
60 This notion of a collective frame is dissimilar from the recent deployment of an "ecumenical frame" to think about sectarianism as coexistence and political collaboration—the transcendence of religious difference. Instead, it focuses on relationality that exceeds political redress or national reconciliation. It is cornered by geographic limit and daily communal accountability (and its lack). On the "ecumenical frame," see Makdisi 2021.
61 Guirguis 2016.
62 Mahmood 2015, 213.
63 Soliman Shafik, as quoted in Fayed 2014.
64 Shortly after the beheading of the twenty-one on the shores of Libya in February 2015, ISIS released its newsletter entitled "Revenge for the Muslimāt Persecuted by the Coptic Crusaders of Egypt."
65 For more on the representational distinction between "sectarian" and "terrorist" violence, see Heo 2018, 244–47.
66 Mahmood 2015, 102.

CHAPTER 3. RELIGIOUS DIFFERENCE AND ASYLUM LAW

1 Sadik 1997.
2 US Department of Homeland Security, Office of Homeland Security Statistics n.d. These statistics do not include religious affiliation. For over a decade, Egypt has been one of the leading countries of nationality of persons granted asylum.
3 See Olmstead 2013; and more recently, see El-Fekki and Malsin 2019.
4 See chapter 1 for more on this development. For a broader historical frame of this narrative, also see Arjana 2015.
5 Tusan 2012.
6 Mahmood 2015, 72.
7 A prominent lawyer of Coptic asylum cases used this phrase several times in conversation with me.
8 For example, see Good 2007 on asylum law and expert testimony in the United Kingdom.
9 Rozakou 2012.

10 Fassin, Wilhelm-Solomon, and Segatti 2017.
11 Fassin and d'Halluin 2007, 309–10.
12 Foucault (1984) 1994, as cited in Fassin and d'Halluin 2007, 325.
13 Indeterminacies also emerge when lawyers and applicants co-produce images of deservingness and victimhood, and there are stakes when applicants fail at the "game." For more on the ethical complexity of asylum law in the context of Greece, see Cabot 2013.
14 Ordóñez 2008, 58.
15 Geertz 1983, 85.
16 Englund 2005, 12; as cited in Malkki 2007, 336.
17 Seemingly acknowledging the lack of specificity regarding this concept, the Ninth Circuit Court of Appeals noted, "Persecution covers a range of acts and harms," and "the determination that actions rise to the level of persecution is very fact-dependent." See Cordon-Garcia v. INS, 204 F.3d 985, 991 (9th Cir. 2000). On the other hand, the Seventh Circuit has noted that "actions must rise above the level of mere 'harassment' to constitute persecution." See Tamas-Mercea v. Reno, 222 F.3d 417, 424 (7th Cir. 2000). And the First Circuit added that the experience "must rise above unpleasantness, harassment and even basic suffering." See Nelson v. INS, 232 F.3d 258, 263 (1st Cir. 2000). Bray n.d.
18 For more on this, see Sedra 2009.
19 Ticktin 2006.
20 Kennedy 2004, 14–15; Wilson 1996.
21 In 2022 Gabriel noted that his approval rates had increased further, adding that 99 percent of his cases are approved, with most of his clients originating from Arab states of the Persian Gulf at that time. He described it to me this way: "It has never been better for Copts applying for asylum." And as of July 2023, Gabriel described how he is "busier now than ever before," with up to two new Coptic clients a week, now mainly "uneducated laborers and farmers from al-Minya" crossing the US-Mexico border after a long journey from the Emirates to Turkey and then on to Colombia and buses to the southern border. If they cross the border, many of them have taken buses to New York and New Jersey, where they are detained by US Immigration and Customs Enforcement, eventually released, and await their turn in the US asylum system. Many have detailed harrowing journeys; some are kidnapped on the way to the border for ransom and become victims of human trafficking, and some are killed by their kidnappers. See "Abandoned Bus" 2023.
22 Ordóñez 2008, 41.
23 For more on the politics of Christian conversion and negotiations of credibility among asylum seekers in Germany, see Rose and Given-Wilson 2021.
24 This is not to say that Coptic applicants do not continue to apply based on a personal story. However, Gabriel has persuaded clients against this, arguing that it is more difficult to win as the government deconstructs the story, poking holes in the narrative. By focusing on structural conditions, Gabriel and other lawyers avoid the possibility of denial.

25 For example, in the mid-1980s, Coptic Christian Farid Ghaly traveled to the United States and applied for asylum, arguing that Christians in Egypt were subject to discrimination and violence because of their religious identity. At a 1987 merits hearing on Ghaly's asylum case, an immigration judge admitted a March 1986 State Department report that concluded that Copts faced prejudice and occasional acts of individual discrimination from Egypt's Muslim majority, but denied that these acts were systemic or initiated by official discourse. Both the Board of Immigration Appeals and the Ninth Circuit Court of Appeals based in San Francisco found that, while Copts are subject to discrimination in Egypt, this was insufficient as a basis to grant asylum. Both upheld the judge's decision denying Ghaly's asylum. See Gordon 2001. For more on the case, see Ghaly v. INS, 58 F.3d 142 (9th Cir. 1995).
26 Soltero 2006, 138.
27 Soltero 2006, 140.
28 Anker and Blum 1989, 70.
29 Anker and Blum 1989, 76.
30 INS v. Cardoza-Fonseca, 480 U.S. 421 (1987).
31 As cited in Anker and Blum 1989, 80.
32 Ordóñez 2008, 43.
33 As noted earlier, this Coptic class distinction in asylum proceedings changed considerably, according to Gabriel; most of his clients as of the late summer of 2023 are from working-class and poor Upper Egyptian backgrounds, those who crossed the US-Mexico border without visas.
34 Fassin 2013, 48.
35 It should be noted that Gabriel's Coptic women applicants have also included female genital mutilation (FGM) as an additional reason for asylum. As Fassin 2013 notes, the FGM group designation is an exception within the French system, since this group is not one based on race, religion, or other recognized categories. In cases of extreme and unusual abuse such as FGM, "humanitarian asylum" is varyingly invoked across state asylum systems. See Gutner 2005.
36 Various local attacks on Copts from the 1970s to the 2000s were organized by Muslim Brotherhood offshoot organizations in Egypt, such as al-Gama'a al-Islamiyya. From 2013, however, bombings and attacks against Copts in Egypt (as well as Libya) have also been claimed by Islamic State (ISIS) affiliates.
37 "Egypt Schoolboy" 2015.
38 Ha 2017, 140.
39 For other examples, see Galal 2012; and A. Shenoda 2010.
40 Mahmood 2005, 44, as cited in A. Shenoda 2010, 145.
41 Mahmood 2005, 45.
42 A. Shenoda 2010, 158.
43 Hirschkind 2006.
44 Gaffney 1994, 90, as cited in A. Shenoda 2010, 177.
45 Asad 2007, 31.

46 Ordóñez 2008, 46.
47 Fassin and d'Halluin 2007.
48 Fassin and d'Halluin 2005, 598.
49 Sedra 1999, 221; Elsässer 2014, 102–35.
50 Makar 2016.
51 M. Tadros 2009, 272.
52 "Egypt Opens Middle East's Biggest Cathedral" 2019.
53 On the detention of Ramy Kamel and Patrick Zaki, see International Christian Concern 2022, a press release from an American evangelical advocacy organization based in Washington, DC.
54 Kårtveit 2017; S. Tadros 2017. For Coptic dissent over this relationship, see "Coptic Activists" 2016.
55 El Khawaga 1997.
56 Oraby 2018.
57 Agrama 2012, 74.
58 M. Ibrahim 2019b.
59 Agrama 2012; Mahmood 2015.
60 Asad 2003.
61 Mahmood 2015, 4.
62 Agrama 2015, 306.
63 Nine people were killed after an armed man opened fire on a Coptic Orthodox church and a nearby shop in Ḥilwān, south of Cairo in December 2017. ISIS claimed responsibility for the attack. See "Egypt's Coptic Christians Targeted" 2017.
64 For more on Washington, DC, and the industry of expertise, see Razavi 2019b.
65 Razavi 2019a.
66 N. Ahmed 2015.
67 Jenkins 2019; Walsh and Youssef 2016; Gaballa and Tolba 2017.
68 Connected to my earlier discussion of the icon concept, the legal iconicity of Coptic Christians is mediated by the theopolitical authority of US asylum procedures to determine the bodies of the persecuted for salvation. As Elizabeth Shakman Hurd has argued, the asylum regime affirms "the possibility of freedom, salvation, and redemption through conversion . . . to the American project itself" (2021, 112). The bodies of the persecuted are saved through asylum, but as persecuted Christians, Copts also share a divine kinship through Christianity that has, of late, been subsumed into "a single imagined category and spiritual community that transcends borders." Bruner 2021, 6. Again I turn to Angie Heo's work on the icon to think about Copts as "icons" of a persecuted people in US asylum procedures: "The holy icon is therefore not simply the bounded portrait image, but rather the image in relation to the larger organizational complex of signs within which it is embedded. . . . Inasmuch that different people share signifying linkages between any given image and its ritual value, they belong to a common realm of imagination." Heo 2018, 182. As discussed in this chapter, judges I encountered during

research "knew the Copts" and understood them through their persecution by Muslims (although this is not to say that *all* asylum judges "know the Copts"). In this way, the Coptic martyr as image of divine intercession in bloodied this-worldly death has linked Coptic asylum seekers to a broader "organizational complex of signs" that enters courtrooms of legal adjudication.

69 Heo 2018, 14, 207–34.
70 Ordóñez 2008, 58.
71 Fassin and d'Halluin 2005, 606.
72 At a master calendar hearing, the immigration judge does not decide on the substance of a case. Instead, they confer with the government attorney to determine a schedule for the case and ask a person to plead to (admit or deny) certain facts as they pertain to the case.
73 Fassin and d'Halluin 2007, 306.
74 Malkki 2007, 342.
75 This phrase is originally taken from William Shakespeare's play *Merchant of Venice*. The pound of flesh implies a lawful but unreasonable recompense; it also connotes vengeful behavior.
76 2 Corinthians 12:10 (New International Version).
77 While the number of Egyptian asylees increased between 2016 and 2018 (during my main fieldwork), there were no official statistics indicating that the US embassy in Cairo lessened its denials of temporary travel. Mossaad 2019.
78 Appadurai 1990, 299.
79 On an "ethical thematization" of religious difference, which I take *tabādul* to gesture toward, see Mahmood 2015, 213.
80 *Hawawshi* is an Egyptian dish consisting of a pita stuffed with minced meat and spiced with onions, pepper, and parsley.
81 Mahmood 2015, chap. 3.

CHAPTER 4. AFFECTIVE BODIES AND SECURITY PRAXIS

Portions of this chapter are derived from Candace Lukasik, "Economy of Blood: The Persecuted Church and the Racialization of American Copts," *American Anthropologist* 123, no. 3 (2021): 565–77; and Candace Lukasik, "Migrating Minority: Persecution Politics in Transnational Perspective," *International Journal of Middle East Studies* 54 (2022): 541–46.

1 Cordoba House, "Founder's Vision," http://cordobahouse.com.
2 "Joseph Nasrallah Speaks" 2010.
3 Stern 2017. While not in attendance at Nasrallah's 2010 speech, I was in attendance at his 2011 appearance at the same rally. Members of the audience around us distinctly asked one another whether Nasrallah was Muslim or not, even after he was introduced as Coptic Christian.
4 Volpp 2002.
5 Hong 2020. See Lukasik 2022b on majority perceptions of minor feelings in Egypt.

6 Rana 2007.
7 Anthropologist Kali Rubaii (2019) has examined how the intersections of sect and place in the global war on terror lead to sectarianism becoming a social fact in Anbar Province, Iraq. Rubaii's idea of "politicized place" aids in the thinking about geography as already enmeshed in certain racialized discourses of threat, suspicion, and danger.
8 E. Goldstein 2006, 5.
9 Kishi 2017.
10 Selod 2018.
11 Mozingo 2001.
12 Puar 2007. On Kurdish racialization in post-9/11 America, see Thangaraj 2022.
13 Winerip 2001.
14 Rana 2016, 119.
15 Winerip 2001.
16 Michael is a pseudonym.
17 Phone interview by author, February 2020.
18 Hanoosh 2019, 111–20; Naber 2014, 1108; Hage 1998, 61.
19 Puar 2007, 167.
20 J. Butler 1993, 17, as cited in Puar 2007, 183.
21 J. Butler 1993, 17, as cited in Puar 2007, 183. See also Rosa 2019.
22 Puar 2007, 184.
23 Conversation, August 2017, Staten Island, New York.
24 Text message correspondence, February 2020.
25 Yellin 2018.
26 Kim 1999.
27 Anidjar 2003.
28 Puar 2007, 187.
29 Dias 2020.
30 Recall the following quote from the US visa officer at the Cairo embassy toward the end of chapter 3: "If a young man comes to me, I see he doesn't have a job, but has a brother who lives in Revere, Massachusetts, I'm going to have to deny him because of the possibility that he would stay in the US. There's too great of a *risk*."
31 Examples of this argument include A. Butler 2021; Gorski and Perry 2022; Jones 2020; and Perry and Whitehead 2020.
32 See Watchmen on the Wall 2016. Recently, Justina has also become more involved in conservative activism focused on gender and sexuality education in public schools, in addition to networking at Trump-affiliated events between New Jersey and Florida.
33 Hage 2021.
34 Rowe 2007.
35 I. Ibrahim 2019.
36 Arraf 2022.

37 For a comparative case in the Chaldean community of Sterling Heights, Michigan, see Hanoosh 2019, 191–95.
38 Interview by author, November 2017, New York.
39 Some news outlets gave the following translations: "I have made my decision. I put my fate in God's hands." Egyptian officials denied this translation because it implied that the pilot purposefully crashed the plane on a suicide mission, but also the translation missed the distinct meaning of the phrase, which focuses on God's will in all matters beyond human control. Langewiesche 2001. See National Transportation Safety Board 1999 for the NTSB's official report on the cause of EgyptAir Flight 990's crash. The report indicates that the crash was due to pilot error, but there was no definitive motive. Of concern for this section are the transnational dynamics of the crash and how Hany's translation of the incident impacted his decision to join the Joint Terrorism Task Force (JTTF). Hany's interpretation of the pilot's error and possible motives is what is crucial to consider.
40 Flores 1993. In 1985 Farag Foda was also invited to visit the American Coptic Association headquarters in Jersey City. ACA members accompanied him on his tour of the New York–New Jersey area. According to the former ACA secretary during a personal interview in May 2017, Foda also wrote a book on his experiences in the United States, among Coptic activists and others, but was banned from publishing it.
41 Coptic securitization in the diaspora is very different from the Egyptian context, where Copts are securitized and sectarianized by the Egyptian state. See Guirguis 2016.
42 ACLU 2013.
43 Aviv 2017.
44 G. Fields 2005, as cited in Aviv 2017.
45 Aviv 2017.
46 St. Mark's Coptic Law Enforcement Officers Society 2021d.
47 St. Mark's Coptic Law Enforcement Officers Society 2021c.
48 McAlister 2021, 267.
49 Hanna 2019. Also see Fallas 2024.
50 For an example of this in the US context, see De Luce 2022.
51 Hanna 2019.
52 Malsin 2015, as cited in Hanna 2019.
53 Elliot 2021.
54 St. Mark's Coptic Law Enforcement Officers Society 2021a.
55 Coptic Orthodox Diocese of the Southern United States 2020a.
56 St. Mark's Coptic Law Enforcement Officers Society 2021b.
57 Richardson 1974, 53, as cited in Muller 2012, 293.
58 Roediger 1991; Guterl 2001.
59 Jacobson 1999.
60 Muller 2012.
61 Ignatiev 1995, 163, as cited in Muller 2012, 294–95.

62 Morrison 1993.
63 Fernando 2019.
64 St. Mark's Coptic Law Enforcement Officers Society 2021b.
65 Right Response Ministries 2023.

CHAPTER 5. DIASPORIC TRANSLATIONS AND GLOBAL CULTURE WARS

1 Abouna Bavly James is a pseudonym.
2 Seikaly 1970; Marzouki 2016.
3 Young 2015; Castelli 2007.
4 Castelli 2007, 162.
5 See the updated page "War on Christianity" on the Jeremiah Project webpage, www.jeremiahproject.com, cited in Castelli 2007. Not only does it describe the threat of an Islamic invasion in the United States, but it explicitly posits Middle Eastern Christians and most specifically Coptic Christians as examples of what Islam and an anti-God America could inflict upon Christians in the United States.
6 Castelli 2007, 173–74.
7 *Asa'l ma'a Mira* [Ask with Mira], Coptic Sat TV, October 23, 2020.
8 Online and offline progressive networks have emerged in diasporic communities that address issues spanning from new immigrant concerns to anti-Blackness in church communities and LGBTQ rights. For more on this, see the websites of the organization Egypt Migrations, https://egyptmigrations.com, and the Elmahaba Center based out of Nashville, TN, www.elmahabacenter.com, discussed further in the conclusion.
9 Thangaraj 2012.
10 Morrison 1993.
11 Connolly 2005.
12 Castelli 2007, 173.
13 C. Ramzy 2015, 652.
14 Examples of "Christian nationalism" in academic discourse include the following titles: A. Butler 2021; Gorski and Perry 2022; Jones 2020; and Perry and Whitehead 2020.
15 J. Scott 1997.
16 For more on this intra-communal debate, see Lukasik 2016.
17 A. Shenoda 2011.
18 Zeidan 1999. Also see R. Scott 2010, esp. chap. 4.
19 Purcell 1998.
20 For more on Christian media in Egypt, see Armanios and Amstutz 2013; and Heo 2013.
21 C. Ramzy 2015.
22 On the idea of Christian citizenship, see O'Neill 2009.
23 A. Shenoda 2011.
24 McCaughey 2023; also see Perkins 2020, chap. 6.

25 McAlister 2023.
26 For more on this, see Dowland 2009.
27 Curtis 2018; Waits 2022; Buss and Herman 2003.
28 Hurd 2015.
29 "Manhattan Declaration" 2009.
30 Riccardi-Swartz 2021; Stoeckl and Uzlaner 2022; Ayoub and Stoeckl 2024.
31 As cited in McAlister 2023, 159.
32 "Manhattan Declaration" 2009.
33 As cited in McAlister 2023, 164. For its position on "conversion therapy," see Family Watch n.d.
34 McAlister 2023, 165.
35 On the late 1990s–early 2000s, see Long 2004.
36 Smith 2017.
37 "Coptic Church Organizes" 2017.
38 Coptic Orthodox Diocese of Los Angeles 2003.
39 After the legalization of same-sex marriage in the United States, Bishop Raphael of the Coptic Orthodox Church noted, "Homosexuality is the result of perverted desires or a sick upbringing, and it needs to be treated." See "Homosexuals Need Treatment" 2015.
40 The conference was initially entitled "The Volcano of Homosexuality." See "Coptic Church Organizes" 2017. Also see the Church's official English-language Facebook page post, US-International Coptic Media Center 2019.
41 For example, see Progressive Copts 2020.
42 For more on the intersection of social media and the spread of "conversion therapy" in places like Egypt, see Asher-Schapiro and Gebeily 2021.
43 Wasfy has appeared on many Egyptian television talk shows over the years. For example, "Cairo Talk" 2022.
44 For more on McHugh, see Nutt 2017. For an example of Wasfy's deployment of such research, see Alkarma TV 2014.
45 Garver 2022.
46 Another example of the reverberations of the Disney controversy in Florida was the demand from Egypt that Netflix and Disney conform with conservative moral norms. See "Egypt Demands" 2022. See also Stoeckl 2020.
47 Bjork-James 2021.
48 Fitzgerald 2020.
49 Matthew Hanna is a pseudonym.
50 Zoom interview by author, October 2021.
51 Coptic Orthodox Diocese of the Southern United States 2020b.
52 Zoom interview by author, October 2021.
53 Comparatively, Muslims in Detroit have also formed alliances with conservative Polish Catholics on LGBTQ issues. See Perkins 2020, chap. 6. In contrast, though, Chaldean Catholics in the Detroit metro area have troubled these intercommunal alliances with American Muslims See particularly Hanoosh 2019, chap. 7.

54 Since the mid-1990s in Egypt, a man by the name of Atef Aziz has led a movement (now termed Shine International) counter to the sanctioned teachings of the Coptic Orthodox Church. In 2016 Coptic bishops of North America issued a statement threatening excommunication for anyone who corresponded with or participated in liturgical services with Aziz, who has taken residence in the United States. For more on this, see Christian Youth Channel 2019.
55 Gollock 1906, 34, as cited in Brooks Hedstrom 2012, 135.
56 Pew Research Center n.d.
57 Coptic Orthodox Diocese of the Southern United States 2021.

CONCLUSION

1 Cave 2005.
2 "Full News Coverage" 2005.
3 Elliott 2005b.
4 "Family, Friends Mourn" 2005.
5 "Funeral of Slain Family" 2005.
6 Conte 2011.
7 Elliott 2005a.
8 S. Saad 2005.
9 Genesis 4:10 (New King James Version), as cited in S. Saad 2005.
10 Translated from S. Saad 2005.
11 Hulsether 2022, 313.
12 The hope and dream of America are at the heart of this book through its focus on the Green Card Lottery, from its inception through its present-day administration, and the contradictions of such a program for Copts and other African migrants to the United States. See also Goodman 2023.
13 Hulsether 2022, 309.
14 Castelli 2004, 203.
15 M. Ibrahim 2023, 12.
16 Morsi 2021. Lydia Yousief estimates this specific figure based on Coptic priest accounts at the parish level in Nashville, although there are no official statistics. See Yousief 2019. The lack of official statistics in Nashville parallels the issue of broader statistics on the Coptic diaspora in the United States discussed in the introduction.
17 For example, this includes recent initiatives to allow for better Arabic-language access (among other languages such as Amharic) to obtain a driver's permit and license. See the website of the Our State Our Languages initiative, www.ourstateourlanguages.org.
18 These Coptic connections have been mapped by the Elmahaba Center. See Elmahaba Center n.d.
19 For more on the uniqueness of the Coptic community in Nashville, see Yousief 2019.

20 *al-maḥaba* means unconditional love, fitting for the ethos of the center, whose mission statement reads, "Culture is Community is Care." See its website, www.elmahabacenter.com.
21 Laughland 2020.
22 For more on these diverse approaches, see Akladios 2020a.
23 See AlSultany and Shohat 2013.
24 For a comparative study, see Beltrán 2020.
25 Lydia Yousief is not a pseudonym; her real name is shared with permission.
26 As noted by Lydia during our conversation.
27 Elmahaba email to supporters, August 16, 2021.
28 Elmahaba Instagram post, March 24, 2021.
29 Elmahaba Instagram post, February 27, 2021.
30 As cited in Roediger 1991, 12–13.
31 For further elaboration, see Myers 2017.
32 For a comparative way of thinking about the concept of *ghurba* through estrangement, exile, and alienation at the axes of destruction and production between Lebanon, Jordan, and Canada, see Eldridge and Iqbal 2022.
33 "Egyptians from poor towns have long crossed the sea to Europe, but those numbers soared dramatically last year [2022]. The International Organization for Migration counted nearly 22,000 Egyptian migrants arriving to Europe mostly by sea last year, topping every other nationality. Including from war-torn countries like Afghanistan and Syria." Batrawy 2023.
34 The Hefleys were American evangelical writers. *By Their Blood* chronicles stories of martyrdom and Christian persecution from fifty countries. It was originally published in 1979.
35 Hefley and Hefley 1996, 639.
36 One example that circulated on social media—among Copts in Egypt and in diaspora—was the shooting of sixty-six-year-old Reda Girgis, who had traveled from Egypt to New York City in May 2023 to celebrate the birth of a grandchild. While in front of the Chop Cheese Deli in Washington Heights making a phone call to his son (the deli's owner), he was shot in the head by a stray bullet. He lay bleeding on the sidewalk with his phone in hand. "He came like three days ago," said a deli worker, Egyptian Gamal Abouelezz. "The man is innocent. He had nothing to do with the life over here. He just came to visit his son and he lost his life." Wassef and Johnson 2023.
37 For more on this concept of the "less-than-lethal," see Rubaii 2023.
38 Anidjar 2019, 145, as cited in Eldridge and Iqbal 2022.

BIBLIOGRAPHY

"Abandoned Bus with More Than 100 Egyptians Found in Southern Mexico." 2023. *Middle East Eye*, August 18, 2023. www.middleeasteye.net.

Abaza, Mona. 2013. *The Cotton Plantation Remembered: An Egyptian Family Story*. Cairo: American University in Cairo Press.

Abbas, Raouf, and Assem al-Dessouky. 2011. *The Large Landowning Class and the Peasantry in Egypt, 1837–1952*. Edited by Peter Gran and translated by Amer Mohsen and Mona Zikri. Syracuse, NY: Syracuse University Press.

Abu El-Haj, Nadia. 2022. *Combat Trauma: Imaginaries of War and Citizenship in Post-9/11 America*. New York: Verso.

Abul-Magd, Zeinab. 2013. *Imagined Empires: A History of Revolt in Egypt*. Berkeley: University of California Press.

Abu-Lughod, Ibrahim. 1967. "The Transformation of the Egyptian Elite: Prelude to the 'Urābī Revolt." *Middle East Journal* 21 (3): 325–44.

ACLU. 2013. "Factsheet: The NYPD Muslim Surveillance Program." June 17, 2013. www.aclu.org.

Agamben, Giorgio. 2013. *The Kingdom and the Glory: For a Theological Genealogy of Economy and Government*. Stanford, CA: Stanford University Press.

Agrama, Hussein. 2012. *Questioning Secularism: Islam, Sovereignty, and the Rule of Law in Modern Egypt*. Chicago: University of Chicago Press.

———. 2015. "Religious Freedom and the Bind of Suspicion in Contemporary Secularity." In *Politics of Religious Freedom*, edited by Winnifred Fallers Sullivan, Elizabeth Shakman Hurd, Saba Mahmood, and Peter G. Danchin. Chicago: University of Chicago Press, 301–12.

Ahmed, Nadia. 2015. "Why Egyptians Are Risking Their Lives to Work in Libya." *Guardian*, February 20, 2015. www.theguardian.com.

Ahmed, Sara. 2014. *The Cultural Politics of Emotion*. London: Routledge.

Akladios, Michael. 2020a. "Heteroglossia: Interpretation and the Experiences of Coptic Immigrants from Egypt in North America, 1955–1975." *Histoire sociale / Social History* 53 (109): 627–50. https://doi.org/10.1353/his.2020.0034.

———. 2020b. "Ordinary Copts: Ecumenism, Activism, and Belonging in North American Cities, 1954–1992." PhD dissertation, York University.

———. 2022. "Critical Events and the Formation of a Coptic Diaspora in North America between Al-Khanka and Al-Zāwiya Al-Hamrā." In *Routledge Handbook on Middle Eastern Diasporas*, edited by Dalia Abdelhady and Ramy Aly, 52–65. London: Routledge.

Alkarma TV. 2014. "Al-jinsiyya al-mithliyya min wijihat nathr 'almiyya" [Homosexuality from a scientific perspective]." YouTube, July 31, 2014. https://www.youtube.com/watch?v=7Yt3VYVvD38.
Alsultany, Evelyn. 2012. *Arabs and Muslims in the Media: Race and Representation after 9/11*. New York: New York University Press.
Alsultany, Evelyn, and Ella Shohat, eds. 2013. *Between the Middle East and the Americas: The Cultural Politics of Diaspora*. Ann Arbor: University of Michigan Press.
"Al-yūm 'aiyydat shuhada' al-aqbāṭ al-suwīs 1952." 2019. *Masihyo Masr (min Amrika)*, January 4, 2019. https://masihyomasrfromamerica.com.
Anidjar, Gil. 2003. *The Jew, the Arab: A History of the Enemy*. Stanford, CA: Stanford University Press.
———. 2009. "The Idea of an Anthropology of Christianity." *Interventions* 11 (3): 367–93. https://doi.org/10.1080/13698010903255718.
———. 2014. *Blood: A Critique of Christianity*. New York: Columbia University Press.
———. 2015. "The Christian Question: A Response to the Blood Forum." *Marginalia*, March 2, 2015. https://themarginaliareview.com.
———. 2019. "On the Political History of Destruction." *ReOrient: The Journal of Critical Muslim Studies* 4 (2): 144–65. https://doi.org/10.13169/reorient.4.2.0144.
Anker, Deborah, and Carolyn Patty Blum. 1989. "New Trends in Asylum Jurisprudence: The Aftermath of the US Supreme Court Decision in INS v. Cardoza-Fonseca." *International Journal of Refugee Law* 1 (1): 67–82.
Anker, Elisabeth Robin. 2014. *Orgies of Feeling: Melodrama and the Politics of Freedom*. Durham: Duke University Press.
Antoon, Sinan. 2017. *The Baghdad Eucharist*. Translated by Maia Tabet. Cairo: Hoopoe.
Appadurai, Arjun. 1990. "Disjuncture and Difference in the Global Capital Economy." *Theory, Culture & Society* 7: 295–310. https://doi.org/10.1177/026327690007002017.
Arjana, Sophia Rose. 2015. *Muslims in the Western Imagination*. Oxford: Oxford University Press.
Armanios, Febe. 2011. *Coptic Christianity in Ottoman Egypt*. Oxford: Oxford University Press.
———. 2016. "Good Evangelicals, Bad Evangelicals? Egypt's Coptic Orthodox Church and the Charismatic Movement." Unpublished paper.
Armanios, Febe, and Andrew Amstutz. 2013. "Emerging Christian Media in Egypt: Clerical Authority and the Visualization of Women in Coptic Video Films." *International Journal of Middle East Studies* 45 (3): 513–33. https://doi.org/10.1017/S0020743813000457.
Arraf, Jane. 2017. "After 2016 Assault, a Coptic Christian Grandmother in Egypt Fights for Justice." NPR, May 26, 2017. www.npr.org.
———. 2022. "Coptic Leader Criticizes Egypt's Building Restrictions on Churches after Deadly Fire." *New York Times*, August 18, 2022. www.nytimes.com.
Asad, Talal. 1993. *Genealogies of Religion: Discipline and Reasons of Power in Christianity and Islam*. Baltimore: Johns Hopkins University Press.

———. 2003. *Formations of the Secular: Christianity, Islam, Modernity*. Stanford, CA: Stanford University Press.

———. 2007. *On Suicide Bombing*. New York: Columbia University Press.

———. 2011. "Thinking about the Secular Body, Pain, and Liberal Politics." *Cultural Anthropology* 26 (4): 657–75. https://doi.org/10.1111/j.1548-1360.2011.01118.x.

Asher-Schapiro, Avi, and Maya Gebeily. 2021. "LGBT+ Conversion Therapy: Banned on Facebook, but Thriving in Arabic." Reuters, June 3, 2021. www.reuters.com.

Atiya, Aziz S. 1968. *History of Eastern Christianity*. Notre Dame, IN: University of Notre Dame Press.

Atiya, Maged. 2018. "Immigration and the Reinvention of Identity: Part I." *Salama Moussa: Reclaiming Egypt Blog*, March 17, 2018. https://salamamoussa.wordpress.com.

Aviv, Rachel. 2017. "The Trials of a Muslim Cop." *New Yorker*, September 11, 2017. www.newyorker.com.

Axel, Brian Keith. 1996. "Time and Threat: Questioning the Production of Diaspora as an Object of Study." *History and Anthropology* 9 (4): 415–43. https://doi.org/10.1080/02757206.1996.9960888.

———. 2001. *The Nation's Tortured Body: Violence, Representation, and the Formation of a Sikh "Diaspora."* Durham: Duke University Press.

Ayoub, Phillip M., and Kristina Stoeckl. 2024. *The Global Fight against LGBTI Rights: How Transnational Conservative Networks Target Sexual and Gender Minorities*. New York: New York University Press.

Baer, Gabriel. 1962. *A History of Landownership in Modern Egypt, 1800–1950*. Oxford: Oxford University Press.

Bahr, Samira. 1984. *Al-Aqbāṭ fi al-Ḥayat al-Siyasiyya al-Miṣriyya*. Cairo: Maktabat al-Anglo al-Miṣriyya.

Bakker Kellogg, Sarah. 2021. "A Racial-Religious Imagination: Syriac Christians, Iconic Bodies, and the Sensory Politics of Ethical Difference in the Netherlands." *Cultural Anthropology* 36 (4): 618–48. https://doi.org/10.14506/ca36.4.08.

Bandak, Andreas. 2014. "Of Refrains and Rhythms in Contemporary Damascus: Urban Space and Christian-Muslim Coexistence." *Current Anthropology* 55 (S10): S248–S261. https://doi.org/10.1086/678409.

Banks, Adelle M. 2016. "Coptic Bishop Seeks Support from Evangelicals." *Religion News Service*, March 11, 2016. https://religionnews.com.

Baron, Beth. 2014. *The Orphan Scandal: Christian Missionaries and the Rise of the Muslim Brotherhood*. Stanford, CA: Stanford University Press.

Batrawy, Aya. 2023. "Egypt Is Suffering Neither War nor Chaos, but People Are Migrating Away Anyway." NPR, July 12, 2023. www.npr.org.

Bayly, C. A. 2012. "Representing Copts and Muhammadans: Empire, Nation, and Community in Egypt and India, 1880–1914." In *Modernity and Culture: From the Mediterranean to the Indian Ocean, 1890–1920*, edited by Leila Tarazi Fawaz and C. A. Bayly, 158–203. New York: Columbia University Press.

Bayne, Brandon. 2021. *Missions Begin with Blood: Suffering and Salvation in the Borderlands of New Spain*. New York: Fordham University Press.

Behrens-Abouseif, Doris. 1982. "The Political Situation of the Copts, 1798–1923." In *Christians and Jews in the Ottoman Empire*, edited by Benjamin Braude, 325–46. Boulder, CO: Lynne Rienner.

Beliso-De Jesús, Aisha. 2015. *Electric Santería: Racial and Sexual Assemblages of Transnational Religion*. New York: Columbia University Press.

Beltrán, Cristina. 2020. *Cruelty as Citizenship: How Migrant Suffering Sustains White Democracy*. Minneapolis: University of Minnesota Press.

Bernal, Victoria. 2004. "Eritrea Goes Global: Reflections on Nationalism in a Transnational Era." *Cultural Anthropology* 19 (1): 3–25. https://doi.org/10.1525/can.2004.19.1.3.

Beshai, Adel. 1998. "The Place and the Present Role of the Copts in the Egyptian Economy: Traditions and Specializations." In *Christian Communities in the Arab Middle East: The Challenge of the Future*, edited by Andrea Pacini, 191–99. Oxford: Clarendon.

Bildhauer, Bettina. 2006. *Medieval Blood*. Cardiff: University of Wales Press.

———. 2013. "Medieval European Conceptions of Blood: Truth and Human Integrity." *Journal of the Royal Anthropological Institute* 19 (S1): S57–S76. https://doi.org/10.1111/1467-9655.12016.

Bishay, Mounir. 2012. *Qaḍāiyya al-qibṭiyya: Afkar w ara'a nahu ghad akthar ishrāqān*. Los Angeles: Organization of Christian California Copts.

Bjork-James, Sophie. 2021. *The Divine Institution: White Evangelicalism's Politics of the Family*. New Brunswick, NJ: Rutgers University Press.

Bland, Weston. 2019. "Copts, the State and the 1949–1950 *al-Majlis al-Millī* Electoral Crisis: Articulating Community in a Time of Anxiety." *Islam and Christian-Muslim Relations* 30 (3): 303–22. https://doi.org/10.1080/09596410.2019.1619978.

Botros, Ghada. 2005. "Competing for the Future: Adaptation and the Accommodation of Difference in Coptic Immigrant Churches." PhD dissertation, University of Toronto.

———. 2006. "Religious Identity as an Historical Narrative: Coptic Orthodox Immigrant Churches and the Representation of History." *Journal of Historical Sociology* 19 (2): 174–201. https://doi.org/10.1111/j.1467-6443.2006.00277.x.

Boulos, Sami I. 2006. *The History of the Early Coptic Community in the USA (1955–1970)*. Self-published.

Boum, Aomar. 2013. *Memories of Absence: How Muslims Remember Jews in Morocco*. Stanford, CA: Stanford University Press.

Braude, Benjamin, and Bernard Lewis, eds. 1982. *Christians and Jews in the Ottoman Empire: The Functioning of a Plural Society*. 2 vols. New York: Holmes and Meier.

Bray, Ilona. N.d. "What Counts as Persecution When Applying for Asylum or Refugee Status." Nolo. www.nolo.com.

Brettell, Caroline. 1986. *Men Who Migrate, Women Who Wait: Population and History in a Portuguese Parish*. Princeton: Princeton University Press.

Bridge Initiative Team. 2019. "Factsheet: European Foundation for Democracy." Bridge: A Georgetown University Initiative, December 5, 2019. https://bridge.georgetown.edu.

Brinkerhoff, Jennifer. 2016. *Institutional Reform and Diaspora Entrepreneurs: The In-Between Advantage*. Oxford: Oxford University Press.

Brinton, Jasper Y. 1926. "The Mixed Courts of Egypt." *American Journal of International Law* 20 (4): 670–88. https://doi.org/10.2307/2188689.

Brodkin, Karen. 1998. *How Jews Became White Folks and What That Says About Race in America*. New Brunswick, NJ: Rutgers University Press.

Brooks Hedstrom, Darlene L. 2012. "Treading on Antiquity: Anglo-American Missionaries and the Religious Landscape of Nineteenth-Century Coptic Egypt." *Material Religion* 8 (2): 127–52. https://doi.org/10.2752/175183412X13346797480998.

Brown, Nathan. 2009. "The Precarious Life and Slow Death of the Mixed Courts of Egypt." *International Journal of Middle Eastern Studies* 25 (1): 33–52. https://doi.org/10.1017/S0020743800058037.

Brown, Wendy. 1995. *States of Injury: Power and Freedom in Late Modernity*. Princeton: Princeton University Press.

Brubaker, Rogers. 2005. "The 'Diaspora' Diaspora." *Ethnic and Racial Studies* 28 (1): 1–19. https://doi.org/10.1080/0141987042000289997.

Bruner, Jason. 2021. *Imagining Persecution: Why American Christians Believe There Is a Global War against Their Faith*. New Brunswick, NJ: Rutgers University Press.

Burton, Elise. 2021. *Genetic Crossroads: The Middle East and the Science of Human Heredity*. Stanford, CA: Stanford University Press.

Bush, George H. W. 1990. "Address before a Joint Session of the Congress on the Persian Gulf Crisis and the Federal Budget Deficit." September 11, 1990. https://bush41library.tamu.edu.

Bush, Luis. 1996. "The 10/40 Window—Getting to the Core of the Core." Luis Bush Papers. https://luisbushpapers.com.

Buss, Doris, and Didi Herman. 2003. *Globalizing Family Values: The Christian Right in International Politics*. Minneapolis: University of Minnesota Press.

Butler, Anthea. 2021. *White Evangelical Racism: The Politics of Morality in America*. Chapel Hill: University of North Carolina Press.

Butler, Judith. 1993. "Endangered/Endangering: Schematic Racism and White Paranoia." In *Reading Rodney King, Reading Urban Uprising*, edited by Robert Gooding-Williams, 15-22. New York: Routledge.

Bynum, Caroline Walker. 2007. *Wonderful Blood: Theology and Practice in Late Medieval Northern Germany and Beyond*. Philadelphia: University of Pennsylvania Press.

Cabot, Heath. 2013. "The Social Aesthetics of Eligibility: NGO Aid and Indeterminacy in the Greek Asylum Process." *American Ethnologist* 40 (3): 452–66. https://doi.org/10.1111/amet.12032.

"Cairo Talk: Open Discussion about Homosexuality." 2022. *Al-Qahira w Al-Nas*, September 17, 2022. https://www.youtube.com/watch?v=cnyL2aKvcTQ.

Carsten, Janet. 1995. "The Substance of Kinship and the Heat of the Hearth: Feeding, Personhood, and Relatedness among Malays in Pulau Langkawi." *American Ethnologist* 22 (2): 223–41. https://doi.org/10.1525/ae.1995.22.2.02a00010.

———. 2019. *Blood Work: Life and Laboratories in Penang*. Durham: Duke University Press.

———, ed. 2000. *Cultures of Relatedness: New Approaches to the Study of Kinship*. Cambridge: Cambridge University Press.
Carter, B. L. 1986. *The Copts in Egyptian Politics*. London: Croom Helm.
Carter, Jimmy. 1985. *The Blood of Abraham: Insights into the Middle East*. Boston: Houghton Mifflin.
Castelli, Elizabeth. 2004. *Martyrdom and Memory: Early Christian Culture Making*. New York: Columbia University Press.
———. 2005. "Praying for the Persecuted Church: US Christian Activism in the Global Arena." *Journal of Human Rights* 4 (3): 321–51. https://doi.org/10.1080/14754830500257554.
———. 2006. "The Ambivalent Legacy of Violence and Victimhood: Using Early Christian Martyrs to Think With." *Spiritus: A Journal of Christian Spirituality* 6 (1): 1–24. http://dx.doi.org/10.1353/scs.2006.0028.
———. 2007. "Persecution Complexes: Identity Politics and the 'War on Christians.'" *Differences: A Journal of Feminist Cultural Studies* 18 (5): 152–80. https://doi.org/10.1215/10407391-2007-014.
Cave, Damien. 2005. "Briefings: Crime; Jersey City Lead." *New York Times*, February 2005. www.nytimes.com.
Chan-Malik, Sylvia. 2018. *Being Muslim: A Cultural History of Women of Color in American Islam*. New York: New York University Press.
Christian Youth Channel. 2019. "The Heresy of Group Led by Atif Aziz Mashrky (Part 2)." Episode 13, *New Heresy*. YouTube, May 20, 2019. https://www.youtube.com/watch?v=KMfZJMHwUIk.
Chu, Julie. 2010. *Cosmologies of Credit: Transnational Mobility and the Politics of Destination in China*. Durham: Duke University Press.
Clements, Henry. 2019. "Documenting Community in the Late Ottoman Empire." *International Journal of Middle East Studies* 51: 423–43. https://doi.org/10.1017/S0020743819000369.
Clifford, James. 1997. *Routes: Travel and Translation in the Late Twentieth Century*. Cambridge, MA: Harvard University Press.
Cohen, Jeffrey H. 2004. *The Culture of Migration in Southern Mexico*. Austin: University of Texas Press.
Collins, Eliza. 2015. "Cruz Defends Plan to Allow Christian Refugees but Ban Others." *Politico*, November 19, 2015. www.politico.com.
Connolly, William E. 2005. "The Evangelical-Capitalist Resonance Machine." *Political Theory* 33 (6): 869–86. https://doi.org/10.1177/0090591705280376.
Conte, Michaelangelo. 2011. "300-Year Sentence for Jersey City Man Convicted in 2005 Quadruple Killing Is Upheld." NJ.com, June 10, 2011. www.nj.com.
"Coptic Activists Criticize Church's Support of Sisi's New York Visit." 2016. *Mada Masr*, September 19, 2016. https://madamasr.com.
"Coptic Church Organizes 'Volcano of Homosexuality' Conference." 2017. *Egypt Independent*, September 28, 2017. www.egyptindependent.com.

Coptic Orthodox Diocese of Los Angeles, Southern California, and Hawaii. 2003. "Coptic Orthodox Church Condemns Homosexuality, Ordination of Homosexuals and Same-Sex Marriage." August 26, 2003. www.lacopts.org.

Coptic Orthodox Diocese of the Southern United States. 2020a. "A Statement on the Death of Mr. George Floyd." June 30, 2020. https://suscopts.org.

———. 2020b. "OCCM Webinar: The Future of Orthodoxy in America by Bishop Youssef." YouTube, September 22, 2020. https://www.youtube.com/watch?v=K95l7Z1bdmo&t=1165s.

———. 2021. "OCCM Webinar: Church vs State: Godly Citizen under a Secular Master by Fr. Moses Samaan." YouTube, March 29, 2021. https://www.youtube.com/watch?v=fVKkF5IPPWU&list=PLkkYZew63JGbgDsvEbvuYaPO8evq_pfoK&index=6.

Coptic Solidarity. 2014. "Coptic Solidarity Mourns Loss of Advocate Reverend Keith Roderick." March 13, 2014. www.copticsolidarity.org.

———. 2020. "Coptic Solidarity Launches Voter Registration Campaign for American Copts." February 12, 2020. www.copticsolidarity.org.

Corrigan, John, Melani McAlister, and Axel R. Schäfer, eds. 2022. *Global Faith, Worldly Power: Evangelical Internationalism and US Empire*. Chapel Hill: University of North Carolina Press.

Cuno, Kenneth. 1993. *The Pasha's Peasants: Land, Society, and Economy in Lower Egypt, 1740–1858*. Cambridge: Cambridge University Press.

Curtis, Heather D. 2018. *Holy Humanitarians: American Evangelicals and Global Aid*. Cambridge, MA: Harvard University Press.

Das, Veena. 2007. *Life and Words: Violence and the Descent into the Ordinary*. Berkeley: University of California Press.

De Luce, Dan. 2022. "CIA Honors Underground Railroad and Civil War Hero Harriet Tubman as a Model Spy with a New Statue." NBC News, October 1, 2022. www.nbcnews.com.

De Luce, Dan, and Julia Ainsley. 2018. "Despite Trump's Promise to Protect Them, Christian Refugees Struggle to Enter US." NBC News, September 12, 2018. www.nbcnews.com.

Deringil, Selim. 2012. *Conversion and Apostasy in the Late Ottoman Empire*. Cambridge: Cambridge University Press.

Derrida, Jacques. 2002. "'Above All, No Journalists!'" In *Religion and Media*, edited by Hent de Vries and Samuel Weber, 56–93. Stanford, CA: Stanford University Press.

Dewachi, Omar. 2017. *Ungovernable Life: Mandatory Medicine and Statecraft in Iraq*. Stanford, CA: Stanford University Press.

Dias, Elizabeth. 2020. "Christianity Will Have Power." *New York Times*, August 9, 2020. www.nytimes.com.

Dowell, Anna. 2015. "Landscapes of Belonging: Protestant Activism in Revolutionary Egypt." *International Journal of Sociology* 45 (3): 196. http://doi.org/10.1080/00207659.2015.1045345.

Dowland, Seth. 2009. "'Family Values' and the Formation of a Christian Right Agenda." *Church History* 78 (3): 606–31. https://doi.org/10.1017/S0009640709990448.

Dulin John. 2017. "Transvaluing ISIS in Orthodox Christian-Majority Ethiopia: On the Inhibition of Group Violence." *Current Anthropology* 58 (6): 785–96. https://doi.org/10.1086/694648.

Earl of Cromer. 1908. *Modern Egypt* Vol. 2. London.

"Egypt Demands Netflix and Disney Conform with Its 'Social Values.'" 2022. *Middle East Eye*, September 8, 2022. www.middleeasteye.net.

"Egyptian Police Raid Cafes during Ramadan Fast." 2016. *Middle East Eye*, June 10, 2016. www.middleeasteye.net.

"Egypt Opens Middle East's Biggest Cathedral Near Cairo." 2019. BBC News, January 6, 2019. www.bbc.com.

"Egypt Schoolboy Dies after Teacher Beating, Ministry Says." 2015. *France24*, March 9, 2015. www.france24.com.

"Egypt's Coptic Christians Targeted in Deadly Attacks." 2017. *Al Jazeera*, December 29, 2017. www.aljazeera.com.

Eldridge, Aaron Frederick, and Basit Kareem Iqbal. 2022. "A Tropics of Estrangement: *Ghurba* in Four Scenes." *Diacritics* 50 (1): 112–40. https://doi.org/10.1353/dia.2022.0004.

El-Fekki, Amira, and Jared Malsin. 2019. "Anti-Christian Violence Surges in Egypt, Prompting an Exodus." *Wall Street Journal*, April 26, 2019. www.wsj.com.

Elgindy, Khaled. 1999. "Diaspora Troublemakers: Is the Organized Coptic Community in the US Doing More Harm Than Good?" *Cairo Times*, February 1999.

Elisha, Omri. 2016. "Saved by a Martyr: Evangelical Mediation, Sanctification, and the 'Persecuted Church.'" *Journal of the American Academy of Religion* 84 (4): 1056–80. https://doi.org/10.1093/jaarel/lfw016.

El Khawaga, Dina. 1997. "The Laity at the Heart of the Coptic Clerical Reform." In *Between Desert and City: The Coptic Orthodox Church Today*, edited by Nelly van Doorn-Harder and Kari Vogt, 142–66. Eugene, OR: Wipf & Stock.

———.1998. "The Political Dynamics of the Copts: Giving the Community an Active Role." In *Christian Communities in the Arab Middle East: The Challenge of the Future*, edited by Andrea Pacini, 172-190. Oxford: Clarendon Press.

Elliot, Alice. 2021. *The Outside: Migration as Life in Morocco*. Bloomington: Indiana University Press.

Elliott, Andrea. 2005a. "A Bloody Crime in New Jersey Divides Egyptians." *New York Times*, January 21, 2005. www.nytimes.com.

———. 2005b. "Rage Explodes at Egyptian Family's Funeral." *New York Times*, January 18, 2005. www.nytimes.com.

Elmahaba Center. N.d. "A Map of Coptic Nashville: An Oral History Project." www.elmahabacenter.com.

Elsässer, Sebastian. 2014. *The Coptic Question in the Mubarak Era*. Oxford: Oxford University Press.

Englund, Harri. 2005. *Prisoners of Freedom: Human Rights and the African Poor*. Berkeley: University of California Press.

Erol, Ali E. 2023. "Delighted for a Dairy Queen in Egypt: US Foreign Policy Leadership Discourse in the Middle East during Arab Spring." *Journal of International and Intercultural Communication* 16: 74–89. https://doi.org/10.1080/17513057.2021.1950198.
Faier, Lieba, and Lisa Rofel. 2014. "Ethnographies of Encounter." *Annual Review of Anthropology* 43 (1): 363–77. https://doi.org/10.1146/annurev-anthro-102313-030210.
Fallas, Amy. 2024. "Sectarian Politics? Securitization, Urban Development, and Coptic Advocacy in Cairo." In *Cairo Securitized: Reconceiving Urban Justice and Social Resilience*, edited by Paul Amar, 401–11. Cairo: AUC Press.
"Family, Friends Mourn Slain NJ Family." 2005. Fox News, January 17, 2005. www.foxnews.com.
Family Watch. N.d. "Family Watch Endorses International Declaration Opposing Bans on So-Called 'Conversion Therapy.'" https://familywatch.org.
Fassin, Didier. 2013. "The Precarious Truth of Asylum." *Public Culture* 25 (1) : 39–63. https://doi.org/10.1215/08992363-1890459.
Fassin, Didier, and Estelle d'Halluin. 2005. "The Truth from the Body: Medical Certificates as Ultimate Evidence for Asylum Seekers." *American Anthropologist* 107 (4): 597–608. https://doi.org/10.1525/aa.2005.107.4.597.
———. 2007. "Critical Evidence: The Politics of Trauma in French Asylum Policies." *Ethos: Journal for the Society for Psychological Anthropology* 35 (3): 300–329. https://doi.org/10.1525/eth.2007.35.3.300.
Fassin, Didier, and Richard Rechtman. 2009. *The Empire of Trauma: An Inquiry into the Condition of Victimhood*. Princeton: Princeton University Press.
Fassin, Didier, Matthew Wilhelm-Solomon, and Aurelia Segatti. 2017. "Asylum as a Form of Life: The Politics and Experience of Indeterminacy in South Africa." *Current Anthropology* 58 (2): 160–87. https://doi.org/10.1086/691162.
Fayed, Hanan. 2014. "Are Copts Fleeing Egypt?" *Egyptian Streets*, September 9, 2014. https://egyptianstreets.com.
Feldman, Keith, and Leerom Medovoi. 2016. "Race/Religion/War: An Introduction." *Social Text* 34 (4) (129): 1–17. https://doi.org/10.1215/01642472-3680834.
Fernando, Mayanthi L. 2019. "State Sovereignty and the Politics of Indifference." *Public Culture* 31 (2): 261–73. https://doi.org/10.1215/08992363-7286813.
Fields, Barbara Jeanne. 1990. "Slavery, Race and Ideology in the United States of America." *New Left Review* 181 (1): 95–118.
Fields, Gary. 2005. "New York Teaches Lesson on Fighting Terror." *Wall Street Journal*, March 2, 2005. www.wsj.com.
Fitzgerald, Mary. 2020. "Welcome to Trump Country: 'We're the Silent Majority.'" Open Democracy, November 2, 2020. www.opendemocracy.net.
Flores, Alexander. 1993. "Secularism, Integralism and Political Islam." *MERIP* no. 183 (July–August). https://merip.org.
Foucault, Michel. (1984) 1994. "L'éthique du souci de soi comme pratique de la liberté." In *Dits et écrits*, vol. 4, 708–29. Paris: Gallimard.
Francis, Pope. 2015. "An Ecumenism of Blood." EWTN, January 30, 2015. www.ewtn.com.

Franke, Katherine M. 2012. "Dating the State: The Moral Hazards of Winning Gay Rights." *Columbia Human Rights Law Review* 44 (1): 1–46.
"Full News Coverage of the Jersey Coptic Family Massacre." 2005. www.coptic-church.org/funeral.htm.
"Funeral of Slain Family Brings Religious Tensions to a Boil." 2005. *Gainesville Sun*, January 18, 2005. www.gainesville.com.
Furani, Khaled. 2019. *Redeeming Anthropology: A Theological Critique of a Modern Science*. Oxford: Oxford University Press.
Gaballa, Arwa, and Ahmed Tolba. 2017. "Palm Sunday Bombings of Egyptian Coptic Churches Kill 44." Reuters, April 9, 2017. www.reuters.com.
Gaffney, Patrick D. 1994. *The Prophet's Pulpit: Islamic Preaching in Contemporary Egypt*. Berkeley: University of California Press.
Gaibazzi, Paolo. 2015. *Bush Bound: Young Men and Rural Permanence in Migrant West Africa*. London: Berghahn.
Galal, Lise Paulsen. 2012. "Coptic Christian Practices: Formations of Sameness and Difference." *Islam and Christian-Muslim Relations* 23 (1): 45–58. https://doi.org/10.1080/09596410.2011.634596.
Gamble, Richard. 2003. *The War for Righteousness: Progressive Christianity, the Great War, and the Rise of the Messianic Nation*. Washington, DC: Regnery.
Gardner, Katy. 1995. *Global Migrants, Local Lives: Travel and Transformation in Rural Bangladesh*. New York: Oxford University Press.
Garver, Rob. 2022. "Florida Battles Disney World over 'Don't Say Gay' Bill." *VOA News*, April 22, 2022. www.voanews.com.
Geertz, Clifford. 1973. "Religion as a Cultural System." in *The Interpretation of Cultures: Selected Essays*. New York: Basic Books.
———. 1983. *Local Knowledge: Further Essays in Interpretive Anthropology*. New York: Basic Books.
George, Sheba. 2005. *When Women Come First: Gender and Class in Transnational Migration*. Berkeley: University of California Press.
Georgy, Joshua Thomas. 2015. "Fragmented Geographies: The See of Alexandria, Its Following, and the Estrangements of Modernity." PhD dissertation, Columbia University.
Ghosh, Amitav. 1999. "The Diaspora in Indian Culture." *Public Culture* 2 (1): 73–78. https://doi.org/10.1215/08992363-2-1-73.
Gillem, Mark L. 2007. *America Town: Building the Outposts of Empire*. Minneapolis: University of Minnesota Press.
Goldstein, Alyosha, ed. 2014. *Formations of United States Colonialism*. Durham: Duke University Press.
Goldstein, Eric L. 2006. *The Price of Whiteness: Jews, Race, and American Identity*. Princeton: Princeton University Press.
Gollock, Minna C. 1906. *River, Sand and Sun. Being Sketches of the C.M.S. Egypt Mission*. London: Church Missionary House.
Good, Anthony. 2007. *Anthropology and Expertise in the Asylum Courts*. London: Routledge.

Goodman, Carly. 2023. *Dreamland: America's Immigration Lottery in an Age of Restriction*. Chapel Hill: University of North Carolina Press.
Goodstein, Laurie. 1998. "A Rising Movement Cites Persecution Facing Christians." *New York Times*, November 9, 1998. www.nytimes.com.
Gordon, Louis A. 2001. "Christians in the American Court System." *Middle East Forum*, Winter 2001. www.meforum.org.
Gorski, Philip, and Samuel L. Perry. 2022. *The Flag and the Cross: White Christian Nationalism and the Threat to American Democracy*. Oxford: Oxford University Press.
Grammich, Clifford, Erica J. Dollhopf, Mary L. Gautier, Richard Houseal, Dale E. Jones, Alexei Krindatch, Richie Stanley, and Scott Thumma. 2023. "Maps and Files for 2020." In *2020 US Religion Census*. Association of Statisticians of American Religious Bodies. www.usreligioncensus.org.
Gran, Peter. 2004. "Upper Egypt in Modern History: 'A Southern Question'?" In *Upper Egypt: Identity and Change*, edited by Nicholas Hopkins and Reem Saad, 79–96. Cairo: AUC Press.
Grewal, Zareena. 2014. *Islam Is a Foreign Country: American Muslims and the Global Crisis of Authority*. New York: New York University Press.
Gualtieri, Sarah. 2001. "Becoming 'White': Race, Religion and the Foundations of Syrian/Lebanese Ethnicity in the United States." *Journal of American Ethnic History* 20 (4): 29–58. https://doi.org/10.2307/27502745.
———. 2009. *Between Arab and White: Race and Ethnicity in the Early Syrian American Diaspora*. Berkeley: University of California Press.
Guirguis, Laure. 2016. *Copts and the Security State: Violence, Coercion, and Sectarianism*. Stanford, CA: Stanford University Press.
Guirguis, Magdi, and Nelly van Doorn-Harder, eds. 2011. *The Emergence of the Modern Coptic Papacy*. Cairo: AUC Press.
Guterl, Matthew Pratt. 2001. *The Color of Race in America, 1900–1940*. Cambridge, MA: Harvard University Press.
Gutner, Rebecca H. 2005. "A Neglected Alternative: Toward a Workable Standard for Implementing Humanitarian Asylum." *Columbia Journal of Law and Social Problems* 39 (4): 413–50.
Ha, Hyun Jeong. 2017. "Emotions of the Weak: Violence and Ethnic Boundaries among Coptic Christians in Egypt." *Ethnic and Racial Studies* 40 (1): 133–51. https://doi.org/10.1080/01419870.2016.1201586.
Hackett, Conrad. 2011. "How Many Christians Are There in Egypt?" Pew Research Center, February 16, 2011. www.pewresearch.org.
Haddad, Yvonne, and Joshua Donovan. 2013. "Good Copt, Bad Copt: Competing Narratives on Coptic Identity in Egypt and the United States." *Studies in World Christianity* 19 (3): 208–32. https://doi.org/10.3366/swc.2013.0058.
Hage, Ghassan. 1998. *White Nation: Fantasies of White Supremacy in a Multicultural Society*. London: Routledge.
———. 2021. *The Diasporic Condition: Ethnographic Explorations of the Lebanese in the World*. Chicago: University of Chicago Press.

Halbwachs, Maurice. 1992. *On Collective Memory*. Chicago: University of Chicago Press.
Hanegraaff, Hank. 2017. *Muslim: What You Need to Know about the World's Fastest-Growing Religion*. Nashville, TN: W Publishing Group.
Haney López, Ian. 1996. *White by Law: The Legal Construction of Race*. New York: New York University Press.
Hanna, Michael Wahid. 2019. "Excluded and Unequal: Copts on the Margins of the Egyptian Security State." Century Foundation, May 9, 2019. https://tcf.org.
Hanoosh, Yasmeen. 2019. *The Chaldeans: Politics and Identity in Iraq and the American Diaspora*. London: I. B. Tauris.
Hasan, S. S. 2003. *Christians versus Muslims in Modern Egypt: The Century-Long Struggle for Coptic Equality*. New York: Oxford University Press.
Hefley, James, and Marti Hefley. 1996. *By Their Blood: Christian Martyrs of the Twentieth Century*. Grand Rapids, MI: Baker Publishing Group.
Heikal, Muhammad Hasanayn. 1983. *Autumn of Fury: The Assassination of Sadat*. New York: Random House.
Heo, Angie. 2013. "'Money and Chandeliers': Mass Circuits of Pilgrimage to Coptic Egypt." *Journal of the American Academy of Religion* 81 (2): 516–28. https://doi.org/10.1093/jaarel/lft018.
———. 2018. *The Political Lives of Saints: Christian-Muslim Mediation in Egypt*. Berkeley: University of California Press
Hertzke, Allen D. 2004. *Freeing God's Children: The Unlikely Alliance for Global Human Rights*. New York: Rowman and Littlefield.
Hirschkind, Charles. 2006. *The Ethical Soundscape: Cassette Sermons and Islamic Counterpublics*. New York: Columbia University Press.
———. 2008. "Cultures of Death: Media, Religion, Bioethics." *Social Text* 26 (3): 39–58. https://doi.org/10.1215/01642472-2008-003.
"Homosexuals Need Treatment: Bishop Rafael." 2015. *Daily News Egypt*, June 28, 2015. www.dailynewsegypt.com.
Hong, Cathy Park. 2020. *Minor Feelings: An Asian American Reckoning*. New York: One World.
Horbury, Mary. 2003. "The British and the Copts." In *Views of Ancient Egypt since Napoleon Bonaparte: Imperialism, Colonialism, and Modern Appropriations*, edited by David Jeffreys, 153–70. London: Routledge.
Hothi, Randeep Singh. 2024. "The Massacre and Martyr(dom)s of Oak Creek: On the Problem of Diaspora, the Economy of Agonism, and the Extimacy of Relation-Making." *Cultural Anthropology* 39 (2): 246–71. https://doi.org/10.14506/ca39.2.04.
Hulsether, Lucia. 2022. "Decolonization ™." In *Religion and US Empire: Critical New Histories*, edited by Tisa Wenger and Sylvester A. Johnson, 298–318. New York: New York University Press.
Hunter, Alistair, and Fiona McCallum Guiney. 2023. "Misrecognised as Muslim: The Racialisation of Christians of Middle Eastern Heritage in the UK." *Journal of Ethnic and Migration Studies* 49 (15): 4014–32. https://doi.org/10.1080/1369183X.2022.2157803.

Huntington, Samuel. 1996. *The Clash of Civilizations and the Remaking of World Order*. New York: Simon and Schuster.
Hurd, Elizabeth Shakman. 2015. *Beyond Religious Freedom: The New Global Politics of Religion*. Princeton: Princeton University Press.
———. 2021. "Freedom, Salvation, Redemption: Theologies of Political Asylum." *Migration and Society: Advances in Research* 4: 110–23. https://doi.org/10.3167/arms.2021.040111.
Ibrahim, Ishak. 2019. "The Reality of Church Construction in Egypt." Tahrir Institute for Middle Eastern Policy, June 27, 2019. https://timep.org.
Ibrahim, Mina. 2019a. "The Invisible Life-Worlds of a Coptic Christian." *Middle East—Topics & Arguments* 13: 89–94.
———. 2019b. "A Minority at a Bar: Revisiting the Coptic Christian (In-)visibility." *Social Compass* 66 (3): 366–82.
———. 2023. *Identity, Marginalisation, Activism, and Victimhood in Egypt: Misfits in the Coptic Christian Community*. Cham, Switzerland: Palgrave Macmillan.
Ibrahim, Raymond. 2013. *Crucified Again: Exposing Islam's New War on Christians*. Washington, DC: Regnery.
———. 2018. *Sword and Scimitar: Fourteen Centuries of War between Islam and the West*. Cambridge, MA: Da Capo.
Ibrahim, Saad Eddin, and Ibn Khaldoun Center for Development Studies. 1996. *The Copts of Egypt*. London: Minority Rights Group.
Ibrahim, Vivian. 2010. *The Copts of Egypt: The Challenges of Modernisation and Identity*. London: I. B. Tauris.
———. 2015. "Beyond the Cross and the Crescent: Plural Identities and the Copts in Contemporary Egypt." *Ethnic and Racial Studies* 38 (14): 2584–97. https://doi.org/10.1080/01419870.2015.1061138.
Ibrahim, Youssef. 1998. "US Bill Has Egypt's Copts Squirming." *New York Times*, April 12, 1998. www.nytimes.com.
Ignatiev, Noel. 1995. *How the Irish Became White*. London: Routledge.
Ikeuchi, Suma. 2019. *Jesus Loves Japan: Return Migration and Global Pentecostalism in a Brazilian Diaspora*. Stanford, CA: Stanford University Press.
Imada, Adria. 2012. *Aloha America: Hula Circuits through the US Empire*. Durham: Duke University Press.
International Christian Concern. 2022. "Coptic Advocate Ramy Kamel Finally Released from Prison." January 10, 2022. www.persecution.org.
Iskander, Elizabeth. 2012. *Sectarian Conflict in Egypt: Coptic Media, Identity and Representation*. London: Routledge.
Issawi, Charles. 1982. "The Transformation of the Economic Position of the Millets in the Nineteenth Century." In *Christians and Jews in the Ottoman Empire: The Functioning of a Plural Society*, vol. 1, edited by Benjamin Braude and Bernard Lewis, 261–85. New York: Holmes and Meier.
Jacobson, Matthew Frye. 1999. *Whiteness of a Different Color: European Immigrants and the Alchemy of Race*. Cambridge, MA: Harvard University Press.

Jenkins, Philip. 2019. "Christian Martyrs in Orange Jumpsuits." *Christian Century*, July 3, 2019. www.christiancentury.org.

Jones, Robert P. 2020. *White Too Long: The Legacy of White Supremacy in American Christianity*. New York: Simon and Schuster.

"Joseph Nasrallah Speaks at the FDI/SIOA Rally 9/11/2010." Eye on the World, YouTube, September 12, 2010. https://www.youtube.com/watch?v=bEJMRDqsMCE.

Karas, Shawky. 1986. *The Copts since the Arab Invasion: Strangers in Their Land*. Jersey City, NJ: American, Canadian, and Australian Coptic Associations.

Kårtveit, Bård. 2017. "Are Copts at Risk Because of Their Sisi Support?" *New Arab*, March 14, 2017. https://english.alaraby.co.uk.

Kashani, Maryam. 2023. *Medina by the Bay: Scenes of Muslim Study and Survival*. Durham: Duke University Press.

Kayyali, Randa A. 2018. "Race, Religion and Identity: Arab Christians in the United States." *Culture and Religion* 19 (1): 1–19. https://doi.org/10.1080/14755610.2017.1402797.

Keating, Susan Katz. 1990. "Keeping Faith with Western Aid." *Washington Times*, November 12, 1990.

Kelly, John D. 2006. *The American Game: Capitalism, Decolonization, World Domination, and Baseball*. Chicago: University of Chicago Press.

Kennedy, David. 2004. *The Dark Side of Virtue: Reassessing International Humanitarianism*. Princeton: Princeton University Press.

Khalidi, Rashid. 2005. *Resurrecting Empire: Western Footprints and America's Perilous Path in the Middle East*. Boston: Beacon.

Khalil, Magdi. 1999. *Aqbāṭ al-Mahjar: Darāsa Midāniyya Ḥuwl Humuwm al-Waṭan w al-Muwāṭina*. Cairo: Dār al-Khiyāl.

Khater, Akram Fouad. 2001. *Inventing Home: Emigration, Gender, and the Middle Class in Lebanon, 1870–1920*. Berkeley: University of California Press.

Kim, Claire Jean. 1999. "The Racial Triangulation of Asian Americans." *Politics & Society* 27 (1): 105–38. https://doi.org/10.1177/0032329299027001005.

Kishi, Katayoun. 2017. "Assaults against Muslims in US Surpass 2001 Level." Pew Research Center, November 15, 2017. www.pewresearch.org.

Kleinman, Arthur, Veena Das, and Margaret Lock, eds. 1997. *Social Suffering*. Berkeley: University of California Press.

Klunzinger, Karl Benjamin. 1878. *Upper Egypt: Its People and Its Products: A Descriptive Account of the Manners, Customs, Superstitions, and Occupations of the People of the Nile Valley, the Desert, and the Red Sea Coast; with Sketches of the Natural History and Geology*. New York.

Knapman, Hugh Somerville. 2018. *Ecumenism of Blood: Heavenly Hope for Earthly Communion*. Mahwah, NJ: Paulist Press.

Kotsko, Adam. 2018. *Neoliberalism's Demons: On the Political Theology of Late Capital*. Stanford, CA: Stanford University Press.

Lane, Edward William. 1871. *An Account of the Manners and Customs of the Modern Egyptians*. London: John Murray.

Langewiesche, William. 2001. "The Crash of EgyptAir 990." *Atlantic*, November 2001. www.theatlantic.com.
Laughland, Oliver. 2020. "'We're Modern Slaves': How Meat Plant Workers Became the New Frontline in Covid-19 War." *Guardian*, May 2, 2020. www.theguardian.com.
Lazali, Karima. 2021. *Colonial Trauma: A Study of the Psychic and Political Consequences of Colonial Oppression in Algeria*. Translated by Matthew B. Smith. Cambridge: Polity.
Leeder, S. H. 1918. *Modern Sons of Pharaohs: A Study of the Manners and Customs of the Copts of Egypt*. London: Hodder and Stoughton.
Lemons, J. Derrick, ed. 2018. *Theologically Engaged Anthropology*. Oxford: Oxford University Press.
Long, Scott. 2004. "In a Time of Torture: The Assault on Justice in Egypt's Crackdown on Homosexual Conduct." Human Rights Watch, February 29, 2004. www.hrw.org.
Lukasik, Candace. 2016. "Conquest of Paradise: Secular Binds and Coptic Political Mobilization." *Middle East Critique* 25 (2): 107–25. https://doi.org/10.1080/19436149.2016.1144910.
———. 2021. "Economy of Blood: The Persecuted Church and the Racialization of American Copts." *American Anthropologist* 123 (3): 565–77. https://doi.org/10.1111/aman.13602.
———. 2022a. "Migrating Minority: Persecution Politics in Transnational Perspective." *International Journal of Middle East Studies* 54 (3): 541–46. https://doi.org/10.1017/S0020743822000678.
———. 2022b. "Majority Perceptions of Minor Feelings in Egypt." Tahrir Institute for Middle East Policy. www.timep.org.
———. 2022c. "Modern-Day Martyrs: Coptic Blood and American Christian Kinship." In *Global Visions of Violence: Persecution and Agency in World Christianity*, edited by Jason Bruner and David Kirkpatrick, 107–24. New Brunswick, NJ: Rutgers University Press.
———. 2022d. "Religious Publicity and Transnational Minority Politics." *Immanent Frame*. http://tif.ssrc.org.
———. 2022e. "Beyond Church and State: Contentions of Minority Citizenship in Egypt." *Journal of Orthodox Christian Studies* 5 (2): 179–201.
Lum, Kathryn Gin. 2022. *Heathen: Religion and Race in American History*. Cambridge, MA: Harvard University Press.
Maghbouleh, Neda. 2017. *The Limits of Whiteness: Iranian Americans and the Everyday Politics of Race*. Stanford, CA: Stanford University Press.
Mahmood, Saba. 2005. *The Politics of Piety: The Islamic Revival and the Feminist Subject*. Princeton: Princeton University Press.
———. 2009. "Religious Reason and Secular Affect: An Incommensurable Divide?" In *Is Critique Secular? Blasphemy, Injury, and Free Speech*, by Talal Asad, Wendy Brown, Judith Butler, and Saba Mahmood, 64–100. Berkeley: Townsend Center for the Humanities, University of California, Berkeley.

——. 2015. *Religious Difference in a Secular Age: A Minority Report*. Princeton: Princeton University Press.

Maira, Sunaina. 2009. *The 9/11 Generation: Youth, Rights, and Solidarity in the War on Terror*. New York: New York University Press.

Majaj, Lisa Suhair. 2000. "Arab-Americans and the Meanings of Race." In *Postcolonial Theory and the United States: Race, Ethnicity, and Literature*, edited by Amritjit Singh and Peter Schmidt, 320–37. Jackson: University of Mississippi Press.

Makar, Johannes. 2016. "How Egypt's Copts Fell Out of Love with President Sisi." *Foreign Policy*, December 9, 2016. https://foreignpolicy.com.

Makdisi, Ussama. 2000. *The Culture of Sectarianism: Community, History, and Violence in Nineteenth-Century Ottoman Lebanon*. Berkeley: University of California Press.

——. 2011. *Artillery of Heaven: American Missionaries and the Failed Conversion of the Middle East*. Ithaca, NY: Cornell University Press.

——. 2021. *Age of Coexistence: The Ecumenical Frame and the Making of the Modern Arab World*. Berkeley: University of California Press.

Malkki, Liisa. 2007. "The Politics of Trauma and Asylum: Universals and Their Effects." *Ethos: Journal for the Society for Psychological Anthropology* 35 (3): 336–43. https://doi.org/10.1525/eth.2007.35.3.336.

Malsin, Jared. 2015. "Christians under Pressure: From Bigotry at School to Imprisonment and Murder." *Guardian*, July 27, 2015. www.theguardian.com.

"Manhattan Declaration: A Call of Christian Conscience." 2009. November 20, 2009. www.manhattandeclaration.org.

Marcos, Anthony. 2021. *A Spring in Sinai: Hieromartyr Mina Abood, His Life, Miracles, and Martyrdom in Post-Revolutionary Egypt*. Sandia, TX: St. Mary and St. Moses Abbey Press.

Marcus, George. 1995. "Ethnography in/of the World System: The Emergence of Multi-Sited Ethnography." *Annual Review of Anthropology* 24: 95–117. https://doi.org/10.1146/annurev.an.24.100195.000523.

Marks, Rachel, Paul Jacobs, and Alli Coritz. 2023. "Lebanese, Iranian and Egyptian Populations Represented Nearly Half of the MENA Population in 2020 Census." US Census Bureau, September 21, 2023. www.census.gov.

Marshall, Paul, and Lela Gilbert. 1997. *Their Blood Cries Out: The Worldwide Tragedy of Modern Christians Who Are Dying for Their Faith*. Dallas: Word Publishing.

Marshall, Paul, Lela Gilbert, and Nina Shea. 2013. *Persecuted: The Global Assault on Christians*. Nashville: Thomas Nelson.

Marshall, Ruth. 2014. "Christianity, Anthropology, Politics." *Current Anthropology* 55 (S10): S344–S356. https://doi.org/10.1086/677737.

Marzouki, Nadia. 2016. "The US Coptic Diaspora and the Limit of Polarization." *Journal of Immigrant & Refugee Studies* 14 (3): 261–76. https://doi.org/10.1080/15562948.2016.1210712.

"Maven Developments' Cali Coasts Accumulates More Than EGP 16bn in Investments." 2022. *Daily News Egypt*, August 1, 2022. www.dailynewsegypt.com.

McAllister, Carlota, and Valentina Napolitano. 2020. "Introduction: Incarnate Politics beyond the Cross and the Sword." *Social Analysis: The International Journal of Anthropology* 64 (4): 1–20. https://doi.org/10.3167/sa.2020.640401.

———. 2021. "Political Theology/Theopolitics: The Thresholds and Vulnerabilities of Sovereignty." *Annual Review of Anthropology* 50: 109–24. https://doi.org/10.1146/annurev-anthro-101819-110334.

McAlister, Melani. 2001. *Epic Encounters: Culture, Media, and US Interests in the Middle East since 1945*. Berkeley: University of California Press

———. 2008a. "The Politics of Persecution." *MERIP*, no. 249 (Winter). https://merip.org.

———. 2008b. "What Is Your Heart For? Affect and Internationalism in the Evangelical Public Sphere." *American Literary History* 20 (4): 870–95. https://doi.org/10.1093/alh/ajn049.

———. 2012. "The Persecuted Body: Evangelical Internationalism, Islam, and the Politics of Fear." In *Facing Fear: The History of an Emotion in Global Perspective*, edited by Michael Laffan and Max Weiss, 133–61. Princeton: Princeton University Press.

———. 2018. *The Kingdom of God Has No Borders: A Global History of American Evangelicals*. Oxford: Oxford University Press.

———. 2019. "Evangelical Populist Internationalism and the Politics of Persecution." *Review of Faith & International Affairs* 17 (3): 105–17. https://doi.org/10.1080/15570274.2019.1644007.

———. 2021. "Established Authorities: Theology, the State, and the Apartheid Struggle." In *At Home and Abroad: The Politics of American Religion*, edited by Elizabeth Shakman Hurd and Winnifred Fallers Sullivan, 249–72. New York: Columbia University Press.

———. 2023. "Evangelicals and Human Rights." In *Reclaiming Human Rights in a Changing World Order*, edited by Christopher Sabatini, 149–81. London: Chatham House.

McCaughey, Betsy. 2023. "Muslims Are Helping Turn the Tide in School Culture Wars." *New York Post*, April 11, 2023. https://nypost.com.

McGranahan, Carole, and John Collins, eds. 2018. *Ethnographies of US Empire*. Durham: Duke University Press.

McKinnon, Susan. 1991. *From a Shattered Sun: Hierarchy, Gender, and Alliance in the Tanimbar Islands*. Madison: University of Wisconsin Press.

McKinnon, Susan, and Fenella Cannell, eds. 2017. *Vital Relations: Modernity and the Persistent Life of Kinship*. Santa Fe, NM: SAR Press.

"MECHRIC Warns from Escalation of Oppression against Christians in Egypt, Lebanon, Iraq, Others." 2001. *Mideast Newswire*, June 28, 2001. www.clhrf.com.

Merry, Sally Engle. 2016. *The Seductions of Quantification: Measuring Human Rights, Gender Violence, and Sex Trafficking*. Chicago: University of Chicago Press.

Meunier, Michael. 1998. "The Egyptian Government Persecutes Coptic Christians." *Washington Times*, April 12, 1998, B2.

Michka, Aaron. 2021. "House, Church, Cave: Coptic Landscapes and the Demands of Pluralism in Upper Egypt." PhD dissertation, University of Michigan.

Mikhail, Kyriakos. 1911. *Copts and Muslims under British Control: A Collection of Facts and a Résumé of Authoritative Opinions on the Coptic Question*. London: Smith, Elder & Co.

Mondzain, Marie-José. 2005. *Image, Icon, Economy: The Byzantine Origins of the Contemporary Imaginary*. Translated by Rico Franses. Stanford, CA: Stanford University Press.

Morrison, Toni. 1993. "On the Backs of Blacks." *Time*, December 2, 1993. https://time.com.

Morsi, Noran. 2021. "Elmahaba Center: Uniting Coptic Egyptians in Nashville's Little Minya." Egyptian Streets, April 1, 2021. https://egyptianstreets.com.

Moss, Candida. 2013. *The Myth of Persecution: How Early Christians Invented a Story of Martyrdom*. New York: Harper Collins.

Mossaad, Nadwa. 2019. "Refugees and Asylees: 2018." Department of Homeland Security, Office of Immigration Statistics, October 2019. www.dhs.gov.

Mozingo, Joe. 2001. "Slain Egyptian Was a Fixture in San Gabriel." *Los Angeles Times*, September 19, 2001. www.latimes.com.

Muller, Christopher. 2012. "Northward Migration and the Rise of Racial Disparity in American Incarceration, 1880–1950." *American Journal of Sociology* 118 (2): 281–326. https://doi.org/10.1086/666384.

Myers, Ella. 2017. "Beyond the Wages of Whiteness: Du Bois on the Irrationality of Antiblack Racism." *Items: Insights from the Social Sciences*, March 21, 2017. https://items.ssrc.org.

Naber, Nadine. 2014. "Imperial Whiteness and the Diasporas of Empire." *American Quarterly* 66 (4): 1107–15. https://doi.org/10.1353/aq.2014.0068.

Naber, Nadine, and Matthew Stiffler. 2013. "Maronite Christians, Orthodox Christians, and Sunni Muslims from the Arab Region: Between Empire, Racialization, and Assimilation." In *MisReading America: Scriptures and Difference*, edited by Vincent Wimbush, 208–71. New York: Oxford University Press.

Napolitano, Valentina. 2015. *Migrant Hearts and the Atlantic Return: Transnationalism and the Roman Catholic Church*. New York: Fordham University Press.

———. 2020. "On the Touch-Event: Theopolitical Encounters." *Social Analysis: The International Journal of Cultural and Social Practice* 64 (4): 81–99. https://doi.org/10.3167/sa.2020.640405.

National Transportation Safety Board. 1999. *Aircraft Accident Brief: EgyptAir Flight 990*. NTSB, October 31, 1999. www.ntsb.gov.

"New Church Strife Reported in Egypt." 1972. *New York Times*, November 15, 1972. www.nytimes.com.

Nucho, Joanne Randa. 2016. *Everyday Sectarianism in Urban Lebanon: Infrastructures, Public Services, and Power*. Princeton: Princeton University Press.

Nutt, Amy Ellis. 2017. "Long Shadow Cast by Psychiatrist on Transgender Issues Finally Recedes at Johns Hopkins." *Washington Post*, April 5, 2017. https://washingtonpost.com.

Oliphant, Elayne. 2021. "The Secular and the Global: Rethinking the Anthropology of Christianity in the Wake of 1492." *Religion* 51 (4): 577–92. https://doi.org/10.1080/0048721X.2021.1971500.

Olmstead, Gracy. 2013. "A Coptic Exodus from Egypt." *American Conservative*, September 6, 2013. www.theamericanconservative.com.

O'Neill, Kevin. 2009. *City of God: Christian Citizenship in Postwar Guatemala*. Berkeley: University of California Press.

Oraby, Mona. 2018. "Law, the State, and Public Order: Regulating Religion in Contemporary Egypt." *Law & Society Review* 52 (3): 574–602. https://doi.org/10.1111/lasr.12353.

Oram, Elizabeth. 2004. "Constructing Modern Copts: The Production of Coptic Christian Identity in Contemporary Egypt." PhD dissertation, Princeton University.

Ordóñez, J. Thomas. 2008. "The State of Confusion: Reflections on Central American Asylum Seekers in the Bay Area." *Ethnography* 9 (1): 35–60. https://doi.org/10.1177/1466138108088948.

Papaconstantinou, Arietta. 2006. "Historiography, Hagiography, and the Making of the Coptic 'Church of the Martyrs' in Early Islamic Egypt." *Dumbarton Oaks Papers* 60: 65–86.

Parks, S. Kent, and John Scott. 2010. "Missing Peoples: The Unserved 'One-Fourth' World: Especially Buddhists, Hindus and Muslims." Lausanne Movement, July 5, 2010. https://lausanne.org.

Pastor, Camila. 2017. *The Mexican Mahjar: Transnational Maronites, Jews, and Arabs under the French Mandate*. Austin: University of Texas Press.

Pedersen, David. 2012. *American Value: Migrants, Money, and Meaning in El Salvador and the United States*. Chicago: University of Chicago Press.

Pennington, J. D. 1982. "The Copts in Modern Egypt." *Middle Eastern Studies* 18 (2): 158–79. https://doi.org/10.1080/00263208208700503.

Pennock, Pamela E. 2017. *The Rise of the Arab American Left: Activists, Allies, and Their Fight against Imperialism and Racism, 1960s–1980s*. Chapel Hill: University of North Carolina Press.

Perkins, Alisa. 2020. *Muslim American City: Gender and Religion in Metro Detroit*. New York: New York University Press.

Perry, Samuel, and Andrew Whitehead. 2020. *Taking America Back for God: Christian Nationalism in the United States*. Oxford: Oxford University Press.

Pew Research Center. 2012. *Faith on the Move: The Religious Affiliation of International Migrants*. March 8, 2012. www.pewforum.org.

———. N.d. "Religious Landscape Study." www.pewforum.org.

Piot, Charles. 1999. *Remotely Global: Village Modernity in West Africa*. Chicago: University of Chicago Press.

Piot, Charles, with Kodjo Nicolas Batema. 2019. *The Fixer: Visa Lottery Chronicles*. Durham: Duke University Press.

Progressive Copts. 2020. "Open Statement against the Coptic Church's Position on the LGBTQI+ Community." Medium, January 15, 2020. https://medium.com.

Puar, Jasbir. 2007. *Terrorist Assemblages: Homonationalism in Queer Times*. Durham: Duke University Press.

Purcell, Mark. 1998. "A Place for the Copts: Imagined Territory and Spatial Conflict in Egypt." *Ecumene* 5 (4): 432–51. https://doi.org/10.1177/096746089800500403.

Ramirez, Anthony. 2005. "Arrests Fail to Mend Muslim-Christian Rift." *New York Times*, March 5, 2005. www.nytimes.com.

Ramzy, Carolyn M. 2015. "To Die Is Gain: Singing a Heavenly Citizenship among Egypt's Coptic Christians." *Ethnos* 80 (5): 649–70. https://doi.org/10.1080/00141844.2014.943260.

Ramzy, Mark. 2023. "One of the 'Progressive Copts' on the Future He Sees for the Coptic Diaspora." *Broadview*, July 4, 2023. https://broadview.org.

Rana, Junaid. 2007. "The Story of Islamophobia." *Souls* 9 (2): 148–61. https://doi.org/10.1080/10999940701382607.

———. 2016. "The Racial Infrastructure of the Terror-Industrial Complex." *Social Text* 34 (4): 111–38. https://doi.org/10.1215/01642472-3680894.

Razavi, Negar. 2019a. "In Times of Crisis: Middle East Policy between the Counterterror State and the Marketplace of Ideas." *Critical Studies on Security* 7 (1): 1–17. https://doi.org/10.1080/21624887.2018.1500053.

———. 2019b. "The Systemic Problem of 'Iran Expertise' in Washington." *Jadaliyya*, September 4, 2019. www.jadaliyya.com.

Reid, Donald. 2002. *Whose Pharaohs? Archaeology, Museums, and Egyptian National Identity from Napoleon to World War I*. Berkeley: University of California Press.

Riccardi-Swartz, Sarah. 2021. "American Conservatives and the Allure of Post-Soviet Russian Orthodoxy." *Religions* 12 (12): 1036. https://doi.org/10.3390/rel12121036.

Richardson, James F. 1974. *Urban Police in the United States*. Port Washington, NY: Kennikat.

Rieker, Martina. 1997. "The Sa'id and the City: Subaltern Spaces in the Making of Modern Egypt." PhD dissertation, Temple University.

Right Response Ministries. 2023. "Christians Are Under Attack in America." YouTube, April 19, 2023. https://www.youtube.com/watch?v=6jxwJafXCjk.

Robbins, Joel. 2013. "Beyond the Suffering Subject: Toward an Anthropology of the Good." *Journal of the Royal Anthropological Institute* 19 (3): 447–62. https://doi.org/10.1111/1467-9655.12044.

———. 2020. *Theology and the Anthropology of Christian Life*. Oxford: Oxford University Press.

Robson, Laura. 2011. *Colonialism and Christianity in Mandate Palestine*. Austin: University of Texas Press.

Roderick, Keith. 1998. "The Egyptian Government Persecutes Coptic Christians." *Washington Times*, April 12, 1998, B2.

Roediger, David R. 1991. *The Wages of Whiteness: Race and the Making of the American Working Class*. New York: Verso.

Rogers, Eugene F., Jr. 2021. *Blood Theology: Seeing Red in Body- and God-Talk*. Cambridge: Cambridge University Press.
Rosa, Jonathan. 2019. *Looking Like a Language, Sounding Like a Race: Raciolinguistic Ideologies and the Learning of Latinidad*. Oxford: Oxford University Press.
Rose, Lena. 2019. "Geometries of 'Global' Evangelicalism." *Global Networks* 19: 86–100. https://doi.org/10.1111/glob.12211.
Rose, Lena, and Zoe Given-Wilson. 2021. "'What Is Truth?' Negotiating Christian Convert Asylum Seekers' Credibility." *Annals of the American Academy of Political and Social Science* 697 (1): 221–35. https://doi.org/10.1177/00027162211059454.
Rothberg, Michael. 2009. *Multidirectional Memory: Remembering the Holocaust in the Age of Decolonization*. Stanford, CA: Stanford University Press.
Rowe, Paul. 2001. "Four Guys and a Fax Machine? Diasporas, New Information Technologies, and the Internationalization of Religion in Egypt." *Journal of Church and State* 43 (1): 81–92. https://doi.org/10.1093/jcs/43.1.81.
———. 2007. "Neo-Millet Systems and Transnational Religious Movements: The Humayun Decrees and Church Construction in Egypt." *Journal of Church and State* 49: 329–50. https://doi.org/10.1093/jcs/49.2.329.
Roy, Arundhati. 2004. *An Ordinary Person's Guide to Empire*. Boston: South End.
Rozakou, Katerina. 2012. "The Biopolitics of Hospitality in Greece: Humanitarianism and the Management of Refugees." *American Ethnologist* 39 (3): 562–77. https://doi.org/10.1111/j.1548-1425.2012.01381.x.
Rubaii, Kali. 2018. "Counterinsurgency and the Ethical Life of Material Things in Iraq's Anbar Province." PhD dissertation, University of California, Santa Cruz.
———. 2019. "Tripartheid: How Sectarianism Became Internal to Being in Anbar, Iraq." *Political and Legal Anthropology Review (PoLAR)* 42 (1): 125–41. https://doi.org/10.1111/plar.12278.
———. 2023. "Decentering Death: The War on Terror and the Less-Than-Lethal Paradigm." *American Anthropologist*, May 2023. https://doi.org/10.1111/aman.13870.
Saad, Reem. 2002. "Egyptian Politics and the Tenancy Law." In *Counter-Revolution in Egypt's Countryside: Land and Farmers in the Era of Economic Reform*, edited by Ray Bush, 103–25. New York: Zed Books.
———. 2006. "The Two Pasts of Nasser's Peasants: Political Memories and Everyday Life in an Egyptian Village." In *History and the Present*, edited by Partha Chatterjee and Anjan Ghosh, 127–48. London: Anthem.
Saad, Saad Michael. 2005. "The Armanious Family: Four Coptic Icons from Thebes Transfigured in New Jersey." [In Arabic]. *Watani*, March 27, 2005, 8.
———. 2010. "The Contemporary Life of the Coptic Orthodox Church in the United States." *Studies in World Christianity* 16 (3): 207–25.
Sadik, Morris. 1997. "Madhbaḥat ʿEzbet Daoud-Najʿ Ḥammādī Qinā 3/13/1997." Markiz al-Kalima al-Masiḥi. https://alkalema.net.
Sahlins, Marshall. 2013. *What Kinship Is—And Is Not*. Chicago: University of Chicago Press.

St. Mark's Coptic Law Enforcement Officers Society. 2021a. "Lt. Mariana Zakhary at the PBA & Coptic community dinner 3031." Facebook, August 9, 2021. https://www.facebook.com/stmarkscopticleos/videos/1885029291656696.

———. 2021b. "Patrick Lynch, NYC PBA President at the PBA & Coptic Community Leaders dinner." Facebook August 9, 2021. https://www.facebook.com/stmarkscopticleos/videos/1699417784448985.

———. 2021c. "PBA and Coptic Community leaders Dinner 2021." Facebook, August 9, 2021. https://www.facebook.com/stmarkscopticleos/videos/172450234955670.

———. 2021d. "Egyptian Community Activists urge the community to support the police." Facebook, August 15, 2021. https://www.facebook.com/stmarkscopticleos/videos/188324333290316.

Saleh, Zainab. 2021. *Return to Ruin: Iraqi Narratives of Exile and Nostalgia*. Stanford, CA: Stanford University Press.

Salomon, Noah. 2021. "When Home Becomes Abroad, and Abroad Becomes Home: Thinking American Empire Through a New Sudan." In *At Home and Abroad: The Politics of American Religion*, edited by Elizabeth Shakman Hurd and Winnifred Fallers Sullivan, 288–303. New York: Columbia University Press.

Schielke, Samuli. 2020. *Migrant Dreams: Egyptian Workers in the Gulf States*. Cairo: AUC Press.

Schneider, David. 1984. *A Critique of the Study of Kinship*. Ann Arbor: University of Michigan Press.

Schwabe, Siri. 2023. *Moving Memory: Remembering Palestine in Postdictatorship Chile*. Ithaca, NY: Cornell University Press.

Scott, Joan W. 1997. *Only Paradoxes to Offer: French Feminists and the Rights of Man*. Cambridge, MA: Harvard University Press.

Scott, Rachel M. 2010. *The Challenge of Political Islam: Non-Muslims and the Egyptian State*. Stanford, CA: Stanford University Press.

Sedra, Paul. 1999. "Class Cleavages and Ethnic Conflict: Coptic Christian Communities in Modern Egyptian Politics." *Islam and Christian-Muslim Relations* 10 (2): 219–35. https://doi.org/10.1080/09596419908721181.

———. 2009. "Writing the History of the Modern Copts: From Victims and Symbols to Actors." *History Compass* 7 (3): 1049–63. https://doi.org/10.1111/j.1478-0542.2009.00607.x.

———. 2011. *From Mission to Modernity: Evangelicals, Reformers, and Education in Nineteenth-Century Egypt*. London I. B. Tauris.

Seikaly, Samir. 1970. "Coptic Communal Reform: 1860–1914." *Middle Eastern Studies* 6 (3): 247–75. https://doi.org/10.1080/00263207008700152.

Selod, Sahar. 2018. *Forever Suspect: Racialized Surveillance of Muslim Americans in the War on Terror*. New Brunswick, NJ Rutgers University Press.

Seteney, Shami. 2009. "Aqalliyya/Minority in Modern Egyptian Discourse." In *Words in Motion: Toward a Global Lexicon*, edited by Carol Gluck and Anna L. Tsing, 151–73. Durham: Duke University Press.

Sharkey, Heather. 2008. *American Evangelicals in Egypt: Missionary Encounters in an Age of Empire*. Princeton: Princeton University Press.
Shea, Nina. 2008. "The Origins and Legacy of the Movement to Fight Religious Persecution." Hudson Institute, June 14, 2008. www.hudson.org.
Shenoda, Anthony. 2010. "Cultivating Mystery: Miracles and a Coptic Moral Imaginary." PhD dissertation, Harvard University.
———. 2011. "Reflections on the (In)Visibility of Copts in Egypt." *Jadaliyya*, May 18, 2011. www.jadaliyya.com.
———. 2012. "The Politics of Faith: On Faith, Skepticism, and Miracles among Coptic Christians in Egypt." *Ethnos* 77 (4): 477–95. https://doi.org/10.1080/00141844.2011.609941.
Shenoda, Matthew. 2005. *Somewhere Else*. Minneapolis, MN: Coffee House.
Shukry, Nader. 2011. "Adly Abadir (1920- 2009)." *Watani*, December 15, 2011. https://en.wataninet.com.
Simpson, Audra. 2014. *Mohawk Interruptus: Political Life Across the Borders of Settler States*. Durham: Duke University Press.
Smith, Samuel. 2017. "Egypt's President Sisi Meets with US Evangelical Leaders for First Time in Cairo." *Christian Post*, November 2, 2017. www.christianpost.com.
Soltero, Carlos R. 2006. *Latinos and American Law: Landmark Supreme Court Cases*. Austin: University of Texas Press.
Spelman, Elizabeth V. 1997. *Fruits of Sorrow: Framing Our Attention to Suffering*. Boston: Beacon.
Steinmetz-Jenkins, Daniel. 2014. "Blood: A Critique of Christianity." *Immanent Frame*, July 15, 2014. https://tif.ssrc.org.
Stern, Marlow. 2017. "Media for Christ, Company Allegedly Behind 'Innocence of Muslims.'" *Daily Beast*, July 14, 2017. www.thedailybeast.com.
Stewart, Kathleen. 2007. *Ordinary Affects*. Durham: Duke University Press.
Stoeckl, Kristina. 2020. "The Rise of the Russian Christian Right: The Case of the World Congress of Families." *Religion, State & Society* 48 (4): 223–38. https://doi.org/10.1080/09637494.2020.1796172.
Stoeckl, Kristina, and Dmitry Uzlaner. 2022. *The Moralist International: Russia in the Global Culture Wars*. New York: Fordham University Press.
Stoler, Ann Laura. 2016. *Duress: Imperial Durabilities in Our Times*. Durham: Duke University Press.
Stoler, Ann Laura, and Carole McGranahan. 2018. "Disassemblage: Rethinking US Imperial Formations." In *Ethnographies of US Empire*, edited by Carole McGranahan and John Collins, 477–89. Durham: Duke University Press.
Stone, Nomi. 2022. *Pinelandia: An Anthropology and Field Poetics of War and Empire*. Berkeley: University of California Press.
Strathern, Marilyn. 1985. "Kinship and Economy: Constitutive Orders of a Provisional Kind." *American Ethnologist* 12 (2): 191–209. https://doi.org/10.1525/ae.1985.12.2.02a00010.

Tadros, Mariz. 2009. "Vicissitudes in the Entente between the Coptic Orthodox Church and the State in Egypt (1952–2007)." *International Journal of Middle East Studies* 41 (2): 269–87. https://doi.org/10.1017/S0020743809090667.

Tadros, Samuel. 2013. *Motherland Lost: The Egyptian and Coptic Quest for Modernity*. Stanford, CA: Hoover Institution Press.

———. 2017. "The Continuing Tragedy of Egypt's Coptic Christians." Hudson Institute, May 30, 2017. www.hudson.org.

Tambar, Kabir. 2019. "Professions of Friendship: Revisiting the Concept of the Political in the Middle East." *Comparative Studies of South Asia, Africa, and the Middle East* 39 (2): 249–63. https://doi.org/10.1215/1089201X-7586775.

Tambiah, Stanley. 1996. *Leveling Crowds: Ethnonationalist Conflicts and Collective Violence in South Asia*. Berkeley: University of California Press.

Thangaraj, Stanley. 2012. "Playing through Differences: Black-White Racial Logic and Interrogating South Asian American Identity." *Ethnic and Racial Studies* 35 (6): 988–1006. https://doi.org/10.1080/01419870.2012.661868.

———. 2022. "'We Share the Same Ancestry': US Kurdish Diasporas and the Aspirational and Ascriptive Practices of Race." *American Anthropologist* 124 (1): 104–17. https://doi.org/10.1111/aman.13698.

Thomas, Martyn, Adly A. Youssef, Heinz Gstrein, and Paul Meinard Strässle, eds. 2006. *Copts in Egypt: A Christian Minority under Siege: Papers Presented at the First International Coptic Symposium, Zurich, September 23–25, 2004*. Göttingen: G2W.

Thomas, Sonja. 2019. "Cowboys and Indians: Indian Priests in Rural Montana." *WSQ: Women's Studies Quarterly* 47 (1–2): 110–31. https://doi.org/10.1353/wsq.2019.0028.

Thomas, Todne. 2021. *Kincraft: The Making of Black Evangelical Sociality*. Durham: Duke University Press.

Thomas, Todne, Asiya Malik, and Rose Wellman, eds. 2017. *New Directions in Spiritual Kinship: Sacred Ties across the Abrahamic Religions*. Cham, Switzerland: Palgrave Macmillan.

Ticktin, Miriam. 2006. "Where Ethics and Politics Meet: The Violence of Humanitarianism in France." *American Ethnologist* 33 (1): 33–49. https://doi.org/10.1525/ae.2006.33.1.33.

Tsing, Anna. 2005. *Friction: An Ethnography of Global Connection*. Princeton: Princeton University Press.

Tsourapas, Gerasimos. 2018. "Egypt: Migration and Diaspora Politics in an Emerging Transit Country." Migration Policy Institute, August 8, 2018. www.migrationpolicy.org.

Tusan, Michelle. 2012. *Smyrna's Ashes: Humanitarianism, Genocide, and the Birth of the Middle East*. Berkeley: University of California Press.

US Department of Homeland Security, Office of Homeland Security Statistics. N.d. "Refugees and Asylees Annual Flow Report." www.dhs.gov.

US Department of State, Bureau of Consular Affairs. N.d. "Diversity Visa Program Statistics." https://travel.state.gov.

US-International Coptic Media Center. 2019. "On Saturday, November 16, His Holiness concluded the fifteenth convention." Facebook, November 20, 2019. https://www.facebook.com/CopticUS/posts/867543490328213.

Vine, David. 2015. *The United States of War: A Global History of America's Endless Conflicts, from Columbus to the Islamic State*. Berkeley: University of California Press.

Volpp, Leti. 2002. "The Citizen and the Terrorist." *UCLA Law Review* 49 (5): 1575–1600.

Waits, Hannah. 2022. "Putting an American God into Public Schools around the World." *Diplomatic History* 46 (4): 701–27. https://doi.org/10.1093/dh/dhac040.

Wakin, Edward. 1963. *A Lonely Minority: The Modern Story of Egypt's Copts*. New York: William Morrow.

Wallace, Bruce. 2013. "Amid Instability in Egypt, Coptic Christians Flee to US." NPR, January 4, 2013. www.npr.org.

Walsh, Declan, and Noor Youssef. 2016. "ISIS Claims Responsibility for Egypt Church Bombing and Warns of More to Come." *New York Times*, December 13, 2016. www.nytimes.com.

Walton, Jeffrey. 2014. "IRD Grieves the Loss of Keith Roderick, Defender of the Persecuted Church." *Juicy Ecumenism*, March 12, 2014. https://juicyecumenism.com.

Wassef, Mira, and Nicole Johnson. 2023. "Innocent Bystander Killed in Drive-By Shooting Was Visiting Family in NYC from Egypt." PIX11, May 24, 2023. https://pix11.com.

Watchmen on the Wall—A Ministry of Family Research Council. 2016. "Brigitte Gabriel Reads the Muslim Brotherhood Plan for America." YouTube, September 6, 2016. https://www.youtube.com/watch?v=SgKfL6M6CpU.

Watson, Andrew. 1904. *The American Mission in Egypt: 1854–1896*. Pittsburgh: United Presbyterian Board of Publication.

Weimer, Adrian Chastain. 2011. *Martyrs' Mirror: Persecution and Holiness in Early New England*. Oxford: Oxford University Press.

Wellman, Rose. 2021. *Feeding Iran: Shi'i Families and the Making of the Islamic Republic*. Berkeley: University of California Press.

Wenger, Tisa, and Sylvester A. Johnson, eds. 2022. *Religion and US Empire: Critical New Histories*. New York: New York University Press.

Westbrook, Donald A., and Saad Michael Saad. 2017. "Religious Identity and Borderless Territoriality in the Coptic E-Diaspora." *Journal of International Migration and Integration* 18 (1): 341–51. https://doi.org/10.1007/s12134-016-0479-8.

Weston, Kath. 1991. *Families We Choose: Lesbians, Gays, Kinship*. New York: Columbia University Press.

Williams, Daniel. 2010. *God's Own Party: The Making of the Christian Right*. Oxford: Oxford University Press.

Wilson, Richard A. 1996. "Representing Human Rights Violations: Social Contexts and Subjectivities." In *Human Rights, Culture and Context: Anthropological Perspectives*, edited by Richard A. Wilson, 134–60. London: Pluto.

Winerip, Michael. 2001. "A Terrorist at the Shell Station? No, but That Goatee Looks Suspicious." *New York Times*, September 30, 2001. www.nytimes.com.

Yellin, Deena. 2018. "Coptic Orthodox Pope Tawadros Visits New Jersey." NJ.com, September 30, 2018. htttps://nj.ccm.

Ye'or, Bat. 1985. *The Dhimmi: Jews and Christians under Islam*. Madison, NJ: Fairleigh Dickinson University Press.

———. 2001. *Islam and Dhimmitude: Where Civilizations Collide*. Madison, NJ: Fairleigh Dickinson University Press

Young, Neil J. 2015. *We Gather Together: The Religious Right and the Problem of Interfaith Politics*. Oxford: Oxford University Press.

Yousief, Lydia. 2019. "Coptic Nashville." *Public Orthodoxy*, April 17, 2019. https://publicorthodoxy.org.

Youssef, Bishop. 2016. *Adapting to a New Place Called Home: The Coptic Immigration Experience in the United States of America*. Sandia, TX: St. Mary & St. Moses Abbey Press.

———. N.d. "The 21 Martyrs of Libya: Videotaped Instantaneous Sainthood." Coptic Orthodox Diocese of the Southern United States. www.suscopts.org.

Youssef, Joseph. 2013. "From the Blood of St. Mina to the Martyrs of Maspero: Commemoration, Identity, and Social Memory in the Coptic Orthodox Church." *Journal of the Canadian Society for Coptic Studies* 5: 61–73.

Zakher Musa, Kamal. 2015. *Qarā'a fi Wāqa'na al-Kinisiy: Shahāda w Ru'iyya*. Cairo: GC Center.

Zeidan, David. 1999. "The Copts—Equal, Protected or Persecuted? The Impact of Islamization on Muslim-Christian Relations in Modern Egypt." *Islam and Christian-Muslim Relations* 10 (1): 53–67. https://doi.org/10.1080/09596419908721170.

Zizioulas, John D. 1985. *Being as Communion*. Yonkers, NY: SVS Press.

Zubovich, Gene. 2022. *Before the Religious Right: Liberal Protestants, Human Rights, and the Polarization of the United States*. Philadelphia: University of Pennsylvania Press.

INDEX

Abaza, Mona, 88
Abbas, Raouf, 80
al-'Abbāsiyya district, in Cairo, 24
Abdel-Masih, Joseph Nasrallah, 151–52
Abu El-Haj, Nadia, 231n72
Abul-Magd, Zeinab, 25
Abū Qurqās, al-Minyā village, 57
ACA. *See* American Coptic Association
ACLJ. *See* American Center for Law and Justice
activism: of Coptic diaspora, 35–36, 48, 53, 239n74; of Muslims in West, 55–56; for persecution of Christians, 58–59
Acts (Book of), 48
Agrama, Hussein, 130
Agrarian Reform Act of 1952, Egypt, 86–87
'Ali, Muhammad, 80–81, 87
American Center for Law and Justice (ACLJ), 66
American Coptic Association (ACA), 40–41, 57, 207, 235n15, 235n18; asylum status influenced by, 129
American Copts: Arab American community and, 59; Armanious family murders, 205, 207; assimilation of, 174–77; Christian conservative movement and, 182, 184; Christian nationalism and, 185–88, 202; collective memory of persecution among, 4, 59; conservative alliances with, 199–202; Coptic American Political Action Committee, 195, 197, 214; *The Copts* newsletter, 40; culture wars and, 188–94, 204; Egypt Migrations organization, 234n7; LGBTQ rights and protections and, 191–94, 204, 252n39, 252n53; marginalization of, 62; martyrdom and, 208; as model minority, 214; in New Jersey, 194–99; pluralism and, 178–79; political support for Trump, 180–82, 184; Progressive Copts, 234n7; racialization of, 152; sectarian legacies for, 199–202; size of community, 232n88; in the South, 210–16; suffering as common bond among, 59–67; US Christian conservative movement and, 182, 184; violence against, 205, 206, 207; wage issues for, 215–16. *See also* immigration; migration
American Presbyterian missionaries, in Egypt, 227n3
Anderson, Leith, 64–65
Angaelos (Bishop), 64–65, 241n95
Anglo-American Protestant movement, 227n3
Anidjar, Gil, 2–3
Anker, Deborah, 115
anthropology: cultural alterity and, 8; theology and, 8
anti-Arab racism, 39, 234n7
anti-Black racism, 61, 219
anti-Muslim racism, 39, 234n7; against Copts, 2; after 9/11, 155
Arab Spring, 1, 24, 198
Armanios, Febe, 13
Armanious family murders, in New Jersey, 205, *206*, 207
Asad, Talal, 9

assimilation, of Copts: exercises in, 209; in US, 174–77, 209–10
Assyrian National Congress, 238n67
asylum, asylum status and, in US: administrative procedures for, 109; American Coptic Association and, 129; appeals for, 245n17, 246n25; bodily hermeneutics and, 123–28; commonsense legality for, 110–11, 116–17; Coptic Orthodox Church role in, 129–31; for Copts, 104–5, 107–11, 245n2; country of origin/regional conditions for, 135–36, 144–48; credibility assessment for, 112–13; for Egyptians, 107, 113; eligibility criteria for, 110; establishment of distance for, 119–23; Green Card Lottery and, 136; group membership proof for, 135; under Immigration and Nationality Act of 1952, 115; *INS v. Cardoza-Fonseca* and, 115–16; International Religious Freedom Act and, 132; judges and, 140–41; legalized suspicion and, 131; *Matter of Mogharrabi* case, 116; media narratives on, 107–8; Migration and Refugee Assistance Act of 1962 and, 115; ministerial influences on, 129–31; after 9/11, 137; non-governmental organizations' role in, 132; during Obama administration, 113; objectivity assessment in, 116; persecution assessment for, 114–19, 142–44; personal stories, 135–44; Refugee Act of 1980 and, 115; religious identity as factor for, 137–38; sectarian violence as factor for, 111–14, 117–13; trial performance as influence on, 131–35; trial testimony for, 110; during Trump administration, 113
Al-Azhar University, 243n51
Aziz, Atef, 253n54

Baer, Gabriel, 80
bahdala (everyday humiliation), 101

Bahjūra village, 69, *70*, 78–87, *89*, 90–91, *102*, *148*; asylum narratives and, 144–45; communal life in, 121; divisions in, 78–79; kidnapping of youth from, 147; migration from, 69–71, *70*, 76; Mounira Takla school, 70; Takla family in, 79–82; violence in, 106; women migrating from, 70–71
Baring, Evelyn, 16
Barrett, Amy Coney, 188
Bat Ye'or. *See* Littman, Gisèle
Behrens-Abouseif, Doris, 84
Being as Communion (Zizioulas), 227n5
belonging: for Egyptian Copts, 184–88; whiteness as form of, 176–77
Berlant, Lauren, 53–54
Beshara, Magdy, 155–57
Bible Answer Man, 63
Biden, Joe, 180
Bieman, Anba, 126
Bildhauer, Bettina, 67
bin Laden, Osama, 157
Bjork-James, Sophie, 194
Black Reconstruction in America (Du Bois), 216
blood: as access, 10; as accusation, 10; Crucifixion of Christ, 68; ecumenism of, 64, 240n93; empire and, 18, 20–23; as ethnographic artifact, 228n9; kinship and, 11–18; martyrdom and, 3, 67–68; "Persecuted Church" and, 9–10; theological importance of, 228n9; theology, 28; theopolitics and, 5–11. *See also* economy of blood
Blood (Anidjar), 2–3, 205
Blood of Coptic martyrs, 23
blood theology, 28
Blue Lives Matter movement, 172
Blum, Carolyn Patty, 115
Boas, Franz, 22
Bolton, John, 151
Breitbart, Andrew, 151
Brown, Wendy, 53–54

Buddhism, 50
Bush, George H. W., 51
Bush, Luis, 50–51
Butler, Judith, 157
al-Butrusiyya Church, 24
Bynum, Caroline Walker, 5, 10
By Their Blood (Hefley, J., and Hefley, M.), 218–19

Cairo, Egypt: al-'Abbāsiyya district in, 24; al-Butrusiyya Church, 24; Christian cathedrals in, 127–28; Coptic Orthodox Church in, 24; Grand Cathedral of St. Mark, 127–28; New Cairo, 127–28; al-Zāwya al-Ḥamra' neighborhood, 42. *See also specific neighborhoods*
Cairo Times, 59
Canadian Coptic Association (CCA), 42
Cartozian, Tatos O., 22
Castelli, Elizabeth, 7, 179, 210
Catholics: culture wars and, 190; Muslims and, 252n53
CCA. *See* Canadian Coptic Association
Christian Coalition, 51–52
Christianity, Christians and: as colonizing force, 236n29; communion in, 228n6; "dhimmi" and, 61–62; Eastern, 3, 108; in Egypt, 38, 72, 208; European perspectives on, 108; in Global South, 53; historical variations in, 3; imperial, 8–9; imperial Christian kinship, 50–53, 68; kinship and, 13; martyr blood and, 67–68; in Middle East, 4, 22–23, 50–51; Muslim-Christian relations, 98–100, 144; narrative of Muslim violence against, 107; persecution narratives for, 38; relationality between Muslims, 144; religious revival among, 123; slavery legacy and, 61; solidarity among American Copts, 214; in South Asia, 4; Syriac, 243n41; tabādul, 146, 248n79; theopolitical variations in, 3; transhistorical role of, 8; violence against, 38; ways of knowing in, 233n105. *See also* Eastern Christianity; persecution, of Christians; Western Christian conservative movement
Christian nationalism, 185–88, 202
Christian Rescue Effort for the Emancipation of Dissidents (CREED), 54–55
Christian Right, in US, Israel supported by, 60
Christian Solidarity International, 54, 57, 61, 237n49
Ciattarelli, Jack, 201
citizenship: in Egypt, 86, 129–30; proximity to whiteness and, 22; religion linked with, 129–30
class. *See* economic class
Clinton, Hillary, 180
Coalition for the Defense of Human Rights, 237n49
Cold War, Western Christian conservative movement after, 51–52
collective memory: American Copts, persecution and, 4, 59; Coptic, 208–9; for landowning Copts, 93–94; shared religious identity and, 91–92; of violence, 54
colonial Egypt: American Presbyterian missionaries in, 227n3; Copts during, 80–87; elites in, 81–85; fellaḥin in, 82–84, 87; land ownership by Copts in, 81–82; Orientalists of, 14; racial science in, 14; segregation of religious minorities in, 144; social status in, 82–85; urban/rural divide in, 83–84
colonialism: Coptic Christians as icons of, 47; icon of, 241n97
colonial trauma, 21
commonsense legality, for asylum, 110–11, 116–17
communal kinship, 12–13
communism, Christian persecution under, 50

community, communal life and: in Bahjūra village, 121; concept of, 243n41; among Copts, 26; Elmahaba Center's role in, 215–16

conversion therapy, 191–93

Coptic American Political Action Committee, 195, 195, 197, 214

Coptic diaspora: activism of, 35–36, 43, 53, 239n74; advocacy in, 144; alternative formations of, 228n14; American Christian communities and, 4, 50–51, 53–54; The Copts, 40–42, 48, 49, 54, 106; diasporic lenticularity, 27, 164; ethnic identity for, 234n4; kinship within, 165–66; in media, 41–42; persecution narratives in, 144; political praxis for, 39–43; Sadat on, 43, 47; securitization in, 167–71, 250n41; transnational translations for, 55, 209; US national security policies and, 153, 161–62, 177; in US, 237n45. See also American Copts

Coptic Law Enforcement Officers Society, 175

Coptic martyrs, martyrdom and, 3–4; American Copts, 208; at al-Buṭrusiyya Church, 23, 23; Era of the Martyrs, 13; in global media, 66; icons of, 37; ISIS and, 5, 6, 7, 64; January 6th US Capitol attacks and, 5, 6, 7; methodological approach to, 7–11; politics of, 7–11; violence and, 97–98. See also Voice of the Martyrs

Coptic memory, 235n19

Coptic Orthodox Christianity: calendar for, 13; in Egyptian society, 161; reconfiguration of, 1–2; Synaxarium, 12; transnational, 179

Coptic Orthodox Church, 227n1; acts of witness in, 13; bodily hermeneutics and, 125; al-Buṭrusiyya Church, 24; in Cairo, 24; Coptic Communal Council, 86; Egyptian Protestants and, 64; emigration and, 103; global focus on, 47; institutional coherence of, 13; as institutional force in Egypt, 130; Karas' criticism of, 45–46; legitimacy of, 13; migration assistance from, 75; moral imaginary of, 13–14; Nasser and, 86–87; of New York and New England, 24; role in asylum applications, 129–31; in Southern US, 212–13; theological competition with, 253n54; transnational Copts and, 44; transnationalism and, 44, 128; transnational religious life through, 128

Coptic Solidarity, 24, 35; diasporic activism at, 36–38

Copts: as ancient race, 14; anti-Muslim racism against, 2; asylum status and, 104–5, 107–11, 245n21; belonging and community among, 26; Christian conservative movement's embrace of, 2; collective memory for, 208–9; collective trauma of, 44; during colonial Egypt, 80–87; commercialization of, 63; communal kinship among, 12–13; concerns over secularization for, 199; construction of churches by, 166–67; definition of, 134; discrimination against, 40, 98–99; in Egyptian Parliament, 236n24; European recognition of, 15; global suffering of, 63–67; homogenization of community of, 92; immigration to US, 44–48, 50; invisibility/visibility dynamic for, 78; ISIS and, 5, 6; as living victims of Arab imperialism, 45; martyrdom and, 3–5, 6, 7; migration from Egypt, 12; as minority, 87–92, 184–88; Muslims as distinct from, 11–12, 17–18; national belonging for, 184–88; persecution in Egypt, 4–5, 39; population in Egypt, 1; precarity of, 100–101; racial purity of, 14–17; relationality among, 12; rights movement for, 57–58; as "sons of pharaohs," 17; suffering as common bond among, 59–63; transnational, 14, 27, 55, 209; at United Nations, 126; US embassy rejection of, 161; victimhood for, 53–56; as victims of Islam, 50; violence against, 5, 97–98. See also American Copts; Bahjūra village; Coptic diaspora; migration; persecution, of Copts; specific topics

Copts and Muslims under British Control (Sayce), 16–17

The Copts (newsletter), 40–42, 48, 49, 54, 106

The Copts since the Arab Invasion (Karas), 44–48

1 Corinthians, 1

The Cotton Plantation Remembered (Abaza), 88

COVID-19 pandemic, 212, 218

CREED. See Christian Rescue Effort for the Emancipation of Dissidents

cults, cult and, in medieval era, 10

cultural alterity, anthropology and, 8

culture wars: abortion issue and, 190–91; American Copts' role in, 188–94, 204; Catholics and, 190; evangelical influence on, 188–89; LGBTQ rights and protections, 191–94; Manhattan Declaration, 191; transnational coalition of conservative religious communities and, 190, 192; UN Family Rights Caucus, 191

Cuno, Kenneth, 87

Dadesho, Sargon, 238n67

Daesh. See Islamic State of Iraq and Syria

Dawood, Mounir, 207

DeSantis, Ron, 193

al-Dessouky, Assem, 80

dhimmi (non-Muslim communities), 61–62

diaspora: lenticularity of, 27, 164; Sikh, 233n104. *See also* Coptic diaspora

diasporas of empire, 27. *See also* Coptic diaspora

Diocletian, 13

discrimination: against Christians, 99; against Copts, 40, 98–99; cultural means of, 155–56; suffering of Copts through, 210

Diversity Visa Lottery. *See* Green Card Lottery

Donatist controversy, 229n23

Dow v. United States, 22

Du Bois, W. E. B., 216

Eastern Christianity: Eastern Orthodox Church, 3; economy of blood and, 3; kinship with Western Christianity, 108

economic class: divisions between American Copts and, 214; kinship and, 92–94, 97

economy of blood, 2; Eastern Christianity and, 3

ecumenism of blood, 64, 240n93

Egypt: Agrarian Reform Act of 1952, 86–87; anti-Christian plight in, 36; Arab Spring, 1, 18, 24, 198; Christianity in, 38, 72, 208; citizenship in, 86; Coptic migration from, 12; Coptic Orthodox Church in, 130; Coptic population in, 1, 74; imperialism in, 25–26; Islamic revival in, 123; land reform in, 87–88; migration from, 12, 69–71, 70, 76–77; Muslims in, 15; national identity of, 15; nationalization movement in, 85; national unity paradigm, 187–88; 1952 revolution in, 46, 69, 85–86, 88, 92–93, 103; Open Door policy in, 87; partitions in, 123; persecution of Copts in, 4; private land ownership in, 80–82, 85, 93–94, 95; privatization of economy in, 87; Protestants in, 64; religion linked with citizenship in, 129–30; revolution in, 1; sectarianism in, 110–11; semiotic ideologies in, 122–

23; Sidarous-Takla family in, 92–94, 97, 241n1; 2011 revolution, 1, 18, 24, 198; Upper region of, 25–26; violence against Christians in, 38. *See also* Arab Spring; Bahjūra village; Cairo, Egypt; colonial Egypt; Copts; Naj' Ḥammādī; *specific topics*
EgyptAir Flight 990, crash of, 168, 250n39
Egyptian Christians for Trump, 181, 183
Egypt Migrations organization, 234n7
Eldahabi, Edward Ghali, 58
Elgindy, Khaled, 59–60
Elmahaba Center, 212–14, 234n7, 251n8; community remapping by, 215–16
emigration, of Copts: asylum-seeking and, 104–5; Coptic diaspora and, 104; Coptic Orthodox Church and, 103; kinship and, 103–4; after 1952 revolution, 103; persecution politics and, 103; private landowning families and, 103. *See also* Green Card Lottery; immigration
empire, imperialism and: Arab imperialism, 45; blood and, 18, 20–23; Christianity and, 8–9; diasporas of, 27; in Egypt, 25–26; expansion of, 20; sovereignty and, 21; transition from, 20; transnationalism influenced by, 27; US as, 20–21, 231n75, 231n79
Empire (Hardt and Negri), 20
enchanted internationalism, 238n52
Era of the Martyrs, 13
Europe: perspectives on Christianity, 108; recognition of Copts, 15
evangelical movement: culture wars and, 188–89; definition of, 227n2; Lausanne Movement, 50, 241n95; National Association of Evangelicals, 64; Second International Conference on World Evangelization, 50. *See also* Western Christian conservative movement
everyday humiliation. *See bahdala*

exchange between Muslims and Christians. *See tabādul*
'Ezbet Daoud neighborhood, 106–7

Faier, Leiba, 233n109
Family Rights Caucus (UN), 191
Family Watch International, 191
Fassin, Didier, 118–19, 124, 238n64, 246n35
fellaḥin (peasants), 82–84, 87
female genital mutilation (FGM), 246n35
Fields, Barbara, 15–16, 153
First Gulf War, 51
First International Coptic Symposium, 61
Floyd, George, murder of, 175
Foda, Farag, 169, 250n40
forced migration, of Copts, 72
Foucault, Michel, 109
France, asylum cases in, 109, 118–19
Francis (Pope), 3, 240n93
Freedom House, 56
Furani, Khaled, 8

al-Gama'a al-Islamiyya organization, 246n36
Geller, Pamela, 151
geopolitical kinship, 11
Ghaly, Farid, 246n25
Girgis, Reda, 254n36
Global North, migration to, 142
Global South, Christians of, 53
Gohmert, Louis, 36–38
Gordon, Ernest, 54
Graham, Billy, 50
Great Britain: Anglo-American Protestant movement, 227n3. *See also* colonial Egypt; colonialism
Greek Orthodox Church, 63
Green Card Lottery (Diversity Visa Lottery/Program), in US, 18, 19, 25–26, 73, 97, 253n12; asylum status and, 136; Egyptian Copts and, 74–75, 232n90; Irish migrants and, 74; Muslim participation in, 76; Naj' Ḥammādī and, 180;

role of chance in, 75–78; in Southern US, 211; women and, 71
Greewal, Zareena, 233n105

Haas, Steve, 5
Hadid, Bobby Farid, 169–70
Hage, Ghassan, 27
d'Halluin, Estelle, 124
Hanegraaff, Hank, 63–64
Hardt, Michael, 20
Hefley, James, 218–19, 254n34
Hefley, Marti, 218–19, 254n34
Heo, Angie, 76, 241n97
hermeneutics, body: asylum process and, 123–28; Coptic Church and, 125; persecution narratives and, 124–25; proof of suffering and, 124; US national security policies and, 157–62
Hinduism, 50
Holy Bible Society, 39
Horowitz, Michael, 58
Hudson Institute, 56, 73
Hurd, Elizabeth Shakman, 247n68

Ibrahim, Mina, 242n11
Ibrahim, Raymond, 63–64
Ibrahim, Saad Eddin, 244n55
icons, iconography and: of colonialism, 241n97; Coptic Orthodox Christianity and, 47, 247n68; of martyrdom, 37
Ignatiev, Noel, 176
Ignatius of Antioch, 229n24
immigration, to US: Coptic, 44–48, 50; Immigration Act of 1990, 73; Immigration and Nationality Act of 1952, 115; INS v. Cardoza-Fonseca, 115–16; Syrian, 22. See also Green Card Lottery
Immigration Act of 1990, US, 73–74. See also Green Card Lottery
Immigration and Nationality Act of 1952, US, 115
imperial Christianity, 8–9; kinship and, 50–53, 68

In the Levant (Warner), 15
Innocence of Muslims, 151
Institute for Religion and Democracy, 56
INS v. Cardoza-Fonseca, 115–16
International Religious Freedom Act (IRFA), US (1998), 58–59, 239n70; asylum and, 132; transnational disagreements over, 240n78
Iran, America as "the great Satan" for, 56
Iranian hostage crisis, 51
IRFA. *See* International Religious Freedom Act
ISIS. *See* Islamic State of Iraq and Syria
Islam: Christian conservative movement and, 52; Copts as victims of, 50; counterpublics for, 123; European perspectives on, 108; as governance system, 64; in Middle East, 55–56; securitization, 167–71. *See also* Muslims
Islamic State of Iraq and Syria (ISIS): Coptic martyrs and, 5, 6, 7, 64; violence and persecution by, 120, 133
Israel, US Christian Right and, 60
Issawi, Charles, 81

January 6th US Capitol attacks, Coptic martyrs and, 5, 6, 7
Jesus Christ: Crucifixion of, 68; kinship and, 11–12; salvation through death and resurrection of, 7–8
Jewish guilt, 10
Joint Terrorism Task Force, 169–70, 250n39
Jubilee Campaign, 54

Karas, Adel, 155
Karas, Leila, 235n11
Karas, Shawky, 40, 235n11, 235n19, 236n24; *The Copts since the Arab Invasion,* 44–48; criticism of Coptic Orthodox Church, 45–46; Sadat and, 47–48; US Copts and, 57. *See also* American Coptic Association

al-Karm, al-Minyā village, 35
Khalil, Elhamy, 44, 235n11, 235n19
al-Khanka, violence in, 39–41
Khomeini (Ayatollah), 42
King, Rodney, 157
kinship: anthropological studies of, 11; blood and, 11–18; Christian, 13; class and, 92–94, 97; communal, 12–13; within Coptic diaspora, 165–66; Coptic emigration and, 103–4; Eastern Christianity with Western Christianity, 108; geopolitical, 11; imperial Christian, 50–53, 68; Jesus Christ and, 11–12; Persecuted Church and, 54; as process of doing, 11; spiritual forms of, 11
Kuwait, 87
Kyrillos (Bishop), 79
Kyrillos VI (Pope), 127

land ownership: collective memory and, 93–94; by Copts in colonial Egypt, 81–82; in Egypt, 80–82, 85, 93–94, 95
land reform, in Egypt, 87–88
Lane, Edward, 84
Lausanne Movement, 50, 241n95
law enforcement: American Copts in, 167–68; Blue Lives Matter movement, 172; Coptic Law Enforcement Officers Society, 175; Muslims in, 157–59, 169–70; NYPD Muslim Surveillance Program, 169–70; Police Benevolent Association of the City of New York, 175; St. Mark's Coptic Law Enforcement Officer Society, 171, 175, 196
legalized suspicion, asylum and, 131
LGBTQ populations: conversion therapy for, 191–93; culture wars and, 191–94; rights and protections for, 191–94, 204, 252n39
Littman, Gisèle (Bat Ye'or), 240n83
A Lonely Minority (Wakin), 235n18
Lynch, Patrick, 175, 177

Macarius III (Pope), 48
Mahmood, Saba, 85, 104, 122
Makdisi, Ussama, 82–85, 236n31
Malkki, Liisa, 142
Manhattan Declaration, 191
Marshall, Paul, 58
martyrs, martyrdom and: blood and, 3, 67–68; historical imagination of, 67; invention of, 229n29; methodological approach to, 28–31; persecution and, 8; theology of, 208–9, 229n21; victimhood and, 210; white, 229n25. *See also* Coptic martyrs
Maspero, Gaston, 14–17
Maspero Massacre, 185
Maspero Youth Union (MYU), 185–87
Matter of Mogharrabi case, 116
Matthew (Gospel of), 1
McAlister, Melani, 52–53, 172, 233n102
McHugh, Paul, 193
MECHRIC. *See* Middle East Christian Committee
medieval era, cult in, 10
memory: reconstruction of, 163–67. *See also* collective memory
Metaxas, Eric, 5, 6, 7
Meunier, Michael, 57–59, 238n67
Middle East Christian Committee (MECHRIC), 238n67
Middle East region: Christian communities in, 4, 50–51; Christians in, 22–23; Islam in, 55–56; migrants from, 22–23
migration, migrants and, Copts and: from Bahjūra village, 69–71, 70, 76; blood of Coptic martyrs and, 23, 23; circuits, 100–101; Coptic Orthodox Church and, 73, 75; demographics of, 232n90; from Egypt, 12, 69–71, 70, 76–77; ethnographic fieldwork on, 26; forced, 72; to Global North, 142; Green Card Lottery and, 73–78; institutional factors for, 71–72; International Organization for Migration, 254n33; intersec-

tional factors for, 72; methodological approach to, 28–31; Middle Eastern Christian, 22; from Najʿ Ḥammādī, 76–77; narratives of, 72–75; Persecuted Church and, 76; studies, 233n97; voluntary, 72. *See also* Green Card Lottery; immigration
Migration and Refugee Assistance Act of 1962, US, 115
Mikhail, Kyriakos, 16
model minority, American Copts as, 214
Modern Egypt (Baring), 16
Mordechai, Victor, 56
Morrison, Toni, 176
Morsi, Mohamed, 107, 244n56
Motherland Lost (Tadros), 73
Mounira Takla school, 70
Mubarak, Hosni, 45
Mummies and Moslems (Warner), 15
Muslim Brotherhood, 127; al-Gamaʿa al-Islamiyya, 246n36; persecution of Copts by, 120, 133, 180; rise to political power, 163
Muslim (Hanegraaff), 63–64
Muslims: activism in West, 55–56; Catholics and, 252n53; Christian-Muslim relations, 98–100, 144; concerns with death among, 230n32; Copts as distinct from, 11–12, 17–18; Egyptian, 15; in law enforcement, 157–59, 169–70; racialization of, 155; relationality between Christians and, 144; religious revival among, 123; *tabādul*, 146, 248n79; violence against Christians, 107
MYU. *See* Maspero Youth Union

NAE. *See* National Association of Evangelicals
Najʿ Ḥammādī, 76–77, 88–89, 119–20; asylum narratives and, 145–48; Christmas massacre in, 151–52; Green Card Lottery and, 180; kidnapping of youth from, 147

Napolitano, Valentina, 227n5
Nashville, Tennessee, Copts in, 210–16
Nasser, Gamal Abdel, 127; Agrarian Reform Act of 1952, 86–87; Coptic Orthodox Church and, 86–87; nationalization policies under, 85–86; 1952 revolution and, 46, 69, 85–86, 88, 92–93. *See also* nationalization movement
National Association of Evangelicals (NAE), 57, 64–65
nationalism. *See* Christian nationalism
nationalization movement, in Egypt, 85–86
Negri, Antonio, 20
neoliberalism, transition from imperialism, 20
New York Times, 208
NGOs. *See* non-governmental organizations
9/11 attacks, in US: anti-Muslim assaults after, 155; asylum cases after, 137; Copts in Egypt after, 61; Islamic threat after, 62; national security policies after, 152–54; racialization of Middle Eastern communities after, 152–53. *See also* World Trade Center site
1952 revolution, in Egypt, 46, 69, 85–86, 88, 92–93; emigration after, 103
non-governmental organizations (NGOs), 132
non-Muslim communities. *See dhimmi*
NYPD Muslim Surveillance Program, 169–70

Obama, Barack, 113
Oliphant, Elayne, 7
Open Door policy, in Egypt, 87
Open Doors USA, 57
Orientalism, Orientalists and, 243n35; colonial Egypt and, 14; modern Egyptian history and, 84
Oriental Orthodox, 115, 190, 224

290 | INDEX

peasants. *See fellaḥin*
Perkins, Judith, 7
Persecuted Church, 237n49; blood and, 9–10; Christian kinship and, 54; definition of, 66–67; global idea of, 9; migration and, 76; moral imaginary of, 1; Prayer for the Persecuted Church, 5; public support for, 52; theopolitics of, 179; US policy and, 51
persecution, of Christians, 38; activism on, 58–59; of American Copts 4; under communism, 50; Copts in Egypt, 4–5, 39; martyrdom and, 8; as narrative in US Christian conservative movement, 57; racialization and, 4; theopolitics of, 10–11, 108–9. *See also* Persecuted Church
persecution, of Copts: of American Copts in the South, 215; asylum status influenced by, 114–19, 142–44; body hermeneutics and, 124–25; Copts in diaspora and, 144; emigration and, 103; by ISIS, 120, 133; by Muslim Brotherhood, 120, 133, 180 myth of, 229n29; patterns of practice of, 143; transnational discourses on, 143; US national security policies and, 171–74
Petrie, Flinders, 16
Phares, Walid, 238n67
Philosophical Investigations (Wittgenstein), 110
Pipes, Daniel, 61
police, policing and. *See* law enforcement
Police Benevolent Association of the City of New York, 175
Politics of Piety (Mahmood), 122
Prayer for the Persecuted Church, 5
precarity: Coptic, 100–101; of Coptic Christianity, 101–10
Progressive Copts, 234n7
Protestants: Anglo-American Protestant movement, 227n3; in Egypt, 64

al-Qaddafi, Muammar, 42
Qinā province, 77, 86, 147

racecraft, 153
racialization: of American Copts, 152–53; of Muslims, 155; after 9/11 attacks in US, 152–53; persecution and, 4. *See also* anti-Muslim racism; racism
racial purity, of Copts, 14–17
racism: anti-Arab, 39, 234n7; anti-Black, 61, 219; of Trump, 21. *See also* anti-Muslim racism
Reagan, Ronald, 58
Rechtman, Richard, 238n64
Refugee Act of 1980, US, 115
relationality: between Christians and Muslims, 144; among Copts, 12
Religious Difference in a Secular Age (Mahmood), 104
religious freedom movement, 57–59; during Cold War, 56; Third International Archon Conference on Religious Freedom, 63. *See also specific topics*
religious identity, collective memory and, 91–92
rights movement: for Copts, 57–58; for LGBTQ populations, 191–94, 204, 252n39, 252n53
Robbins, Joel, 238n64
Robertson, Pat, 51–52
Robson, Laura, 236n31
Roderick, Keith (Father), 52–53, 57, 61, 237n49, 238n52, 239n70; role in global Christian solidarity, 62. *See also* Coptic Solidarity
Rofel, Lisa, 233n109
Romans (Epistle to the), 172
Romney, Mitt, 238n67
Rothberg, Michael, 235n19
Rubaii, Kali, 249n7

al-Sadat, Anwar, 40–41, 46; on Coptic diaspora as threat, 43, 47; Karas and,

47–48; mass arrests under, 42; Open Door policy under, 87; privatization of economy under, 87; sectarian logics under, 122
Said, Edward, 14
Saint Shenouda Church, 106
Saleh, Tarek Yousof (Sheikh), 207
Saleh, Zainab, 233n109
salvation, death of Christ and, 7–8
Saudi Arabia, 87
Sawiris, Naguib, 35
Sayce, Archibald Henry, 16–17, 243n35
Schneider, David, 11
Second International Conference on World Evangelization, 50
sectarian violence. *See* violence
secularism, secularization and: Coptic concerns over, 199; frameworks of, 8; religious regulation and, 130
security praxis, US national security policies and: assimilation of Copts and, 174–77; Coptic diaspora and, 165–66; Coptic protests and, 164; Coptic securitization, 167–71, 250n41; Copts in law enforcement, 167–68; cultural means of discrimination and, 155–56; EgyptAir Flight 990 crash, 168, 250n39; Joint Terrorism Task Force, 169–70, 250n39; memory of reconstruction and, 163–67; Middle Eastern bodies and, 157–62; Muslims in law enforcement, 157–59, 169–70; after 9/11 attacks, 152–54; NYPD Muslim Surveillance Program, 169–70; perception of Middle Eastern persons as threats, 154–55; persecution of Copts and, 171–74; policing institutions, 171–74; securitization of Islam, 167–71; as transnational forms of injury, 162–63; under Trump administration, 159–61, 164
Sedra, Paul, 243n46
Sekulow, Jay, 66

Sekulow, Jordan, 66, 151
September 11th attacks. *See* 9/11 attacks
Shakespeare, William, 248n75
Shalaby, Alex, 35
Shea, Nina, 35–36, 58
Shenoda, Anthony, 122, 186–87
Shenouda III (Pope), 39–42, 45, 167, 192, 196–97, 200
Sikh diaspora, 233n104
SIOA. *See* Stop Islamization of America
al-Sisi, Abdel Fattah, 112, 125–28, 244n56
Slater, Sharon, 191
slavery, Christianity and, 61
Society of St. Stephen, 237n49
South Asia, Christian communities in, 4
Southern US, American Copts: Coptic Orthodox Church, 212–13; during COVID-19 pandemic, 212; economic class divisions among, 214; Elmahaba Center, 212–16, 234n7, 251n8; Green Card Lottery and, 211; as model minority, 214; in Nashville, 210–16; politics of persecution and, 215; relation to Muslim populations, 212; social isolation of, 214; solidarity with marginalized people, 214; as students, 211–12; wage issues for, 215–16
sovereignty, US imperialism and, 21
Spelman, Elizabeth, 52–53
Spencer, Robert, 151
St. Mark's Coptic Law Enforcement Officer Society, 171, 175, 196
Steinmetz-Jenkins, Daniel, 3
Stevens, John Paul (Justice), 115–16
Stewart, Kathleen, 27–28
Stop Islamization of America (SIOA), 151
Stückelberger, Hansjürg, 61
students, American Copts as, 211–12
Suez Massacre, 46
suffering, of Copts: bodily hermeneutics and, 124; as common bond between American Copts, 59–67; through discrimination, 210

Sūhāj, 44, 46, 77, 235n11
Synaxarium, of Coptic Orthodox Church, 12
Syria, immigration to US, 22
Syriac Christians, 243n41

tabādul (exchange between Muslims and Christians), 146, 248n79
Tadros, Samuel, 73
Takla, Daoud, 70
Takla, Ibrahim, 94
Takla, Kamal Bek, 79
Tawadros II (Pope), 126, 128
Tertullian, 8
Thabet, Suad, 35
theology: anthropological approach to, 8; blood, 28; of Christ's blood, 228n9; of martyrdom, 208–9, 229n21
theopolitics: blood and, 5–11; of Persecuted Church, 179; of persecution, 10–11, 108–9
Thomas, Todne, 12
traditional values, retention and protection of, 30, 179
transnational Copts, 55, 209
transnationalism: Coptic Orthodox Christianity and, 179; Coptic Orthodox Church and, 44, 128; imperialism and, 27; International Religious Freedom Act and, 240n78
Trump, Donald, 66, 238n67; American Coptic support for, 180–82, 184; asylum cases under, 113; Egyptian Christians for Trump, 171–73, 181, 183; national security policies under, 159–61, 164; racism of, 21; in 2020 US presidential election, 5, 7, 180–82; "war on Christians" and, 180
2020 US presidential election, 5, 7, 180–82; Egyptian Christians for Trump, 171–73, 181, 183

UAE. *See* United Arab Emirates
UN. *See* United Nations

United Arab Emirates (UAE), 119
United Nations (UN): Copts at, 126; Family Rights Caucus, 191; Human Rights Council, 191–92
United States (US): Anglo-American Protestant movement, 227n3; anti-Black racism in, 61; Arab Spring and, 18; assimilation of Copts in, 174–77, 209–10; Blue Lives Matter movement, 172; citizenship in, 22; Coptic diaspora in, 237n45; Coptic migration to, 12; Diversity Visa Program, 19, 25, 71; as empire, 20–21, 231n75, 231n79; First Gulf War, 51; as gatekeeper of mobility, 20; Green Card Lottery, 18, 25–26, 73–78; Immigration Act of 1990, 73; Immigration and Nationality Act of 1952, 115; International Religious Freedom Act, 58–59, 132; Iranian hostage crisis, 51; Migration and Refugee Assistance Act of 1962, 115; promise of religious freedom in, 217; Refugee Act of 1980, 115; 2020 US presidential election, 5, 7; "war on Christians" in, 180–82, 184; "war on terror," 249n7; whiteness in, 22, 176–77. *See also* immigration; security praxis; Southern US; Western Christian conservative movement; *specific topics*
United States v. Cartozian, 22
US. *See* United States
US Copts (organization), 57

victimhood: commodification of, 56; for Copts, 53–56; martyrs and, 210
violence: against American Copts, 205, 206, 207; asylum status influenced by, 111–14, 117–18; in Bahjūra village, 106; collective memory of, 54; against Copts, 5, 97–98; by ISIS, 120, 133; in al-Khanka, 39–41; martyrdom and, 97–98; during al-Sisi administration, 125–26; Suez Massacre and, 46; during

"war on terror," 249n7; in al-Zāwya al-Ḥamra' neighborhood, 42
Voice of the Martyrs, 54, 57
voluntary migration, of Copts, 72

wage issues, for American Copts, 215–16
Wakin, Edward, 235n18
Warner, Charles Dudley, 15
war on Christians, 180–82, 184
war on terror, 249n7
Wasfy, Awsam, 193, 252n43
Washington Post, 235n15
Watson, Andrew, 84
Western Christian conservative movement, in US: American Copts and, 182, 184; Christian Coalition, 51–52; Christian Right, 60; after Cold War, 51–52; Copts embraced by, 2; international Christian communities and, 4; Islam and, 52; pain narratives and, 10–11; persecution narrative in, 57; political ascendancy of, 38; "war on Christians," 180–82, 184
white martyrdom, 229n25

whiteness, in US: ascension into, 176–77; citizenship and, 22; as compensation, 216; definitions of, 22; as form of belonging, 176–77; as political project, 176
white supremacy, 153–54
Wilders, Geert, 151
Wissa, Philip, 193
Wittgenstein, Ludwig, 110
women: Diversity Visa Program and, 71; female genital mutilation, 246n35; migration from Bahjūra village, 70–71. *See also specific topics*
Wonderful Blood (Bynum), 5
World Lebanese Organization, 238n67
World Trade Center site, 151–52, 154, 158
wound culture, 53–54

Yousief, Lydia, 213, 222, 253n16, 254n25. *See also* Elmahaba Center
Youssef (Bishop), 11, 198, 240n80
Yu'anis, Anba, 126–27

Zakhary, Mariana, 175
al-Zāwya al-Ḥamra' neighborhood, 42
Zizioulas, John D., 227n5

ABOUT THE AUTHOR

CANDACE LUKASIK is Assistant Professor of Religion and affiliated with Anthropology and Middle Eastern Cultures at Mississippi State University.

www.ingramcontent.com/pod-product-compliance
Lightning Source LLC
Chambersburg PA
CBHW020357080526
44584CB00014B/1051